V&R

Forschungen zur Religion und Literatur des Alten und Neuen Testaments

Herausgegeben von
Dietrich-Alex Koch, Matthias Köckert,
Christopher Tuckett und Steven McKenzie

Band 225

Vandenhoeck & Ruprecht

Ryan O'Dowd

The Wisdom of Torah: Epistemology in Deuteronomy and the Wisdom Literature

Vandenhoeck & Ruprecht

Bibliografische Information der Deutschen Nationalbibliothek

Die Deutsche Nationalbibliothek verzeichnet diese Publikation in der Deutschen Nationalbibliografie; detaillierte bibliografische Daten sind im Internet über http://dnb.d-nb.de abrufbar.

ISBN 978-3-525-53089-4

Printed in Germany.
Druck und Bindung: ⊕ Hubert & Co., Göttingen

Gedruckt auf alterungsbeständigem Papier.

Table of Contents

Preface

"He who thinks he knows does not yet know as he ought to know [...]"

So the apostle Paul exhorts an ancient Corinthian audience childishly infatuated with its own *epistemology*. Paul goes on to suggest that "anyone who knows God is loved by him". The study that follows will, among other things, show how an ancient Jewish mind like Paul's would be inclined to think of knowledge in such holistic and religious terms. Not only does Paul submit knowledge to love, but he places "the one who thinks he knows" in communion with and submission to God and neighbor. Knowledge is rarely so conditioned today; in fact, a purified, rational and objective pursuit of expert-knowledge tends to rule our Google-CNN-text-message-front-page-e-mail world. This concern characterises the train of ponderings that gave life to this study.

What I present here is a slightly adapted version of my PhD thesis from the University of Liverpool in 2005. Its main purpose is to explore the conditions and contexts for knowing in the ancient Hebrew world, focused particularly on the literature in the traditions of wisdom and torah (law). But a secondary purpose of this volume is to provide a "meta-critique" of modern epistemology; how do we "modern," post-Enlightenment people think about knowledge and what are the consequences? I raise many of these questions in the first chapter and provide some possible reflections on the issues in my conclusion. My hope is that this manuscript will promote creativity, reflection and flourishing in the many fields into which it journeys: biblical studies, theology, religion, philosophy, sociology, ethics and hermeneutics.

A project like this a product of a diverse community: family members, academic colleagues, friends, and neighbours. I am not ashamed to say that few of the ideas in this study originated in my own mind and that, in many ways, I share the achievements (and missteps) with those who have journeyed with me. Still, the writing and the final formulations are mine and I accept the guidance and critique which will come from it, hoping that it will lead our communities forward.

I thank all of those friends and family members who encouraged and helped to finance our studies in Britain. Mom and Dad, Brendon and Devin and your families, my parents-in-law and Stacy – a special debt of gratitude for all your sacrifices. I had world-class guidance and supervision during my studies. My thanks to those in Chester and Cheltenham: Anthony Thiselton, Gordon McConville and Eric Christianson. I salute Craig Bartholomew (St. Bart), my main supervisor who encouraged this project in its infancy and has seen it through to its publication. In the process Craig has gone from my supervisor, to colleague, friend and co-author. Thank you for the modelling, fellowship, service and much ruminating over good food and wine. My thanks also to the intellectual and spiritual communities in the U.K. and Canada who have nourished my work and my humanity: Robby, Aubrey, Heath, William, Chad, Christine, Jamie, Victor, Don, David, Cal, Sean and many more. I extend my gratitude to Gordon Wenham and Christopher Partridge who examined the original thesis and provided many helpful suggestions for improvement. This project would never have come together were it not for Steve Siebert's tireless work on the format, as well as the rest of the staff at Nota Bene software. Finally, my thanks to my editor, Steve McKenzie, who recommended this thesis for the FRLANT series.

I am long overdue in giving appropriate acclamation to those closest to me. I hope that seeing this in print gives back some of the honor due to my wife and children who have journeyed much of the world with me without complaint or hesitation. To Patrick, Annie and Aidan – thanks for giving your dad time and space to read another book, finish another paragraph and, too often, only half listen to your stories of surprise, discovery and sometimes despair. Your love and imaginations have fueled mine. And to Amy, my dear wife, who has lovingly shared every bump and groove of this educational and scholarly road. You bring me endless joy, confidence and happiness. This book is dedicated to you – may all who read it marvel at the beautiful and gifted woman who made it possible.

Ryan O'Dowd
Ontario, Summer 2008

CHAPTER ONE

Introduction
The Epistemology of Religion

"Faith Seeking Understanding" Anselm

"Thus, I was unable to choose someone whose views seemed to me to be preferable to those of others, and I found myself forced to take on the task of guiding myself."[1] René Descartes

"It was upon this threshold that the strange figure of knowledge called man first appeared [...] In attempting to uncover the deepest strata of Western culture, I am restoring its rifts, its instability, its flaws; and it is the same ground that is once more stirring under our feet."[2] Michel Foucault

Our table has been set by our ancestors: Plato, Aristotle, Augustine, Descartes, Kant and countless others. From Hebraic and medieval knowledge set within the context of faith, and Enlightenment knowledge of rational certainty, to postmodern skepticism and doubt of knowledge altogether, epistemology has been on a journey through human history. The purpose of this study is to chart this path with the particular focus of a phenomenology of ancient Hebrew religion. In a narrative style, we will ask questions about the possibility and nature of knowledge – of God and his world within this religious tradition and its worldview.

But how is this done in our own day? In light of the political, social, global and ethical nature of pluralisms, rapid change and conflict in our world today, a phenomenology of religion is complex and heavily charged. But for this reason it also deeply urgent. If we approach our study carefully, we can minimize the charge and attend more helpfully to matters that bear upon the urgent. We set out, then, with an attitude which combines "rigor and humility", and "passionate conviction plus a sedulous respect for the convictions of others."[3]

---

1 *Discourse on Method and Related Writings* (London/New York: Penguin Books, 2003), 15.

2 M. Foucault, *The Order of Things* (New York: Vintage Books, 1994), xxiv.

3 D.F. Wallace on the "democratic spirit" in "Tense Present: Democracy, English, and the Wars Over Usage", *Harpers* (April 2001) 39–58, on pp. 41–2.

Perhaps nowhere is it more appropriate to engage these religious and philosophical questions than through the luminous history of Hebrew wisdom and law. These two textual traditions have long been associated with what it means for humans to know: they form the core of Israel's ancient sense of theology, cosmology and self-understanding; they dominate the writings in the Second Temple period; and they are the primary foundation for the books of the Christian New Testament and countless critical writings of the medieval era. In our own day they stand both as an antiquated source against which new modern models of knowing are imagined and more recently in postmodern accounts as a source for critiquing modernity. Our study is, therefore, a conversation between ancient Hebrew religious writings and the vast history of commentary on those texts since that time.

1. Methodological Considerations

Because this study draws upon such a diverse history and wide range of disciplines, several issues must be clarified up front. To begin, this study is primarily a study of the epistemology of religion – how people go about knowing God and the world.[4] So, while questions of historical, social, psychological, political and aesthetic perspectives will always be in play, we will make our decisive statements about the epistemological issues before us, often leaving other questions open or unanswered. Such a trajectory is best followed if we first set out our taxonomy through a brief history of epistemology and then proceed to state the hermeneutical assumptions that will guide us between this history and the biblical texts in question.

1.1 A History of Ideas in Epistemology and Religion

We begin with a brief introduction to the broad contours of epistemology over the course of human history. This is essential, as we will argue, because of the common tendency for interpreters to project modern ideas of *knowing* back into ancient cultures. Such projections lead to poor and often mistaken assumptions about the values, beliefs, and motivations behind the writing of these ancient texts and thus, as Stephen Toulmin suggests, to see too much of oneself in the historiographical mirror that reflects the ancient culture.[5] Toulmin rightly guides the historian's attention not just to the

---

[4] The philosophical discipline of epistemology can, of course, be described in much greater detail: modes of knowing, belief, faith, certainty, justification etc. See D. Hamlyn, "History of Epistemology", in Paul Edwards (ed.), *Encyclopedia of Philosophy 3* (8 Volumes; New York/London: Macmillan, 1967) 8–38.

[5] S. Toulmin, *Cosmopolis: The Hidden Agenda of Modernity* (Chicago: University of Chicago, 1990), 22.

ancient world under study, but to our own historiographical mirror, on guard for distortions which obscure our perceptions about knowledge.[6] Thus following Ricoeur's monumental study, *The Symbolism of Evil*, we should start our project with the recognition that we are asking Hellenic, western questions of the ancient Near Eastern, Hebraic world. The conversation will by nature always be provisional and open to further interpretation and revision. Following the historical review here, the next section will revisit these concerns and propose a hermeneutic for meeting the challenges inherent to our study.

Our review charts a chronological path, beginning with ancient Hebrew thought. While the specific details of Hebraic epistemology are yet to be explored in subsequent chapters, we should still make note of the overall context of ancient Israel which set it apart amidst the history of ideas which follows. Most notably, Hebrew religion, like ANE religion in general, is not theoretical in its approach to life and worldview. Rather, ancient Hebrew thought communicates through a holistic approach to life: ethics, history and worship are grounded in a mythical, narrative framework.[7] Israel's self-understanding and ethics thus grow out of her participation in a created world and her status in a covenant relationship with the creator God. Even in the wisdom literature, where evidence of the covenants and salvation history is non-existent, or implicit at best, we still find a strong sense that ethics and knowledge are grounded in the cosmic order of Yahweh's creation. Knowledge, therefore, is intrinsically participatory, or a product of discovering God and his world by living in it. To know is to live in ethical conformity with God's ordered reality,[8] not to escape from it into objective analysis. It is only in late wisdom literature that we find the slightest of allusions to Greek knowledge in an abstract sense.

For this reason, it is important to mark the major shift in epistemology from ancient Near Eastern myths and holisms to the more familiar Greek way of theoretical and abstract thought. Plato's *idealist* philosophy, arguably the foremost in the Greek world, established a divide between the material world of human life and the rational world of Ideas (or Forms).

---

[6] Or, to restate Heisenberg's observation, the observer always influences or interferes with the object under study. My point is not to eliminate perspectives in search of some kind of objectivity, for I do not believe that can be done, but rather to raise our awareness of *perspectives* to the level of our awareness of *observation* itself.

[7] See M. Buber, "People Today and the Jewish Bible: From a Lecture Series", in M. Buber/F. Rosenzweig (ed.), *Scripture and Translation* (Bloomington: Indiana University, 1994) 4–21, on pp. 4–21 where he locates the Hebraic sense of reality in a distinctively holistic worldview; creation, revelation, story, and encounter with the divine are all integrated. Cf. Ricoeur's discussion on ancient myth in *The Symbolism of Evil* (Boston: Beacon, 1967), 161–75.

[8] Ricoeur, *Symbolism of Evil*, 130–1, locates the Jewish sense of imagination within ethics, or the written and oral Torah. See chapters two and eight below.

Knowledge is found only in the latter. Thus human "participation" for Plato is not in the material world, but rather something done rationally and ontologically.[9] Ethics too are separated from the material ontology of mythical human origins, and relegated instead to the ontology of *nous* – of abstract reason and contemplation of the Ideas. Plato's dialogues favor reason, evidence and objectivity over mythos, faith, and revelation.[10]

Aristotle's more *realist* epistemology is a notable exception to the dominant idealism in Greek philosophy. Aristotle does not abandon Plato's assumption that all knowledge is related to universals, but his primary concern is to locate human knowledge in the immanent (practical) aspects of the real, natural world.[11] In this way, the senses and reason lead us to knowledge; Plato's strong, transcendental separation of the material world from the Ideas is abandoned in favor of an immanentism.[12] Because he aligns knowledge with our experience of nature, Aristotle is also inclined to associate ethics with knowledge (an interesting parallel with the Hebraic tradition). He discusses the "Intellectual Virtues" at length where knowledge is an aspect not just of reasoning, but of wisdom and *phronesis* – of discernment in the timely and particular.[13]

Plato's academy is typically regarded as the stronger historical force. It was clearly adopted within Jewish and Christian theology for several centuries after his death, most notably by Augustine. Platonic ontology and theory also dominates Medieval scholasticism as well as setting the foundation for the Enlightenment return to reason, science, and astronomy three centuries later. At the very least we have several significant turning points in history which are grounded in the onto-theological model of reason in Platonic philosophy. During these eras, the ambiguities and poetics of myth, the ethics of religion, and cosmic symbolism are replaced with "being" and the "what *is*?" of Hellenic rationalism.Yet because of these major foci of Platonic renewal in the West, many assume that the intervening Medieval era was also guided by Platonism or neo-Platonism. One possible reason for this opinion is the fact that most Medieval history has been written in the wake of Modernity, which itself renewed the Greek emphasis on reason and its ontological and epistemological dualisms. Nevertheless, there is also a less appreciated, or at least a less acknowledged stream of

---

9 See R. Kearney, *The Wake of Imagination* (New York: Routledge, 1988), 49–52.

10 Plato, *The Republic* (New York/London: Penguin Books, 2003), Books II and X. Cf. also R. Tarnas, *The Passion of the Western Mind: Understanding the Ideas That Have Shaped Our World View* (New York: Ballantine Books, 1991), 8–9.

11 C. Taylor, "Aristotle's Epistemology", in S. Everson (ed.), *Epistemology* (Cambridge: Cambridge University, 1990) 116–44, provides a careful analysis of Aristotle's theoretical and practical concerns with knowledge.

12 Tarnas, *Passion*, 61.

13 Aristotle, *The Nicomachean Ethics* (New York: Penguin Books, 2004), VI.v,vii.

Medieval thought, influenced not so much by Augustine's neo-platonism as by his classical liberalism and indebtedness to Cicero, Homer and Virgil.[14] This poetic (aesthetic), religious and more discursive way of knowing owes its vision to Augustine but also to the four-fold way of interpretation initiated by Origen, Jerome and the Latin Fathers. Thus, Abelard, Boethius, Gregory, Basil, Bede, Bonavanture, Valla and Erasmus are among a long tradition of spiritual philosophy which is far less theoretical and systematic than neo-Platonist Christianity.[15] In fact, in the Renaissance and humanist eras at the end of the Medieval period we find a decisive turn away from the rational, onto-theological categories of Medieval neo-platonism and late scholasticism back towards a strong affirmation of the classical love of texts, poetics, aesthetics, realism and limits in human philosophy.[16] Here the non-systematic blend of knowledge with ethics, theology, philosophy and nature is another resurgence of holistic worldviews of the Medieval mystics, theology and the Hebraic religion to which they both are indebted. Furthermore, Thomas Aquinas, despite his strong onto-theological leanings, also revived Aristotelian immanent realism, affirming access to the knowledge of God both in reason *and* nature.

Amid their differences, what Greek, Medieval and ancient Hebraic epistemology have in common is that they all orient the knower to a transcendent *other* outside of the self. There is, in other words, a divine reality beneath which (or whom) we find ourselves as knowers. This was all to change in Modernity.

More than anything else, the Modern era is distinguished by its anthropological turn *inwards* and scientific move from below to *above*. René Descartes is undoubtedly the most representative and foundational figure of this shift.[17] In the sixteenth century his search for truth and certainty leads him to dismiss poetry, history, story and tradition[18] in favor of the logic of critique and doubt within individual reason. Descartes' experience of seemingly irresolvable pluralities in philosophy, science and religion in his day, com-

[14] M. McLuhan, *The Classical Trivium* (Corte Madera, CA: Gingko, 2006), 87–99.

[15] H.D. Lubac, *Medieval Exegesis* (Grand Rapids, MI: Eerdmans, 1998) and McLuhan, *The Trivium* (cited above) provide similar accounts of the grammatical-rhetorical traditions which formed the foundations of the liberal arts. R. Kearney's *Wake of Imagination*, 114–49, has an illuminating portrait of the more Platonic categories which, while they often dominate the official church language in Christendom, are matched by the artistic and poetic rhetoric of the popular world and the arts throughout the Medieval era; a Hebraic worldview maintains its influence in the midst of the official rhetoric.

[16] According to Toulmin, "Human modesty", and not "certainty" provided their motto for life and doctrine, *Cosmopolis*, 23–7.

[17] Cf. C. Stephan Evans who points to Descartes' acceptance of "*scientia* in the medieval sense" and therefore credits John Locke with the most radical form of "evidentialist" certainty regarding knowledge, *The Historical Christ and the Jesus of Faith* (Oxford: Clarendon, 1996), 208.

[18] Descartes, *Discourse*, 8.

pelled him to go at it alone: "I was unable to choose someone whose views seemed to me to be preferable to those of others, and I found myself forced to take on the task of guiding myself."[19] And, not just his "self" in general but the reliable, immaterial self of reason: "After all, whether we are awake or asleep, we should never allow ourselves to be convinced of anything except by the evidence of our reason [...]."[20] The individual human mind, its scientific method and its ethical conscience become the new location of ultimate reality. The transcendent is now *in here* rather than *out there* and inward autonomy replaces the outward divinity of the pre-modern world.[21]

Whereas Descartes trusted reason over sense and imagination, empiricism made an Aristotelian turn to the scientific necessity and reliability of the senses. This empirical method of knowing is certainly different than Descartes' rationalism; yet both share a confidence in individual (subjective) verification within a systematic and scientific paradigm. And, both traditions are deeply concerned with assuring the knower that our experiences of the world are real and that we can have confidence in the knowing process. The Enlightenment, in effect, amplifies rationalism into a new, scientific and objective pursuit of "evidence" in search of propositions of truth and knowledge. Knowledge comes when we disengage from history, community, ontology, worldviews,[22] and from faith in the pursuit of knowledge. Enlightenment epistemologies also generally promote the *regionalisation* of knowledge,[23] rather than the holistic and immanent epistemologies of Hebraism and Aristotelianism.

At the peak of the Enlightenment project, Immanuel Kant proposed a transcendental way of uniting reason and experience within the subjective mind. While the details of his philosophy are beyond the scope of this study, it is notable that his work is opposed by the powerful *Sturm und Drang* movement of the eighteenth century, which sought to re-engage knowing with faith, religion, poetics, music and history. J.G. Hamann, typically considered the founder of the *Sturm und Drang* and Kant's most significant interlocutor, responded to weaknesses in Kant's epistemology and

---

19 Ibid., 15.

20 Ibid., 29.

21 While Descartes has much to say about God, it is a rational theism even less theological than Plato's. God is the perfect representation of reason and truth whose existence gives us confidence in our own internal ability to reason and understand.

22 D.K. Naugle, *Worldview: The History of a Concept* (Grand Rapids, MI/Cambridge: Eerdmans, 2002), xix defines a worldview a "system of narrative signs that establishes a powerful framework within which people think (reason), interpret (hermeneutics), and know (epistemology)".

23 P. Ricoeur, *Hermeneutics and the Human Sciences* (Cambridge: Cambridge University, 1981) describes Gadamer's philosophy as a "synthesis of two movements [...] from regional hermeneutics to general from epistemology of human sciences to ontology". (60) and "The obsessive concern with radicality thus blocks the return route from general hermeneutics towards regional hermeneutics: towards philology, history, depth-psychology, etc." (90).

proposed "faith" as a type of knowledge which involves belief, rather than something opposed to knowledge.[24]

The Enlightenment project does not retain its progressive and humanistic form of rational optimism, failing to deliver the intercultural harmony, scientific certainty, and human flourishing which it promised. The result is a post-Enlightenment world of increasingly diverse views of knowledge. We can, however, loosely identify several kinds of responses to the demise of individual autonomy and rational certainty: denial and reaffirmation (fundamentalism, rationalism, and scientism), ambivalence (modern analytical philosophy), reaction, revolt, re-construction (postmodernism) and finally various forms of critical realism. In is important that we see how the most extreme postmodern[25] thinkers renew ancient historical expressions of Epicureanism, Stoicism, and Skepticism.[26] Here we encounter a turn from confidence to suspicion and even the death of knowledge in the death of the modern "Man" (Foucault). Postmodern suspicion and doubt are aimed at the whole arsenal of Western ideals which gave unity to pre-modern religion and Modern science: universals, the divine, story, history, poetry and art.[27] The energy behind the postmodern mood is typically directed away from foundations and meaning and toward doubt, despair and the *deconstruction* of knowledge.[28]

In our own day many if not most people operate somewhere between the radical postmodern rejection of knowledge and naive optimism in science and individual human autonomy. C.S. Evans describes this in-between area as holding a "modest" epistemology because it assumes a "common-sense" approach to knowledge. It is modest because it agrees with the skeptical conclusion that ambitious attempts at epistemological justification and certainty have failed to achieve a consensus, but also because it recognizes the

---

24 Hamann's epistemology also appealed to Aristotelian realism, grounding knowledge and language in society, aesthetics, politics. etc. Cf. F.C. Beiser, *The Fate of Reason: German Philosophy from Kant to Fichte* (Cambridge, MA/London: Harvard University, 1987), 24–43.

25 J.A. Kirk, et al., "The State of Claims to Rationality", in A.J. Kirk and K.J. Vanhoozer (ed.), *To Stake a Claim* (New York: Orbis Books, 1999) 35–52, on pp. 46–52 helpfully divides the postmodern approach to knowledge into four categories: Practice (the pragmatic approach of Rorty); Poetry (following Heidegger's search for truth in "Being"); Play (Derrida's deconstruction which, at the loss of a stable center to language, shows the faulty rhetorical structures behind it); and Power (Foucault's reduction of rationality to the "sociopolitical" forces of the day).

26 Tarnas, *Passion*, 78.

27 S.J. Grenz, *A Primer on Postmodernism* (Grand Rapids, MI/Cambridge: Eerdmans, 1996), 5f who limits the mood to the postmodern period. However, Tarnas, *Passion*, rightly sees both the classical (78) and Renaissance (276) roots of postmodern ideas, particularly in Michel Montaigne. Cf. also Toulmin, *Cosmopolis*, 36–42 and R.H. Popkin, "Michel Eyquen de Montaigne", in P. Edwards (ed.), *Encyclopedia of Philosophy 5* (New York: Collier-Macmillan, 1972) 366–68, on p. 368.

28 G. Steiner, *Real Presences* (Chicago: University of Chicago, 1989), 116–27.

obvious fact that most of the world assumes that "knowledge is possible, indeed that it is actual".[29]

The nature of the epistemological project we have embarked upon here demands a kind of modest epistemology – a confidence in knowledge without resorting to dogmatism or scientific precision. Knowledge is real and possible, but it is not always easily acquired and is often distorted or obscured by our personal preferences and the cultural and social contexts which surround us. In order to sustain this careful balance, we will need to say more about the hermeneutic method which will bring interpretation and epistemology together.

1.2 Hermeneutical Concerns

A modest approach to knowing dovetails with our remarks from the beginning of the chronological history above, setting the tone for our study as descriptive rather than prescriptive – an attempt to identify the framework within which ancient Hebrew *knew* things and trusted their knowledge. For, as we have said, the Hebraic worldview is not theoretical; its views are expressed narratively, mythically and poetically. Critical and theoretical concerns, therefore, must be tempered towards a focus on the cohesion in these ancient texts – those narrative dimensions of belief out of which epistemological observations can be made. The following hermeneutical assumptions will help us to keep us focused on our purpose.

Our overarching hermeneutical outlook seeks to situate the literary and historical dimensions of our study within the full, interdisciplinary understanding of *meaning*. Paul Ricoeur suggests the helpful metaphor of a "conflict of interpretations",[30] which seeks not to override the literary with the historical – or vice versa – but to allow perspectives from history, aesthetics, and worldview (ideology) to be sustained in endless, open conversation.[31] For an historian the text is primarily an artifact and for the aesthete the text is primarily a source of beauty. But for the hermeneutician, the *collection* is an artifact, discourse, and a poetic source of beauty, as all inform

---

[29] *Christ*, 205.

[30] "Existence and Hermeneutics", in *The Conflict of Interpretation* (Evanston, IL: Northwestern University, 1974) 3–24. Here Ricoeur argues that the "epistemology of interpretation" wrongly favored a Kantian objective approach to knowledge. An "ontology of knowledge", on the other hand, reflects phenomenologically on the problem of hermeneutics; rather than closing down questions of meaning and knowledge, it orients the interpreter to the many levels of interpretation involved in coming to meaning.

[31] Meir Sternberg suggests that biblical interpretation is not *a* discipline, but the "intersection of the humanities par excellence". *The Poetics of Biblical Narrative* (Bloomington, Indiana: Indiana University, 1987), 21. He goes on to describe how biblical texts are typically studied from either historical, poetic, literary or philosophical perspectives, but rarely from all of them at once, which is what the biblical text requires, p. 36.

the meaning and value of the text.[32] Hermeneutics therefore reminds us how the ancient world viewed these texts as aesthetic and hierophanic tales which are *true* in the way they set apart a unique way of knowing God and other things about the world.[33] In other words, attention to the conflict of interpretations requires us to suspend literary, sociological and historical critiques, relevant as they are, long enough to propose another way of reading the text – epistemological, ethical and formative.

When discourse, poetics and worldview are set in conversation, they allow us to raise more critical questions about the mythical and narrative way of knowing. Meir Sternberg's work attends to this very intersection of disciplines. Yet I suggest that Sternberg is too ready to conflate all philosophy, religion, and epistemology into "ideology." As we will argue in chapter four below, such a reductive move is not consistent with the historical origins of "ideology." It also obscures the texture within ancient worldviews and their ability to have an awareness that certain ideologies can be resisted in favor of something else, namely wisdom, truth or the like.[34]

We should finally note the important way that the conflict of interpretations makes us aware of the tradition of meta-critique in continental philosophy. As we suggested above, our historiographical and literary-critical mirrors must be examined for their tendency to reflect too much of the observer. Here we note Ricoeur's citation of Hans Gadamer's critique of *Forschung,* or inquiry: "Scientific research does not escape the historical consciousness of those who live and make history. Historical knowledge cannot free itself from the historical context which conditions it."[35] Hermeneutics, therefore, must simultaneously retain postures of critique and self-critique, allowing the text to speak into our world with its own questions and perspectives, and, at times, to remain beyond our comprehension.

2. The Epistemologies within Wisdom and Law

We turn now to set our course for the chapters which follow. The relationship between torah and wisdom in the Old Testament has fueled a vibrant

---

[32] P. Ricoeur, "Structure and Hermeneutics", in *The Conflict of Interpretations* (Evanston, IL: Northwestern University, 1974) 27–61, on p. 32; P. Ricoeur, "The Problem of Double Meaning", in *The Conflict of Traditions* (Evanston, IL: Northwestern University, 1974) 62–78, on p. 68; *HHS*, 146f; and *Interpretation Theory: Discourse and the Surplus of Meaning* (Fort Worth, TX: Texas Christian University, 1976), 12–14. Cf. S. Carmy/D. Schatz, "The Bible as a Source of Philosophical Reflection", in D.H. Frank/O. Leaman (ed.), *History of Jewish Philosophy* (London: Routledge, 2003) 13–37, on pp. 13–37.

[33] See L. Kass, *The Beginning of Wisdom* (Chicago: University of Chicago, 2003), 7, 10.

[34] Leon Kass' preference to seek "wisdom" implies a for more personal and involved view of the textual content than Sternberg's almost objective "ideology," *Beginning of Wisdom*, 2.

[35] *HHS*, 76.

discussion in the last half-century. Eckhard Schnabel's study from 1985 helpfully summarizes eight theories about how these two traditions came to be equated in post-exilic Israel, the book of Sirach in particular.[36] Our study is not immediately concerned with their theological alignment in late Judaism and early Christian thought, but rather with the development of those traditions prior to that point.[37]

The next chapter begins our study with the literary evolution of torah in the Hebrew Bible, briefly describing the way in which the cosmic myths in Genesis and the historical narratives in Exodus form a basis for knowing God and the world. The chapter ends with an introduction to Deuteronomy. As we will see, Deuteronomy is undoubtedly a later addition to these early myths and narratives, designed to establish the torah as a definitive Mosaic tradition. While the historical accounts of the Deuteronomist's work are a matter of general consensus, our concern is more hermeneutical and intertextual. That is, Deuteronomy is increasingly valued as a rhetorical masterpiece,[38] and chapters three through five of our study demonstrate the way it advances the mythical and ethical framework of knowing which originates in the Genesis narratives. While highlighting some of the discontinuities between Deuteronomy and the Tetrateuch, our primary aim is to ask how the aesthetic and theological fabric of Deuteronomy also evidence important epistemological threads coming out of the earlier narratives.

Chapters six and seven seek to describe the epistemology of the wisdom literature, beginning with Proverbs. Despite the close attention given to epistemology in the wisdom literature, wisdom scholarship so far has failed to produce an independent study of epistemology in this book. Proverbs, after all, is generally agreed to be the original form of wisdom, grounded in cosmic orderliness and retributive optimism. We will argue that much of what has been stated about proverbial epistemology has been based upon readings which neglect and/or undervalue the synthetic theological and literary force brought to bear by the order and arrangement of the final collection.

In chapter 7 we briefly introduce the epistemological studies in Ecclesiastes and Job. As "late" or "critical" responses traditional Jewish religion, these books are typically pitted against torah (Deuteronomy) and early wisdom (Proverbs). However, there is also an aesthetic and rhetorical richness

---

[36] E.J. Schnabel, *Law and Wisdom from Ben Sira to Paul: A Tradition Historical Inquiry Into the Relation of Law, Wisdom, and Ethics* (Tübingen: Mohr Siebeck, 1985), 1–4.

[37] Perhaps closer to what is done in G.T. Sheppard, *Wisdom as a Hermeneutical Construct: A Study in the Sapientializing of the Old Testament* (Berlin/New York: BZAW de Gruyter, 1980) and chapter eight below.

[38] See J.-P. Sonnet, *The Book Within the Book: Writing in Deuteronomy* (Leiden/New York: Brill, 1997).

in these books which invites more interpretation and reflection. Drawing on the epistemological aspects of these books we will propose a more nuanced way to describe the relationship between their content (Job and Ecclesiastes) and these two traditions (torah and wisdom).

After these independent, textual studies in torah and wisdom, chapter eight finally asks how our understanding of the relationship between wisdom and law has been affected by the epistemological studies of these individual books. The previous chapters will also put us in a position to consider questions about the deuterocanonical literature and the gradual move in Jewish and Christian interpretations of the Hebrew Bible to begin with a Greek perspective on knowledge, myth and ethics.

3. Conclusion

Questions of epistemology and ideology have rarely been the focus of biblical scholarship, relegated instead to hermeneutical and sociological specialists. This study draws these disciplines together in order to enrich them all in some way. Our short rehearsal of the history of epistemology in this chapter also demonstrates how the phenomenological reflection which follows will provide an opportunity for meta-critique: descriptive analysis invites historiographers, sociologists, literary critics and theologians to reflect on their own methods and assumptions and to initiate conversation where it did not exist before. All of this will become apparent as our exploration progresses.

CHAPTER TWO

Mythos, Cosmos and Episteme
Mythical and Cosmic Origins to Hebraic Knowledge

1. Introduction

> [T]he stories in Genesis address our current concern with man's relation to nature and the earth, to the animals, and to the divine – ultimate questions in any pursuit of wisdom.[1]

In a rare interdisciplinary venture, bioethicist Leon Kass has released a massive work on Genesis which invites religious, literary, historical, political, and philosophical-minded folk alike to join in hearing the most popular Jewish book as *wisdom*. The rarity of such work has been created by the tendency among modern scholars to press Genesis into molds of revelation, *or* history, *or* literature. But as F. Rosenzweig helpfully notes, the biblical narrative has a grand, ancient "epic narrative" quality that bridges revelation, teaching and poetics.[2] The creation account, for example, strikes readers from every outlook in life with its claims to the order in the world and the place of humanity within that order, regardless of its religious origins.

What we have to say about Deuteronomy and the wisdom literature below depends largely upon a mytho-poetic unity between Genesis, the Pentateuch narratives and the wisdom literature. This chapter will, therefore, rehearse the epistemological worldview that is laid down in these stories and then provide a framework for relating them to Deuteronomy in chapters three through five.

2. Cosmos and Knowledge: Genesis 1–11

Like Kass, Ricoeur's reading of the Pentateuch enters through a hermeneutic of ancient mythology. He explains,

> myth will here be taken to mean what the history of religions now finds in it: not a false explanation by means of images and fables, but a traditional narration, which

[1] L. Kass, *The Beginning of Wisdom* (Chicago: University of Chicago, 2003), 21.

[2] F. Rosenzweig, "The Secret of Biblical Narrative Form", in M. Buber/F. Rosenzweig (ed.), *Scripture and Translation* (Bloomington/Indianapolis: Indiana University, 1994) 129–42.

relates to events that happened at the beginning of time and which has the purpose of providing grounds for the ritual actions of men of today and, in a general manner, establishing all the forms of action and thought by which man understands himself in his world.[3]

While ancient myths are our way into ancient worldviews, Ricoeur recognizes that we do not have immediate access to the original sense of myths, their symbols and their power of "discovering and revealing the bond between man and what he considers sacred".[4] We stand in a cultural and historical gap, needing to balance the "cosmic", "oneric" and "speculative" dimensions of symbolic interpretation. Critical methods are prone to overemphasise speculation, allowing demythologization to overpower the hierophanic, cosmic,[5] aesthetic and religious dimensions. In our search for epistemological significance, therefore, we must be on guard not to demand only speculative, direct or theoretical explanation of the human experience in the world. Creation, evil and the divine remain embedded in a symbolic, complex fabric within which people came to know and understand the local world and its manifestations of sin and injustice.

An interdisciplinary hermeneutics is thus essential to this project, for it was within *this* symbolic and cosmic world that the Torah was first received. In other words, the mythical world of torah is rooted in the creation accounts in Genesis 1–3 where nature, divinity, humanity and morality are first understood. In Genesis 1–2 we encounter two parts of an ancient, origin myth. The first (1:1–2:3) is cosmic and slowly builds a picture of perfect order and goodness. The second part (2:4–3:25) is a ranging, personal story of human freedoms and divine fellowship which rises to a climax of epistemological uncertainty, doubt and rebellion. There are obvious discontinuities between the stories, but from the mythical and poetic perspectives of interpretation, these create a space for emplotment and conflict around the nature of good and evil.[6]

The strongest sense of unity between the two creation plots[7] comes at the point of humanity being made in God's image (1:27) and his breathing life into it (2:7). The movement is from general creation to particularity within the creation. Both stories thus elevate woman and man to near-divine status: in Genesis 1:1–2:3, humans end the intensive progress from days one to six and are given universal responsibility for creation-care; in Genesis 2–3 Adam's giving particular names to the animals symbolizes this same

---

3 P. Ricoeur, *The Symbolism of Evil* (Boston: Beacon, 1967), 5.

4 Ibid.

5 Ibid., 9, cf. also Keel, *Symbolism*, 8.

6 M. Buber, *Good and Evil* (New York: Scribner, 1952), 67–80 provides just such an explorative reading of these two myths.

7 See G.T. Sheppard, *Wisdom as a Hermeneutical Construct: A Study in the Sapientializing of the Old Testament* (Berlin/New York: BZAW de Gruyter, 1980), 22–6.

authority over the other creatures (2:19–20). The plot thickens, forcing us to imagine how the universal limits, boundaries and order in the first creation account in the life of the local and timely real-world garden of the second.

The climax of this inter-narrative conflict comes in Genesis 3, formed primarily by the problem of particularity. That is, the *cosmic* and *universal* images of "beasts" (הַבְּהֵמָה) in Genesis 1:25 and "every green herb" (כָּל־יֶרֶק עֵשֶׂב) in Genesis 1:30 become *particular*: vegetation (2:8–9), animals (2:19–20) and humans (2:20–25) are all named. When the symbolic creation images in chapter 1 are particularised, order and harmony become dynamic and vibrant, but also ambiguous. The new polarities of Life and the Knowledge of Good and Evil create a climactic epistemological tension – what anthropologist Van Gennep, calls "liminal". Liminality describes the universal intra-cultural power of "rights of passage" where "Transitions from group to group and from one social situation to the next are looked on as implicit in the very fact of existence, so that a man's life comes to be made up of a succession of stages with similar ends and beginnings: birth, social puberty, marriage [...]."[8] Adam and Eve stand on the threshold of ethical and vocational identity before these two deeply enticing agricultural symbols of the created order. The perplexing tension is an epistemological teaching point as it forces the audience to speculate about the conditions which lead Adam and Eve to cross the sacred thresholds. These epistemological thresholds are also ethical, derived from the larger symbolic, narrative-nexus which blends universal cosmic boundaries (Gen 1) with the particularity of practical ethics and human and divine wisdom (Gen 2–3).

The interpretation of the imagination (יצר) in Genesis, rising out of Talmudic commentary, helps us to appreciate the mythical-epistemological significance of these two narratives.[9] The first and last words of Genesis 2:7–8 come from the root יצר:

> Yahweh God fashioned the man (**וַיִּיצֶר** יְהוָה אֱלֹהִים אֶת־הָאָדָם) ... and he put there the man whom he fashioned (אֶת־הָאָדָם אֲשֶׁר **יָצָר**).

This is the man who had been *created* in the "image of God" (1:27) to govern God's world. Although the root יצר means to "form" or "create," Genesis uses it in a way that provides ethical and epistemological nuance; like

---

8 A.v. Gennep, *The Rites of Passage* (London/Henley: Routledge and Kegan Paul, 1977), 3, 10–21. Cf. N. Stahl, *Law and Liminality in the Bible* (JSOTSup; Sheffield: JSOT, 1995), 11–2 who sees liminal situations in the tensions of a society marked by "new beginnings" and "critical phases": "All liminal moments, however, share some defining characteristics: they are concerned with transition, and function as focal points of the biblical vision of the often tenuous, always dynamic relationship between God and his elect." Liminality is central to our study and will be discussed at several points in chapters below.

9 See R. Kearney, *The Wake of Imagination* (New York: Routledge, 1988), 39–49; Ricoeur, *Symbolism of Evil*, 130–1; and E. Fromm, *You Shall be as Gods: A Radical Reinterpretation of the Old Testament in Its Tradition* (Chicago/New York: Holt, Rinehart and Winston, 1966), 67–72.

their Creator, humans are called to their own creative work in the form of imitation and imagination. Erich Fromm helpfully connects the symbols of creation and divine image with the rabbinical doctrines of divine *imitation*[10] and *knowledge* of the divine: "This imitation of God by acting the way God acts means becoming more and more like God; it means at the same time *knowing* God."[11] Indeed it is knowledge of good (טוב) and evil (רע) which first seduces the woman to be *like* God (3:5). Overcome by a desire for "wisdom" (שׂכל) and the savory pleasures of taste and sight, epistemology and divine command appear to be at odds (3:6); Eve is unable to interpret the symbols and carry out her יצר vocation. Unable to "know" Good and Evil, humanity overshoots its privilege and *imitates* God in a profane way.

The epistemological *Leitwörter* of Genesis 1–3 all reappear in two noahic passages, and complete the development of the mythical-ethical imagination. The first passage is Genesis 6:5 where God expresses regret for his original creation. The second comes after the flood and serves to return favor to the divine image:

> And Yahweh saw all the wickedness (רָעַת) of humanity on the earth and that all the intentions (יֵצֶר) of the thoughts of his heart were only evil (רַע) continually. (Gen 6:5)

> When Yahweh smelled the pleasing aroma, Yahweh said in his heart, "I will never again curse the ground because of humanity for the intention (יֵצֶר) of man's heart is evil (רַע) from his youth. Neither will I ever again strike down every living creature as I have done". (Gen 8:21)

Buber perceptively notes that it is not "man" which God declares evil, but the יצר within him (cf. Ps 73:7).[12] It is the imagination, the epistemological freedom to act as co-creator, that has become evil. The extended narrative in Genesis 1–8 leaves us with a complex theology of cosmic boundaries, ethics and epistemology (imagination as imitation). Ricoeur explains the rabbinical interpretation:

> Nevertheless, what underlies this ethical vision of the world is the idea of a liberty entirely responsible and always at its own disposal [...] we find this in the writings of the rabbis in two themes, the first of these is the theme of the two "inclinations" (or *yetzer*): man is subject to the duality of two tendencies, two impulses – a good inclination and an evil inclination. The latter-yetzer *ha-ra* is implanted by the Creator in man; he is one of the things that God has made and of which he has said that they were "very good".[13]

---

10 See Fromm, *You Shall be as Gods*, 63–5.
11 Ibid., 167.
12 Buber, *Good and Evil*, 91.
13 *Symbolism of Evil*, 130–1.

The theological connections between the cosmic intentions for humanity and the Mosaic Torah foreground the next three chapters of our study. For law-keeping – in the full context of the Torah – is always connected to human knowledge of the divine sense of "good." Fromm explains, "The practice of the law is true religiosity, the knowledge of the law is the substitute for theology."[14] The Patriarchal narratives stand between the cosmic, creation mythology and the Mosaic law-proper. As we visit the Patriarchs, we will identify several more narrative connections between the creation myth and the laws in Exodus and Deuteronomy.

3. Primordial and Patriarchal Connections

The narratives in Deuteronomy and Exodus have been written with both divisions of Genesis in mind: they affirm the cosmic imagery in Genesis 1–11 and they show a theological respect for the Patriarchal narratives. The lynch-pin for all of these connections is in Genesis 12. D.J. Clines' study of Genesis 12:1–3 illustrates the role of the Abrahamic promise as the "theme" of the Pentateuch, uniting the patriarchs with the law.[15] Yet he fails to develop the relationship between the human primeval vocation as co-creators (Gen 1:26–8) and the patriarchal narratives (Gen 12–50).[16] Countless symbols and mythical parallels, however, make this relationship clear: the sins of Adam, Abraham, Babel, and Sodom; the "land" and the "garden;" Adam as father of humanity and Abram as the father of Israel; and Eve's "seed" and Abram's "seed." Wenham rightly concludes that Genesis 12 naturally unites creation with the Patriarchs.[17] Kass also confirms the relationship, calling this text the "turning point in human history" and "a new human alternative": "In a word, the new human way – the way of the Children of Israel, launched as a light to the nations" is "built" on the principles of justice and righteousness (law).[18] God has selected Abraham, not to abandon

---

14 Fromm, *You Shall be as Gods*, 191.

15 D.J. Clines, *The Theme of the Pentateuch* (JSOTSup 10; Sheffield: Sheffield Academic, 1978). Cf. S.D.J. McBride, "The Yoke of the Kingdom: An Exposition of Deuteronomy 6:4–5", *Interpretation* 27 (1973) 273–306, on p. 273 for a confirmation of the "universal" nature of Yahweh's kingdom in OT theology.

16 This is Gordon Wenham's critique of Clines in *Story as Torah: Reading the Old Testament Ethically* (Edinburgh: T&T Clark, 2000), 23–4.

17 G.J. Wenham, *Genesis 1–15* (Word Biblical Commentary; Waco, TX: Word, 1987) says that the "editor's interests" lie in patriarchal history which is "background to the story of Israel's exodus from Egypt and the lawgiving at Sinai which forms the subject matter of Exodus to Deuteronomy" (xlv). Furthermore the primordial history "shows how the promises made to the patriarchs fulfill *God's original plans for humanity*" (li, emphasis added) and "The promises of blessing to the patriarchs are thus a reassertion of God's original intentions for man" (275).

18 Kass, *Beginning of Wisdom*, 17, 12.

the nations and the original creation, but to focus on the cosmic vocation of a single family as the means for universal redemption.[19]

M. Kline sees the patriarchal narratives united to law by way of the covenant. The covenant is Yahweh's means to gather the nations around Israel and, therefore, in his own presence as the "cultic" centre of his world.[20] Taking the primordial and universal themes together, Genesis sets Israel apart in a legal and binding relationship with Yahweh in order to gather and bless the nations in a re-created garden. The covenant, of course, knits the theologies of Genesis 12 together with Exodus and Deuteronomy which follow.

4. Knowledge in Exodus

Just as Genesis 12 is the bridge between creation and Patriarchs, so Exodus is the bridge between the patriarchs and the Deuteronomic covenant. Like Genesis 1–11, this bridge is supported by the towers of epistemology, ethics and divine presence.

The combination of theophany (divine appearance) and knowledge in Exodus have received a great deal of attention in recent decades. Polak points to the "supra-textual" nature of theophany which stands at the centre of the Exodus plot.[21] The theophanic appearances occur in stages, according to Polak, which in turn progressively reveal both the nature of Yahweh's revelation and the uniqueness of Moses' mediatorial role.[22] Zimmerli and Eslinger also make note of the unique collocation of ידע and יהוה in Exodus 1–15 (Zimmerli's "*Erkenntnisformel*") which are combined with a causative intention: "that you (he, they) might know that I am Yahweh".[23]

---

19 See also G.v. Rad, *Genesis* (Philadelphia: Westminster, 1961), 155–6.

20 *The Structure of Biblical Authority* (Grand Rapids, MI: Eerdmans, 1972), 46–7. Cf. S.D. McBride, "Polity of the Covenant People; The Book of Deuteronomy", in D. Christensen (ed.), *Song of Power* (Winona Lake: Eisenbrauns, 1993) 62–77.

21 "Theophany and Mediator: The Unfolding of a Theme in the Book of Exodus", in M. Vervenne (ed.), *Studies in the Book of Moses* (Leuven: Leuven University, 1996) 113–47, on pp. 113, 117. Cf. also J.J. Niehaus, *God at Sinai: Covenant and Theophany in the Bible and Ancient Near East* (Grand Rapids, MI: Zondervan, 1995), 26–7.

22 Polak, "Theophany", 122–3.

23 Exodus 5:2; 6:7; 7:17; 8:10; 9:14, 16; 10:1; 14:4, 18. See W. Zimmerli, "I Am Yahweh", in W. Brueggemann (ed.), *Yahweh* (Atlanta: John Knox, 1953) 1–28, "Knowledge of God According to the Book of Ezekiel", in W. Brueggemann (ed.), *I Am Yahweh* (Atlanta: John Knox, 1954) 29–98, on pp. 29–98 (47) and L. Eslinger, "Exod 6:3 in the Context of Genesis 1-Exodus 15", in L. Regt/J. de Waard/J.P. Fokkelman (ed.), *Literary Structure and Rhetorical Strategies in the Hebrew Bible* (Assen: Van Gorcum, 1996) 188–98 and "Freedom or Knowledge? Perspective and Purpose in the Exodus Narrative (Exodus 1–15)", *JSOT* 52 (1991) 43–60. Although the roots ידע and יהוה occur together variously throughout the OT (e.g. "I know says Yahweh"), what is at issue here is the combination of forms in a way that implies "knowing Yahweh".

Together these themes of theophany and knowledge play a progressive role in four stages of Exodus.

In the first stage, these themes control the narrative in the call of Moses and the revelation of the divine name in Exodus 3–6.[24] Moses' role as the mediator of Yahweh's essence and his activity in history[25] become the central themes for the following narrative, for Moses will carry his burning bush-experience at Horeb (Sinai) down to Egypt and back with his people to the mountain.[26] In this context, the first in a subsequent string of *Erkenntnisformel*-phrases (יהוה-ידע) comes in Pharaoh's question:

Exod 5:2
וַיֹּאמֶר פַּרְעֹה מִי יְהוָה אֲשֶׁר אֶשְׁמַע בְּקֹלוֹ לְשַׁלַּח אֶת־יִשְׂרָאֵל לֹא יָדַעְתִּי אֶת־יְהוָה וְגַם אֶת־יִשְׂרָאֵל לֹא אֲשַׁלֵּחַ׃

Not only does this collocation of ידע and יהוה appear here for the first time in the Pentateuch, but its frequency in these chapters is unmatched in the OT aside from Ezekiel 1–40 – a book with similar goals.[27] In Exodus, Pharaoh's question implicitly stands in bold contrast to Yahweh's emphatic (fiery) revelation to Moses in chapter 3 and creates a gap for the following narrative to fill. The gap is initially filled in chapters 5–12 by Yahweh's answer of ten plagues. But this only begins the narrative development of Yahweh's identity/glory in the events at the Sinai (ch. 19–24; 31–34) and tabernacle (ch. 40) theophanies which foreground the rest of the Pentateuch. In the context of the answer to Pharaoh (Exod 5–12), Yahweh's acts of judgment and redemption in Egypt serve a higher epistemological purpose, striking at the heart of Pharaoh's claim on divinity and wisdom (*Ma'at*). Eslinger thus states, "Freeing Israel from Egypt's power seems the point of the whole affair, but a careful look at the overall shape of the

---

[24] The name "Yahweh" appears first in Genesis, of course, but this does not mean that the writer(s) of Exodus is unaware of the textual tradition (Jahwist). Rather Exodus' point is that the divine name comes to Israel with additional revelation of his acts in Egypt and at Horeb. Cf. Eslinger, "Exod 6:3", 192 and C.R. Seitz, "The Call of Moses and the 'Revelation' of the Divine Name", in idem.; *Word Without End* (Grand Rapids, MI: Eerdmans, 1998) 229–47.

[25] Zimmerli, "Knowledge", 47, limits the knowledge of Yahweh to his activity and not his essence. The very meaning of the divine name (no matter how it is translated) undeniably implies something about his essence which will be evidenced by his actions. Cf. B.S. Childs, *The Book of Exodus* (Louisville, KY: Westminster, 1974), 88f on God's "being" and "activity" in history and revelation.

[26] Zimmerli, "Knowledge", 12–3 and M. Fishbane, *Text and Texture: Close Readings of Selected Biblical Texts* (New York: Schocken, 1979), 68–9 both illustrate the connections between Moses' intermediary status and divine knowledge.

[27] Eslinger, "Exod 6:3" counts nine collocations of ידע and יהוה outside of Exodus and Ezekiel (Deut 29:5 [6]; 1 Kgs 20:13, 28; Isa 45:3; 49:23, 26; 60:16; Hos 2:22 [20]; Joel 2:27; 4:17 [3:17]. Nine are found in Exod 1–15 alone and six more in Exod 16–33). Zimmerli, "Knowledge", 30, 47 counts between 78 and 86 uses of the "monotonous turn of phrase" in Ezekiel.

events [...] leads me to believe that liberation is subordinate to the *manifestation of the divine name* through the miraculous interventions."[28]

Yahweh's revelatory aims are sustained throughout the rest of Exodus. Although there is no explicit theophany at the sea (Exod 13–15), the theophanic themes of water, power and judgment[29] converge to form the basis of a universal declaration wherein Yahweh's victory over Pharaoh shows his "incomparable power and thereby establishes his divine authority" (cf. 14:4, 18).[30] In the larger context of the Pentateuch, Yahweh is exercising a re-creative power to fashion Israel out of the chaos of Egypt and prepare them for a new typological garden hope of a promised land.[31] The re-creating God leads Israel back to Horeb, the place of Moses' first theophanic experience,[32] where he uses his mediator to give Israel his law (or ten דברים, Exod 19–34) as a new pattern for good and evil.

Here we find the next two stages of narrative and epistemological development. The first is in the initial giving of the law and the Book of the Covenant (ch. 19–24). The second is during the failure of the golden calf in Exodus 32–34 where Yahweh reestablishes his relationship with Israel with a mysterious appearance to Moses in the cleft of the rock. Coming from the victory at the sea, the first episode carries power and authority into a covenant ceremony which binds Israel in a redemptive relationship with clear legal overtones.[33] The subsequent failure with the golden calf performs at least two functions. First, it builds upon Yahweh's power and authority with his forgiving and loving nature (34:6), a new revelation which is appropriately highlighted by the repetition of the divine name יהוה יהוה who is a God who: רחום וחנון ארך אפים ורב־חסד ואמת. Second, Israel's ethical failure at Horeb also reinforces the corresponding implications for divine distance and limits to human knowledge of Yahweh.[34] The latter move is central to the Pentateuchal narrative both because it confirms a place for eschatologi-

---

[28] "Exod 6:3", 189, emphasis added. Cf. also G. Fischer, "Exodus 1–15 – Eine Erzählung", in M. Vervenne (ed.), *Studies in the Book of Exodus* (Leuven: Leuven University, 1996) 149–78, on p. 153 who says: "Pharaos Frage 'Wer ist Jahwe?' in 5,2 ist Triebfeder für das weitere Tun Gottes [...]". See also pp. 159 and 176. Although less emphatically, Childs, *Exodus*, 104–5, 114–5 also notes the centrality of Yahweh's name and nature in the narrative.

[29] On these theophanic themes, see Polak, "Theophany", 113 and Niehaus, *Sinai*, 23, 25, 205–17.

[30] Polak, "Theophany", 137.

[31] T.E. Fretheim, *Exodus* (Interpretation; Louisville, KY: John Knox, 1991) 13–5 and "The Reclamation of Creation: Redemption and Law in Exodus", *Interpretation* 45 (1991) 354–65, argues that creation theology lies at the heart of the book of Exodus and defines what it means for Israel to be redeemed out of the water. See also Niehaus, *Sinai*, 198–9 who shows how the six-day covenant meal in Exod 24 also enacts creation imagery and secures Israel's place as a new creation.

[32] See Childs, *Exodus*, 59–60.

[33] Kline, *Structure*, 117–20 convincingly ties ANE covenant treaty patterns (Hittite or Assyrian) to the Yahweh's royal status over Israel giving him both "ownership" and "authority" (cf Exod 31:13–17).

[34] Stahl, *Law*, 63–4.

cal hope but also because it secures Moses' uniqueness as the sole covenant mediator between Yahweh and his people.[35]

The fourth theophanic episode comes when Yahweh's כבד fills the tabernacle and, in effect, makes his Sinai presence among Israel permanent and transportable (Exod 40:34–38). Lohfink here sees a pattern of what we are calling actualisation as the tabernacle and the retelling of the story allow the Sinai experience of one generation to become "transferable" to future generations in future places.[36] As the narrative closes, its reference to theophany echoes Moses' place at Sinai and at the burning bush at Horeb (Exod 3) as evidenced by sixteen references to Israel's obedience: "as Yahweh commanded Moses".[37] That is to say, by obeying the command of Yahweh *through Moses* future Israel can access to the mountain and tabernacle glory of her ancestors: obeying the good יצר leads to knowledge of God.

In the end, we can see that Yahweh's self-revelation, in his essence, his activity and his relational nature, drives the Exodus narrative along. The plot mimics the narrative in Genesis 1–12 as it moves from power (creation), authority, ownership, righteousness to a patient, forgiving love. As such, we find that Exodus reinforces not only the progressive knowledge of this God and his covenant stipulations, but that his revelation will be mediated, at least for now, through a return to Sinai via Moses, the covenant mediator. The creation theme also produces a noticeable resonance with Genesis 1–3 and God's presence in garden (Gen 3:8). In both stories the presence and knowledge of God stand as a stable centre for God's people.

The intervening material between Exodus and Deuteronomy continues the story of God's purpose for Israel, yet it also sustains a momentum from Exodus which heightens a rhetorical turn of wordplay in Deuteronomy 1:1 and 1:5. That is, Leviticus and Numbers report the words of Yahweh through a distant narrator: "And Yahweh called (קרא) to Moses and said (דבר) to him ..." (Lev 1:1); "And Yahweh spoke (דבר) to Moses ..." (Num 1:1). Yahweh's voice controls the narrative in Numbers especially, where the repetition of the phrase "Yahweh spoke to Moses" occurs 44 times. Deuteronomy 1:1, on the other hand, is the first disjunctive introduction (דברים אשׁר דבר משׁה) which turns from Yahweh's to Moses' words.

5. Deuteronomy in the Pentateuch

Not only does Deuteronomy link Moses' words to Yahweh's revelation, but it also begins with immediate references to the "land", "fathers", "promise"

---

35 Polak, "Theophany", 141–43.

36 *Theology of the Pentateuch: Themes of the Priestly Narrative and Deuteronomy* (Edinburgh: T&T Clark, 1994), 128–34.

37 Exod 39:1, 7, 21, 26, 29, 31, 32, 42, 43; 40:16, 19, 23, 25, 26, 29, 32.

and "seed" to establish a rhetoric of continuity with historical narrative of the Pentateuch. Epistemologically, the point of the Pentateuchal history has been to establish Yahweh's revelation and identity – signified by recurring theophanies – at the centre of Israel's worldview. Deuteronomy's main purpose is to establish Moses as the ontological and epistemological link between Israel in Egypt and Israel's monarchies. Deuteronomy's unique role will be studied over the next three chapters and this chapter will conclude by laying out a map for our investigation.

Needless to say, Deuteronomy's dating and textual tradition are one of the most complex in the whole OT. However, we are not immediately concerned with confirming or advancing the major thrusts of these issues, but with drawing upon those aspects which contribute to our epistemological questions. Our main point of dialogue with traditional and source-criticism is a hermeneutical appeal to the history of religions which would give the myth and narrative genres the weight they do not carry in a western worldview. That is to say that the textual-layering, unsighted quotations, and thematic borrowing evident in Deuteronomy, rather than implying a manipulative power-play,[38] are primarily evidence of a hierophanic, mythical and religious effort to find national and religious identity through storytelling.

In order to give the narrative foundations of society their due, we will focus primarily on Deuteronomy *as a part of the Pentateuch*. Jean-Pierre Sonnet is among a growing number of scholars who have drawn our attention back to the magnificent rhetorical and aesthetic power of this book. Sonnet suggests that Deuteronomy is a part of the Pentateuch not only in its canonical "position", but also in its narrative "texture".[39] His work illumines for us the poetics of "intra-Pentateuchal connections"[40] which stand in conversation with the historical hypotheses surrounding the book, its

[38] As H.V. Bennett has argued, it is possible and even likely that higher social classes benefited from the laws in Deuteronomy, *Injustice Made Legal: Deuteronomic Law and the Plight of Widows, Strangers, and Orphans in Ancient Israel* (Grand Rapids, MI: Eerdmans, 2002). This does not, however, imply authorship or intent. As we argue in chapter four below, there is just as much evidence to suggest the opposite.

[39] J.-P. Sonnet, *The Book Within the Book: Writing in Deuteronomy* (Leiden/New York: Brill, 1997), 23. Cf. also M. Sternberg, "Time and Space in Biblical (Hi)Story Telling: The Grand Chronology", in R. Schwartz (ed.), *The Book and the Text: The Bible and Literary Theory* (Oxford: Blackwell, 1990) 81–145, on pp. 137–8.

[40] Sternberg, "Time and Space". Cf. also W. Brueggemann, "The Travail of Pardon: Reflections on *slh*", in B.A. Strawn/N.R. Bowen (ed.), *A God So Near* (Winona Lake, IN: Eisenbrauns, 2003) 283–97, on p. 288 who ties this to a post-exilic reading. Pentateuchal readings are also offered by Childs, *Introduction*, 215; T.E. Fretheim, "Law in the Service of Life: A Dynamic Understanding of Law in Deuteronomy", in B.A. Strawn/N.R. Bowen (ed.), *A God So Near* (Winona Lake, IN: Eisenbrauns, 2003) 183–200, on p. 198; P.D. Miller, *Deuteronomy* (Interpretation; Louisville, KY: John Knox, 1990), 22; and D.T. Olson, *Deuteronomy and the Death of Moses: A Theological Reading* (Minneapolis, MN: Fortress, 1994), 201–02.

covenant structure and its law codes.[41] Our study of knowledge in Deuteronomy focuses on these poetic connections and the "liminal" world they create.[42]

The liminal shape of the text's themes and metaphors is crucial to its interpretation but also to its comparison with the wisdom literature. As a "book on the boundary",[43] Deuteronomy stands poised before an aggregate of boundaries or thresholds which are geographical, ethnic, moral, religious and social.[44] Israel will cross the Jordan into the promised land and, with the imminent death of Moses, must cross into the future with new leadership and new encounters with Yahweh. At the same time, Israel must *not cross* into the abominable worship of the nations; she must *not* make alliances with nations who are nearby; and she must only worship in the way and in the place Yahweh chooses. Boundary crossing – future change, challenges and prohibitions – are common to all humanity, giving these thresholds a trans-generational appeal; readers are meant to sympathise with the story, identify with the characters and apply its message in new times and places. In the midst of this journey, Horeb (Sinai) represents a fixed and celebrated point in Israel's past. God met face to face with Moses there and gave his law to Israel. Deuteronomy's journey, as we will see, centres upon the memory of Horeb as the present and future symbol of God's glorious presence with his people.

In order to draw fully upon these literary and liminal dimensions of the book, we will need to approach the next three chapters of our thesis with

---

[41] Deuteronomy's parallels with treaty forms should not go unrecognised, particularly as it creates an authoritative rhetoric for Moses. Cf. e.g. Kline, *Structure*, 131–53; P.C. Craigie, *The Book of Deuteronomy* (NICOT; Grand Rapids, MI: Eerdmans, 1976), and more recently E.H. Merrill, *Deuteronomy* (NAC; Nashville, TN: Broadman & Holman, 1994). At the same time, recent scholarship also illustrates Deuteronomy's uniqueness and the mutual presence of the law-code and treaty genres which sharpen Deuteronomy's sense of counter-cultural awareness. Cf. J.G. McConville, *Deuteronomy* (AOTC; Leicester/Downer's Grove, IL.: InterVarsity, 2002), 24f ; C.J.H. Wright, *Deuteronomy* (NIBC; Peabody, MA: Hendrickson, 1996), 2–5; D.L. Christensen, "Form and Structure in Deuteronomy 1–11", in Norbert Lohfink (ed.), *Das Deuteronomium* (Leuven: Leuven University, 1985) 135–44, on p. 135; and M. Weinfeld, *Deuteronomy and the Deuteronomic School* (Winona Lake, IN: Eisenbrauns, 1992 (Oxford: Clarendon, 1972)), 146–57.

James Barr, "Biblical Law and the Question of Natural Theology", in T. Veijola (ed.), *The Law in the Bible and in Its Environment* (Helsinki: Finnish Exegetical Society, 1990) 1–22 takes the parallels between ancient cultures and the Mosaic law as evidence for ancient natural law or natural theology. I argue that this discounts the essential capacity of OT revelation to oppose natural law in ancient legal systems and ideology – a form of *cultural critique*; what he takes as synthesis might just as well be be antithesis. I do not deny the divinely created or naturally existing continuity in all human cultures, it is rather to say that Barr has unnecessarily flattened the Torah and missed one of its fundamental uniquenesses – its definitive claim to be divine revalation.

[42] Cf. R.P. O'Dowd, "Memory on the Boundary: Epistemology in Deuteronomy", in M. Healy/R. Parry (ed.), *The Bible and Epistemology* (Carlisle, UK: Paternoster, 2007) 3–22. With the permission of Paternoster Press, some of that material is reused here.

[43] Wright, *Deuteronomy*, 9; also Miller, *Deuteronomy*, 4, 9.

[44] In addition to Wright and Miller (cited above), see N. MacDonald, *Deuteronomy and the Meaning of 'Monotheism'* (Tübingen: Mohr Siebeck, 2003), 155 and Olson, *Deuteronomy*, 95–6, 181–2.

structure, *rhetoric* and *theology* of Deuteronomy foremost in our mind. We will, therefore, work within the following framing elements of the book:[45] the commanding presence of Moses' four speeches (1:6; 5:1; 29:2; 33:2); the concentric frame of the narrator's speeches (1:1; 4:44–5; 28:69; 33:1);[46] the spatial frame of travel from Horeb (ch. 1–3), to Moab (4:1; 5:3 etc.) to the "land" (ch. 31–34);[47] and the theological and legal wordplay between תורה and דבר which moves Deuteronomy from speech to writing – from words of torah (1:1–5) to a book of the torah (17:19; 31:24–26).[48] The next three chapters are organised in a way that keeps these structural and theological factors central to our epistemological interpretation.[49]

Chapter 3 (Deuteronomy 1–11): From Horeb to Moab: Actualising Israel's History. This chapter traces Israel's covenant history focusing on the events at Horeb where God reveals his glory to Moses as he delivers the law to Israel. This torah represents the means to future encounters with and knowledge of God.

Chapter 4 (Deuteronomy 12–26): Ideology and Epistemology in the Deuteronomic Laws. Deuteronomy 12 "stops" in a sense, as Moses outlines an ideal image of Israel's future dwelling in the land. In this way, the Torah serves as the means to reproduce the realities at Horeb (and Moab) while resisting the ideologies of the foreign nations.

Chapter 5 (Deuteronomy 27–34): Re-Actualisation in Future Covenants. In these chapters the spoken words (Yahweh's and Moses') are transformed into a ceremony on stones (ch. 27) and a Torah book (30–31) creating future images of continuity, compromise and promise.

6. Conclusion

This chapter has introduced us to the mythical and narrative foundations of ancient Hebrew epistemology. We have found that Israel's way of knowing

---

45 For more on the literary background of frames, see R.P. O'Dowd, "Frame Narrative", in D. Reid/T. Longman/P. Enns (ed.), *Dictionary of Old Testament Wisdom, Poetry and Writings* (Downers Grove: InterVarsity, Forthcoming).

46 Most scholars identify three speeches, but see Sonnet, *Book*, 17–8, for the inclusion of the fourth speech at 33:1. Olson, *Deuteronomy*, 14f, too, sees the structural break at 33:1, however, he also adds another division at 6:1 for the same reason. This is a possible break, but is different from the others in that it is not a part of the narrator's speech.

47 See Wright, *Deuteronomy*, 4–5 and D.L. Christensen, *Deuteronomy 1:1–21:9* (WBC; Dallas, TX: Thomas Nelson, 2001), 4–5. Christensen also shows how the book has a concentric Menorah structure ideal for the 11 weekly divisions for Jewish recitations of the book (xciii–xciv).

48 See Sonnet, *Book* and S.D. McBride, "Polity", 64–5.

49 Deuteronomy has almost endless layers in its structure. As Christensen warns, no single structure can capture a work of art and too much attention on the form can inhibit the intended experience; in the end one should 'enjoy the music', "Form", 139.

is grounded in a storied, ethical, and religious way of life. *Knowing*, in fact, is a matter of divine-imitation where creating, or imagining, is at one and the same time obeying God and knowing God. The laws thus fit naturally into this ethico-epistemological nexus; obeying God's commands is to be like him and know him. Deuteronomy's laws, meanwhile, take us a long way from the laws in Exodus and the first trip to Horeb. All new political and social demands nurture the Deuteronomist's work, and our interpretation has been structured to get at the liminal/epistemological nature of the final collection of the Mosaic tradition. Our next three chapters will progressively illumine this work.

CHAPTER THREE

From Deuteronomy to Horeb: Actualising Israel's History Deuteronomy 1–11

1. Introduction

As we will see, Deuteronomy 1–11 intentionally oscillates between Israel's history, her present (at Moab), and her future life in the land. This undergirds the book's overall narrative strategy of depicting Israel in a liminal journey where the events of the past and promises of the future continually (re-)shape her present worldview. "Actualisation" describes this process wherein the climactic events of the past are renewed in the present and future.[1] Actualisation grounds Israel's life, purpose and knowledge in a unfolding narrative of redemption. This chapter will consider the four dominant actualising mechanisms in Deuteronomy 1–11: rhetorical wordplay, history telling, memorisation and writing metaphors.

As we argued in the last chapter, our reading gives particular attention to the rhetorical and structure framework of the book: Deuteronomy continues the narrative development of the Pentateuch where Moses has become Israel's prophet and mediator. Israel's failures at Sinai and in the desert accentuate his new, exclusive access to Yahweh and his revelation. Deuteronomy also intensifies the narrative with several allusions to Moses' imminent death (1:37; 3:26; 4:21), thus creating an immediate suspense in the Pentateuchal plot. Readers are lead to wonder how Israel will retain their access to Yahweh, his presence and his guidance after Moses is gone. This anticipation is meant to bring liminal urgency to Israel in her need to actualise her past and sustain her relationship with her saving God.

2. From Horeb: Moses' "Words" and God's Promises (Deuteronomy 1–3)

Deut 1:1
אֵלֶּה הַדְּבָרִים אֲשֶׁר דִּבֶּר מֹשֶׁה אֶל־כָּל־יִשְׂרָאֵל בְּעֵבֶר הַיַּרְדֵּן בַּמִּדְבָּר בָּעֲרָבָה מוֹל סוּף בֵּין־פָּארָן וּבֵין־תֹּפֶל
וְלָבָן וַחֲצֵרֹת וְדִי זָהָב׃

[1] See B.S. Childs, *Memory and Tradition in Israel* (London: SCM, 1962), 53.

Deut 1:8
רְאֵה נָתַתִּי לִפְנֵיכֶם אֶת־הָאָרֶץ בֹּאוּ וּרְשׁוּ אֶת־הָאָרֶץ אֲשֶׁר נִשְׁבַּע יְהוָה לַאֲבֹתֵיכֶם לְאַבְרָהָם לְיִצְחָק וּלְיַעֲקֹב
לָתֵת לָהֶם וּלְזַרְעָם אַחֲרֵיהֶם׃

The first eight verses in Deuteronomy introduce two keys to the narrative progress of the book. First, the appearance of the "land", "promise", "fathers" and "Horeb" (Sinai) (v.8) serve to keep Deuteronomy's narrative in the flow of the Pentateuchal drama and ground Israel's epistemology in her historical identity.[2] This is accentuated by the narrator "telling" about the דברים which Moses spoke at Horeb (1:1–4) and then "showing" Moses speaking to his audience in verse 5.[3] Much like the book of Job, this tool of shifting perspectives adds a persuasive tension to the plot and draws readers into the story. Second, the reference to the דברים in verse 1 and the תורה in verse 5 begins a pattern of rhetorical wordplay that will continue through chapter 32. Patriarchal themes and wordplay are integrated in Deuteronomy and represent Israel's need to actualise her history. We will study these integrated keys individually.

2.1 Primordial and Patriarchal Themes in Deuteronomy 1–3

First of all, the larger Pentateuchal drama is immediately apparent by the references to Yahweh's promise (נשׁבע) to the "fathers" (v. 8). Deuteronomy makes almost 50 references to the patriarchs: 47 to the fathers (naming them on occasion) and two more independent references to "Abraham, Isaac and Jacob" (9:27 and 34:4).[4] The inclusion of these several themes, (land, promise, fathers, and seed) strategically places Deuteronomy in the

---

[2] J.G. Millar, "'A Faithful God Who Does No Wrong: History, Theology, and Reliability in Deuteronomy", in P. Helm/C. Trueman (ed.), *The Trustworthiness of God* (Leicester, UK: Apollos, 2002), argues that Deuteronomy 1–11 depends on the Exodus tradition "to demonstrate the trustworthiness of God both in action and in word".

[3] On showing (direct evidence) verses telling (indirect), see Sonnet, *Book*, 121, 245–6; W.C. Booth, *The Rhetoric of Fiction* (Chicago: University of Chicago, 1983 (1961)), 3–19; Sonnet, *Book*, 13; Sternberg, *Poetics*, 122; Alter, *Narrative*, 155–8.

[4] On the patriarchal theme in Deuteronomy, see G. Braulik, "Deuteronomy and the Birth of Monotheism", in idem.; *Theology* (1994) 99–130, 237–47, on pp. 110–4; N. Lohfink, "Verküngkigung Des Hauptgebots in der Jüngsten Schicht des Deuteronomiums (Dt 4, 1–40)", in idem.; *Studien Zum Deuteronomium und zur Deuteronomistischen Literatur 1* (Stuttgart: Katholisches Bibelwerk, 1990) 167–91, on pp. 186–7; N. Lohfink, "Dtn 12,1 und Gen 15,18: Das dem Samen Abrahams Geschenkte Land als der Geltungsbereich der Deuteronomischen Gesetze", in idem.; *Studien zum Deuteronomium und zur deuteronomistischen Literature 2* (Stuttgart: Katholisches Bibelwerk, 1991) 257–85, on p. 257 and Sonnet, *Book*, 205. Cf. however, the different views of W.E. Lemke, "Circumcision of the Heart: The Journey of a Biblical Metaphor", in B.A. Strawn/N.R. Bowen (ed.), *A God So Near* (Winona Lake, IN: Eisenbrauns, 2003) 299–319, on pp. 302–3 and T.E. Fretheim, "Law in the Service of Life: A Dynamic Understanding of Law in Deuteronomy", in B.A. Strawn/N.R. Bowen (ed.), *A God So Near* (Winona Lake, IN: Eisenbrauns, 2003) 183–200, on p. 184 (in the same volume).

full stream of Genesis' theological flow from creation and fall to the table of nations and the call of Abram. Genesis 12:1–3 as we saw above marks a transitional point in the narrative. The laws for the land in Deuteronomy reflect God's primordial intention for humanity (all nations) to live before him in a re-created garden.[5] In other words, there is a momentum behind this universal divine purpose which fuels the developing narrative as it continues from Exodus to Deuteronomy,[6] and this Pentateuchal agenda lies at the heart of our epistemological investigation. Deuteronomy's efforts to establish continuity lie in its interest in developing the primeval and patriarchal "story" of Israel in the world. The introduction to Moses' words alerts the reader to the ontological foundations which Moses' words have with Yahweh's identity and revelation.

2.2 Rhetorical Wordplay in Deuteronomy 1

The disjunctive turn between Yahweh's word and Moses' words signals a second clue to actualisation in Deuteronomy, initiating a rhetorical wordplay which continues to the end of the book. Here in the beginning (1:1), Moses' דברים identify, and therefore anticipate, the sermons that follow. As we will see, the anticipatory role is enhanced by a wordplay in verse 5:

בְּעֵבֶר הַיַּרְדֵּן בְּאֶרֶץ מוֹאָב הוֹאִיל מֹשֶׁה בֵּאֵר אֶת־הַתּוֹרָה הַזֹּאת לֵאמֹר׃

This verse closes the narrator's brief introductory address by placing Moses at Moab where his explanation of תורה sits in parallel with his דברים (v. 1).[7] Although the wordplay and themes continue through verse 8, the narrator's words stop at verse 5 and create a frame for his introduction:[8]

---

[5] See W. Brueggemann, *Deuteronomy* (AOTC; Nashville: Abingdon, 2001), 104 and my analysis of Deuteronomy 8 below.

[6] T.E. Fretheim, "The Reclamation of Creation: Redemption and Law in Exodus", *Interpretation* 45 (1991) 354–65, on p. 356 says that "The placement of Genesis shows that God's purpose in redemption is not finally centered on Israel". See also Wright, *Deuteronomy* (NIBC; Peabody, MA: Hendrickson, 1996), 11–4 and M. Fishbane, *Text and Texture: Close Readings of Selected Biblical Texts* (New York: Schocken, 1979), 76 who identifies the intentional echo between Moses and Israel in Exodus and the calling of Abraham in Gen 12:10–20 (Pharaoh, Egypt, desert etc.).

[7] The wordplay between דבר and דברים can be seen progressively as follows: 1:1, 34; 4:2, 12–15, 32–36; 5:1, 4–5, 22–31; 6:4, 6; 9:10; 11:18–18; 12:28; 13:3–4; 17:19; 18:18–20; 27:3, 8, 26; 28:14, 28; 28:69 (29:1); 30:14; 31:1, 12; 31:24, 28, 30; 32:44–47, 48; 34:5.

[8] D.L. Christensen, *Deuteronomy 1:1–21:9* (WBC; Dallas, TX: Thomas Nelson, 2001), 9, 13; J.G. McConville, *Deuteronomy* (AOTC; Leicester/Downer's Grove, IL: InterVarsity, 2002), 60; J.H. Tigay, *Deuteronomy, Debarim* (JPSTC; Philadelphia, PA: Jewish Publication Society, 1996), 5; and P.C. Craigie, *The Book of Deuteronomy* (NICOT; Grand Rapids, MI: Eerdmans, 1976), 92. But, see A. Mayes, *Deuteronomy, NBC* (Grand Rapids, MI/London: Eerdmans/Marshall, Morgan & Scott, 1979), 113 whose arguments are directed against Lohfink's chiastic structure (and not a frame per se).

The דברים that Moses דבר (v. 1)
    Place: Beyond the Jordan (v. 1)
        Time: Eleven days journey (v. 2)
            Moses דבר all that Yahweh had commanded him (v. 3)
        Time: After he had defeated Sihon (v. 4)
    Place: Beyond the Jordan (v. 5)
Moses began באר this תורה saying (אמר) v. 5

This rhetorical wordplay is central to our phenomenological reading. That is, the combination of Moses' דברים (1:1), the דבר Yahweh commanded him (1:3), and the תורה (1:5) forms a rhetorical bridge between Moses' speech, Yahweh's speech, the developing "book" and Israel's own writing and speaking activity in the land – i.e. their future actualisation of Yahweh's original words. Our immediate concern is with the theological and communicative device in chapter 1, but the rhetorical wordplay will illumine our reading of the whole book.

(1) First of all, we make note of the linguistic and structural complex created by the wordplay between תורה in verse 5 and its counterpart דברים in verse 1. In a linear reading (the surrounding context of the Pentateuch), תורה has been used with fairly limited reference to "law" or "commandment." In these first verses, however, Deuteronomy makes תורה the subject of his speeches (דברים) and introduces a more nuanced meaning for "torah" than in the Pentateuch thus far.[9] Here the internal and external order of the narrative is essential to its meaning.[10] Approaching this text from the first four books of the Pentateuch, one senses a new application for תורה and the beginning of a wordplay which corresponds to a progressive set of allusions meant to entice the reader into hearing these "words."[11]

(2) As a result of this wordplay, Deuteronomy gradually achieves a blending effect between Moses' words and Yahweh's words.[12] As already

---

[9] G. Braulik, "Die Ausdrücke Für 'Gesetz' Im Buch Deuteronomium", in idem.; *Studien Zur Theologie Des Deuteronomiums* (Stuttgart: Katolisches Bibelwerk, 1988) 11–38, notes the limitations of a standard lexicon in this case. Cf. also P. Enns, "Law of God", in W.A. Van Gemeren (ed.), *NIDOTTE, 5 Vols. 4* (Grand Rapids, MI: Zondervan, 1997) 893–900 (895–7), and B. Lindars, "Torah in Deuteronomy", in P.R. Ackroyd/B. Lindars (ed.), *Words and Meanings: Essays Presented to Winton Thomas* (Cambridge: Cambridge University, 1968) 117–36.

L. Wittgenstein, *Philosophical Investigations* (2nd ed.; Oxford: Blackwell, 2001 (1958)) makes a helpful distinction between the "use" (*Gebrauch* I.30, 41, 43) of words and the "training" (*Abrichtung* I.5, 6, 7) of social contexts which also influence the meaning of a word. In this sense, Deuteronomy is training its readers by using torah with "blurred edges" (I.71) as a part of its epistemological and rhetorical agenda.

[10] Cf. Braulik, "Ausdrücke"; F. Crüsemann, *The Torah: Theology and Social History of Old Testament Law* (Edinburgh: T&T Clark, 1996), 332; Mayes, *Deuteronomy*, 116–7; and Tigay, *Deuteronomy*, 5.

[11] Cf. Strawn's attention to rhetorical repetition in Deuteronomy which has the dual effect of "disorienting" and then "sharpening", "Keep/Observe/Do – Carefully – Today! The Rhetoric of Repetition in Deuteronomy", in B.A. Strawn/N.R. Bowen (ed.), *A God So Near* (Winona Lake, IN: Eisenbrauns, 2003) 215–40, on pp. 234–6.

[12] See Brueggemann, *Deuteronomy*, 26. I. Cairns, *Deuteronomy: Word and Presence* (ITC; Grand Rapids, MI: Eerdmans, 1992), 55 and N. Lohfink, "Das Deuteronomium: Jahwegesetz oder Mosegesetz?" in

noted, the preceding context between Exodus and Numbers recorded Yahweh's words to Moses. Deuteronomy 1:1–5 makes an emphatic point of ascribing this book (these "words") to Moses. Yet at the same time, the narrator is careful to qualify Moses' teaching as they express Yahweh's authoritative command (1:3).

D. Olson does not see blending here, arguing that Moses' speeches in Deuteronomy are "secondary" and "less authoritative" human words (particularly Deut 12–26) when compared to Yahweh's speech and Decalogue. Moses' words appear less fixed, and in need of "interpretation and adaptation."[13] Yet Olson overlooks both the obvious and sustained wordplays in the book and the theological themes which grant Moses' divine authority as he speaks. Because this blend between Yahweh and Moses is central to my entire analysis of Deuteronomy, it is necessary to engage Olson further and introduce how these (wordplay and themes) will operate throughout the rest of Deuteronomy.

First of all, we have already noted that Deuteronomy clearly portrays Moses' words as commanded *by Yahweh* (1:3; 5:31) and therefore as explicitly, divinely authorised. Second, in his concluding speech, Moses' דבר is *elevated* in Israel's eyes as that which is both near (קרב, 30:14) and their very "life" (הייכם, 32:47). Taking these two points together allows us to suggest another theological implication: Moses' "life-giving" דבר correspond to Yahweh's authoritative דבר in his creative acts (Gen 1:4–31).[14] In this way, Stahl and Fretheim acknowledge not just this creative power in Yahweh's דבר but also its theological capacity to address Yahweh's law as the design for his created order[15] – a law which Moses sets out to explain carefully (1:5) in his own divinely commanded (1:3), but fully human *words* (1:1). Finally, we add to this our previous observation that the narrative from Exodus to Numbers (cf. Deut 5:22–28) reinforces Moses' unique access to Yahweh and his presence in theophany when receiving these words (e.g. Exod 31–33; Num 11–16). We therefore have very good reason to accept the "divinely authoritative" nature of Moses' דברים in Deuteronomy's narrative.

(3) Finally, it is important to note how the combination of באר and תורה in verse 5 introduce Deuteronomy's use of both oral and written worlds of

---

idem.; *Studien Zum Deuteronomium und Zur Deuteronomistischen Literatur 3* (SBAB 20; Stuttgart: Katholisches Bibelwerk, 1995) 157–65.

13 *Deuteronomy and the Death of Moses: A Theological Reading* (Minneapolis, MN: Fortress, 1994), 32, 46.

14 S. Greidanus, "The Universal Dimension of Law in the Hebrew Scriptures", *Sciences Religieuses* 14 (1985) 39–51, on pp. 39–43.

15 T.E. Fretheim, *Exodus* (Interpretation; Louisville, KY: John Knox, 1991), 14; N. Stahl, *Law and Liminality in the Bible* (JSOTSup; Sheffield: JSOT, 1995), 16f, 23, 45. Maimonides frequently emphasised this connection between law and created order, H. Kreisel, "Moses Maimonides", in D.H. Frank/O. Leaman (ed.), *History of Jewish Philosophy* (London: Routledge, 2003) 245–80, on pp. 256–58.

communication.[16] Chapter 1, of course, only envisions the *oral* dimension, but this is the side most often overlooked in modern commentary whenever it wrongly assumes that oral cultures are necessarily less developed than literate cultures.[17] We will find that the narrative in Deuteronomy progressively uses oral and written means of communication to enhance the delivery and longevity of its message through future *actualisation*.[18] Furthermore, the oral world of communication places the תורה (v. 5) of Moses' speeches (teaching/law) in the urgent parenetic context signified by באר ("explain carefully"). There is a parenetic urgency; Moses sets out to be *persuasive*[19] in his last speech to Israel and together this urgency and wordplay begin the alluring and suspenseful nature of this narrative.

We have now made several references to Moses' unique mediatorial role and the urgency brought about by the anticipation of his death (1:37; 3:26; 4:21).[20] Like Deuteronomy 1:2–4 and 8, the material in 1:9–3:29 appropriates the context of the surrounding Pentateuchal narrative and history,[21] including Israel's inherent tendency to covenant unfaithfulness (Deut 1:19–46)[22] to sustain the growing tension. That is, Moses' death and Israel's unfaithfulness pose urgent questions for future Israel: "How will the presence and revelation of Yahweh continue after Moses is gone?"[23] (i.e. "How will Yahweh be known?", and "Who will give Israel her future commands?"). The next 30 chapters are designed, in part, to resolve the tension created by the future death of Israel's mediator and thus create a theology of actualising ancient realities in later generations.

In sum, we have found that the wordplay and theological (Pentateuchal) themes in Deuteronomy 1:1–8 are beginning to give a divinely authoritative dimension to Moses' words. Just as Yahweh's identity and revelation figured centrally in Israel's worldview between Genesis and Numbers, it will do so in Deuteronomy through his mediator Moses. What Israel knows is dependent on the knowledge she receives from God's chosen mediator and the laws he commands. Yet it is also clear that these words are communicated with a vocabulary that is explicitly oral and urgent. In what follows we see that this oral component begs for future writing and repetition.

---

16 Sonnet, *Book*, 12–3, 29–32.

17 See S. Niditch, *Oral World and Written Word* (Louisville, KY: Westminster John Knox, 1996), 78–88.

18 Ibid., 100, cf. especially the remarks on Deut 32 in chapter 5 below.

19 See Christensen, *Deuteronomy*, 9; McConville, *Deuteronomy*, 62; and C.J.H. Wright, *Deuteronomy*, 21.

20 See G.W. Coats, "Legendary Motifs in the Moses Death Reports", in D. Christensen (ed.), *Song* (1993) 181–91, on p. 185 on the uniqueness of Moses' relationship with Yahweh.

21 See Tigay, *Deuteronomy*, 4.

22 P. Barker, "Faithless Israel, Faithful Yahweh in Deuteronomy", PhD DissertationBristol University, 1995.

23 Cf. M. Weinfeld, *Deuteronomy 1–11* (AB; New York: Doubleday, 1991), 221.

3. Moses' Words at Moab about Yahweh's Words at Horeb (Deut 4–11)

3.1 Deut 4: Transition from Past to Present and Future

Chapter 4 stands as both a transition between 1–3 and 5–11 and an introduction to the rest of the book. Because of its unique content, it is the theological heart of Deuteronomy and our close attention to its linguistic, rhetorical and theological aspects will allow us to demonstrate the growth of the actualisation imperative in Deuteronomy. These aspects include (1) the nature of Israel's history, (2) the continued and expanded wordplay among the *Ausdrücke* (legal terms), (3) theophany (divine presence) and its universal dimensions, and (4) the teaching functions in the community. Together, these aspects undergird Deuteronomy's summons for Israel not only to recall her history but to enter it and actualise her relationship with Yahweh through obedience to the torah.

3.1.1 Time, History and Actualisation

As suggested in the first chapter Israel's epistemology is grounded in the ontological and ethical nexus of the creation myth. Deuteronomy's unique role in the OT is one of historic specificity, to ground Israel's knowledge and ethics in the covenantal history of the Tetrateuch. In Deuteronomy 4 this history is brought to the fore as Moses makes his first explicit move from past to present:

Deut 4:1
וְעַתָּה יִשְׂרָאֵל שְׁמַע אֶל־הַחֻקִּים וְאֶל־הַמִּשְׁפָּטִים אֲשֶׁר אָנֹכִי מְלַמֵּד אֶתְכֶם לַעֲשׂוֹת לְמַעַן תִּחְיוּ וּבָאתֶם וִירִשְׁתֶּם
אֶת־הָאָרֶץ אֲשֶׁר יְהוָה אֱלֹהֵי אֲבֹתֵיכֶם נֹתֵן לָכֶם׃

This passage in Deuteronomy 4:1 is Moses' first significant use of "today" and introduces us to his obsessive concern with the present through his repetitive use of "today" and "now" throughout the rest of Deuteronomy. Depending on how one interprets the various contexts there are about 60 significant occurrences of היום and היום הזה in Deuteronomy.[24] There are also are eight to ten integral uses of עתה and ועתה.[25] One effect of Moses' continual reference to the present is to signal the formal commencement of

[24] I count 74 occurrences of יום, 60 of which are significant. J.G. Millar, "Living at the Place of Decision: Time and Place in the Framework of Deuteronomy", in J.G. McConville/J.G. Millar; *Time and Place* (Sheffield: Sheffield Academic, 1994) 15–88, on p. 153 counts 62 references. It is not clear why Olson, *Deuteronomy*, 32f and J.v. Goudoever, "'The Liturgical Significance of the Date in Dt 1,3", in N. Lohfink (ed.), *Das Deuteronomium* (Leuven: Leuven University, 1985) 145–8, on p. 148 only cite 27 occurrences. For a detailed analysis, see S.J. DeVries, *Yesterday, Today and Tomorrow: Time and History in the Old Testament* (London: SPCK, 1975).

[25] Deut 4:1, 32; 5:25; 6:1; 10:12, 22; 26:10; 27:1; 31:19 and 32:39.

applied "teaching"; but it is a mistake to leave it in the past.[26] Rather, the repetition in Deuteronomy is so excessive that it leads to another conclusion. That is, this rhetoric emphasises the performative nature of these sermons which begs for Israel's participation in the narrative.[27] The call to "today" is "liturgical,"[28] for every generation to renew or to *actualise* the covenants at Horeb and Moab. Actualisation in Deuteronomy's rhetoric is commonly accepted in modern study;[29] yet we must nevertheless be clear about the nature of Jewish "time" and "history" as they effect the memory and ceremonies in the OT.[30]

In particular, it is important to maintain Deuteronomy's affirmation of a progressive nature of history in its use of memory and repetition.[31] That is, the actualising features in Deuteronomy, as applied in chapters 4–11, are signified with anachronistic imagery while also affirming progressive history. In four places Deuteronomy anachronistically positions the second generation at Horeb (Sinai) for the first delivery of the law:

Deut 4:9
רַק הִשָּׁמֶר לְךָ וּשְׁמֹר נַפְשְׁךָ מְאֹד פֶּן־תִּשְׁכַּח אֶת־הַדְּבָרִים אֲשֶׁר־רָאוּ עֵינֶיךָ וּפֶן־יָסוּרוּ מִלְּבָבְךָ כֹּל יְמֵי חַיֶּיךָ
וְהוֹדַעְתָּם לְבָנֶיךָ וְלִבְנֵי בָנֶיךָ׃

(cf. also 5:22–27; 6:20; 11:2–7).

---

[26] As done by S.R. Driver, *A Critical and Exegetical Commentary on Deuteronomy* (ICC; Edinburgh: T&T Clark, 1902), 62–3; Tigay, *Deuteronomy*, 40–3 and Weinfeld, *Deuteronomy 1–11*, 199. Some consider it a problem in 4:5 that Moses reminds Israel of what he "has taught" (למדתי) Israel (the הקים והמשפתים) *before* his teaching. Weinfeld, *Deuteronomy 1–11*, 201 notes how Semitic languages use the perfect (*qatal*) to express a present rather than a completed event. Cf. Seow's remarks in chapter 7 of this thesis regarding the timeframe of Qohelet's reign. In any case, the grammar alone is not decisive and the point seems to be, given Deut's use of היום, that Moses wants to renew the Horeb covenant for each generation in the present. Cf. both Cairns, *Deuteronomy*, 56 and McConville, *Deuteronomy*, 104.

[27] See S.C. Barton, "New Testament Interpretation as Performance", *SJT* 52 (1999) 179–208, on p. 183 who critiques NT interpretation which places an unnecessary wall between meaning "then" and application today. Similarly, Deuteronomy wants future generations to enter its history in their own day and, in this way, find the ongoing meaning of the text. Cf. Strawn, "Keep/Observe/Do", 236, who says, "In the case of Deuteronomy, this would entail giving ourselves over to its repetitive rhetoric with the possibility, perhaps even the likelihood, that we would emerge on the other side transformed by that rhetoric – suddenly attuned to the suasive mood, the content of the actions enjoined, and the objects of the verbal commands, not to mention to the One who commands".

[28] See DeVries, *Yesterday*, 178 and Goudoever, "Significance", 148.

[29] See G. Braulik, "Wisdom, Divine Presence and Law: Reflections on the Kerygma of Deut 4:5–8 (1977)", in idem.; *Theology* (1–25, 199–214, 1994); Cairns, *Deuteronomy*, 56, 68; Childs, *Memory*, 52; Goudoever, "Significance", 148; Millar, "Place", 79-80; P.D. Miller, *Deuteronomy* (Interpretation; Louisville, KY: John Knox, 1990), 67, 209 J.G. McConville, "Time and Place and the Deuteronomic Altar-Law", in J.G. McConville/J.G. Millar; *Time and Place* (Sheffield: Sheffield Academic, 1994) 89–139, on p. 125; and J.G. McConville, "Metaphor, Symbol and the Interpretation of Deuteronomy", in C.G. Bartholomew/et al. (ed.), *After Pentecost* (Carlisle, UK/Grand Rapids, MI: Paternoster/Zondervan, 2001) 329–51, on p. 344.

[30] On time in both Jewish and Christian theology, see N. Wolterstorff, "The Remembrance of Things (Not) Past: Philosophical Reflections on Christian Liturgy", in T.P. Flint (ed.), *Christian Philosophy* (Notre Dame, IN: University of Notre Dame, 1990) 118–61; Y.H. Yerushalmi, *Zakhor: Jewish History and Jewish Memory* (Seattle/London: University of Washington, 1996) and the four essays in G.E. Ganssle, *God and Time: Four Views* (Carlisle, UK: Paternoster, 2001).

[31] As compared to "perfectionist" or "skeptical" views of history, cf. Holmes, *Listening to the Past*.

Clearly the "you" who saw with their "eyes" alludes to the fathers who, by the time of Deuteronomy, would have already died in the desert (cf. Num 14:28–35).[32] Most of the second generation would have been children or not yet born during theophany at Sinai. Still, Moses addresses the children as witnesses of these events. The repeated anachronism does more than simply remember the events for the younger generation, but gives all future generations a memory in which the realities and unique identity of the original participants become their own.[33] Sonnet says, "Actually the play between the two generations represents Moses' rhetorical way of addressing his audience as the trans-generational Israel: the sons were, through their fathers, Israel present at Horeb [...]."[34] In this way Deuteronomy is saying that each generation can realise the original relationship between God and their fathers. This is to remember Horeb in a way that it becomes present, powerful and real.[35] So even though Deuteronomy never portrays an explicit theophany at Moab, this does not mean that it substitutes God for a symbolic presence or name theology. Rather, Deuteronomy sustains the Exodus motif of the ידע יהוה through the actualisation of the divine presence at Horeb. As O'Donovan says, "Yhwh is immediately present in conquest; his presence is mediated in judgment; and he is present in a kind of concealed immediacy in the law."[36]

In this use of history, we can begin to see Deuteronomy's ability to engage readers in the face of their own liminal boundaries through its own significant moments in creative and redemptive history. The intention is for Israel to *realise* past liminal boundaries or thresholds in the present and the future. Israel's living tradition is thus a matter of perpetual *actualisation* of her relationship with Yahweh in new and changing contexts. Childs suggest the following explanation for the process in Israel:

To remember was to call to mind a past event or situation, with the purpose of evoking some action [...]. To remember was to actualize the past, to bridge the gap of time and to

---

[32] According to Geller, "Wisdom", 47 this is not "accidental," but "an association of past and present through the faculty of sight, a kind of syllogism of experience rather than strict logic" 47.

[33] Cf. Wolterstorff's warning that Jewish views of history were progressive, not "timeless" nor a "time machine", Wolterstorff, "Remembrance", 128.

[34] *Book*, 11. Both Miller, *Deuteronomy*, 67 and Millar, "Place", 58 connect this with "actualisation". Millar in particular, recognises the intention to make the covenant at Horeb not "mere memory, but as "*a memory which is actualized in the present at Moab*". B.M. Levinson, *Deuteronomy and the Hermeneutics of Legal Innovation* (Oxford: Oxford University, 1998), 151–2 sees the obvious intentional anachronism but assigns it to ideological transformation by later (Josianic) editors – an unwarranted logical leap in this case. Only a few interpreters make note of this anachronistic technique. Cf. McConville, *Grace*, 126–33; DeVries, *Yesterday*, 176–7. and Cairns, *Deuteronomy*, 58.

[35] Sonnet, *Book*, 142–3 says that the Horeb event is reproduced by reading the torah; cf. Stahl, *Law*, 92. On the combined effect of "Today" (4:1) in this context, see: Braulik, "Wisdom", 24; and Olson, *Deuteronomy*, 37. See also Yerushalmi, *Zakhor*, 113–15 on remembering the Torah and preserving *halakhah* at the heart of national and theological memory.

[36] *DN*, 50.

form a solidarity with the fathers. Israel's remembrance became a technical term to express the process by which later Israel made relevant the great redemptive acts which she recited in her tradition. The question of how to overcome the separation in time and space from the great events of the past became the paramount issue.[37]

As such it seems clear, even at this early stage in Deuteronomy, that this "torah" is not an archaic story with empty moral principles. Yahweh's actions in Israel's midst (redemption, judgment, presence, law, revelation) are directed towards a renewal of the divine-human relationship. Israel must, therefore, pursue knowledge by renewing the redemptive events of the past and *hermeneutically closing the historical distance* with the past.[38] This actualising tradition continually reaffirms the ontology undergirding Yahweh's created world, which in the Pentateuch, includes the order, "vocation" and primordial purpose for Israel in history.[39] History and memory for Israel have a "transcendent meaning" or story in which subsequent generations find their identity.[40]

3.1.2 Deuteronomic Wordplay and the Role of this "Book"

We have already suggested that Deuteronomy's legal terms intermingle in a way that results in a rhetorical summons to actualise the past (Deut 6, 8, 27–32). In Deuteronomy 4–11 the legal *Ausdrücke* appear more frequently and densely than any other part of Deuteronomy. Here we will see how these terms come alive in the teaching, memorisation and learning of the individual Israelites (ch. 6–8, 11). As the Israelites take up these didactic roles of handling the *Ausdrücke* (read, say, teach, remember, etc.) they

---

37 *Memory*, 74–5. Cf also DeVries, *Yesterday*, 347 and Millar, "Place", 15.

38 This is, of course, the hermeneutical problem in Descartes, Kant, Lessing and Schleiermacher's suspicion of ever truly recovering the past. In response, Gadamer (following Heidegger) answers with the need to "fuse" the historical horizons. H.G. Gadamer, *Truth and Method* (2nd ed.; New York: Crossroad (Sheed and Ward), 1985 (1975 English Translation; 1960 German)), 263–74. See also Ricoeur's notion of a "living" tradition over against a "politicising" tradition, *Hermeneutics and the Human Sciences* (Cambridge: Cambridge University, 1981), 72.

39 See Fretheim, "Law", 191. Cf also Yerushalmi's insightful observations, "There are sufficient clues to indicate that what was suddenly drawn up from the past was not a series of facts to be contemplated at a distance, but a series of situations into which one could somehow be existentially drawn. This can perhaps be perceived most clearly in that quintessential exercise in Jewish group memory which is the Passover Seder. Here, in the course of a meal around the family table, ritual, liturgy, and even culinary elements are orchestrated to transmit a vital past from one generation to the next. The entire Seder is a symbolic enactment of an historical scenario whose three great acts structure the Haggadah that is read aloud: slavery-deliverance-ultimate redemption. Significantly, one of the first ritual acts to be performed is the lifting up of a piece of unleavened bread (matzah) before those assembled, with the declaration: *Ha laḥma 'anya* – "*This is the bread of affliction* which our forefathers ate in the Land of Egypt." Both the language and the gesture are geared to spur, not so much a leap of memory as a fusion of past and present. Memory here is no longer recollection, which still preserves a sense of distance, but reactualization. It is this quality that impels the "I" in the *Tish'ah be-'Ab* lament as well, and nowhere is the notion brought forth more vigorously than in a Talmudic dictum central to the Passover Haggadah itself. 'In each and every generation let each person regard himself as though he had emerged from Egypt.'" *Zakhor*, 44–5.

40 Yerushalmi, *Zakhor*, 5–26.

actualise the historical realities behind the initial appearance of the *Ausdrücke*: i.e. Yahweh's theophany and giving of the Decalogue to Moses.

The rhetorical emphases in this chapter are signaled by the fact that after 1:5 none of the *Ausdrücke* appear again until 4:1–8. This passage represents an introduction to chapter 4 and the material in chapters 4–26[41] and, as Deuteronomy returns to this pattern of terminological interchangeability ("*Austauschbarkeit*"),[42] it advances the imagery in a way that undergirds everything to follow. It does so by introducing the Hebrew root חק and extending the wordplay in 1:1–5 from two to five terms:

1:1 דברים	4:1 חקים משפטים
	4:2 דבר, מצות
	4:5 חקים ומשפטים
	4:6 כל־החקים האלה
1:5 תורה הזה	4:8 חקים ומשפטים, כל התורה הזאת

These new parallels create "blurred edges" around the legal terms which are becoming increasingly obvious with their continued use. The "*Doppelausdruck*" (חקים משפטים) in 4:1 introduces the *content* of Moses' teaching (למד)[43] corresponding to the תורה (1:5) as the *content* of his דברים (1:1).[44] This is even more clear when we see the nature of the content is identified by דבר in 4:2 which also resonates with דברים in 1:1 (and the דבר in 6:5). Furthermore, the totality of the following contents marked by כל־החקים האלה in 4:6 parallels כל התורה הזאת in 4:8.[45] These parallels and wordplays are well noted, but their precise function is a matter of dispute.

Because of the historical nature of this context, and the narrative clues in Deuteronomy 30–31, the wordplays should be understood in the light of the rhetorical and theological relationship between the Horeb and Moab covenants. That is, the Horeb covenant (ברית, 5:2) is represented by the עשרת

41 A point argued by Braulik, "Wisdom", 2–3. See Christensen, *Deuteronomy*, 72–5 for a summary of views on this chapter's structure. I am primarily interested in the density of legal terms between vv. 1 and 8 which sets them apart with 4:40, 45 as the proper frame for the chapter.

42 Braulik's "Ausdrücke", examines the interchangeable use of ten terms as they all have contexts in which they refer to the entire Deuteronomic promulgation in ch. 5–26, 28: ברית, דב־, דרך, הקים, הקת, מצוה, מצות, משמרת, משפתים, עדות, תורה.

43 Referring either to Deut 4–26 or 12–26, see below.

44 Christensen, *Deuteronomy*, 80 and E.H. Merrill, *Deuteronomy* (NAC; Nashville, TN: Broadman & Holman, 1994), 137 are among many who note the parallel between דבר, and תורה, equating the "book" of Moses with Deuteronomy; yet this overshoots not only the point in Deut 4, but it also misinterprets the rhetorical nature of Moses' book *within* the book of Deuteronomy. See chapter 5 below.

45 N. Lohfink, "Die *Huqqîm Ûmišpātîm* im Buch Deuteronomium und ihre Neubegrenzung durch Dtn 12,1", in idem.; *Studien Zum Deuteronomium und Zur Deuteronomistischen Literatur 2* (Stuttgart: Katholisches Bibelwerk, 1991) 229–56, on pp. 249–51 argues that the asyndentic חקים in 6:1 exists in a tension with 4:45 and 11:26–32 and the later addition in 4:1–40 serves to limit the intended reference of the *Doppelausdruck*. Thus, contrary to Braulik, the *Doppelausdruck* applies to ch. 12–26 and not 5–26. McConville, "Place", 126–7 examines the uncertainties in Lohfink's grammatical and theological assumptions and draws his conclusions into question. Added to this, Lohfink undervalues the progressive correspondence being built into these terms through the linearity of Deuteronomy's narrative.

דברים of Yahweh written on two tablets of stone (4:13; cf. Exod 34:28)[46] and placed *in* the ark of the covenant (Deut 10:5). Deuteronomy's audience is renewing the Horeb covenant *at Moab* where Yahweh's ten דברים come through Moses' דברים which will be written in a book and placed *by* the ark (31:9, 26). The significance of the book and the ark will be discussed in chapter 5 below, however, the end of Deuteronomy helps us to see where these semantic tools are gradually going. In Deuteronomy 4, their meaning is "open" and alluring, leading readers to conclude that Moses' place in issuing *words* and a *torah* are fully in line with *Yahweh's words* in the Horeb covenant, and thus a part of Yahweh preparing his people for entry into new contexts.[47] In these "words," then, Israel can begin to see that Moses is giving the second generation the means to renew the events at Horeb; his דברים are the תורה by which they will be able to prosper under Yahweh's hand and draw near to Yahweh in the future (4:1, 6–8) – *after the death of Moses*.

As such, Israel has a continuity with the past. This continuity, however, is also protected and limited by the "canon" formula in Deuteronomy 4:2. This formula must be clarified in light of the obvious echo in 5:22:

Deut 4:2 (Cf. 13:1 [12:32])
לֹא תֹסִפוּ עַל־הַדָּבָר אֲשֶׁר אָנֹכִי מְצַוֶּה אֶתְכֶם וְלֹא תִגְרְעוּ מִמֶּנּוּ לִשְׁמֹר אֶת־מִצְוֹת יְהוָה אֱלֹהֵיכֶם אֲשֶׁר אָנֹכִי מְצַוֶּה אֶתְכֶם׃

Deut 5:22
אֶת־הַדְּבָרִים הָאֵלֶּה דִּבֶּר יְהוָה אֶל־כָּל־קְהַלְכֶם בָּהָר מִתּוֹךְ הָאֵשׁ הֶעָנָן וְהָעֲרָפֶל קוֹל גָּדוֹל וְלֹא יָסָף וַיִּכְתְּבֵם עַל־שְׁנֵי לֻחֹת אֲבָנִים וַיִּתְּנֵם אֵלָי׃

In the first instance (4:2), Moses commands Israel not to add to the חקים and משפטים that he is preparing to teach to them (4:1). We have already seen that, besides the reference to דבר in verse 2, the close of this context also equates the commands to תורה הזה (4:8). In the second instance (5:22) it is Yahweh, at the conclusion of the 10 words, who "adds no more".

These "canon" formulas are, as we will see, a part of the continuing rhetoric which envisions boundary markers for the future life in the land. So, part of this formula is surely limiting, or cautionary as it reflects the common legal formulations in both treaties[48] and law-codes of the ANE.[49] Yet, the legal prohibition leads scholars to pursue a number of theological meanings for 4:2.

---

46 On this use of ברית see Braulik, "Ausdrücke", 15–7.

47 Cf. McConville, *Deuteronomy*, 41 who says, "In theological terms, Deuteronomy makes a claim that God not only spoke, but goes on speaking by means of the teaching and interpretation of his word in believing communities." Cf. also R. Polzin, *Moses and the Deuteronomist: A Literary Study of the Deuteronomic History* (Bloomington: Indiana University, 1980), 9–11.

48 Kline, *Structure*, 36, 152.

49 Tigay, *Deuteronomy*, 43.

Notably, Olson's division between divine and human words emerges again here, pointing to a distinction between Yahweh's "ten words" at Horeb and Moses' "statutes and ordinances" at Moab where only Yahweh's words are the object of 4:2.[50] In quite a different perspective, Weinfeld rejects the context of legal-treaty associations and assigns this passage to a purely "sapiential ideological" origin with no "juristic" or legal connotation.[51] This lifts Deuteronomy out of the obvious Pentateuchal and covenantal context found in a canonical reading and is fairly easily eliminated.[52] Kline, meanwhile, is careful to preserve the covenantal framework of the book, yet believes that this makes Deuteronomy a treaty which is "not susceptible to ready modification."[53] The options are not mutually exclusive and we need to achieve a balance between the formulas in 4:2 and 12:32 [13:1] and the imperatives of future actualisation which will require the law to be applied in a variety of circumstances.

Thus, on the one hand, actualisation requires the law to be interpretively modified. We see this in a subtle transition which occurs between Deuteronomy 5:22 and 6:1 where, after giving the Decalogue, Yahweh speaks no more (5:22). He then sends Israel to their tents before continuing to reveal "commandments," "statutes" and "rules" to Moses. In other words, Yahweh has more commands to add and chooses to communicate them privately in a way that authorises the continuation of Moses' speech in 6:1.[54] The narrator has, therefore, preserved the signs of transition that uphold Moses' divine agency[55] and allow Moses to add to the דבר in a way that the law itself requires.[56]

On the other hand, the prohibitions aim at more than just limiting matters of simple adaptation to the law, but rather of the temptation to change the law by profane distortion – or to let Israel's national and religious story be tainted by foreign ideologies. This is argued throughout the next chapter, but here we can see that both instances of the prohibition (4:2; 12:32 [13:1]) are set in the context of the danger of false worship on the basis of assimilation of foreign gods and idols (4:15–31; 12:29–13:11 [10]).[57] It is the very nature of constantly changing future threats and temptations which will test

---

50 *Deuteronomy*, 32–3. Cf. also Sonnet, *Book*, 45–7 who sees here a closing of the Horeb covenant.

51 *D&DS*, 262–3.

52 For a critique of Weinfeld's sapiential interpretation, see Tigay, *Deuteronomy*, 43.

53 Kline, *Structure*, 153.

54 Sonnet, *Book*, 45–8 calls this Moses' "rhetorical manoeuvre" whereby 6:1ff is a "*didactic reformulation* of God's legal communication" for a new generation.

55 In fact, Deuteronomy itself, as a voice within a voice (within a voice) only strengthens the case for the a careful blending of authority. Cf. Sonnet, *Book*, 10–3 and chapter 5 below.

56 Christensen, *Deuteronomy*, 80; G. Braulik, *Deuteronomium* (NEB; 2 vols.; Würzburg: Echter Verlag, 1986–1992), 39; and McConville, *Deuteronomy*, 103. This ambiguous overlap between Moses' words and the words commanded forbid drawing a definitive line between them.

57 Christensen, *Deuteronomy*, 80; Tigay, *Deuteronomy*, 44 and Geller, "Wisdom", 36.

Israel's loyalty to Yahweh as they reinterpret and apply the law to these contexts.[58] In sum the threat to "this word" is not "modification" of just any kind, but the assimilation of anti-covenantal influences of the surrounding society.[59] In fact, as McConville recognises, Deuteronomy itself is a contextual adaptation of the Book of the Covenant which "canonizes the activity of reinterpreting the tradition."[60]

Therefore, the tension in 4:2 is "more apparent than real, since all fresh hearing of Deuteronomy is bound to entail translations into new situations."[61] In reality, the prohibition, combined with the actualising nature of the trans-generational call to "today," are Deuteronomy's way of reminding future generations that their understanding (knowledge) of the present must be engaged in the hermeneutical activities of keeping the law amidst the contextual threats to their own covenant faithfulness. 4:2 serves as a reminder that this is a dangerous and yet unavoidable enterprise.

3.1.3 Theophany, History and the Universal Aims of the Torah

Thus far, I have argued that the wordplay among the legal terms in Deuteronomy 4–11 represent Israel's future means of renewing past realities. We will now see that these realities are redemptive and theophanic in nature, derived from events of the past which disclose to Israel the uniqueness of Yahweh in his identity and presence with his chosen people. To make this epistemological move, Deuteronomy explicitly appropriates both sides of the theophany pattern in Exodus: (a) Yahweh's acts in creation and throughout history are confirmed by a series of questions posed to Israel about their purpose (Deut 4:32–34; cf. 6:20–24; 32:1–14). Referring to Exodus 1–15, these texts remind Israel that Yahweh's essence and his acts have no comparison in the history of the world,[62] and (b) Deuteronomy combines these acts with powerful imagery witnessed by Israel at Horeb (4:33; 4:36-37; 5:22–28; cf. 29:2–3). Creation, redemption and the mountain are all tied to theophany.

Moses then reminds Israel of how they feared death as the result of hearing and seeing Yahweh on the mountain (5:22–28). They Israelites, in turn, urge Moses into a mediatorial role:

---

[58] Craigie, *Deuteronomy*, 130 emphasises the "*essence* of the law, not the *letter* of the law".

[59] Driver, *Deuteronomy*, 63 suggests that the prohibition is against anything "weakening" or of "inferior authority" to the effect of "neutralising" this command. Christensen, *Deuteronomy*, 80 allows for the need for "necessary legal innovations," and Tigay, *Deuteronomy*, 43 says this is "not intended to stymie legal innovation." Cf. also Cairns, *Deuteronomy*, 55.

[60] "Metaphor", 347.

[61] Ibid.

[62] See Lohfink, "Verküngdigung", 187–91. Referring to 4:33f Lohfink says, "Die spielt auf alle Ereignisse an, die wir in Ex 1–15 lesen, zuerst die Plagen, dann den Sieg am Schilfmeer. Der Forschungsauftrag gibt auch sogleich an [...] daß diesen Ereignissen in der gesamten Menschheitsgeschichte nichts Vergleichbares an die Seite gestellt werden könnte: 4, 35." (188)

Deut 5:27
קְרַב[63] אַתָּה וּשֲׁמָע אֵת כָּל־אֲשֶׁר יֹאמַר יְהוָה אֱלֹהֵינוּ וְאַתְּ | תְּדַבֵּר אֵלֵינוּ אֵת כָּל־אֲשֶׁר יְדַבֵּר יְהוָה אֱלֹהֵינוּ אֵלֶיךָ וְשָׁמַעְנוּ וְעָשִׂינוּ׃

Moses thus receives the torah and teaches it to Israel as a direct expression of his exclusive ability to withstand the danger that comes from the fiery theophany and the voice of Yahweh (cf. 2 Cor 3:7–18).[64]

The entire thrust of Deuteronomy 4, in fact, pivots around the theophanic experiences in Exodus (at Horeb); both sides of the chapter's "inner-frame" (vv. 5–8 and 32–39)[65] employ the theophanic divine knowledge gained in the past as a means to highlight the universal implications of Israel's obedience to the law.

(1) Deuteronomy 4:5–8
The opening of the frame (vv. 5–8) promises Israel that if she keeps these commandments it will be חכמתכם and בינתכם in the sight of the nations (v. 6a). The point is emphatically repeated through the mouth of the nations at the end of the verse: רק עם־חכם ונבון (6b). It is important to notice that the torah (statutes, commandments, etc.) are a witness to the nations of wisdom, understanding and greatness.[66] Note that in a book focused on *Israel's* future social order over against surrounding nations, the universal promise of Genesis 12:1–3 has not been lost; the words of Yahweh promising to make Israel a גוי גדול in Genesis 12:2 are the very words the nations will use to bless her if she obeys the torah (4:7).[67]

Furthermore, the words of the nations incorporate the "nearness" and "righteousness" which law-keeping has the potential to reveal. First, the law will demonstrate the קרב of Israel's God:

כִּי מִי־גוֹי גָּדוֹל אֲשֶׁר־לוֹ אֱלֹהִים קְרֹבִים אֵלָיו כַּיהוָה אֱלֹהֵינוּ בְּכָל־קָרְאֵנוּ אֵלָיו׃
(v. 7)

The root קרב is rare in Deuteronomy, especially in the parenetic sections,[68] which makes the echo in Israel's mouth in 5:27 significant: "קרב אתה and hear all that Yahweh our God will say to us, and all that Yahweh our God will speak to you, we will do it." Israel's pleading with Moses is based on their inability to withstand the glory of Yahweh's presence (5:22–27). Yet

63 On the Hebrew קרב, cf. Deut 4:7 and 30:14. See below.

64 I. Wilson, *Out of the Midst of the Fire: Divine Presence in Deuteronomy* (SBLDS; Atlanta: Scholars, 1995), 56–66 shows that Deuteronomy adds the phrase "out of the midst of the fire" to the Exodus accounts of Sinai in order to solidify not only Moses reception of the words, but also Israel's almost fatal experience of the fire which testifies to the divine source behind Moses's words.

65 Olson, *Deuteronomy*, 33ff.

66 Contrary to Weinfeld, *D&DS*, 254–6, I do not take this to be a matter of "ideological conflict" between wisdom and torah schools (257), but evidence of their shared worldview. See chapters 4 and 8 below.

67 Braulik, *Deuteronomium*, 40; Weinfeld, *Deuteronomy 1–11*, 202; C.J.H. Wright, *Deuteronomy*, 48–9.

68 Cf. also 13:8; 21:3, 6; 22:2; 30:14; 32:17, 35.

in 4:7 Israel sees that keeping the torah allows her to re-create Moses' nearness to Yahweh before the nations. This draws the admiration of the nations and confirms for Israel that a powerful God who can draw near like Yahweh is without equal.

Second, Israel's obedience will confirm the צדיק of the rules and statutes (4:8b) and torah (4:8c) which Moses "sets before them this day". Wisdom, understanding, righteousness, greatness and nearness are all future benefits contained in the law.[69] As such, Yahweh's tabernacle glory (Exod 40) corresponds not only to the righteousness of the torah itself, but to his continued presence on the basis of Israel's perseverance in pursuing צדק through it.[70] Moses' words to Israel are a torah which will enable the future presence of Yahweh for Israel.[71] God's presence with his people is inseparably tied to their knowledge of Yahweh's declared realities in her political and social realms: wisdom, understanding and righteousness.

The most dramatic epistemological implication of this text arises from the fact that these words are in the mouth of the surrounding nations (cf. Deut 32:27–43) who bless Israel for her greatness, the superiority of their law in wisdom[72] and, therefore, the superiority of their God.[73] This suggests, in conjunction with Genesis 11–50, that "God had a purpose for Israel"[74] in history. By keeping the torah, the nations look to Israel and her law as "normative"[75] and "paradigmatic"[76] for the created order. Surely, Israel's universal witness is often overlooked because it is a witness of "being"[77] and not of "going." Yet, just as the mountain and the tabernacle represented the glory of Yahweh in Israel's midst, Israel as a nation represents that same place of glory in the midst of the nations. These laws and statutes, then, are not just social accommodations for living in the land; they are a paradigm of God's re-creative initiative to bring righteousness,

---

69 See MacDonald, *Deuteronomy*, 199; McConville, *Deuteronomy*, 104–6; Miller, *Deuteronomy*, 56–7; Brueggemann, *Deuteronomy*, 51–3 and Merrill, *Deuteronomy*, 116–8. Cf. however, Craigie, *Deuteronomy*, 130f; Mayes, *Deuteronomy*, 150f; Weinfeld, *Deuteronomy 1–11*, 202; and Tigay, *Deuteronomy*, 44–5 who miss the theophanic connections altogether.

70 Niehaus, *Sinai*, 203. See Merrill, *Deuteronomy*, 117 who shows the law-keeping nature in the use of צדיק here.

71 Miller, *Deuteronomy*, 56, however, misses the connections with Exodus and Horeb, describing the law as a "surrogate" rather than an enabler of divine presence.

72 Braulik, *Deuteronomium*, 41.

73 On this basis MacDonald, *Deuteronomy* drastically underestimates the monotheistic intentions of this book. Deuteronomy aims to universalise its God before the nations. MacDonald fails to discern the cosmic and mythical framework in the book. Cf. however, O'Donovan, *DN*, 72; Olson, *Deuteronomy*, 181–2; C.J.H. Wright, *Deuteronomy*, 10–1; N. Wright, *Jesus and the Victory of God* (Minneapolis, MN: Fortress, 1996), 204; Keil/Delitzsch, "Pentateuch", 875; and Tigay, *Deuteronomy*, xii–xiii who says, "The fundamental principle underlying Deuteronomy is monotheism [...]. An aspect of Deuteronomy's monotheism is its teaching that Israel's God guides the history of all peoples."

74 O'Donovan, *DN*, 29.

75 Ibid., 28. See also Fretheim, "Law"; and Greidanus, "Dimension", 39.

76 C.J.H. Wright, *Ethics*, 62–4.

77 C.J.H. Wright, *Deuteronomy*, 12.

justice and wisdom into this world.[78] As such, they represent the moral and religious requirements for sustaining a relationship with the creator God. Deuteronomy will build upon this insistence that *how* and *what* one knows is tied to the ethics of obedience. There is an inherent virtue required to know this God of the nations: he is near and known when his torah is obeyed, and – at the same time – his presence is required for knowledge to be successfully acquired.[79]

(2) Deuteronomy 4:32–39

We also make note of the close to the inner frame in chapter 4 (vv. 32–39) which rejoins the motifs of Yahweh's uniqueness and his revealed law. The passage is introduced by a series of rhetorical questions which invite Israel to contemplate history[80] since היום אשר ברא אלהים אדם אל הארץ (4:32b) in order to draw the particular conclusion repeated at the beginning and end of the subsection:

FROM CREATION – uniqueness of Horeb and deliverance (4:32–34)

CONCLUSION – (4:35)

[81] אַתָּה הָרְאֵתָ לָדַעַת כִּי יְהוָה הוּא הָאֱלֹהִים אֵין עוֹד מִלְבַדּוֹ׃

PROMISE TO FATHERS – uniqueness of Horeb and deliverance (4:36–38)[82]

CONCLUSION – (4:39)

וְיָדַעְתָּ הַיּוֹם וַהֲשֵׁבֹתָ אֶל־לְבָבֶךָ כִּי יְהוָה הוּא הָאֱלֹהִים בַּשָּׁמַיִם מִמַּעַל
וְעַל־הָאָרֶץ מִתָּחַת אֵין עוֹד׃

Significantly, 4:32–39 appeals to both senses where Israel's "seeing" signs and "hearing" testimony of God's works testify to his uniqueness.[83] In verses 32–34, Israel is led to conclude that no such acts as the Horeb revelation or the Egypt deliverance have occurred since creation. Verses 37–38 place this same lesson in the context of patriarchal promises, leading to the conclusion that Yahweh has treated Israel like no other nation in history

---

78 Fretheim, "Creation", 361–2.

79 Cf. the study on the first commandment by D. Patrick, "Is the Truth of the First Commandment Known by Reason?" *CBQ* 56 (1994) 423–41 where he shows how the truth in the content of the story of Israel's relationship with Yahweh depends upon Israel's obedience to the command (436).

80 C.J.H. Wright, *Ethics*, 48 draws the same conclusion.

81 Most translations assume a "monotheistic" reading of the Hebrew אין עוד מלבדו (v. 35) and אין עוד (v. 39) – "there is no other besides him." MacDonald rejects these on the basis of his view of monolatry in Deuteronomy, *Deuteronomy*, 81–5. He has shown that these grammatical constructions are possible and at best probable. Yet, MacDonald's translation and theology of monotheism fail to do justice to the ontological nature of the Pentateuchal and OT story. Cf. R.P. O'Dowd, "Nathan MacDonald: Deuteronomy and the Meaning of 'Monotheism'", *EJT* 13 (2004) 66–7.

82 Some take the reference to hearing Yahweh's voice 'out of heaven' (4:36) as the basis for a "name theology" in the Deuteronomy. Wilson, *Midst*, 9–15 shows how "name theology" overlooks the nature of לפני יהוה as it represents actual divine presence in the book.

83 The allusions to seeing and hearing emerge again in Deut 29 and will be discussed specifically in chapter 5 below.

that they might know that he is Yahweh (cf. Ps 147:20). Or, as Sternberg puts it, "God shapes the world plot with a view to getting his creatures to 'know' him."[84] And, in light of 4:1–8, the lesson can be seen to have a resonating effect on the surrounding nations if Israel would only keep the torah.

Positioned in this way, the knowledge of Yahweh prefaces and qualifies the ensuing legal discourse which, as argued below, extends from 4:1 to 31:23. The implication for Israel is that the knowledge of Yahweh, of his activity in history, and of his universal uniqueness are the foundation of her knowledge of the world.[85] The knowledge of Yahweh is part and parcel with the moral, social and ethical commandments which he reveals.[86] That this same union of creation and salvation events is used to justify Yahweh's uniqueness in 32:39–43 – and his concern for the testimony of the nations (32:27) – reinforces the fact that epistemology is grounded in the ontology of divine presence and divine power and the ethics of obedience.

Finally, this careful juxtaposition of theophany with torah and the קרב of Yahweh constitutes the first instance of a transcendence/immanence motif that is sustained throughout Deuteronomy.[87] It is Israel's obedience to the rules and statutes of *torah* which demonstrates to the nations the *nearness* of Yahweh and the righteousness of the law (4:6–8). Yet it is also the *words* of this *torah* which express both the reality and the content of Yahweh speaking "out of heaven" and acting "on earth" (4:36). Torah allows Israel to experience the nearness and transcendence of Yahweh[88] in future times and thus has the potential to replace Moses' unique ministry in Israel.

3.1.4 Introduction to Teaching Functions in the Community

So far in chapter 4 we have seen how the use of time (history), wordplay and theophany create a platform for actualisation of the divine relationship. The fourth component of actualisation is the performative roles in which Israel will bring the torah to life. These four components will be expanded upon and applied throughout the rest of Deuteronomy, yet at the heart of the performative or participatory function is the "teaching" role in chapter 4 which we will find broadened in several later chapters.

Specifically, chapter 4 enjoins Israel to teach (למד) the next generation as a means to actualise her relationship with Yahweh. למד is used more than

---

[84] Sternberg, *Poetics*, 48.

[85] Cf. Maimonides' similar conclusions, Kreisel, "Maimonides", 248.

[86] See McConville, *Deuteronomy*, 36–7 and Niehaus, *Sinai*, 21–3.

[87] Thus Deuteronomy 4 parallels Deuteronomy 12 as the place where Yahweh meets his people and the transcendent nature of Yahweh which stands over Israel, See Millar, "Place", 35–6 and McConville, "Place", 130–36. Cf. also Stahl, *Law*, 53; N. Lohfink, *Theology of the Pentateuch: Themes of the Priestly Narrative and Deuteronomy* (Edinburgh: T&T Clark, 1994), 130; Olson, *Deuteronomy*, 39 and Geller, "Wisdom", 57–8.

[88] See McConville, *Grace*, 125–6.

80 times in the Old Testament; yet in the Pentateuch it is found only in Deuteronomy, and its 17 occurrences are not incidental.[89] While Olson goes too far in saying that *torah* in Deuteronomy is "catechesis" his overall point is valid.[90] Exodus shows that though Moses was a prophet slow of speech (Exod 4:10), Yahweh gives him the words to confront Pharaoh (7:1–2) and thereby transform him into the principle mode of communication between Yahweh and Israel. In Deuteronomy, Moses' speech is communicated as דברים, תורה and now למד.

What is significant in Deuteronomy 4 is not just that the first four references to teaching occur (vv. 1, 5, 10, 14), but that this takes place in the context of both the influence of the legal wordplay in 4:1–8 and massive movements between past, present and future. Braulik helpfully captures the teaching rhetoric in Deuteronomy as a part of the overall torah-wordplay, in this case through the various *Promulgationsätze* of the law.[91] Thus, in addition to the wordplay in the ten *Ausdrücke*, we have four semi-synonymous promulgation verbs for the law: צוה, נתן, דבר, and למד.[92] It is no mistake that these verbs occur particularly in phrases with the *Ausdrücke*, for – it is well recognised – torah in Deuteronomy carries as much of a force of "teaching" as of "law" in Deuteronomy.[93] So while the individual promulgation words and phrases have the potential to signal minor nuances, the overall thrust of the vocabulary is the same: to give the "blurred edges" of *torah* an overwhelmingly didactic and performative character.

Secondly, the power of this semantic artistry is enhanced by the historical movements in chapter 4. The four references to למד move through a past-present-future timeline while embracing Moses and Israel in the acts of teaching. The effect is to enmesh people, teaching and torah in a transgenerational paradigm:

4:1	PRESENT (מלמד)	Moses
4:5	PAST (למדתי)	Moses commanded by Yahweh
4:10	FUTURE (ילמדון)	Children's children
4:14	PAST (ללמד)	Moses commanded by Yahweh

[89] Deut 4:1, 5, 10, 14; 5:1, 31; 6:1; 11:19; 14:23; 17:19; 18:9; 20:18; 31:12, 13, 19, 22. MacDonald, *Deuteronomy*, 134 notes that only the book of Psalms has more occurrences than Deuteronomy (27), mostly in Psalm 119.

[90] *Deuteronomy*, 6, 9–16. On the other hand, S.D. McBride, "Polity of the Covenant People; The Book of Deuteronomy", in D. Christensen (ed.), *Song of Power* (Winona Lake, IN: Eisenbrauns, 1993) 62–77, on p. 65f emphasises the "political policies" and "jurisprudential" character of torah. Catechesis and/or teaching should not be set against the legal or constitutional. Torah is both. Cf. C.J.H. Wright, *God's People in God's Land: Family, Land, and Property in the Old Testament* (Exeter/Grand Rapids, MI: Paternoster/Eerdmans, 1990), 83.

[91] Braulik, "Ausdrücke", 13–4.

[92] See chapter 5 for my argument that כתב should be included among these terms.

[93] Braulik, "Wisdom", 5–6; Miller, *Deuteronomy*, 12, 25; Olson, *Deuteronomy*, 11.

Olson states, "The chapter provides a model of ongoing interpretation and reflection on past tradition that keeps the tradition alive and adaptable [...] the heart of the chapter is a set of *three teaching paradigms* from past, present, and future that exemplify the recurring movement of God's people through judgment to hope, curse to blessing, life to death."[94] Significantly, God is never said to "teach" in Deuteronomy;[95] rather Moses access to Yahweh and unique prophetic role are distributed throughout Israel for in teaching roles which will reproduce the torah in future generations. Family (Dt. 4:9–10; 6:4–9, 20–25; 11:19), kings (17:19), priests (31:12–13), and people (31:19–22) will all bear the post-Mosaic responsibility for teaching Moses' (and Yahweh's) word. Again we cite McConville's observation above that Yahweh's word goes on speaking in future "teaching" and "interpretation" in the community.[96] Deuteronomy envisions an essentially incarnational eschatology of Yahweh's word in Israel in the mouths of the people.

In Deuteronomy 1–4 we have seen the theological, rhetorical and structural development use actualisation as the means for each generation of Israelites to find their knowledge of the present identified with generations of the past. Israel's history thus yields an ontological, spiritual and redemptive reality as the context within which future generation of knowers must be engaged to know Yahweh. We turn now to Deuteronomy 5–11 where the teaching roles and rhetoric from the first four chapters reproduce the Mosaic office in the future.

3.2 Oral and Written Worlds: Memory and the Great Commandment

The teaching motif in Deuteronomy 4–5 continues into the next six chapters where the oral and written worlds combine with memory motifs in a way that allows us to give further consideration to the epistemological nature of Deuteronomy's living tradition. Our focus is on chapters 6 and 8 which fit into the overall structure of 4–11 as follows:

Deut 5:1–6:3 – The עשׂרת דברים of Yahweh and Israel's Required Response
  Deut 6:4–25 – Love Yahweh: Teaching and Tradition in the דברים
Deut 7 – A Chosen People: The Context of Israel's Life in the Land
  Deut 8:1–20 – Remember and Do not Forget your Tradition
Deut 9:1–10:11 – A Stubborn People: The Context of Israel's Life in the Land
  Deut 10:12–11:32 – Love, Fear, Teach, Obey[97]

---

94 Olson, *Deuteronomy*, 30–1, emphasis original. Cf. also Miller, *Deuteronomy*, 109.

95 Sonnet, *Book*, 37–8.

96 McConville, *Deuteronomy*, 41.

97 The structure here is hard to tie down given the extensive thematic and semantic overlapping. Nevertheless the basic pattern of past-present-future tied into the future teaching and tradition in the land dominates this section. Cf. especially Christensen, *Deuteronomy*, 64 and S.D.J. McBride, "The Yoke of the Kingdom: An Exposition of Deuteronomy 6:4–5", *Interpretation* 27 (1973) 273–306, on p. 289.

Epistemologically, we see that this creates a perspective forged by a mixture of existential and historical observations about Israel's past and future (5:1–22; 7:1–26; 9:1–10:11) which alternates injunctions to teach, remember, fear and love (6:4–25; 8:1–20; 10:12–11:32). In this way, the last section (10:12–11:32) acts as a climactic summary to chapters 4–11 and a final preparation for the legal material (Deut 12–26). In what follows we are interested in exploring those contributions in chapters 6 and 8 which transition the *Ausdrücke* and *Promulgationsätze* into the oral and written worlds of Deuteronomy 6–34.

3.3 Speech and Writing in the Great Commandment

According to McConville, Deuteronomy 6 "puts into effect the relationship between the Decalogue on Horeb and the Deuteronomic teaching that is to characterize the life of Israel in its entire future [...]."[98] As a whole, the chapter can be divided into three parts: the Shema (vv. 4–9, cf. 11:18–20), a contextual and historical warning about life in the land (vv. 10–19), and a return to the teaching injunction based upon this future context (vv. 20–25). As such, the chapter begins and ends with parents and children – in community – continuing the tradition bearing process, while the middle of the chapter sets the motivation and context that inspires obedience. The actualising potential created by Deuteronomy's rhetoric and theology are evident in the three following aspects: (1) the oral and written worlds, (2) the place of parents and children and (3) the content of the new tradition.

(1) The oral and written worlds emerge most prominently in the Shema and the larger context of chapter 6. Specifically the Shema is a group of דברים, commanded by Moses (v. 6), which are the subject of six commands in verses 6–9: being (היה) on your heart, teaching (שׁנן)[99] them to your children, speaking (דבר) them in the community, binding (קשׁר) them on your hands, being (היה) as frontlets between your eyes, and writing (כתב) them on the family dwellings. There is a general progression from oral to written/permanent vocabulary in these commands which, as Sonnet suggests, imagines a "forthcoming tradition" a "text" and a given body of "words".[100]

This progression supports the Shema's overall function in Deuteronomy 1–11 of *divine imitation*, following Yahweh's activity in Deuteronomy 5 of

98 McConville, *Deuteronomy*, 145.

99 שׁנן is a synonym for למד. The piel of שׁנן in 6:7, "teach your children diligently" is hapax, but the meaning is confirmed by the Arabic, Targum and Peshitta, see Weinfeld, *Deuteronomy 1–11*, 332–3 and G. Fischer/N. Lohfink, "Diese Worte sollst du Summen: Dtn 6,7 wedibbartā bām – ein Verlorener Schlüssel zur meditativen Kultur in Israel", in N. Lohfink (ed.), *Studien zum Deuteronomium und zur deuteronomistischen Literatur 3* (Stuttgart: Katholisches Bibelwerk, 1995) 181–203, on p. 187.

100 Sonnet, *Book*, 57.

speaking (דבר) the commands to Israel and *writing* (כתב) them on two tablets of stone (5:4–5; 5:22). There is a sense of permanence in the stones that are placed in the ark. But it is also true that the stones correspond to the theophanic fire (אשׁ הגדלה) that Israel saw with their eyes (4:36; 5:24). Because Israel feared the fire (5:4, 25–27), and because Yahweh approved of their response (5:28), we have good reason to assume that the fire represents Yahweh's presence on the mountain[101] and, therefore, a combined representation of oral and written revelation. Thus, the divine writing and speaking in chapter 5 constitutes not so much a closure of Yahweh's revelation as a pattern of divine behaviour humanly mimicked in the Shema as Israel responds to Yahweh[102] and actualises the Horeb realities in future generations.

In order to depict the proper response to God, the commands in the Shema employ ritualistic metaphors which envision all-encompassing devotion to Yahweh. Some scholars prefer to isolate these commands to a physical "iconic" exercise[103] over against the metaphorical implications which arise from the ambiguities in the command.[104] That is, we find an open-ended nature of these דברים in the narrative that suggests that the writing commanded refers to more than just the contents in 6:6–9.[105] Even if one could write 6:4–9 in the described locations, the point, as Niditch puts it, is "more on the oral end of the continuum" recalling not only the "words" in chapters 4–5, but the *growing* body of Moses' oral delivery.[106] Added to this, the literacy rate of the average Israelite in Moses' day[107] discourages a literal reading, at least any literal reading which does not serve the larger purpose of fully devoted love to Yahweh.[108] Rather, Deuteronomy 6:6–9 unites writing and speech – "ritual" and "recital"– as the two "channels" of Jewish memory.[109] This becomes more clear in our examination the Shema's content below.[110]

---

101 Wilson, *Midst*, 64–5. Cf. also Lohfink, *Theology*, 130 and Niehaus, *Sinai*, 217–29.

102 Barker, "Israel", 151; MacDonald, *Deuteronomy*, 151 and Olson, *Deuteronomy*, 51.

103 Niditch, *Oral World*, 87, 100 the "iconic" form of the writing imagery is a "memorial" of Yahweh's ten words in chapter 5. Tigay, *Deuteronomy*, 442f, argues for the literal use of teffilin relying on the historical discoveries, particularly at Qumran, which solidify the practice in Second Temple Judaism. Yet the first temple evidence is quite uncertain and Tigay's points do not help us all that much.

104 Sonnet, *Book*, 57.

105 See Fischer/Lohfink, "Worte", 182–3.

106 Niditch, *Oral World*, 87. Cf. Keil/Delitzsch, "Pentateuch", 885.

107 Although literacy increased in post-exilic Israel, the "represented world" in Deuteronomy is much earlier and probably illiterate. Cf. Crenshaw, *Education (1998)*, 38–40 and Niditch, *Oral World*, 100–02.

108 See D.I. Block, "How Many is God? An Investigation Into the Meaning of Deuteronomy 6:4–5", *JETS* 47 (2004) 193–212, on pp. 201–08.

109 Yerushalmi, *Zakhor*, 11.

110 In Jacques Derrida's postmodern theory of texts there is a real tension between speech and writing and texts and meaning, especially in the Western ideal of the logos. Without resorting to Greek logocentrism, Deuteronomy's oral and written worlds perpetually unite speech and writing through a living tradition; word and text are mutually effective in sustaining meaning.

(2) This of course leads us to the place of families (parents and children) at the beginning and end of chapter 6. These share many parallels with the injunctions in the wisdom tradition: the father-son relationship, the "binding" (קשׁר) on the heart, teaching, and the "way" (דרך) (cf. Prov 1:8; 2:1; 3:1–3; 6:21; 7:3). However, the parallels are not sufficient to posit a purely sapiential origin.[111] Rather, the strengths of the wisdom tradition are employed in Deuteronomy to accentuate the rhetorical and parenetic aims of the torah. In this way, Yahweh and Israel can exist in a father-son and mother-son relationship in Deuteronomy (Cf. 32:6, 13),[112] which sets a paradigm for parent-child relationships in the community.

Moreover the interaction of paternal instruction (6:6–9) and pedagogical inquiry (6:20) depicts not just one-way teaching, but a corporate conversation which acts to sustain the memory through an interaction with contemporary world events. In this exercise, the children learn the meaning of the החקים and משפטים as they are located in the history of Yahweh's activity in the world (6:21–24). As such, the revelatory nature of the law gives the tradition a norming authority, but in doing so it does not oppose opposing the exercise of premised and logical thinking which the children and parents are sure to pursue.

(3) Finally, the Shema has many implications for the nature of the divine knowledge transferred throughout future generations. The beginning of the Shema, שמע ישׂראל יהוה אלהינו יהוה אחד (6:4) resonates with the *monotheistic* proclamations in 4:32–39 which assures Israel of Yahweh's uniqueness and his historical purposes for Israel while at the same time reinforcing the uniqueness of Yahweh's nearness (4:7) evidenced by what Israel saw (4:34). The conclusions in chapter 4 were a part of the עשׂרת הדברים of the covenant delivered by *Yahweh* (4:13); yet this repeated creed uniquely prefaces the great commandment issued by *Moses*:[113]

Deut 6:5

וְאָהַבְתָּ אֵת יְהוָה אֱלֹהֶיךָ בְּכָל־לְבָבְךָ וּבְכָל־נַפְשְׁךָ וּבְכָל־מְאֹדֶךָ׃

It is fairly well agreed that the commands in 6:4–9 not only embody an expression of the first commandment, but in doing so, also represent the very heart of the Deuteronomic law.[114] The nature of devotion required of Israel is expressed in the threefold demand for all of the "heart," "life," and "ability." This unique requirement has generated a substantial amount of discussion on the nature and extent of Israel's response.

[111] So, Weinfeld, *D&DS* and less emphatically, Weinfeld, *Deuteronomy 1–11*, 55–7.

[112] See J. McKay, "Man's Love For God in Deuteronomy and the Father/Teaching – Son/Pupil Relationship", *VT* 22 (1972) 426–35 and G.v. Rad, *Deuteronomy* (OTL; Philadelphia: Westminster, 1966), 64.

[113] Millar, "Place", 63 says, "Without ch. 4 and 5, then, the Shema is cut loose from its moorings and basic meaning [...] the Shema affirms the theological coherence of ch. 4–6."

[114] Cf. Miller, *Deuteronomy*, 10; Tigay, *Deuteronomy*, 75–6; and S.D.J. McBride, "Yoke", 296–7.

The most popular theory is that the Shema qualifies the outward obedience which dominates the legal discourse with a need for an internal character.[115] The internal devotion/disposition of the heart is certainly relevant in the OT, especially in Israel's future ability to sustain both the devotional and cultic requirements of the law.[116] Yet, Brueggemann and McBride draw attention to the fact that the literary device also imagines a "singularity" of devotion corresponding to the exclusive nature of Yahweh and his oneness.[117] This observation helps us to avoid the false conclusion that what Moses is commanding is some kind of private or mystical devotion which isolates the spiritual from the physical or the individual from the community. This is confirmed by the fact that the Shema precedes the very physical and memorial practices which are entrenched in the dialogical context of community tradition and that it resonates with the Passover and exodus memorial in Exodus 13:7–10.

MacDonald suggests that the nature of this command is expressed in the metaphorical *herem* command in chapter 7. This confirms for him that "monotheism" is not merely a truth to be "comprehended" but a relationship to be "committed."[118] Mayes' work on the purpose of Deuteronomy expands on this tradition-bearing mode of relationship in Deuteronomy. For his own part, Mayes wants less of a poetic reading of "relationship" and more of an "objective appreciation of Deuteronomy" which he finds in positivist historical method.[119] MacDonald's sensibilities are more suited to Deuteronomy's rhetoric; what Deuteronomy offers is a truth-construct grounded in a poetics of history and not in a science of history. It requires a relative open hermeneutic in time and is not anxious about ambiguity in application. The community changes as does its context and reception of the text, but Yahweh's unchanging identity (and not historical positivism) opposes the relativis*ing* of the truth which comes from him.

Working with MacDonald's notion of love in action, we can see that law is not just a group of rules or set of teachings, but a mysterious and sacramental torah through which Israel *actualises* her relationship with Yahweh by obedience to the covenant. Torah places Yahweh at the centre of Israel's world and therefore conditions her knowledge by the cosmic structure and stability of his created order. By obeying the torah, Israel conforms to the

---

115 See McConville, *Deuteronomy*, 142 and Millar, "Place", 55–6. Cf. also Sonnet's reference to "interiorization," *Book*, 58.

116 Cf. 1 Sam 16:7; Pss 50; 147:10–11; Jer 9:23; 11:8, 20; 17:10.

117 Brueggemann, *Deuteronomy*, 91 and S.D.J. McBride, "Yoke", 304. Cf. also Block, "How Many", 202–12.

118 *Deuteronomy*, 97. Cf. also his statements on p. 136. This is taken up again below.

119 "On Describing the Purpose of Deuteronomy", *JSOT* 58 (1993) 13–33, on pp. 22–5.

universal created order as an expression of her love for Yahweh; her participation in creation enables her to know Yahweh through imitation.[120]

Significantly, the imagery of covenant actualisation is only emerging now, at the beginning of the legal material, and it is not until the end of Deuteronomy that we understand fully what it means to perform the torah. Yet this memorable passage in Deuteronomy relationally conditions the nature of teaching and revelation communicated in throughout the book.[121] Commenting on the unity in Deut 6–12 Nathan MacDonald says:

> The sort of knowledge that Israel is to acquire is more than purely intellectual, for it is a knowledge that, correctly acquired, results in obedience of the commandments [...]. Whatever may or may not be said about the extent of divine knowledge, there is a basic congruence between the knowledge YHWH seeks and the knowledge he desires for Israel, for both may be described as relational.[122]

This relational knowledge cascades across past, present and future generations as parents teach children through perpetual cycles of life in the land. Furthermore, the relationship with Yahweh which unites these generations is grounded in the climactic events in Egypt and at Horeb as they are actualised perpetually in obedient Israel.[123] In sum, we find that the Shema accentuates the liminal nature of Deuteronomy's appeal to readers in new times and places to face their own boundaries in the knowledge of Yahweh as he relates to his world.[124]

3.4 Remember and Do Not Forget: Wordplay and Actualisation in Deuteronomy 8

> Yet the Hebrew Bible seems to have no hesitations in commanding memory. Its injunctions to remember are unconditional, and even when not commanded, remembrance is always pivotal [...]. For here as elsewhere ancient Israel knows what God is from what he has done in history. And if that is so, then memory has become crucial to its faith and, ultimately, to its very existence.[125]

Between the major injunctions to teach (ch. 6 and 11), Moses frames another command to remember (ch. 8) – situated between two parallel (historical) chapters (7, 9) which identify Israel as a (rebellious) object of Yahweh's choice. Memory is a salient characteristic of OT theology, a selective

---

[120] Cf. Zimmerli, "Yahweh", 89–90. O'Donovan, *Resurrection*, 87, argues that "participation" is necessary to perceive the transcendent knowledge of God,

[121] See Miller, *Deuteronomy*, 10, 97, 107.

[122] MacDonald, *Deuteronomy*, 136.

[123] Sonnet, *Book*, 10, notes how Moses' words create the image of a trans-generational Israel.

[124] See variously, Childs, *Memory*, 53; MacDonald, *Deuteronomy*, 155; Millar, "Place", 32, 43, 60–1; Olson, *Deuteronomy*, 89–112; C.J.H. Wright, *Deuteronomy*, 8–9.

[125] Yerushalmi, *Zakhor*, 5, 9.

transmission of the meaningful events in Israelite history. The sheer design and vocabulary in Deuteronomy 8 make it the most memorable of memorial texts in Deuteronomy and the OT – what Yerushalmi calls the "*locus classicus*" of memory and forgetting.[126]

The chapter is crafted in a sophisticated chiasm,[127] recalling two parallel incidents where Yahweh provided manna and water in the context of Israel's unfaithful, grumbling attitude (Num 11, 21). This appropriates the same epistemological event in Exodus towards a different purpose:

Exod 16:12b

וִידַעְתֶּם כִּי אֲנִי יְהוָה אֱלֹהֵיכֶם

Deut 8:3b

לְמַעַן הוֹדִעֲךָ כִּי לֹא עַל־הַלֶּחֶם לְבַדּוֹ יִחְיֶה הָאָדָם כִּי עַל־כָּל־מוֹצָא
פִּי־יְהוָה יִחְיֶה הָאָדָם׃

In Exodus, the purpose of the manna lesson is applied to the *identity* of Yahweh as Israel's saving and providing God. In Deuteronomy, the purpose is applied to Yahweh's *provision* through "all that comes out" of his mouth. The poetics in Deuteronomy 8 weave the assurance of Yahweh's provision into a memorial sermon. This is primarily accomplished through a doubling structure which balances three elements:

- Two allusions to the lesson in the desert (vv. 2–5; 14–16)
- A twofold injunction to remember (זכר vv. 2, 18) and not forget (שׁכח, vv. 11, 14)
- A play between "commandment", "command" and "what proceeds out" (מצוה, vv. 1, 2, 6, 11; צוה, vv. 1, 11 and מוצא, vv. 3, 15).

Similar to the wordplay between תורה and דבר, this play equates what God gives in the exodus (vv. 2–5) and what he does in nature (with water, vv. 14–16) with what (מוצא) out of his mouth.[128] The lesson Israel should remember from her history is one of continuity: just as Yahweh supplies food and water (past), land and victory (future), he supplies the life-giving commands that will sustain Israel as a nation. Thus, the climax or purpose of the passage is recognised as the lesson in verses 11 and 19–20 pleading with Israel to remember – or not forget.[129]

To "remember," according to Yerushalmi, is that nature of *halakhah* in Jewish tradition which transforms history into memory.[130] Memory, then, is not history in the "ambitious" or Enlightenment sense, but the imaginative

126 Ibid., 109.
127 Ibid.
128 This follows the treatment by Van Leeuwen, "Mouth".
129 C.J.H. Wright, *Deuteronomy*, 121 and Craigie, *Deuteronomy*, 184.
130 Yerushalmi, *Zakhor*, 115.

way which past events give identity and continuity to a society. In other words, memory upholds and unites both the historical recollection and an associated response of obedience or faith.[131] MacDonald places this lesson in the context of the great commandment (Deut 6:4–9; 10:12–11:32) to establish that memory is active and relational: "[...] both chapters [7–8] describe the active ways in which "love" to YHWH is to be expressed".[132] Memory therefore recalls the source of Israel's life in Yahweh alone as the motivation for Israel to respond by keeping his torah.

What is more significant, epistemologically, is the repetition of creation themes and a corresponding return to Pentateuchal and universal implications. McConville notes that "whatever comes out of Yahweh's mouth" is sufficient for האדם (v. 3a) recalling the provision for אדם in the garden as signified by the land as the place of obedient reward (ch. 7, 9) and the desert as the place of forgetfulness and disorder (ch. 8).[133] Similarly, Brueggemann, say of 8:19–20: "This is "creation theology"; Deuteronomy anticipates that a land rightly ordered by Torah will become fruitful, blessed by the *shalom* anticipated already in the doxologies of creation" (Gen 1:22, 28).[134]

Thus, like the Shema, Deuteronomy 8 uses history to expand the teaching devices in Deuteronomy 4 into a living tradition and thereby unite subsequent generations. Playing on the language of Exodus 16, Israel's historical failure and Yahweh's provision, this chapter constructs a memorial pattern which unites the facts of history with obligation – ritual with response. History thus becomes liturgy and liturgy imagines and motivates obedience. In the end, what Israel would hope to know in the future can be found by relying on what comes out of Yahweh's mouth (torah) and hand (land). What comes out of Yahweh's mouth (torah) is a story within which Israel finds renewal and hope in a time of rebellion and loss. In the memory of past and future failures Israel is led to trust the words and teaching that will come from Yahweh's mouth (through the mouths and pens of Yahweh's servants) as the ultimate epistemological authority and the foundation for their worldview.

4. Conclusion

This chapter tracked four actualising mechanisms in Deuteronomy 1–11 which serve to renew Israel's historical relationship with Yahweh in each

[131] McConville, *Deuteronomy*, 168 and C.J.H. Wright, *Deuteronomy*, 128. Craigie, *Deuteronomy*, 184–7 makes note of the "double-themes" of "immediacy and contingency" of the present and "all future present moments". Remembering is more than recalling facts but a "living memory".

[132] MacDonald, *Deuteronomy*, 139.

[133] *Deuteronomy*, 170.

[134] *Deuteronomy*, 104.

generation. The use of history which predominates chapters 1–4 is not intended as a chronicle of past events but as the soil within which Moses' poetic and sacramental sermons call Israel to actualisation.

The wordplay between the *Ausdrücke* and Moses' words (דברים) is the primary form of the historical poetics in these chapters. Israel's ability to know Yahweh's identity and revelation abides within living images of these "words" in the mouths and lives of a trans-generational community. The communal functions of teaching, writing, obeying and remembering Moses' messages enrich the narrative but ultimately act rhetorically to draw Israelites into participation. Loving Yahweh (6:5) and remembering his provision (chapter 8) sit in parallel as a further means to inspire Israel's participation in this story.

The result is that "words" and "torah" become oral and written symbols for the story and relationship into which Israel is drawn. Torah thus takes on a sacramental and poetic shape in Deuteronomy. At one and the same time, knowing God is cosmically rooted in the eternal designs for humanity (Deut 1–4, 8), historically transmitted by the community (Deut 6:4–9; 8:1–20), divinely initiated in a covenant, and ethically conditioned by Israel's response. At its heart Torah as Fromm suggests, is an ethical mode of divine knowledge worked out in divine imitation.[135]

---

[135] *You Shall be as Gods*, 167.

CHAPTER FOUR

Ideology and Epistemology in the Deuteronomic Laws Deuteronomy 12–26

1. Introduction

The main body of laws in Deuteronomy 12–26 are framed to be read within the historical and parenetic material in chapters 1–11 and 27–34. In the last chapter, we saw how Deuteronomy's first 11 chapters place these laws in a structure of authority, tradition and memory which join present, future and historical Israel together in their relationship with Yahweh. At the centre of that relationship, Moses' words, or torah, become a living tradition by which each generation of Israel actualises this relationship in new times and places. Chapters 12–26, therefore, can be seen as the legal core of this living tradition – the torah script for divine imitation.

Yet, as seen in Deuteronomy 4:2, Israel's tradition (worldview) has to be carefully preserved and protected from addition and distortion by profane and foreign "ideologies." Like Deuteronomy 4:2, chapters 12–26 have a pronounced concern for the ideological confrontations which await future generations living in new cultural and religious contexts. As such, this chapter aims first to expand on the nature of "worldviews" and "ideologies" as they relate to Israel's tradition in Deuteronomy. Second, we will demonstrate the way in which the structure and content of Deuteronomy 12–26 betray a peculiar sensitivity to ideological confrontation in Israel's future.

2. Ideology and Epistemology

A number of insightful works by Mayes and Miller help us to set "ideology" in the context of OT and Deuteronomic studies.[1] Both scholars make creative use of sociological studies in the OT and pursue their goals through social analytical models adapted from more recent studies in ideology and

---

1 Mayes, "Purpose"; "Deuteronomistic Ideology and the Theology of the Old Testament", *JSOT* 82 (1999) 57–82; *The Old Testament in Sociological Perspective* (London, UK: Marshall Pickering, 1989). Cf. P.D. Miller, "Faith and Ideology in the Old Testament", in F. Cross/W.E. Lemke/P.D. Miller (ed.), *Magnalia Dei: The Mighty Acts of God* (New York: Doubleday, 1976) 464–79.

"ideology critique." Interacting with these studies requires us to step back and review ideological and sociological studies of the OT.

2.1 The Enlightenment and the Turn to Sociological and Ideological Study

Our narrative of epistemology in the first chapter alluded to the Enlightenment ethos as a renewed emphasis individual and reason-based epistemology over against the inferior knowledge of nature, history or religion. The developing preference for rational certainty and purity[2] at the individual level and a corresponding aversion to history/historicity, authority and community tradition. Authority itself became connected with "blind obedience"[3] and an emerging world of empirical and scientific inquiry combined with the tradition of the Kantian critique to place truth in the hands of the human scientific methodology. Knowledge and truth were thus sought through individualistic, ahistorical, objective and rationalistic avenues.

At the end of this Enlightenment era, the concept of "ideology" developed as a fairly neutral reference to a body of ideas usually deriving from a social or cultural tradition.[4] Karl Marx, however, suspicious of the prominence given to the "objectified mind," put the term to use in a derogatory fashion through his critique of ideological materialism.[5] For Marx, ideology, "signified a false consciousness of social and economic realities".[6] Focused on the social and political critique of capitalism and authoritarian governments, Marx posited within history the tendency to *distort* and *dominate* through power, tradition, religion and dogmatism. Freud and Nietzsche adopted Marx's social perspectives to expose the social, linguistic and religious undercurrents in the "ideologies of consensus". Their ideas have come to be known as the "hermeneutics of suspicion." Though they opposed the Enlightenment's mood towards community and history as such, they did apply its emphasis on scientific methodology to critical social sciences (sociology, psychology, anthropology, and economics) in an effort to reveal the distortions in popular views of reality. Their "positivist" and "materialist"[7] methodologies become the foundation for Weber's "conflict tradition" in the study of the OT which is focused primarily on the "subjec-

---

2 Where tradition and authority are viewed as finite and sinful, M. Westphal, "Taking St. Paul Seriously: Sin as an Epistemological Category", in Thomas P. Flint (ed.), *Christian Philosophy* (Notre Dame, IN: University of Notre Dame, 1990) 200–26, on p. 208.

3 P. Ricoeur, *Hermeneutics and the Human Sciences* (Cambridge: Cambridge University, 1981), 71.

4 See Koyzis, *Visions*, 17–8.

5 Marx actually borrowed the connotation from Napoleon's diminutive "idéologues." See D. Braybrooke, "Ideology", in P. Edwards (ed.), *The Encyclopedia of Philosophy 4* (London/New York: Collier Macmillan, 1972) 124–7, on p. 125.

6 Braybrooke, "Ideology", 125.

7 On positivism and materialism, see below.

tive intentions and actions of individuals" as they formed the social basis of ancient societies.[8]

Besides Weber's conflict tradition model, Durkheim's "structural-foundationalist" model, which focused on the "social phenomena" in ancient cultures, represents the second major foundation for OT sociological study.[9] What is most significant in these two models is the way in which they advance the "disengaged" and certainty driven (positivist) emphases of the Enlightenment to critique historically and socially engaged views of the individual, society and religion. They thus regard all religion as an ideological expression of individuals and societies trying to cope with reality.

Yet, as Mayes points out, these two lines of sociological study operate under the influence of positivist and materialist philosophies inherited from Enlightenment scientific methodology and leave "little room for the significance of the interpretative role of the historian or sociologist".[10] He rightly notes that this "confuses a modern social science understanding of the nature and function of religion with what the Israelites themselves believed" – and, we might add, what the social scientist believes.[11] Mayes' attention to the interpreter's perspective will be important when we review his position below. In any case, he affirms the concerns within post-Kantian philosophy related to the ambitions of the objectified scientist to account comprehensively for the complex interrelationships between the individual and the society – in both the ancient and the scientists world – without distorting those worlds through their methods.[12]

2.2 The Hermeneutics of Tradition

Philosophies within the continental and Romantic traditions to which Mayes makes reference critique the analytical, cognitive and individualistic moods of the Enlightenment and of "objectified" social science. In many ways, Heidegger stands as a climactic figure in the challenge to the Enlightenment's tendency to over-privilege epistemology.[13] He confronted the assumption that subjects *in history* could somehow transcend their finite nature and objectify history via scientific investigation. He therefore turned his attention to the historical and ontological nature of the subject *within* history.[14] But Heidegger never worked out his ontology of understanding,

---

8 Mayes, *Old Testament*, 27, 36–77.

9 Ibid., 27, 78–117.

10 Ibid., 119.

11 Ibid., 121f.

12 See Mayes important critique, Ibid., 128–138.

13 Though Dilthey was just as central in shifting concerns to the historical nature of knowing, it was Heidegger who sparked shift to the ontology of understanding itself.

14 Ricoeur summarises Heidegger, "Hermeneutics is not a reflection on the human sciences, but an explication of the ontological ground upon which these sciences can be constructed [...] So understanding is

leaving room for others like Gadamer to develop an ontology of historical consciousness in history, language and aesthetics. Gadamer's means for addressing this nature of "situated" knowledge is the concept of the "horizon".[15]

These horizons are Gadamer's way of accounting realistically for the prejudices and pre-understandings which all cultures have as a result of their confined places in history.[16] This horizoned approach to knowledge exposes the weaknesses in the positivist and materialist sociological models and their presumed immunity from ideologies and prejudices of their own. As Gadamer explains, the objectivist posture proceeds out of a naive and view of objectivity, "Historical analysis shows that it is not until the enlightenment that the concept of prejudice acquires the negative aspect we are familiar with." And, "the fundamental prejudice of the enlightenment is the prejudice against prejudice itself".[17] According to Gadamer, prejudice should be recognised not merely as a possible source of distortion, but as that aspect of historical horizons through which all reason, language and expression necessarily originate and proceed; prejudices are natural and unavoidable even if they distort reality. Gadamer's hermeneutics, therefore, seeks explain one's finite position in a limited historical horizon and the associated prejudices which shape individual and cultural modes of understanding. Hence our appeal to Ricoeur's "conflict of interpretations" in chapter one and the need for us to balance our critique of the text with meta-critique of our hermeneutic.

In sum, the hermeneutical tradition allows us to place scientific epistemology within the phenomenology of human understanding. Such a phenomenology illumines the perspectives and prejudices which led Enlightenment epistemology to regard "religion" as a social and ideological creation of the culture.[18] As Mayes aptly notes, this excludes the ontological possibility that religion exists because it is *natural to humanity*, rather than a cultural construct.[19] In sum, Mayes' critique frees us from the two false assumptions that (1) all religions are ideologies and (2) that all social scientific models are not.

Working with Mayes in the hermeneutic tradition thus allows us to ask the very important and overlooked question: how do we define "ideology" in the light of the religion and worldview of the OT? In other words,

---

not concerned with grasping a fact but with apprehending a possibility of being". Understanding is "a *projection* with in a prior *being thrown*". *HHS*, 55–6.

15 Cf. also Steiner, *Real Presences*, 177.

16 Or what we describe as "worldviews" and "paradigms" elsewhere in this manuscript. Cf also Kuhn, *Structure* and the historical consciousness described by Steiner, *Real Presences*, 164, 176.

17 *Truth and Method*, 239–40.

18 See Sternberg, *Poetics*, 35–7.

19 Mayes, *Old Testament*, 138.

hermeneutical meta-critique returns us to the purpose of this chapter, which is explicitly *not* an attempt to describe Israel's religious ideology from within a worldview of western capitalist materialism, but as far as possible to understand the nature of – and response to – ideology as evident in the OT and in Deuteronomy in particular.

3. Ideology in the Old Testament

Our aim now is to describe Deuteronomy as it represents an aesthetically constructed story of Israel's reality and particularly as it shows an awareness of ideological confrontation in her own historical context. We will first return to a closer examination of the studies by Miller and Mayes where we can identify some internal lacunae between their methodological approach and the study of ideology in Deuteronomy.

Most significantly, the studies by Miller and Mayes share the common tendency of analysing the social contexts and cultural forces of historical critical reconstructions rather than on the aesthetically *represented* world within the texts. They place the Deuteronomic materials in sixth or seventh-century Judah, in what Mayes calls the "century-long culture shock" which provokes a response to the "material" and religious conditions of that era.[20] Miller depicts several ideological stages between the early ideologies of election and conquest and the later ideologies in the eras of the Davidic covenant of Zion.[21] Together they take the "pre-Deuteronomistic" book of Deuteronomy, the Pentateuch, the Deuteronomistic history and the prophets as all representing independent and conflicting ideologies. Thus, despite their (supposed) awareness of modernist paradigms,[22] they fail to submit their own hermeneutics to a self-critique and thus under-privilege ideology in Deuteronomy's own aesthetic and represented world.

A second major aporia for these scholars concerns the relationship between ideology, religion, faith and the content of the biblical books themselves. Mayes states that "Religion as ideology is a function of social relations",[23] assuming that it is therefore impossible to distinguish between ideology and faith or theology.[24] Similarly, for Miller ideology is expressed in

---

20 "Purpose", 25 and "Ideology", 73. This is strange in light his splendid critique of the tendency to over-privilege archaeological and materialist methods of interpretation, *Old Testament*, 128–9.

21 "Faith", 471–74.

22 Both scholars recognise that all ideologies have a "philosophy of history" which impacts their interpretation of events: Miller, "Faith", 467 and Mayes, *Old Testament*, 119. However, what they fail to address is the fact that they too are making interpretive decisions on their own philosophy of history.

23 "Ideology", 62.

24 Ibid., 75–6.

the unavoidable factors in every culture which distort truth through "unintentional error" when conveying information or recording history.[25] As social constructs, faith and theology are thus conceived as self-correcting ideologies to the distorting currents within other "popular" ideologies.[26] The message of the latter prophets, while theologically ideological can still be described as an "attack upon popular ideology" pursued in the name of true religion.[27] For both scholars, then, religion, faith and ideology are inseparably intertwined[28] such that the biblical narrative can be no more than an artifact of Israel's ideological conflict – rather than a response or buffer to it.

But a meta-critical hermeneutic reminds us not only of our own limited horizons, but it also gives serious attention to the biblical text as a story about ideological conflict in its ancient context.[29] Like the exegetical interpreter and the social scientist, the Bible too is a participant in ideological commentary. Its voice is formed by the narrative structure in its story as it creates an opposition between God and humanity, which aims to foster assent and acknowledgment to the divinely omniscient view of reality.[30] In this way, Sternberg states, "God ultimately figures not only as the norm and source but also as the tester of knowledge."[31] In other words, the biblical narrative holds God – and the knowledge of God – over against the human tendency to distort reality – both in ancient and modern worlds.[32]

All this is to say that in Deuteronomy we want to know how the pentateuchal story of a people with a dying prophet, without a knowledge of Jerusalem and without a king represents Israel's story of reality. Furthermore, we want to see how this story relates to the future anticipated horizons of ideological conflict, including our own.[33] The effects of history must therefore flow in both directions such that the modern documentary construction of the text – within an historically conditioned consensus – is susceptible to the ancient story itself.[34] The following investigation

25 "Faith", 466. Cf. Mayes, "Ideology", 66.

26 "Faith", 473–5.

27 Ibid., 474.

28 Cf. Ibid., 467, 477.

29 See I.W. Provan, "Ideologies, Literary and Critical", *JBL* 114 (1995) 585–606, on p. 586.

30 Sternberg, *Poetics*, 46.

31 Ibid., 48.

32 Extending Thiselton's development of "two horizons", Bartholomew suggests the need for a third, the theological horizon, "Three Horizons: Hermeneutics from the Other End – An Evaluation of Anthony Thiselton's Hermeneutic Proposal", *EJT* 5 (1996) 121–35 Thus readers are concerned not just with the ancient horizon of the text, but with the present and God-ward horizons which impact the understanding of the text. On the third horizon, cf. also Steiner, *Real Presences*, 223–32.

33 See especially a statement of this tension between Deuteronomy's claim to authority and interpretive re-writing of that authority in modern methods in Millar, "Faithful God", 4–5.

34 This is not to say that Deuteronomy does not have a history of redactions, but it is to say that the final form requires the reader to read and understand the whole before seeking to divide it. "These are the words" must remain a rhetorical, ethical and theological criteria for reading.

explores the represented social and political world in Deuteronomy 12–26 and gives the world of Horeb, Moab and the promised land literary and theological priority in judging the book's perspective on ideology and worldviews.

4. Ideology and Deuteronomy 12–26

Moses' words in Deuteronomy 12–26 have a structural unity and a theological continuity which we will see is focused on preserving Israel's story from (ideological) distortion. In what follows, we will first survey the literary and ideological nature of the material in chapters 1–26 before turning to three particular sets of legal/ideological material.

4.1 Unity and Continuity in Deuteronomy 12–26

In the last chapter, we briefly made note of the *Doppelausdruck* as structural and thematic brackets for the intervening material. That is, the phrase החקים והמשפטים, and its variants, appear only between 4:1 and 26:16 and create a nexus of several interpenetrating aspects.[35] One the one hand the didactic nature of chapters 4–11 give the ten uses of the *Doppelausdruck* there something of an introductory and parenetic sense to what follows. This of course relies on the fact that the repetition of the *Doppelausdruck* at 11:32; 12:1 and 26:16 – and nowhere in between – creates a frame and label for material contained within (ch. 12–26). Together, parenesis (4–11) and law (12–26) can be distinguished within this larger structure of the whole. This is reinforced by the repetition of דבר at 4:1, 12:32 (13:1) and 26:16, and its proximity to the *Doppelausdruck*, which also creates a correspondence between Moses' words, or speech, and the anticipated content (החקים והמשפטים) in chapters 12–26. We also find the statutes and ordinances (12–26) framed by the blessing and curse at Gerizim and Ebal as follows:

(11:29) את־הברכה על־הר גרזים and את־הקללה על הר עיבל
Deuteronomy 12–26
(27:12) אלה יעמדו לברך את־העם על־הר גרזים
(27:13)[36] אלה יעמדו על־הקללה בהר עביל

In sum, this material, while notably distinct as a legal code (12–26), is prefaced and intermingled with teaching and memory devices in Moses'

---

[35] Braulik, "Ausdrücke", 11–38.
[36] On the framing effect in chapters 12–26, see Olson, *Deuteronomy*, 60.

sermon (4–11).[37] Following Braulik, we can say that "statutes and ordinances" have the poetic flexibility to refer both laws themselves (12–26) and their embedded parenetic context (4–28), while allowing for a vague distinction between the two.[38]

Given these verbal and thematic framing elements, we can now point out several other features in this context which provide a sense of the continuity and exclusivity for this material. For example, the primary focus of the law is on the future conduct in the land and references to the past are made in the context of future memorials (sabbath, Passover, tabernacle) and not in Mosaic parenesis as in chapters 4–11. We also notice that while the use of some parenetic vocabulary is diminished or absent (i.e. תורה and דבר), the application of זכר remains constant. The rhetorical or literary reasons for the change in vocabulary are not always clear, but they seem to reinforce the liturgical ethos of the laws. In fact, the chapters maintain a future focus which reinforces the memorialising and actualising character of the parenetic section within the law code itself; the law prepares for a future memory which will enable constant access to the existential and relational foundations in Israel's history.[39]

As for the legal vocabulary, we find that like החקים והמשפטים, the root תורה is not used in these chapters except in 17:19–20. The significance of this central appearance in the kingship laws will be discussed separately. We also note a decreased use of דבר and דברים with reference to Moses, except in his speech in 12:32 (13:1) – an echoed warning from 4:2 that Israel should not add to this דבר. This of course closes the outer frame in chapter 12 as a wordplay upon the reference to החקים and משפטים in 12:1 and acts as an introduction to chapters 13–26 (see below). The only other significant references are to the דברים of prophets (13:3–4) and the future prophet(s) (13:3–4 [5–6] 18:18–22). Interestingly, after forbidding future profane modification to "all this torah" (12:32), Moses nevertheless gives the expectation of future oral revelation in the shadow of his own ministry (18:15). This draws the prophetic דברים into relief and this will also be treated separately below.

This material lacks two other traits which otherwise dominate the parenetic sections. On the one hand, there is almost no reference made to the

---

[37] Tigay, *Deuteronomy*, 117. Cf. also, Driver, *Literature*, 77–8.

[38] Braulik, "Ausdrücke", 34 labels these the "paränetischen Teil und das Gesetzkorpus als das ganze von Moses promulgierte 'Gesetz' [...]". Similarly, for Millar, "Place", 57, the *Doppelausdruck* is a "hortatory" and "legal" designation for Deut 5–26. Wright, *Deuteronomy*, 158–9 describes the "interpenetration" between 1–11 and 12–26.

[39] Cf. the comments in the last chapter on Deut 4 and the existential effects of obedience and remembering to renew the divine presence and divine knowledge in Israel's midst. See also Yerushalmi, *Zakhor*, 9–13, 44–5.

"promises" or the "fathers."[40] This might be expected given the parenetic nature of the fathers as used by Moses both to motivate future obedience and to situate this revelation along the journey to the promised land. Second, where the Decalogue was given through divine speech (5:6–31), this section is conspicuously short of divine speeches. Labuschagne counts 30 references to divine speech in Deuteronomy which are distributed as follows:

Chapters 1–3 – 10 References
Chapters 4–11 – *8 References*
Chapters 12–26 – *2 References*
Chapters 27–31 – 10 References [41]

In this way, 12–26 can be seen as unique; yet when it is combined with chapters 4–11, the section also balances the two other thirds of the book with ten instances each and is further evidence of a careful and artistic use of literary and rhetorical devices in the book which distinguishes 12–26 within its literary context. Furthermore, a relationship exists between the divine speech of the Decalogue, ending at 5:31, and Moses' legal speech in 12–26 which Yahweh dictated at the end of his own discourse. This movement from divine speech to divinely commanded human speech, meanwhile, takes place within the larger context of Moses' words to Israel (the words of this torah, 1:5) and the framing context of the words of Moses under the pen of the narrator (1:1). The final product is a voice, within a voice – within a voice – and the function is to reinforce the fact that Deuteronomy is "showing" rather than "telling"[42] Israel about Yahweh and his revelation through Moses. It is also a subtle indication that actualisation has already begun, making the laws rhetorically persuasive in the way they draw readers to believe in Moses' words as the means to knowing Yahweh after his (Moses') death.[43]

---

40 Of the 49 references to the "promise" and the "fathers' in Deuteronomy, only two occur between in 12–26 in 19:8 and 26:3.

41 C.J. Labuschagne, "Divine Speech in Deuteronomy", in Christensen (ed.), *Song* (1993) 375–93, on p. 375.

42 Sonnet, *Book*, 13.

43 Millar, "Place", 55–6 captures this similarly: "The concept of law in Deuteronomy is thus much broader than the Decalogue, and it is this law which the rest of the book expounds. At 5:31, then, we are still waiting strictly for the *content* of the new revelation to begin. The preamble of ch. 4–5 has been concerned with demonstrating the continuity of the new with the old. The phrase the 'laws and statutes' has been used with an air of vagueness, to facilitate the new dynamism in the Deuteronomic view of law, and to create an air of tense expectation as the book unfolds [...]. There is a very definite new beginning, and yet this new phase of החקים והמשפתים cannot be separated from what has gone before. This device forges a link between the law-code and the parenesis of ch. 6–11. But it does more than that – it ties the legal stipulations of ch. 12–26 inextricably to the long meditation on the need for obedience to be rooted in love, and beyond that to the Decalogue itself. The lawcode is to be understood as 'the laws and statutes' in the same way as both the Decalogue and the preaching of ch. 6–11."

The combination of these linguistic, thematic and theological factors provides the means to analyse the rhetorical and epistemological content of the material in Deuteronomy 12–26. A brief summary will help set the stage for what follows. In the last chapter, we established the correspondence between דבר, דברים, תורה, and החקים והמשפטים and the rhetorical overlap between Moses' words and Yahweh's words. The Decalogue sits at the heart of chapters 1–11 – communicated by a lengthy divine speech (5:6–31). The speech ends or pauses in verse 22 with Moses telling Israel that Yahweh spoke and "added no more" (5:22); yet Moses' speech continues to quote the details of his own private conversation with Yahweh. The privacy of this exchange is accentuated by the mention of Israel's own fear of the theophany and their retreat to their tents, leaving Moses alone to hear the additional divine instructions (5:23–31). The narrative thus creates an intentional gap, withholding the content of the conversation in 5:31 until it is revisited in chapters 12–26 where the torah and words of Yahweh slip into the background and the words of Moses in the statutes and ordinances rise to the fore. The closing of the gap unites Moses' words with his experience of Yahweh on the mountain and suggests that Moses not only takes up a new revelation or interpretation of law, but does so in the authority of Yahweh's command and in continuity with Yahweh's laws themselves.[44]

In this way, McConville is justified in saying that "the close relationship between Decalogue and subsequent laws inaugurates a hermeneutical process, according to which its provisions may be adapted to new situations, the authority to do so being invested in the appropriated institutions, represented in Deuteronomy by Moses."[45] In other words, what Moses does in his legal speech is a divinely authoritative hermeneutical shift whereby Yahweh's Decalogue gives way to the Mosaic law-for-the-land (12–26). Put another way, Yahweh's ten words have been the moral foundation behind Israel's journey to this point. As Yahweh brings Israel into the land, the extended law in Moses' "words" actually represents what Israel will "bring" before Yahweh (לפני יהוה) in sacrifice, obedience and worship[46] as a mirrored reflection of Yahweh's ten words – divine imitation. Although many of the laws were given in Exodus and Leviticus, the focus in Deuteronomy is on the law for the future. The newness of the land and the surrounding nations make this an especially novel and challenging responsibility, involving epistemological and ideological encounters which Israel must face.

---

44 On the authority of Moses' words in 12–26 (4–33), see S.D. McBride, "Polity of the Covenant People; The Book of Deuteronomy", in D. Christensen (ed.), *Song of Power* (Winona Lake: Eisenbrauns, 1993) 62–77, on pp. 66–7 and Brueggemann, *Deuteronomy*, 26.

45 *Deuteronomy*, 217. Cf. also Driver, *Deuteronomy*, xxv.

46 Wilson, *Midst*, 146. The symmetry between God's acts and Israel's response is also observed by McConville, *Theology*, 33–6 and Wright, *Deuteronomy*, 3.

4.2 Time and Place in Israel's Theological Worldview

Moses' legal speech begins in chapter 12. The position, content and structure of this chapter set a tone for the 14 chapters which follow. Yet, as noted above, the chapter also resonates with the material in 4–11 which established the cross-cultural or missiological standards by which Israel will relate to the land and the nations in the land. Deuteronomy's ideological concerns – in the laws of the central sanctuary in chapter 12 – are addressed through an indivisible tapestry of law, parenesis and history.

The basic thrust in chapter 12 is to regulate the future *nature* and *place* of worship as conceived by a repetition of phrases:

Deut 12:5
כִּי אִם־אֶל־הַמָּקוֹם אֲשֶׁר־יִבְחַר יְהוָה אֱלֹהֵיכֶם מִכָּל־שִׁבְטֵיכֶם לָשׂוּם אֶת־שְׁמוֹ שָׁם לְשִׁכְנוֹ תִדְרְשׁוּ וּבָאתָ שָּׁמָּה׃
(Cf. Deut 12:11, 13–14, 18, 21, 26; 14:22, 24; 16:2, 6–7, 11, 15, 16; 17:8; 26:2)

The majority of modern commentary focuses on Jerusalem or Zion as the implied objective of the מקום, or sanctuary laws. McConville challenges this line of interpretation and, whether or not Jerusalem was intended as the ultimate referent for the chosen place of worship – or whether a single place was ever intended – he is, in my view, right to focus on the more important issues of the ambiguous referent and rhetorical dimensions of this text as they control its meaning and implications. Several observations bear mentioning here.

To begin, there are several facts which resist or diminish what would be a Jerusalem-oriented agenda in Deuteronomy 12: (1) Not only are Jerusalem and the Temple never mentioned in Deuteronomy, but Shechem is authorised in Deuteronomy 27 and the OT and Jewish tradition both propose Shiloh as a possible central sanctuary.[47] (2) This prompts us to recognize Deuteronomy's intentional ambiguity regarding future places.[48] The book's preference for Horeb over Sinai seems to deny that the book has a "supremacy" of one place in mind.[49] (3) Furthermore, Deuteronomy is noticeably ambiguous about worship, having both pro-sanctuary and anti-sacral aspects in its law.[50] Thus, any attempt to align Deuteronomy definitively with a single reformation or Jerusalem tradition is tenuous at best.[51] (4) Moreover, besides a range of Rabbinic interpretations (including a Shiloh sanctuary) New Testament evidence reveals its own ambiguity towards

[47] J.G. McConville, "1 Kings Viii 46–53 and the Deuteronomic Hope", *VT* 42 (1992) 67–79, on pp. 72–3 and McConville, "Place", 103. Cf. Psalm 15:1 with its juxtaposition of tabernacle and temple imagery.

[48] Miller, *Deuteronomy*, 131.

[49] McConville, "Metaphor", 335.

[50] McConville, "Place", 106–7; cf. Weinfeld, *D&DS*, 210–24.

[51] McConville, "Place", 107–8. Cf. Driver, *Literature*, 85–7 and J. Wellhausen, *Prolegomena to the History of Ancient Israel* (Gloucester, MA: Peter Smith, 1973 (1885)), 32–5.

the Temple, often favouring tabernacle imagery at the heart of Israel's worship (Acts 7:44–53; Hebrews);[52] journey and permanence are corresponding themes.

On the contrary what *is* central to this artistic, rhetorical and concentrically designed text[53] is a "place formula," continuing through chapter sixteen, which focuses both on the future adaptability of centralised worship[54] and the prohibition of profane practices. These are clearer when the chiastic structure of this chapter are illustrated as follows:

A – Do (עָשׂה) the Statutes and Ordinances in the Land (ארץ) 12:1
  B – Opposition to Nations (גוים), their Places (מקמות) and their Practices 12:2–4
    C – Go to the Place (מקום) Yahweh Chooses 12:5–7
      D – Do Not Do What is Right in Your Own Eyes (עיניו) 12:8
        E – Offerings and Sacrifices in the Place (מקום)Yahweh Chooses 12:10–25
      D' – Do What is Right in the Eyes (עיני) of Yahweh 12:28
    C' – Yahweh Cuts off the Nations in the Land (ארץ) 12:29
  B' – Do not Follow the Abominable Practices of the Nations (גוים) 12:30–31
A' – Do (עָשׂה) Everything (כל־דבר) I command you 12:32 (13:1)[55]

Together, the structure and language in this chapter lead to several important conclusions. One, there seems to be a greater emphasis on journey imagery[56] and a corresponding succession of places that will represent Yahweh's potential to meet with his people throughout the conquest than there is on a single place.[57] In other words, the place symbolises "life with Yahweh"[58] where, even if at one place in a particular time,[59] the larger thrust is to communicate the "succession of places"[60] in which Yahweh will be present with his people according to his own conditions.[61] The mobile nature of Yahweh's presence is also much more in line with the actualising context of chapters 4–11. Those chapters, like this one, are content to leave future locations ambiguous in order to emphasise the potential to renew the Horeb and Moab covenant realities in future places.

---

52 McConville, "Place", 104f.

53 See Christensen, *Deuteronomy*, 232–7.

54 Which, itself, points towards the hermeneutical and epistemological process envisioned by the application laws over against an unchanging standard.

55 The chiastic structure in this chapter can be represented in various levels of detail. See Christensen, *Deuteronomy*, 239–44 and McConville, *Deuteronomy*, 212–17.

56 Millar, "Place", 32.

57 McConville, "Place", 131–2.

58 Miller, *Deuteronomy*, 32.

59 Or 'one place at a time' Christensen, *Deuteronomy*, 243 and Craigie, *Deuteronomy*, 217.

60 McConville, "Place", 131–2.

61 The juxtaposition of מקום (12:7, , 13–14, 18, 21, 26; 14:22, 24; 16:2, 6–7, 11, 15, 16; 17:8; 26:2) with the emphasis on activities לפני יהוה (12:7, 12, 18; 14:23, 26; 15:20; 16: 11; 18:7; 19:17; 26:5, 10) express the presence of Yahweh at the place over against the identity of the location, Wilson, *Midst*, 157–59.

Tigay also correctly points to the exclusivity in Yahweh s choice in Deuteronomy 17:8–13, yet goes on to classify it as evidence for a single place.[62] However, it could mean that Yahweh will choose many places or even a succession of places as each case of judgment demands. More likely, the point is "a reiteration of the basic instruction of the Book of Deuteronomy: that is, total allegiance to the one Lord, your God,"[63] by deferring to Yahweh's choice.

Further still, by not naming Jerusalem as "the place," the Deuteronomic and Deuteronomistic history actually undercuts the centralisation reform by recording several legitimate alternatives to Jerusalem. Notably, Yahweh chooses a Shechem as a place in of legitimate worship well before the land is occupied or the Israelites approach Jerusalem. The "place" is, in fact, something of a red herring. The point, when the structure and content of Deuteronomy 12 is taken in consideration with chapter 27, is that Yahweh's *choice* stands behind the law. Wright affirms that the obsession with the place has "inverted the priority of the text, which is concerned not so much with the *location* of the place as with its *election* by Yahweh."[64] McConville's insights help us to relate the theology in this text to its function in enabling future actualisation in Israel: "As the 'today' of Moses' exhortation is made a model for Israel's response to Yahweh in all future times, so the encounter at Horeb is given an entry into all future time through Israel's worship at the chosen place – wherever and whenever that might be."[65] Finally, this chapter shows a strong opposition between the nations, their places of worship and their abominable and idolatrous practices over against Yahweh's laws, his chosen place and his chosen people (12:2–4, 30–31).[66] Deuteronomy 4:5–8 promises Israel that her obedience to the torah will become her wisdom, understanding and righteousness in the sight of the nations. Israel and her worldview are permitted – even intended – to influence the nations. Yet, here in chapter 12, in the spirit of Deuteronomy 7 and 20, the direction of influence is limited to one-way as worked out in the violent opposition aimed at the unrighteousness of the Canaanites. The chapter ends where it began – with emphatic opposition to the corrupting influences of the nations (12:2–5, 31). We can safely conclude that the universal or missiological concerns for the nations are not unconditional; Yahweh's declared place and ways of worship represent God's intention to

---

[62] Cf. *Deuteronomy*, 119, 163–4, 364.

[63] Miller, *Deuteronomy*, 131.

[64] *Deuteronomy*, 163. McConville, *Deuteronomy*, 220; cf. 225 says, "Yahweh's prerogative in choosing the place is more important than any identification of it."

[65] McConville, *Deuteronomy*, 223.

[66] Cairns, *Deuteronomy*, 125.

reglate Israel's future interaction with the surrounding nations,[67] where Israel's worldview is universally normative.

In sum, historical and ideological arguments for a Jerusalem centralisation law in Deuteronomy cannot be sustained in light of Deuteronomy's intentional ambiguity towards future places, and the more central fact, synchronically, that the place where Yahweh's name will dwell is grounded in the promise of Yahweh's nearness (קרב) to Israel and Moses on the basis of obedience to the torah itself (Deut 4:6–8; 5:26–7).[68] So, the primary and controlling implication is that Yahweh has placed ethical, temporal and spatial conditions on his presence with Israel in the land. Loyalty to Yahweh means rejection of idolatry.[69] It is a loyalty of "theonomy" over against the individual "autonomy" and ideological "heteronomy" which reject Yahweh's sovereignty.[70]

Furthermore, these constraints for worship are grounded in Israel's historical consciousness through which she understands and responds to the behaviours and culture of the indigenous nations. Israel's torah forms the foundation of an authoritative worldview and protects her religion[71] by opposing the ideological pressures and temptations she will encounter.[72] This nature of ideological opposition is even clearer in Deuteronomy 30:19 where Yahweh's choice of a people and a place are reflected by Moses' command for Israel to *choose* life and uphold the tradition of this torah and actualise Israel's relationship with Yahweh.[73] The epistemological deference Israel is required to give to Yahweh in Deuteronomy 12 also prefaces the law of future prophets whose function it is to guide the people back to her God.

4.3 Hermeneutics and Prophecy

Future prophetic guidance accentuates the need for Israel's loyalty and, like the place formula in chapter 12, "challenges the pretensions of all human institutions".[74] The fact that Yahweh will have to send future guidance and revelation (Deut 13:1–5[2–6]) implies for Israel that life in the land will be characterised by ambiguities. It also implies both that Yahweh already knows the nature of those ambiguities and that he has the resources to guide Israel safely through them.

---

67 Brueggemann, *Deuteronomy*, 143.

68 McConville, "Place", 122.

69 Koyzis, *Visions*, 15. See idolatry and prophecy below.

70 Brueggemann, *Deuteronomy*, 148–9.

71 O'Donovan says that, taken together, Exodus and Conquest give the torah a moral and transcendent authority for Israel, *Resurrection*, 190.

72 On torah becoming a living tradition, see Brueggemann, *Deuteronomy*, 22–3 and Yerushalmi, *Zakhor*, 109.

73 Cf. Millar, "Faithful God", 15.

74 McConville, *Grace*, 27.

The introduction to the prophet in chapter 13 is revisited in the corresponding expression of the prophetic office in chapter 18, following the laws of the king, and the effect of both passages is the same: the expectation of a future prophet creates an openness and ambiguity in Deuteronomy's future tradition, making Moses' words particularly urgent. These two passages (Deut 13:1–5[2–6]; 18:15–22) also provide the means to extend our observations about the ideological awareness in Deuteronomy's epistemology.

Deuteronomy 18:15–22 can roughly be divided into two overlapping sections: the future prophet like Moses (vv. 15–19) and the interpretation and response to future prophets (vv. 19–22). The latter parallels Deuteronomy 13:1–5 [2–6] as both texts raise the possibilities of a future נביא (or חלם חלום in 13:1f [2f])[75] who will appear with a message for Israel. However, the conditions and emphases have striking differences. The key to their meanings and correspondences can be expressed diagrammatically as follows:

Deut 13:2–6 (Hebrew verses)	**Deut 18:19–22**
A. Prophet or dreamer (2)	D. Divine Test: Obedience to prophet (19)
B. Sign: Fulfilled (3)	E. Death to Prophet (6)
C. Human Test: Against Yahweh? (3f)	C. Human Test: Is the word true? (21)
D. Divine Test: Love and Fear Yahweh? (4–5)	B. Word (sign): Not Fulfilled (22)
E. Death to prophet (20)	A. Do not listen or fear the Prophet (22)

The parallels are not exact, but together the order and criteria of content suggest that the passages emphasise a dual-sided test of a future prophet.[76] On the one hand Israel must measure the words (דברי, 13:3[4]), dreams or signs presented by prophets who arises in her midst. On the other hand, Israel must weigh the content of the prophetic counsel and whether it is loyal to Yahweh's name or Yahweh's words (דברי, 18:18) In both cases, Israel and the prophet will be tested: the prophet by Israel and as a result, Israel's heart by Yahweh. The essential criteria is whether the דברים are

[75] Throughout the OT, prophets and dreams are a common way for Yahweh to reveal himself to Israel, cf. Tigay, *Deuteronomy*, 129. Already in the Pentateuch Abraham (Gen 15) and Joseph (Gen 37, 40–41) stand as testimonies to Yahweh's revelation through dreams in addition to Yahweh's declaration to Moses, Miriam and Aaron in Num 12:6.

[76] Or "two criteria", Miller, *Deuteronomy*, 154. Cf. also, Braulik, *Deuteronomium*, 137–8 and Cairns, *Deuteronomy*, 133–4.

from Yahweh or the false prophet (cf. 18:18; 13:3).[77] And while chapter 13 may only raise the possibility of a prophet (כי־יקום),[78] chapter 18 makes it clear that Yahweh will raise up future prophets and give them "my words" (דברי).

As noted earlier in the chapter, these are the only "revelatory" uses of the Hebrew root דבר in chapters 12–26 which correspond to the building pattern of the *Ausdrücke* in Deuteronomy 4–11.[79] Certainly one implication is that, while Moses represents the supreme prophet and Israel's fundamental connection to Yahweh,[80] his "words" and the "words of this torah" will require future supplementation in the land; what is lacking will be added by Yahweh through his choice of a prophet (18:15, 18). Yet, it is Israel who must use Moses' present "words" in Deuteronomy as the standard to measure and confirm the nature of future "words." In what follows, we will consider the way this informs our understanding of ideology and the hermeneutical nature of Israel's present and future tradition.

4.4 Authority and Prophecy

First of all, these two passages establish the authority behind the prophetic office; the דברים determine whether future prophecies come from Yahweh or from the misleading intentions of a pseudo-prophet (13:3; 18:18). Likewise, a true prophet is not self-appointed, but one raised up by Yahweh (18:15, 18) and therefore given Yahweh's message (18:18). At its core, the future prophetic pattern is embedded in the current situation with Moses; Moses stands at the centre of this book and his words overlap with Yahweh's in a way that the torah retains divine authority.[81] Accordingly, the divine authority in the future prophet is one "like Moses" (כמני v. 15; כמוך, v. 18), speaking the דברי of Yahweh.[82]

---

77 Or one who speaks falsehood (דבר סרה, 13:6). The context seems to indicate that false prophets will speak in Yahweh's name to encourage worshipping other gods, cf. Tigay, *Deuteronomy*, 131 and McConville, *Deuteronomy*, 234–5.

78 I agree with the Christensen's rare interpretation of כי־יקום as "When a prophet" rather than "If a prophet," *Deuteronomy*, 268. This admittedly appears to be a casuistic introduction and Deuteronomy does use both כי־ and the more common אם־ to introduce such phrases. Nevertheless, the certainty of future prophets guaranteed in 18:15–22 makes it unlikely that chapter 13 is trying to communicate such ambiguity. Therefore, "when" for כי־ communicates the more certain nature of this text than connoted by the more conditional English "if". Cf. also B. Waltke/M. O'Connor, *An Introduction to Biblical Hebrew Syntax* (Winona Lake, IN: Eisenbrauns, 1990), 637 for the introduction of a "major" *casus pendens* as "when".

79 דבר is repeated here in vv. 18, 19, 20, 21, 22. On its significance and relation to revelation, see Miller, *Deuteronomy*, 152.

80 Cf. Deut 34:10–12 as discussed in chapter 5 below.

81 In Deuteronomy, Moses intermediary role is exemplified by 5:23–27, cf. Num 12. See McConville, *Deuteronomy*, 304; Sonnet, *Book*, 251; Olson, *Deuteronomy*, 85.

82 Brueggemann points out the extraordinary series of imperatives in vv. 3–4 (5–6) "follow, fear, keep, obey, serve, hold fast" which, as presented in inverted word order, accenting the object of the verbs, i.e. Yahweh. *Deuteronomy*, 150, cf. Deut 6:5–9; 10:12–13.

Divine authority also guides the true prophet who receives *knowledge* of the future from Yahweh. Certainly the nature of divine omniscience cannot be settled by these passages alone, but with Beckwith I see the Deuteronomic texts aiming to reinforce Yahweh's supremacy in and over creation (cf. Deut 4:32–39) which allows him to predict events perfectly.[83] The prophetic contexts (Deut 13; 18) portray Israel in a position threatened by the limits of human knowledge – both of reality and of the future. Unlike other gods, Yahweh's universal and trans-temporal apprehension of knowledge allows him to send Israel a prophet with foolproof authentication and divine authority.

Yahweh's authority is also explicit in the requirement of capital punishment for false prophets (13:5[6]; 18:20). The connection between capital crimes and those laws which uphold or emphasise the first commandment is well attested.[84] As such, false prophecy is counsel in the name of other gods or counsel to go after other gods, (18:20; 13:2[3]) – or idolatry, the "suppression" of God's honor by "substitution" with another.[85] False prophecy is, therefore, an embrace and sanction of ideology.[86] True prophecy, meanwhile, affirms the great commandment (Deut 6:4–9) by hermeneutically applying the first commandment (Deut 5:6–7) to the future world of international religious discourse. Both sets of passages require attention to the דברים (6:6 and 13:3[4]; 18:19) in order to remain faithful to Yahweh, and they also portray urgency in the extreme requirements of this devotion – death (13:5[6]; 18:20) and whole-hearted love (6:5).[87] Faithfulness to Yahweh is humanity's highest goal and is evidenced by whole-hearted resistance to idolatry.

Finally,Yahweh's authority is apparent in the way prophetic mediation retains God's presence and absence through multiple voices. That is, the prophet's voice becomes an agent through which Yahweh achieves his mutual desire for both self-revelation and concealment.[88] The effect of multiple voices has often gone unrecognised in Deuteronomic research and Polzin was really the first to analyse the way in which Moses' voice overlapped and replaced the voice of Yahweh in Deuteronomy. Yet he also went on to argue that the narrator's voice served as a final trump for Moses, revealing the narrator as the "prophet like Moses".[89] However, the oppo-

---

[83] "Limited Omniscience and the Test for a Prophet: A Brief Philosophical Analysis", *JETS* 36 (1993) 357–62. Beckwith's arguments against limited omniscience are very persuasive, especially in light of texts like Deut 13 and 18 whose very point is to uphold Yahweh's uniqueness and authority.

[84] Cf. McConville, *Deuteronomy*, 238; Olson, *Deuteronomy*, 85–6; Braulik, *Deuteronomium*, 101–2 and G.M. Tucker, "Deuteronomy 18:15–22", *Interpretation* 41 (1987) 292–7, on p. 294.

[85] Westphal, "Sin", 210.

[86] See Koyzis, *Visions*, 15–7.

[87] Maimonides rightly identifies idolatry as main obstacle to knowledge of God, Kreisel, "Maimonides", 273.

[88] See Niehaus, *Sinai*, 223–5.

[89] Polzin, *Moses and the Deuteronomist*, 27–9.

sitions he sets up between Yahweh, the narrator and Moses – and subsequent exaltation of the narrator – have been subsequently challenged by both Olson and Sonnet. Sonnet argues that Deuteronomy does nothing to diminish Moses' status as Deuteronomy's prophet "*par excellence*" an עבד־יהוה (34:5), "In his omniscience the narrator bows to Moses' prophetic status [...]."[90] Olson is more intent to develop what he calls the "decentering" effects of deaths, multiple voices and broken covenants. He argues that in the end, it is Yahweh's voice, and not the narrator's (so Polzin), which is the "decentering center" of Deuteronomy (cf. Deut 32:39).[91] Moses' identity as Israel's supreme prophet (Deut 34:10–12) is not then denied through the overlap of voices, but rather ushered into its function as an intermediary for Yahweh's presence and absence through prophets. The fuller picture of Moses' role is treated again in the next chapter yet, for now, Moses – and his prophetic activity – are a model for the future need of revelation and interpretation on the part of a prophet, but in such a way that Yahweh's final authority is upheld,[92] his presence is renewed and ideologies are exposed and condemned.

4.5 The Hermeneutical Tradition of Prophecy

There are several pathways into the hermeneutical dimensions of the prophetic office in Deuteronomy 13 and 18. These dimensions are particularly power in the light of the context in Deuteronomy 12–19. Noting the parallels with Chapter 12, McConville has drawn out the trans-generational nature of Deuteronomy 13 and its reference to Egypt in the past (vv. 5[6], 10[11]), Moses' speech in the present (v. 18[19]), the general future reference to the land, and the image of a future city of "perpetual ruin" having been devoted to destruction (v. 16[17]).[93] The chapter thus surrounds the prophet in a context which spans Israel's life at all times and in all places. Moses' intermediary role, and the prophets "like him" in that role, can be seen as a tradition-bearing model for Israel from Egypt into the promised land and beyond. By understanding the future international context and the nature of future ambiguities, we will gain an appreciation for the hermeneutical character prophets bring to Israel's tradition.

First of all, the overwhelming threats to future prophecy are in the religions and (idolatrous) cultures of the Canaanite nations. Both chapters forewarn Israel about the temptation to follow after "other gods," undoubtedly encountered in Israel's international relations (13:8, 13-14; 18:9–14, 20). The abominable practices (תועבת) of the nations are forbidden for Israel

90 Sonnet, *Book*, 251, cf. 235–37.

91 Olson, *Deuteronomy*, 180–1.

92 See Sonnet, *Book*, 252.

93 McConville, "Place", 125.

(18:9, 12) and should be "purged" from their midst (13:6). This reference to purging evil (בער רע) is unique to Deuteronomy[94] and serves to reinforce the absolute holiness Israel must maintain *in the midst* of the nations.[95] That is where Yahweh wants them to live a faithful life, exemplary in righteousness and wisdom before their neighbours.[96] In order to do so, Israel is commanded to devote the current residents to destruction (חרם, Deut 7, 20). The חרם does not eliminate the surrounding nations, nor does it remove the constant exposure Israel will have to competing religions and ideologies; these will continue to come with the power and attractiveness with which Yahweh first came to his people (cf. Exod 3–6).[97] Israel will need the future interpretive nature of prophecy to sustain her in a changing international and religious climate.

Second, as evidenced by the dual test of future prophets, these future contexts and climates will be saturated with ambiguities and uncertainties and the brokenness of Israel's covenant infidelity. Olson calls the prophet a "wild card" and presents a synthetic reading of these two passages:

> [Deut. 18:20–22] deals with the problem inherent in charismatic prophecy. How does one tell a true prophet like Moses from a false prophet claiming to speak a word from God? The criteria are set forth, but they leave room for ambiguity [...]. The definitive guideline is that the word is false if "the thing does not take place or prove true" (18:22). Unfortunately, this guideline is not always self-evident in the immediate circumstance; the hearer must simply wait and see whether the prophet's words come true [...]. There is one more potential problem. What if a prophet predicts something that comes true while speaking in the name of another God? Once again limits are placed on the exercise of authority [...]. Prophets who speak in the name of the divine are to be honored but not worshipped. Their words must be tested. The reality is that sometimes such tests of truth will be ambiguous and may require the hearer to wait and see, remaining open to the new truth that may be revealed through the prophets. Even with the prophets as guides, the Deuteronomic community of faith is not removed from the ambiguities and struggles of real human existence in a broken world.[98]

The extent of ambiguities and brokenness in the world is self-evident to Israel. She has already failed Yahweh in idolatry (Exod 32:1–10; Deut 9:13–29) and insulted him through rebellion, complaint and fear (Numbers 12–27). The difficulties of the future virtually ensure a return to future fail-

---

94 McConville, *Deuteronomy*, 238.

95 See Deut 17:7; 12; 19:13, 19; 21:9, 21; 22:21, 22, 24; 24:7. Cf. Thompson, *Deuteronomy*, 174.

96 This is argued in chapter 3 above.

97 See A. Millard, "Story, History, and Theology", in A.R. Millard/J.K. Hoffmeier/D.B. Baker (ed.), *Faith, Tradition, and History* (Winona Lake, IN: Eisenbrauns, 1994) 37–64, on p. 64 on the way Yahweh's redemptive acts eliminate the "impetus" to follow the "more attractive and so much less demanding" religions.

98 Olson, *Deuteronomy*, 85–6. Cf. to what Lohfink calls the "charismatic [...] counterbalance to all other authorities." "Distribution of the Functions of Power: The Laws Concerning Public Offices in Deuteronomy 16:18–18:22", in D. Christensen (ed.), *Song of Power* (Winona Lake, IN: Eisenbrauns, 1993).

ures (Deut 4:23–31; 31:27; 32:5–18). The history of God's displeasure and future threats of judgments (Deut 4:26–28; 28:15–68) make the hermeneutical task urgent for Israel. That is, although torah promises future actualisation of her relationship with Yahweh, it is her ability to interpret and respond to prophecy faithfully which represents the essential difficulty of life in the world. This response involves the many ambiguous variables which are laid out in two kinds of tests and which signify the endless task of renewing past horizons in the future horizons.[99]

In light of these relationships with nations and the ambiguities of future prophetic oracles, we can see that Deuteronomy-as-torah is the truth standard for future prophetic tests. But in order for the interpretive efforts to succeed in actualising Israel's relationship with Yahweh, torah must be used *correctly*. "Religion," as Tucker recognises it, is at the heart of the search for truth and in order for Israel to discern the nuances between a prophet speaking in the name of Yahweh and speaking by another god, Israel must in some sense become a community of "theologians".[100] Braulik, too, senses the religious requirement in prophetic interpretation which demands that Israel have "faith",[101] what Deuteronomy describes as a circumcised heart (10:16; 30:6)[102] which obeys the torah. Returning to Miller's appreciation for the ideological contexts of Israel's prophetic office, the prophet stands against the ideologies of popular consensus with have abandoned the "imperatives of justice, mercy, and righteousness".[103] Or as Lohfink says, "[...] the prophets seem to be seem to be thought of as a means of concretizing and actualizing the will of God, as set out in general terms in the Torah."[104] Prophecy, then, provides for the continuing relevance and justification of torah into whatever climate Israel may journey. Israel must approach the torah with a theological commitment – doing so maintains, or promises to renew, her relationship with Yahweh. Like the prophetic office, the king's role in Deuteronomy provides the means to resist the influences of the surrounding nations and the vices of human nature which would threaten her worldview.

---

[99] Thus, Braulik sees the torah as applicable for all time while the prophet acts in "Kontinuität" to interpret torah, or speak for Yahweh, in his particular time, *Deuteronomium*, 137. On this general relation between torah and prophecy, see also Crüsemann, *Torah*, 365–67 and Driver, *Deuteronomy*, lxi. Cf. however, von Rad who, in failing to read the two passages together, thinks the author naive for offering such a simple test for a prophet in 18:9–22, *Deuteronomy*, 124–5.

[100] Tucker, "Deut 18:15ff", 296, 297.

[101] Braulik, *Deuteronomium*, 104 says, "Gottes Selbstmitteilung ist nur durch das Wort des Glaubens zugänglich."

[102] This is similar to the *halakhah* at the heart of torah obedience, Yerushalmi, *Zakhor*, 115. In another interesting parallel, Neusner argues that the theology in *Sifre to Deuteronomy* requires human reason to be disciplined by torah, *A Theological Commentary to the Midrash: Sifré to Numbers and Sifré to Deuteronomy* (Studies in Ancient Judaism; Lanham/New York/Oxford: University Press of America, 2001), 151–4.

[103] Miller, "Faith", 473–76.

[104] "Distribution", 351.

4.6 The King as Deuteronomy's Arch-Interpreter of Torah

The kingship laws in Deuteronomy 17:14–20 are significant not only for their anti-ideological content but also for the structural role they play in the linear progression of the book. Notably, chapters 16–18 stand at the centre of the book of Deuteronomy and Lohfink has made note of the structural design in the centre of the statutes and ordinances (12–26), describing it in a pattern of A-B-A2, where the thematic movement is from "A", the original concerns of judicial laws (16:18–17:7), to an aside "B," about the priest, king and prophet, and back to "A," the original concern with judicial matters.[105] At the same time, the linear reading emphasised in the last chapter draws our attention to the content in 17:18 where the king is to write (כתב) a copy of the torah (תורה) in a book or scroll (ספר). While we have already established that this is the only appearance of תורה in 12–26, כתב and ספר are also rare in 12–26 – only used elsewhere in 24:1–4 in the writing of a certificate of divorce.[106] That these words all occur together here – and nowhere else in 12–26 – exhibits an extraordinary string of coincidences and provides ground for readings which look for rhetorical, poetic and theological significance.

The content of the passage will be considered below, yet we can safely say that the book has paused in a sense to depict something unique about these offices. Lohfink's structure can be expanded as follows:

A – Judges appointed and judicial concerns 16:16–17:7
  B – Supremacy of the Judges and Priests 17:8–13
    C – The Law of the King – Write this torah in a book 17:14–20
  B2 – Provisions for the Priests and a Future Prophet 18:1–22
A2 – Return to judges and judicial laws 19:1

While this structure may seem to diminish the significant role of the prophet in 18:15–22, Lohfink's attention to the rhetorical and thematic nature of these chapters accentuates the centrality of the king laws Added to that, this structure shows that the three offices themselves are joined together in this central portion of chapters 12–26 and of the book as a whole. Christensen agrees that this passage is the structural centre of Deuteronomy, concluding that "a primary concern of the book of Deuteronomy, and perhaps the Pentateuch as a whole, is the matter of leadership of the people of God".[107] Looking more closely at the king laws illuminates certain hidden depths of this passage in its overall role in the book. The passage begins with the future desire of the people to appoint a king ככל־הגוים. Moses' response creates an intentional sense of ambiguity.

---

[105] Ibid., 344.
[106] See chapter 5 below on the use of these two terms.
[107] Christensen, *Deuteronomy*, 381.

Deut 17:15

שׂוֹם תָּשִׂים עָלֶיךָ מֶלֶךְ אֲשֶׁר יִבְחַר יְהוָה אֱלֹהֶיךָ בּוֹ מִקֶּרֶב אַחֶיךָ תָּשִׂים עָלֶיךָ מֶלֶךְ
לֹא תוּכַל לָתֵת עָלֶיךָ אִישׁ נָכְרִי אֲשֶׁר לֹא־אָחִיךָ הוּא׃

Although the people appear to want to be like the nations, Yahweh's own opinion about this desire is not altogether clear, and, following the pattern in chapter 12, the main emphasis is on Yahweh's *choice* of the leader and that this choice will be an Israelite – בו מקרם אחיך.[108]

Verses 16–19 then record the four requirements by which this king will be bound. The first three prohibitions (vv. 16–17) can be grouped together in their opposition to the typical corruptions in kingship.[109] In fact, the laws are more like wisdom than laws, as they guard the king's heart from the temptations in his daily conduct (cf. 17:20).[110] The temptations are variously described by the categories of militarism, moral licentiousness and economic power.[111] Two important textual resonances appear here. The first is between the prohibition from going to Egypt to multiply horses in 17:16 and Yahweh's promise that Israel would not return to Egypt again in Exodus 14:13. The prohibition not to pursue military power – horses from Egypt – also has the image of a "moral reversal" of the exodus from Egypt – a place where the torah did not govern the people with righteousness and justice.[112] Thus Israel's history is one of forward progress to be a better nation in a better land. The second resonance is internal to Deuteronomy as the three restrictions parallel the same warnings to Israel in Deuteronomy 7–10 against "the gods of *militaristic power*, *materialism*, and *self-righteous moralism*".[113] What is significant epistemologically is that this parallel keeps the king on the level of the people and their need for moral purity to continue knowing their God.

The fourth and final requirement is a set of commands regarding the king's handling of "this torah," noticeably referring to a not yet completed product (17:18, 19). This text stands as a climax to the king laws as they embrace the key to complying with the moral requirements and "commands" (17:19–20). Not only does תורה appear here for the first time since chapter 11, but it also draws the readers' attention back to the didactic references of Moses' דברים and the wordplay among the *Ausdrücke* in chapters 1:1, 5 and 4–11.[114] Thus in the midst of the Deuteronomic law code, after wading deeply into legal details, Moses makes a strategic echo to the sus-

[108] McConville, *Deuteronomy*, 293.
[109] Driver, *Deuteronomy*, 209.
[110] Cf. especially Prov 31:1–9, Tigay, *Deuteronomy*, 167.
[111] Cf. Brueggemann, *Deuteronomy*, 186–7; Olson, *Deuteronomy*, 82–5; Tigay, *Deuteronomy*, 167–8 and Wright, *Deuteronomy*, 209.
[112] McConville, *Deuteronomy*, 294. Cf. Tigay, *Deuteronomy*, 167–8.
[113] Olson, *Deuteronomy*, 82. Cf. Wright, *Deuteronomy*, 209.
[114] Driver, *Deuteronomy*, 212; Mayes, *Deuteronomy*, 273–4.

penseful and enticing vocabulary of his didactic speeches. This book and these laws have an extraordinary purpose and it behooves the reader to pay attention and stay involved as exemplified by the king. So, not only is the king (like the Israelite families) to write (כתב) the torah onto a ספר of some kind, but he is also to קרא and learn (למד) it.

The use of קרא in verse 19 is worth exploring further as its meaning calls to mind the idea of reading, speaking, or calling out.[115] Whatever the more precise meaning – and it may be intentionally ambiguous – it resonates with the speech and writing commands in 6:6–9 and 11:18–20 thereby reinforcing that the torah is to be appropriated by the individual and community by a combination of oral and written means.[116]

Finally, the twofold objective of this torah command is that the king might ילמד ליראה את־יהוה (17:19) and לבלתי רום־לבבו מאחיו (17:20). The reference to ירא, coupled with כל־דברי התורה provide an echo from 6:2 and 5:23–29 where the proper response of an Israelite to the torah, Yahweh and his powerful theophany at Horeb, is to fear him.[117] So not only is the king to respond as one of the Israelites – and not like Moses as such – but this also continues the developing motif from the last chapter that the torah serves, when obeyed, to actualise and sustain Yahweh's presence among his people in future times and future places.[118] We can now use this exegetical analysis to explore the way the ambiguity in the king laws serves the larger purpose of establishing a model Israelite who is rightly opposed to idolatry (ideology).

4.6.1 Ideology Critique in Israel's Kingship Law

First of all, it is important to appreciate how the king law stands in opposition to the corrupting ideologies of Israel's future neighbours. On the one hand, Moses reveals Israel's natural desire for a king like the nations around her: אשימה עלי מלך ככל־הגוים (17:14). Yet Israel's intentions are complicated by the fact that she wants to be *like* (כ) the nations who have a king who rules "over them." In contrast to the nations, Israel's king must fear Yahweh, and the four laws in 17:15–20 are all intended to keep the heart of Israel's king from being רום [...] מאחיו. Thus a *future* king is not prohibited as much as a king who would act *like* the kings of the nations or one that would be enthroned by the whims of the people. Rather, Yahweh will choose the king (שׂים עליך מלך אשר יבחר יהוה, v. 15) who will reflect back to God his own reverent service.

[115] *BDB*, 894.

[116] Grant, *King*, 206–10. See more below.

[117] Sonnet, *Book*, 81; Fischer/Lohfink, "Worte", 195–97 and Braulik, *Deuteronomium*, 129.

[118] Or Horeb in a new "time and place", Sonnet, *Book*, 81.

The impact of the opposition is made more clear by the comparison of this king to the Mesopotamian kings or Egyptian pharaohs who stood over their kingdoms and had the preeminent role of leading armies into war. Deuteronomy 17 is silent about the regal, militaristic responsibilities of the king and makes an emphatic counter-cultural point by listing its king in the middle, rather than the head of the civil and social offices.[119] Furthermore the typical Mesopotamian king, represented as the mediator between the people and God as the law-giver, stood over the law itself.[120] But Deuteronomy's king is neither the mediator of nor authority over this torah. Therefore, in the absence of a domineering king, Yahweh stands out as Israel's true king,[121] whether or not a chosen Israelite exercises this office in the future.[122]

4.6.2 The Ambiguity of Kingship in Deuteronomy

Besides the king's military role, other aspects of his office exhibit a sense of ambiguity and, from a rhetorical and theological point of view, it can be argued that these are intentional. Needless to say, some scholars view Yahweh's response to Israel's request in a negative light;[123] and Israel's future words admittedly request the capricious desire to be "like the other nations" (v. 14). Yet the obvious negative associations in this request are balanced by Yahweh's emphatic consent: שׂוֹם תָּשִׂים ("You shall *surely* set," v. 15). Contrary to our expectations, Yahweh *seems* to intend a human kingship, but only of the origin and character which he chooses.

Several other factors give a sense of ambiguity to this text. This king has a conspicuous lack of governing authority or responsibility. It is the judges and priests who can be seen ruling over the application of torah to the civil affairs of the people.[124] The king is not mentioned in 19:1–6 and is noticeably left out of the שֹׁטְרִים address to troops going out to war (20:9; cf. 19:17). Instead, the king laws focus on "attitudes and characteristics"[125] and the reader is led to conclude, despite the noble attitudes imagined here, that Israel does not really need a human king.[126] So why does Yahweh so em-

---

119 See Lohfink, "Distribution", 345, 347 and Grant, *King*, 201–2.

120 Tigay, *Deuteronomy*, 166; Cairns, *Deuteronomy*, 165 and Craigie, *Deuteronomy*, 254–56.

121 Grant, *King*, 194. Cf. also O'Donovan, *DN*, 62.

122 McConville, "Metaphor", 334. Cf. however, R.E. Clements, *God's Chosen People: A Theological Interpretation of the Book of Deuteronomy* (London: SCM, 1968), 40–2 who places the ideology critique of the kingship law in the context of a reform against Judean ideologies of a late provenance. The sense of a dilemma is significant. Is Deuteronomy 17 anti-Canaanite, anti-Judah, or both? And, hermeneutically, can it be the latter without being the former first?

123 Though they are not strong on the point, see Cairns, *Deuteronomy*, 165 and Tigay, *Deuteronomy*, 166.

124 Craigie, *Deuteronomy*, 253; N. Lohfink, "Das Deuteronomium: Jahwegesetz oder Mosegesetz?" in idem.; *Studien Zum Deuteronomium und Zur Deuteronomistischen Literatur 3* (SBAB 20; Stuttgart: Katholisches Bibelwerk, 1995) 157–65, on p. 157; Braulik, *Deuteronomium*, 127–8; and Lohfink, "Distribution", 345.

125 Craigie, *Deuteronomy*, 253.

126 Braulik, *Deuteronomium*, 128.

phatically intend to grant such a culturally compromising desire? The ambiguity is in most if not all senses explained by the model nature of the king.

4.6.3 The King as Arch-Torah Reader

The larger point of the cultural critique and ambiguity in this text is to reduce or eliminate any sense of superiority or human transcendence in this king. The law itself places the king as an object of Yahweh's choice בו מקרב אחיך (v. 17) and makes the purpose of the kingship laws to keep the kings heart from מאחיו [...] רום (v. 20). The repetition of אח in verses 15 and 20, and the absence of governing responsibilities serve as rhetorical cues which encourage Israel to identify with the nameless and faceless king of this law.

The parallel noted by Olson between Deuteronomy 7–10 and the three prohibitions in 17:16–17 stand as a further link between the king and the average Israelite.[127] The king shares the same proclivity towards idolatry as his "brother" and is therefore in no less need of this torah. In fact, the appropriation of the torah in verses 18–20 – and its resonances with 6:6–9 and 11:18–20 – make this an obvious editorial return to the didactic and parenetic nature of this torah for all Israel. In light of this the Deuteronomic king is as much an independent eschatological figure as it is a model for all Israelites to emulate.

As a model, the king is under Yahweh's torah[128] and the method prescribed for his handling of the torah is a literary embedded model[129] for every Israelite.[130] Specifically, we noted that the king was to "write for himself a copy" of this torah "before the Levitical priests" (17:18), which parallels the writing of the דברים in chapters 6 and 11. Yet in addition to the writing behaviour the king is to have a daily pattern of reading or calling out the torah (v. 19). The oral nature of קרא here combines with the "day" metaphor (כל־ימי חייו) and thus follows the patterns of all day speaking (דבר) and the metonomic pattern of sitting, standing and walking in 6:7 and 11:19. These patterns are also picked up in Joshua and the Psalms where the vocal הגה is used to signify orality on a daily basis.[131]

Joshua 1:8

לֹא־יָמוּשׁ **סֵפֶר הַתּוֹרָה** הַזֶּה מִפִּיךָוְהָגִיתָ בּוֹ **יוֹמָם וָלַיְלָה** לְמַעַן תִּשְׁמֹר לַעֲשׂוֹתכְּכָל־הַכָּתוּב בּוֹ כִּי־אָז תַּצְלִיחַ אֶת־דְּרָכֶךָ וְאָז תַּשְׂכִּיל׃

Psalm 1:2 (cf. Ps 2:1)

כִּי אִם **בְּתוֹרַת** יְהוָה חֶפְצוֹ וּבְתוֹרָתוֹ **יֶהְגֶּה יוֹמָם וָלָיְלָה**׃

---

[127] *Deuteronomy*, 82–3.

[128] Brueggemann, *Deuteronomy*, 186; McConville, *Deuteronomy*, 295–6.

[129] Or "embedded representation", Sonnet, *Book*, 79–80 – the same embedded technique achieved in the wise woman of Prov 31 (chapter 6 below).

[130] See Grant, *King*, 198–213.

[131] Here Niditch observes that the "king who writes down the law [...] continues in the tradition of Moses [...]" Niditch, *Oral World*, 102.

Although these passages are often translated with "meditate" for הגה, the parallel with קרא in Deuteronomy 17:19 illustrates the definitive oral dimension imagined by this collection of canonical echoes.[132] Thus both the "days" metaphor and the oral imagery represent a pattern throughout these OT texts for the individual repetition and intake of the torah.[133] This kind of king is a "model Israelite" as the "Torah's arch-reader"[134] which should be emulated by future Israelites who do not know Moses except by his book.[135]

It should be noted that here, more than anywhere else, Deuteronomy evidences a very singular portrait of the *individual* torah reader/reciter. Still, this must be held in balance with the OT emphasis on community. Deuteronomy and the OT often focus on the individual person.[136] In fact, it is the value of the individual which emerges from these passages; yet the individual here, and in most individual texts, is clearly not portrayed opposing the community as a means to knowledge. The king writes his copy of the torah מלפני הכהנים הלוים as a sign that the individual reading of the law is also public and communally accountable. The Enlightenment era popularised a distrust of tradition and community; but here tradition becomes the torah-bearing agent throughout history, and community is the place *where the individual finds identity* and the proper environment for coming to knowledge. Knowledge in this picture must be both individual and corporate without pitting one against the other.[137] This emerges clearly in the collection of offices in Deuteronomy 16–18.

4.7 Yahweh's Authority and the Distribution of Israel's Offices

The offices of priest, king and prophet stand at the centre of 12–26 and of Deuteronomy as a whole. Israel's request for a king seems to be granted by Yahweh, yet the kingship itself is in turn diminished and turned into a

---

[132] On the oral function of הגה, see H. Wolf, "הגה", in R.L. Harris/G.L. Archer/B.K. Waltke (ed.), *Theological Wordbook of the Old Testament 1* (Chicago: Moody Press, 1980) 205, on p. 205; M.V. Van Pelt/Walter C. Kaiser, "הגה", in W. VanGemeren (ed.), *NIDOTTE 1* (Grand Rapids, MI: Zondervan, 1997) 1006–8.

[133] On the parallels between Deut 6:6–9; 11:18–20; 17:18–20; Josh 1:8 and Pss 1 and 2, see Fischer/Lohfink, "Worte", 200–1; Braulik, *Deuteronomium*, 129–30; Christensen, *Deuteronomy*, 386–7 and Sonnet, *Book*, 77.

[134] Sonnet, *Book*, 71, 82, 234. Cf. also Crüsemann, *Torah*, 237; Lohfink, "Distribution", 349 and Braulik's "Musterisraelit," *Deuteronomium*, 129.

[135] Cf. however, Cairns, *Deuteronomy*, 168 who sees the king as "Yahweh's representative" which clearly misses the point both of the ambiguity in the text and the obvious resonances within Deuteronomy and the OT.

[136] Cf. Job, Psalms, Ecclesiastes, Jonah, etc.

[137] As I argue in chapter 7, Qohelet deconstructs individualism, yet the book's enticing rhetorical speciality lies in the *common* individuality of suffering, hope, despair and joy he shares with all Israelites. Qohelet is a representative individual of community who, although he despairs at the brokenness of community, cannot, in the end, find any meaning apart from it.

vehicle for reinforcing the foremost theme of the book – *all* the words of this torah for *all* Yahweh's people. Surely the silence regarding the king's regal responsibilities in Deuteronomy 17 are not meant to imply that the torah reading is purely an academic exercise. On the contrary, adherence to the torah is what will prolong the "days of his kingdom" (17:20) that one's "ways" might be successful (Josh 1:9). In other words, the picture imagined here captures the reading and the interpretive engagement through which torah is applied to daily life. The juxtaposition of the prophet balances the picture of the king and stands as a continued reminder of future tests, future revelation and the need for future interpretation.

There emerges, then, a combined effect from the depiction of these three, or five offices (including the שׁפטים and שׁטרים) in Israel's social and political structure. It helps to remember that the main content of Deuteronomy is the דברים משׁה (1:1) and the book is framed by the prediction and report of Moses' death. This key figure who represents Israel's access to Yahweh at Horeb, Sinai and Moab is going away and Israel's need for revelation, leadership and discipline is provided for in his swan song.

How, then, are the Mosaic responsibilities continued? For one, it is obvious that Moses has no true or, at least, no single successor.[138] O'Donovan suggests that there is a "residuum" of Mosaic authority which the "monarch's authority could not absorb or occlude".[139] Even Joshua, whose role is considered in the next chapter, does not retain the Mosaic access to theophany or torah.[140] Rather the enviable power and access in this heroic figure is distributed throughout the Israelite community, in what Olson refers to as a distribution of voices including kings, priests, prophets, judges, elders, officials, parents, heaven and earth (31:28), and other nations (Deut 32).[141] Children and mothers (cf. Prov 31) should also be included if this picture is to retain the fullness of the Mosaic succession developing in these first 26 chapters.

As for the continuing hermeneutical character of torah, Lohfink makes the observation that, "In virtue of the fact that all offices are subordinate to the Torah, God rules in Israel through the revelation he had given in the course of Israel's earlier history [...]."[142] Thus, by means of the prophetic office, God maintains the ability to exercise authority "in ever new ways, as occasions arise".[143] As such, future authority is not only guaranteed through

138 O'Donovan, *DN*, 52 and Sonnet, *Book*, 139–40.

139 *DN*, 62.

140 Although Joshua's commissioning does occur in the theophanic context of the tent of meeting (31:14–15), it is *with Moses* and a one time event for Joshua as mediator/leader. Thus, MacDonald suggests three successors to Moses: the torah, Moses' Song and Joshua, *Deuteronomy*, 142, 144.

141 *Deuteronomy*, 180–1. Cf. also Miller, *Deuteronomy*, 141 and Stahl, *Law*, 95–6 for her reference to the generations of Israelites who succeed Moses' office.

142 "Distribution", 350.

143 Ibid.

this range of community social interaction, but the threat of prophets gives a special urgency to the need for a performative response in interpreting the torah. This contributes to the building urgency and enticing nature of the torah as a means to actualise the greatest benefits of the Mosaic history perpetually.

5. Conclusion

Whereas Deuteronomy 1–11 was preeminently concerned with persuading Israel to actualise her Horeb-relationship with Yahweh in future times and places, Deuteronomy 12–26 aims to preserve and protect Israel in the midst of those future contexts. That is, Deuteronomy prepares Israel for international encounters which will test her faith and worldview. This chapter introduced "ideology" to describe the idolatries which suppress or distort the true knowledge of Yahweh and the proper understanding of his intended world order. And, in contrast to the insightful studies by Miller and Mayes, this chapter sought to listen to Deuteronomy for its own perspective on these ideologies.

The מקום, or sanctuary-laws, in chapter 12 preface the next fourteen chapters by setting conditional limits on the actualisation of Yahweh's presence with his people; they also situate Israel's future knowledge and identity in place; the laws imagine Yahweh present at a succession of places, so long as Israel properly resists the distorting ideologies of the Canaanite religions. The actual place itself turns out to be a red herring, distracting modern interpreters from Yahweh's "choice" in the place and, more importantly, from Yahweh's desire to be the present and guiding factor in Israel's faith and epistemology. In fact, although we find Israel continually warned to resist ideology, her torah stands as a universal norm which reveals Yahweh's wisdom and righteousness to the nations (Deut 4:5ff); Yahweh's – and therefore Israel's – epistemological influence is totalising.

The counter-cultural threat of the nations continues into the prophetic office in Deuteronomy 13:1–5[2–6]. Like the ambiguity of future places, this passage imagines the ambiguity of future revelation from unknown prophets. Together 13:1–5 and 18:15–22 issue the future challenge to all generations to learn and interpret torah, not only to live life with righteousness and justice, but also to be able to discriminate true from the false prophets. The key to this interpretative discrimination is to acknowledge the prophet's דבר as a symbol of faithfulness to Yahweh's torah. The prophet mediates Yahweh's epistemological priority in all of Israel's future life.

Finally, the prophetic office sits in the structural centre of Deuteronomy, alongside the king laws. Deuteronomy 16–18, therefore, not only envisions a future balance and distribution of civil offices, it diminishes the offices through the king laws in a way that the public leader is conceived as a "brother" or public servant who lives as a deliberate student of the torah. The king is as much a future office as it is a model to all Israelites to perform the roles of speaking and writing the torah as a means to a strong kingdom, a successful future and the epistemological exaltation of Yahweh in "fear" (Deut 17:17–20; cf. Deut 6:6–9; 11:18–20; Josh 1:8–9; Ps 1:1–6). The enticing and appealing incentives flow out of the first eleven chapters as Israel remembers the hope of actualising her relationship with Yahweh by performing this torah with the hermeneutical sensitivity to the threats and challenges of the abominable practices of the nations. The final eight chapters of Deuteronomy continue the momentum building throughout these chapters, drawing most of the rhetorical, theological and linguistic puzzles to a dramatic closure.

CHAPTER FIVE

Re-Actualisation in Future Covenants Deuteronomy 27–34

1. Introduction

The last two chapters explored the way Deuteronomy's rhetorical use of history-telling is a means to actualise the knowledge and presence of Yahweh in the future (Deut 1–11). Deuteronomy also equips Israel with the means to resist ideological and moral corruption in future contexts (12–26). These final chapters (27–34) draw these rhetorical and epistemological themes to a conclusion in three interrelated ways which we will examine here. First, the oral and written worlds – and rhetorical wordplay – move Moses' words from speech to writing. As such, Deuteronomy becomes a permanent book with the capacity to perdure and speak again and again for Yahweh and Moses in future times and places. Second, the covenants at Shechem (Deut 27–28) and Moab (Deut 29) renew the realities of the covenant with Moses at Horeb (Deut 5). Third, the blessings and curses in these covenant ceremonies remind Israel of the threatening potential for future of ideological and moral forces to distort her worldview, as seen in Deuteronomy 12–26. In this way Deuteronomy 27–34 blends covenant ceremonies with legal and communication rhetoric to encourage future renewal in Israel. The epistemological implications of this blending are analysed in three sections: (1) The Words and the Book, (2) The Witnesses and Epistemological Virtue, and (3) Beyond Deuteronomy.

2. The Words and the Book: The "Metamorphoses" of Moses' Words[1]

We first encounter "this book" in Deuteronomy 17:18 where it is a sign that Moses' speeches have been completed and preserved in written form. Similarly, the covenant ceremony in chapter 27 introduces several rhetorical and theological devices which lead to the writing of this book in 31:24.

[1] See Sonnet's chapter, "The Metaphorphoses of the *Sēper*" *Book*, 85–116.

Here we will examine the epistemological implications of Moses’ דברים *literally* transforming his speeches into a ספר and *functionally* transforming Israel’s behaviour from hearing the torah at Horeb and Moab to speaking, hearing and doing the torah in future generations. Thus, on the one hand, the move from Moses’ speech to Moses’ writing imitates Yahweh’s movement from speech to writing (5:22), leaving us with a sense of finality and permanence. On the other hand, the metamorphoses beginning in chapters 27–28 (cf. 17:18) are used metaphorically by Moses and the narrator to transform Yahweh’s speaking and writing into community roles for Moses, the priests, Israel and Joshua (Deut 31 – Josh 1:8-9; 24) where future speaking and writing continue. So, in one sense the words will be written (closed), but in this form they will also live on as the book is read, heard and obeyed in the future.

2.1 Rhetoric and Artistry in Deuteronomy’s Use of Orality and Literacy

In order to appreciate the transformative effects in Deuteronomy’s “book,” chapters 27–31 must be considered in the light of unique mode of communication developed in the first 26 chapters. That is, given the interchangeability of the *Ausdrücke* between the “statutes and ordinances” in chapters 12–26 and the תורה and the דברים in 1:1, 5 and 4–11, these final chapters introduce new dimensions to this strategy through the use of כתב and ספר. In the last two chapters I made reference to the emergence of these terms in Deuteronomy 12–26 and their rhetorically “open” capacity to capture future family and community acts of handling the emerging material of the “book.” The distribution of these terms throughout Deuteronomy helps us to perceive its progressive rhetorical ambitions:

Chapters	כתב	ספר
1–3	0	0
4–11	**7**	**0**
12–26	**1**	**1**[2]
27–31	**12**	**8**
32–34	0	0[3]

The fact that the seven occurrences of כתב in 4–11 and twelve between 27–31 are all used with reference to the handling of the *Ausdrücke* signals their

[2] The two uses in 24:1, 3 do not appear be part of Deuteronomy’s rhetorical strategy.

[3] Precisely, כתב: 4:13; 5:22; 6:9; 9:10; 10:2, 4; 11:20; 17:18; 24:1, 3; 27:3, 8; 28:58, 61; 29:19, 20, 26; 30:10; 31:19, 22, 24; and ספר: 17:18; 24:1, 3; 28:58, 61; 29:19, 20, 26; 30:10; 31:24, 26.

status as torah-*Promulgationssatz*.[4] Like the other *Promulgationssatz*, כתב is used by Moses and Yahweh as a model for Israel. Deuteronomy's narrative sequentially portrays each of these characters moving from speaking to writing the torah: first Yahweh (5:6–22; cf. 4:13; 9:10, etc.), then Moses (1:1, 5; 30:10; 31:9, 24), and finally the people who are yet to write in future contexts (6:9; 11:20) and a future ceremony (27:1). In the linear reading, this movement is understood progressively; its gradual revelation maintains a tension and suspense by which Yahweh's and Moses' speaking and writing are epitomised in a way that gives exigency to Israel's own corporate responsibility to carry out this behaviour in the future. Thus we should not overlook the intentional differences between Yahweh and Israel in Deuteronomy 4–11.

That is, both *permanent* and *literal* writing expressions are used with reference to Yahweh's activity on Horeb where he wrote the ten words on the two tablets of stone that Israel physically received – at a point in time – and placed in the ark (4:13; 5:22; 9:10; 10:2, 4). The family (corporate) writing activity is, however, embedded in a poetic series of verbs (דבר, פשר היה, שנן,) which have a *metaphorical* and *all-encompassing sense*.[5] While Yahweh's writing is also metaphorical, the community writing is a mimetic symbol of their daily entrance into writing as moral way of life. That is, even though Israel's writing may have literal dimensions, the major point is to portray the need for divine-imitation through obedience to the torah. In fact, in both 6:6–9 and 11:18–20 the writing imagery moves from internal (לב) to external places (doorposts and gates) whereby torah is appropriated, actualised and applied as continuing social exercise. In sum, we have many reasons to resist a literal reading of commands in 6:9 and 11:20, but chiefly because it eliminates the intentional ambiguity in the overall rhetorical strategy (*sujet*).[6]

When the suspense of the emerging writing metaphor is kept in place, the return to writing in 17:18–20 expands and enriches the writing imagery as the king על־ספר [...] כתב and קרא the torah all his days. The command to write intensifies the literal sense in 4–11 as made evident by the reference to על־ספר. But the king's activity is simultaneously oral (קרא) and also still all-encompassing (כל־ימי חייו), providing a smooth overlap with the corpo-

---

4 While this is not one of Braulik's *Promulgationssatz* "Ausdrücke", 13–4, his criteria are based upon the connection between Yahweh's activity, Moses' activity and the people's future activity in the land. Certainly this verb belongs to Deuteronomy's promulgation strategy.

5 See chapter 4 of this thesis for my arguments on the metaphorical sense.

6 On the *sujet* and *fabula*, see Sonnet, *Book*, 18 M. Sternberg, "Time and Space in Biblical (Hi)Story Telling: The Grand Chronology", in R. Schwartz (ed.), *The Book and the Text: The Bible and Literary Theory* (Oxford: Blackwell, 1990) 81–145, on p. 89 says, "the Bible's adherence to the arrow of time follows from its complex of strategic goals: the historical, the ideological, the artistic proper, along with the rhetorical or communicative pattern designed to bring them home".

rate activity (6:6–9; 11:18–20) and yet an explicit sense of progression with the mention of a future ספר (as argued in the last chapter). The king law thus reinforces the oral, written and all-encompassing necessity for future torah handling throughout the society. In fact, the improbability that the Israelites had high levels of literacy and the strong theology of divine imitation in the Tetrateuch (see chapter 2) make it natural to read the metaphorical representation of writing as ethical imitation. In sum, orality and literacy are integrally combined in a variety of cultural activities such that Yahweh's words continue to speak and effect obedience amidst his people.[7] As we demonstrate now, this rhetoric peaks in chapters 27–31.

2.1.1 Covenant Ratification at Shechem: Deuteronomy 27

The narrator's voice in Deuteronomy 27:1 and the reappearance of the *Ausdrücke* in 27:3 signals a break from chapters 12–26 in order to "show" Moses in the act of exhorting the elders and Israel to keep the "whole commandment" (כל־המצוה, 27:1). That is, at the close of the statutes and ordinances (12–26), the *Ausdruck* מצוה refers to all of Moses' torah between 1:5 and 31:24.[8] The narrator's voice strategically shapes Israel's understanding of time and place by a shift of perspectives[9] as it depicts Moses in the act of speaking. As such, Israel "sees" that the words which were once spoken (oral) are later read or heard to the same effect that they had for the narrator, and for the generation at Moab. We can also see this effect in the way the commandments in Moses' words are given "today" (היום, v. 1) which, for future readers, creates an epic memory of Moses before the second wilderness generation. Meanwhile the substance of the commands themselves refers to a future day and a future ceremony where Moses' words will be heard by countless generations.[10] Overlapping generations, therefore, participate in uniting ceremonies which eclipse the distance between "today" and Moses' days on Horeb with Yahweh. This gives future generations a sense of confidence in the epistemological reliability of their torah as grounded in the ontological, even cosmic continuity between Moses' day and their day. Moses is going away, yet the torah still offers the capacity for future generations to actualise ancient realities through the proper handling of the torah.

---

[7] Niditch, *Oral World*, 3–4, 100; J.G. McConville, *Deuteronomy* (AOTC; Leicester/Downer's Grove, IL: InterVarsity, 2002), 41. Cf. Sonnet, *Book*, 56–8.

[8] McConville, *Deuteronomy*, 388; Millar, "Place", 71; Braulik, "Ausdrücke", 26–8.

[9] On the rhetorical function of changing perspectives, see Sternberg, *Poetics*, 153–85 and chapter 2 above.

[10] Sonnet says that this transcends time and space *Book*, 95, thus extending the potential for actualisation.

The particular commands in this chapter (27:1–8) require Israel to establish an altar at Shechem on "the day"[11] that Israel crosses the Jordan and to set up "large stones" (אבנים גדלות, v. 2) and write on them כל־דברי התורה הזאת (27:2–3). This is the second of seven uses of this phrase (כל־דברי התורה הזאת) in Deuteronomy, echoing the first use in the transitional text in Deuteronomy 17:19.[12] Just as the king was to write "all the words of this torah", so the people will write them in covenant renewal. It is certainly possible that the meaning of "torah" is limited here, only referring to the blessings and curses of 27:15–28:68 or only to the laws in Deuteronomy 12–26.[13] Still, it seems more likely that the reference to [...] כל־דברי implies all the Deuteronomic law (1:5–31:24), including the blessings and curses in chapters 27–28,[14] especially in light of the parallels in 31:12 and 32:46 which close any question or gap about the phrase as applied to the writing on these stones.[15]

Moreover, the covenant ceremony itself continues a series of climactic occasions in the Pentateuch where Yahweh's relationship with Israel and the fathers is actualised through stones, altars and sacrifices (Gen 12:6–7; 15:7–21; 28:11, 18, 22; 31:45; 33:20; 35:14, 20; 33:20; Exod 24). Significantly, Israel's future covenant ceremony at Shechem echoes the first altar built by Abraham – also at Shechem – to confirm Yahweh's promise to give his descendants this land (Gen 12:6–7).[16]

The altar and the stones symbolise the permanence and normativity in Israel's law. Just like the ceremonies with the patriarchal fathers and with the first wilderness generation at Sinai, the second generation will confirm Yahweh's covenant promises and its own covenant responsibility in a new time and place by enacting the role established for them in Moses' book.[17] Yahweh's words, as written on the stones (4:13), were fixed: "do not add or take away from the word I command you today" (4:2). So also Moses' law was fixed at Horeb (12:32 [13:1]) which parallels the ceremony in Exodus where Yahweh wrote the תורה on tablets of stone (אבן, 24:12) and where twelve stones (אבנים) are used as a sign of covenant ratification at the foot of Mount Sinai (28:21). Yet, whereas in Exodus the twelve stones erected

---

[11] Though this may refer to the immediacy of the ceremony rather than the exact day McConville, *Deuteronomy*, 388; Tigay, *Deuteronomy*, 486.

[12] Cf. also 27:8; 28:58; 29:28; 31:12; 32:46.

[13] Or Deut 5–26, see Driver, *Deuteronomy*, 296 and Craigie, *Deuteronomy*, 328. Merrill seems to miss the point of the echoes in 17:18; 27:1; 28:58, etc, when he suggests that only the Decalogue could have been written on stones *Deuteronomy*, 342.

[14] Sonnet, *Book*, 102.

[15] Cairns, *Deuteronomy*, 231; Miller, *Deuteronomy*, 191; McConville, *Deuteronomy*, 388; Tigay, *Deuteronomy*, 248.

[16] Tigay, *Deuteronomy*, 249; G.J. Wenham, "Deuteronomy and the Central Sanctuary", in Christensen (ed.), *Song* (1993) 94–108, on p. 97.

[17] Kline, *Structure*, 34–6.

by the Levites are a secondary witness[18] to the covenant – and the torah is the primary witness – the stones (אבנים גדלים) in Deuteronomy 27 have torah written on them, merging the witness into a single image.[19] In this way, they mimic Yahweh's stones (4:13; 5:22) and attain a corresponding function in the ceremony. Israel's writing not only actualises the Mosaic covenant at Moab, but it engages all the people as active participants in the covenant of this torah.[20] They assume a Mosaic type of intimacy with Yahweh and establish their decision to trust Yahweh and possess the land.

Finally we can make some important observations about the rhetorical and theological function of the ceremony. In the future at Shechem – where Abraham first worshipped – the realities of these historical events will be actualised as the cumulative revelation of torah is written on large stones (27:1–8; cf. Josh 8:30–35). Significantly, the attention given to writing is emphasised by באר (27:8) which echoes Deuteronomy's only other use of this word in 1:5 where Moses set about to באר את־התורה הזאת. Now, towards the end of his sermons, the people are granted partnership and participation with Moses in the careful writing of (i.e. obeying) the torah.[21] McConville states that this relationship between Horeb, Moab and Shechem "symbolizes the theology of covenantal re-realization".[22] Each generation is given a ceremonial means by which to identify with the historic Israel and actualise the certainty of the promises and commands in the torah; Torah is a new and adaptable means for Israel to access Yahweh's nearness and blessing.

2.1.2 The Covenant and the Book at Moab: Deuteronomy 28–30

The covenant at Shechem and the narrative of a future journey are temporary and return to the present somewhere between 28:1 and 28:69[29:1] for Moses' final address to Israel at Moab, "this day" (29:4). There are, in fact, several difficulties in any attempt to locate the break between Shechem and Moab. Notably, the word "today" in 28:69 is also present in 28:1 leading some to argue that the narrator's return to the present at Moab occurred there.[23] Yet 28:69[29:1] also states quite clearly that this is a "covenant" at Moab (בארץ מואב) as commanded (צוה) by Moses "besides" (מלבד) the covenant at Horeb.[24] Despite the ambiguities in 28:1–69[29:1] it is hard to evade this decisive turn to the narrator "showing" Moses commanding all

---

18 The stones in Exodus bore the names of the 12 sons of Israel.

19 Craigie *Deuteronomy*, 328; Cairns, *Deuteronomy*, 230.

20 McConville *Deuteronomy*, 391.

21 Wright *Deuteronomy*, 275. Cf. Tigay, *Deuteronomy*, 250 Miller, "Moses", 247; Thompson, *Deuteronomy*, 263.

22 *Deuteronomy*, 395. Cf. Tigay, *Deuteronomy*, 488.

23 McConville, *Deuteronomy*, 395, 401; N. Lohfink, "Moab oder Sichem – wo wurde Dtn 28 nach der Fabel des Deuteronomiums proklamiert?" in idem.; *Studien zum Deuteronomium und zur Deuteronomistischen Literatur 4* (Stuttgart: Katholisches Bibelwerk, 2000) 205–18. But cf. Driver, *Deuteronomy*, 319 and Mayes, *Deuteronomy*, 348.

24 On the ambiguities in the use of צוה here see Lohfink, "Moab oder Sichem", 207, 213–4.

the words of this torah to the second generation.[25] It therefore seems most likely that the break occurs later (28:69) and not in 28:1, making the blessings and curses a part of the Shechem covenant.

That said, it does not eliminate the rhetorical and temporal blending that has occurred between the two covenants.[26] Dismissing the ambiguity as careless redaction only diverts our attention away from the larger rhetorical effect of the text.[27] The overlap portrays the blessings and curses uttered first at Moab and then ratified in the Land at Shechem.[28] The words are heard in both locations and McConville is right to notice an intentional "blurring of temporal horizons"[29] which unites these covenant ceremonies in a way that gives corporate continuity to the trans-generational people of Israel.[30] Because these ceremonies allow subsequent generations to share an identity, the rhetorical and theological implication is that Yahweh's torah at Horeb has a timeless and normative quality which stands over the people across boundaries of space and time. In this light, the covenants at Horeb, Moab and Shechem are united through the strategic repetition of the *Ausdrücke*.

הדברים דבר יהוה (5:22; 9:10)
כל־דברי התורה הזאת (17:19; 27:3, 8; 28:58; 29:28; 31:12; 32:46)
דברי התורה הזאת (17:18; 27:26; 31:24)
דברי הברית (28:69)

In the past, Yahweh spoke and then wrote the words of a covenant (4:13; 5:22). These are repeated in Moses' own words. Then, as Moses' words draw to an ultimate closure, they too become a covenant in the pattern of Yahweh's covenant (28:69).[31] It is helpful to see the *Ausdrücke* in chapters 27–29 operating according to Kierkegaard's notion of "repetition" – as remembered events that becomes new – and not dying "recollection" of events that are old.[32] The break is not one which separates Horeb from Moab as different historical covenants, but part of a larger communicative

25 See Cairns, *Deuteronomy*, 253–6; Olson, *Deuteronomy*, 131; Miller, *Deuteronomy*, 199; Sonnet, *Book*, 105–6.

26 See Lohfink, "Moab oder Sichem".

27 Cf. Braulik, *Deuteronomium*, 210–11 and Mayes, *Deuteronomy*, 358–61 who ascribe many of the ambiguities to the history of editorial layers. This is somewhat historically egocentric, supposing that the final shapers of the book were not careful or studious enough to shape this text rhetorically. For an example of a reversal of interpretations based on poor estimates of literary quality in Deut 28, see Tigay, *Deuteronomy*, 489–90.

28 Lohfink, "Moab oder Sichem", 216–7. Cf. Craigie, *Deuteronomy*, 327.

29 *Deuteronomy*, 401.

30 Cf. Mayes, *Deuteronomy*, 361 and Cairns, *Deuteronomy*, 255 who describes Israel's "experiences [...] re-presented to successive generations" in way that they become "contemporary realities".

31 On the role of ברית among the *Ausdrücke*, see Braulik, "Ausdrücke", 15–7.

32 Where "repetition" is "recollection forward","Recollection is a discarded garment that does not fit [...]", and "Repetition is an indestructible garment that fits closely and tenderly [...]" S. Kirkegaard, *Fear and Trembling/Repetition* (Princeton, NJ: Princeton University, 1983 [1843]), 131–2.

pattern in which Moses imitates Yahweh and Israel imitates Moses in renewal of an ancient relationship and eternal realities.[33]

2.1.3 Moses Writes the Torah-Book: Deuteronomy 30–31

In chapters 30–31 the many legal terms in Deuteronomy are drawn together into a definitive and mobile "book." The first explicit signal that these words will become a book is in Deuteronomy 28:58:

אִם־לֹא תִשְׁמֹר לַעֲשׂוֹת אֶת־כָּל־דִּבְרֵי הַתּוֹרָה הַזֹּאת הַכְּתוּבִים בַּסֵּפֶר הַזֶּה לְיִרְאָה אֶת־הַשֵּׁם הַנִּכְבָּד וְהַנּוֹרָא הַזֶּה אֵת יְהוָה אֱלֹהֶיךָ׃

The use of ספר here is only the second in Deuteronomy, following the king's responsibility to write a copy of a "this torah" on a ספר (17:18). The word also emerges later in the reassurance Yahweh gives to Israel after her fall and restoration, that she can again prosper if she keeps all the commandments and statutes "which are written in this book of the torah" (הכתובה בספר התורה הזה, 30:10). It is significant that in 17:18, 28:58 and 30:10 the end of this ספר has not yet come and that we do know who wrote it or when.[34] This enigmatic book/scroll and Moses' awaited death are rhetorical and narrative tools which prepare for the material in Chapter 31.

Although there are several acceptable ways to outline chapter 31, it seems best to do so in a way that accentuates the alternating motifs of Joshua's succession and the writing of the book with Yahweh's speech and Moses' speech.[35]

31:2–6	Moses	Exhorts the people based on Yahweh's faithfulness.
31:7–8	Moses	Exhorts Joshua
31:9–13	Moses	Writes the **Torah in a Book** and exhortation to obey
31:14–15	Yahweh	Theophany for Moses/**Joshua**
31:14–15	Yahweh	Commands a **Song** for witness to Israel's unfaithfulness
31:23	Yahweh	Commands and exhorts **Joshua** alone.
31:24–29	Moses	Writes **Torah in a Book**, witness to Israel's unfaithfulness
31:30	Moses	Begins the Song to Israel

The integration of these various themes allows us to make four important observations. (1) First of all, a conceptual gap is closed, to some degree, when the narrator records Moses' own writing of the torah and gives it to the priests in verses 9 and 24–26.[36] As Sonnet recognises, this is the first

[33] Millar says, "Mt Ebal is thus to become the new Moab, standing in continuity in the land with the succession of places of significance without, and taking its place in the journey of the nation." "Place", 72. Cf. also Miller, *Deuteronomy*, 196, 200.

[34] After all, the introduction to Deuteronomy comes from the words of an anonymous narrator who relays the words that Moses *spoke* (דבר) to Israel (1:1).

[35] Olson, *Deuteronomy*, 133–4; Sonnet, *Book*, 126; McConville, *Deuteronomy*, 436–7.

[36] Cf. Braulik *Deuteronomium*, 223; Cairns, *Deuteronomy*, 231; Sonnet, *Book*, 139–40; Miller, *Deuteronomy*, 192f; Wright, *Deuteronomy*, 275.

use of the *wayiqqtol* form of כתב in Deuteronomy where Yahweh is not the subject[37] and, therefore, the first indication that the book in question is Moses'.[38] Moses thus emerges as the supreme parallel for Yahweh's activity (5:22)[39] and his own ספר is accordingly placed next to the ark containing Yahweh's own tablets (31:26).[40] Moses' words are portrayed as Yahweh's words and written with Yahweh's authority.[41] (2) Second, the frame of the chapter elevates Joshua both in his central position between the two references to the book (vv. 9 and 24), but also in his selection to join Moses before Yahweh's theophany at the tent of meeting (31:14–15),[42] thereby signifying Joshua's successional role after Moses. The final section of this chapter will return to this succession theme. (3) Third, in the middle of the chapter between the two reports of Moses finishing (כלה, v. 24) his writing (31:9, 24), Yahweh commissions the writing of a song (שׁירה) to be an additional witness (31:19). This is the first mention of a שׁירה[43] and the closure brought about by Moses writing creates a false stop. One book closes, but another continues suggesting that the contexts of future times and places require adaptation to the torah. The song is also a witness to accompany the book as signs of Israel's future unfaithfulness. Thus, it is common to recognise Moses as succeeded by Joshua, the book and the song.[44] However, this overlooks the community of Israel who, in their hearing, internalising, reading and singing, become another successor.[45] The closure to the book therefore captures Israel in her corporateness, leadership and individuality as human agents of torah-obedience and divine-imitation.

(4) Finally, the succession of characters in their faithfulness to the torah retain the assurance of Yahweh's presence among them in the future. With Moses' death looming, divine presence and divine favour have become a primary concern for Israel and their fears are answered here. This reassurance is achieved by the three parallels between the exhortations to Joshua and Israel: (1) A reminder of God's presence in the past (against Og and Sihon, v. 4; according to the promise to the fathers, v. 7), (2) an exhortation to be strong and courageous (vv. 6 and 7), and (3) the assurance that

---

37 *Book*, 135.

38 McConville, *Deuteronomy*, 439.

39 As the king in Deut 17:18–20 is only writing a *copy* of a preexistent ספר.

40 McConville, *Deuteronomy*, 38; Niditch, *Oral World*, 87; Sonnet, *Book*, 171. Olson points out that the tablets in the ark were 'deconstructed' in the golden calf incident (Deut 9–10) and that by the time of the Babylonian exile, only the book remains as a derivative of the original revelation thus indicting Israel for her predicted unfaithfulness as a failure to keep the torah *Deuteronomy*, 176–7.

41 Millar, "Faithful God", 5; Miller, "Moses", 247.

42 What Sonnet calls the "turning point in the whole picture" *Book*, 120. Cf. also Braulik, *Deuteronomium*, 222 and McConville, *Deuteronomy*, 440.

43 The assonantal resemblance to תורה has often lead some to see scribal mistakes in which all the references in this chapter should be either שׁירה or תורה. In the scope of the book, it makes just as much sense to ascribe poetic skill to the author, especially in light of the ensuing poetic material (ch. 32–33).

44 MacDonald, *Deuteronomy*, 142, 144; Sonnet, *Book*, 156. Cf. also Clements, *People*, 68, 92 who recognises that the priests are successors, but also fails to include the people themselves.

Yahweh will be with you (ההלך עמך, v. 6; ההלך לפניך הוא יהיה עמך, v. 8). In this way, the tables in the ark and the torah book next to the ark, along with the song, together represent the pattern not only for education[46] (reminding Israel about the uniqueness of Moses and the desert generations), nor only renewal of the covenant,[47] but most especially the actualisation of Yahweh’s presence amidst the people – to “perpetuate the Horeb experience”.[48] The next three chapters counter the highly optimistic imagery of actualisation with the threat of future moral failures.

3. Witnesses and Epistemological Virtue in Deuteronomy 30–32

As we argued in chapters 3 and 4 above, Deuteronomy 4:2 and 12–26 indicate that future efforts to actualise the past will be threatened by Israel’s ideological and ethical temptations. In this way, Westphal helpfully recognises that epistemology is conditioned not only by the proper recognition of ideologies, but by the moral limitations brought about through sin.[49] By sin, he means “neither sins nor the tendency to commit sins but the fundamental project of which both sins and the tendency to commit them are expressions [...] best described as *pride*, the *self-assertion* which usurps a role in life not proper to me, depriving God and neighbor of their rightful places as, respectively, my absolute superior and my equal”.[50] In other words, sin is not bad methods – missing the mark – (though this may be symptomatic), but volitional, moral and emotional independence which is manifested in pride and self-deception and bears upon cognitive perspectives, processes and decisions. Westphal cites the failure of the Enlightenment to achieve its goal to free thinkers from the “situated character of all cognition”[51] but at the same time the more fundamental failure to account for passions or moral *interest* which lead the interpreter/knower into folly and self-deception:

> The collapse of foundationalism offers new opportunity for making sin a significant epistemological variable. But this is no more inevitable for post-foundational reflection than it was for foundationalism. For it is entirely possible to find in the ashes of foundationalism only finitude and not sinfulness, to discover preunderstandings that are perspectival but not perverse.[52]

---

45 McConville, *Deuteronomy*, 437, 439 and S.D.J. McBride, “Yoke”, 291.

46 See Craigie, *Deuteronomy*, 371 who sees this as the primary purpose of torah reading.

47 Kline, *Structure*, 119–24 in wanting to uphold the genre of Deuteronomy as covenant over against law, fails to note the connection to Horeb which the torah envisions and enables. In this way the torah is covenantal, educational and ontological.

48 Sonnet, *Book*, 128. Cf. also Cairns, *Deuteronomy*, 273–4; Clements, *People*, 97–9; O’Donovan, *DN*, 50–1. Cf. however Barker, “Israel”, 222–3, who rejects this position. His view is discussed in the section on Deut 30–32 below.

49 “Sin”, 207.

50 Ibid., 200 (emphasis added).

51 Ibid., 210.

52 Ibid., 211.

The last chapter primarily explored the nature of torah as it anticipates and responds to ideological or paradigmatic cultural influences which threaten to distort Israel's knowledge from *without*. Now, looking to Deuteronomy 29–32 (cf. Deut 1–4; 9–10) we find the clearest expression of the corresponding moral problem with Israel's past and future failures, or deception from *within*, which, as I have shown in the last two chapters, is inseparably tied to what and how Israel goes about knowing and imitating Yahweh. Thus, we turn our attention in these penultimate chapters to the moral or virtuous side of knowledge, or the perversive character in the fallen human perspective which leads to distortion.

3.1 The Morality of Israel's Knowledge in Deuteronomy 4–32

In the last section we described the transition from Shechem to Moab (Deut 27–29) and the distinctive beginning of Moses' speech in 29:1 [28:69] which make Deuteronomy 29–32 the next major structural unit in the book.[53] We find significant moral overtones in these chapters apparent in the witness(es) (עד) which are also conspicuously and structurally positioned throughout Deuteronomy:

4:26 "I call heaven and earth as witness"[54]
    19:15–21 (17:6) – Three witnesses required to render judgment
30:19 "I call heaven and earth to witness against you today"
    31:19, 21 Song as witness
    31:26 Book as witness
31:28 "(I) call heaven and earth as witness" (cf. 32:1,40, 43)

In the first reference to "heaven and earth" as a future witness (4:26), Yahweh establishes his means to testify against Israel's future apostasy (4:15–28; 6:10–19; 9:10). 19:15–21 then records a law for the judges to require three witnesses to validate the guilt of a fellow Israelite. It seems significant then, that in chapters 30–31, Yahweh combines these two aspects and combines three separate witnesses to testify to Israel's future covenant infidelity. The dense collection of witnesses in these two chapters (30–31), and Israel's inability to remain faithful, are concepts grounded in a paradox which emerges in the unique narrative features of Deuteronomy 4–29.

That is, chapters 4 and 29–30 form an inclusio[55] whereby the former first raises the possibility of Israel's future forgetfulness (פן־תשכחו, 4:23), and

---

[53] Assuming another new start in 33:1, [...] וזאת הברכה אשר ברך משה. Cf. Olson, "Theology", 203–5 and N. Lohfink, "Der Bundesschluss im Land Moab: Redaktionsgeschichtliches zu Dt 28:69–32:47", *BZ* 6 (1962) 32–56.

[54] Hiphil of עוד also in 30:19 and 31:28.

[55] Deuteronomy 4 and 30 can be seen as summaries of the book. On the resonances between chs 4 and 29–30, see Wright, *Deuteronomy*, 45; Millar, "Place", 82; Driver, *Deuteronomy*, lxxvi, 328; Craigie, *Deuteronomy*, 363.

the latter promises its inevitability. In the process a paradox arises between chapters 4 and 29 through the repetition of three words which are used only in 29:2–3[1–2] and 4:34: מפתים, אתת and מסת. In both contexts, these are witnesses for Israel's benefit – things done "before your eyes" (לעיניך, 4:34; 29:1[2]) and things that your "eyes saw" (ראו עיניך 29:3[2]) – designed for Israel to know (דעת) that Yahweh is God alone (4:34, 39; 29:6[5]). The paradox arises when Yahweh says that he did not give Israel לב לדעת ועינכים לראות ואזנים לשמע, 29:3[4]. In other words, a distinction is made between Israel's literal physical perception and the kind of perception that gives way to true knowledge[56] where Yahweh is apparently in the position of both condemning Israel and yet withholding knowledge.

The implications and resolution of the tension here begin with an understanding of the nuances in "seeing" and "hearing" introduced in Deuteronomy 4. As Geller points out, chapter 4 is rhetorically designed to give seeing and hearing special epistemological connotations (4:11–12 32–36). "Heaven" and "earth" and "seeing" and "hearing" are depicted as oppositions with reversed pairs that represent two kinds of knowledge: heaven (typically representing transcendence) is the place of God's voice and earth (typically associate with immanence) is the place of God's theophany (4:36; cf. Exod 19:11–20).[57] The effect, according to Geller, asserts "the dominance of one over the other: "hearing from heaven" over against and absolutely over "seeing on the earth".[58] The priority is not a dogmatism,[59] but rather a rhetorical and epistemological device; Yahweh's theophany testifies adequately to his uniqueness. Yet to counter the "seeing is believing" attitude of empiricism, God here tells Israel that the historical tradition of his words and works should be held as a more reliable testimony to his unperceived presence in their midst. The (oral) tradition is adequate to assure Israel of the realities which she cannot "see."

Chapter 29, however, interestingly relates the oral revelation of redemption in Deuteronomy 4:36 in purely visual terms (29:2–3) and concludes that Israel did not have "a heart to understand or eyes to see or ears to hear" (v. 4). This reinforces the earlier lesson that "seeing is not necessarily believing".[60] There are many ways to try and resolve this difficult tension between seeing and understanding.[61] Nevertheless, the reference "to this day"

---

[56] On *seeing* without *faith*, see Miller, *Deuteronomy*, 205 and Barker, "Israel", 80, 140–3. On the NT use of this same language, opening the minds of the disciples, see J. Marcus, "Mark 4:10–12 and Marcan Epistemology", *JBL* 103 (1984) 557–74.

[57] Geller "Wisdom", 39–40.

[58] Ibid., 40–41.

[59] As is done by Weinfeld, *Deuteronomy 1–11*, 212–3 and Tigay, *Deuteronomy* 56 to deny Yahweh's presence in the fire. But cf. MacDonald, *Deuteronomy*, 193–4 and Wilson, *Midst*, 68.

[60] Miller, *Deuteronomy*, 204.

[61] Cf. Ibid., 204ff; Tigay, *Deuteronomy*, 275; Cairns, *Deuteronomy*, 255–6.

(v. 4) combined with the entire history of God's acts for Israel (vv. 2–3), suggest that the failure is attributed to the sum of Israel's corporate failures in all of her historical generations.[62] Yahweh seems to lament this same historical tendency in 5:29 wishing that Israel would *always* fear him as they did at the mountain (5:28). Moses, too, declares Yahweh's impression of Israel as a "stiff-necked people" (עם־קשה־ערף, 9:6, 13; 10:16) who need to "circumcise your hearts and be no longer stubborn" (10:16).[63] There is in fact, throughout the Deuteronomic narrative, a consistent connection between לב, עיני and דעת (4:9, 35, 39; 8:2–3, 5; 29:3[4]) which indicates that the primary source of the limits of Israel's knowledge is her own culpable, moral and volitional recalcitrance. Yahweh's withholding (לא־נתן) of eyes that see and a heart that understands (29:3[4]), in the fuller scope of Deuteronomy, is not so much *preventative* as *non-restorative*. "Sin" has consistently interrupted moments of faith and blinded Israel to knowledge. Yahweh alone has the power to refresh her sight (29:4).[64] We find this same tension in Israel's access to the "secret" and "revealed things" in 29:29[28] where, like Job 28, Yahweh is shown to have given humanity conditions for accessing true wisdom and knowledge.[65]

3.1.1 Human Responsibility and Divine Intervention in Deuteronomy 30

The tension created in Deuteronomy 29 between Yahweh's redemptive acts and Israel's continual return to unfaithfulness continues in chapter 30. Structurally, the chapter is often divided into two parts, either between verses 1–10 and 11–20[66] or 1–14 and 15–20.[67] However another alternative, arising from the transition in verse 11 to the "commandment" given "today", suggests a division into the three following sections:[68]

30:1–10	The paradox of future grace and turning
	30:11–14 The ability to do the law commanded "today"
30:15–20	Final exhortation to choose "life" rather than "death"[69]

---

62 Miller, *Deuteronomy*, 206. Cf. Brueggemann, *Deuteronomy*, 260f; Wright, *Deuteronomy*, 284–86.

63 Tigay, *Deuteronomy*, 275. Cf. also this generation's failure at Beth Peor (Deut 3:29; 4:3–4) S.W. Hahn, "Kinship by Covenant: A Biblical Theological Study of Covenant Types and Texts in the Old and New Testaments", PhD dissertation, Marquette University, 1995).

64 McConville, says Israel lacks "the moral understanding that can produce right action" *Deuteronomy*, 415.

65 Barker, "Israel", 164; Braulik, *Deuteronomium*, 216; Cairns, *Deuteronomy*, 262; Mayes, *Deuteronomy*, 367; Merrill, *Deuteronomy*, 385; Miller, *Deuteronomy*, 212.

66 Driver, *Deuteronomy*, 328–30; Thompson, *Deuteronomy*, 284–88; Merrill, *Deuteronomy*, 386–94; Keil/Delitzsch, "Pentateuch", 975–77.

67 Mayes, *Deuteronomy*, 367–71; Miller, *Deuteronomy*, 212–15.

68 McConville, *Deuteronomy*, 423; Craigie, *Deuteronomy*, 362–6; von Rad, *Deuteronomy*, 182–85 Wright, *Deuteronomy*, 289–93.

69 On "life", see Braulik, *Deuteronomium*, 220 and McConville, *Deuteronomy*, 430.

Within this structure, verses 1 and 19 form an inclusio where the דברים of "blessing and curse" – which testifies to future Israel to provoke repentance (שׁוב, v. 2) – and Moses calling the heavens and the earth as witness before Israel, provoke their choice (בהר) of the right path "today" (30:19). In other words, the chapter is framed by the intention for these "words"[70] to inspire an obedient response embodied in שׁוב and בהר in the present and future. A close examination of this chapter will allow us to make several observations about the epistemological nature of Israel's covenant unfaithfulness and Yahweh's restoration.

(1) Deuteronomy 30:1–10. This section follows the climax of the "secret" and "revealed" things in 29:28[29] to form a paradox or tension between divine grace and Israelite repentance.[71] The pericope is distinguished by the juxtaposition of Israel's response and Yahweh's divine initiative or divine restoration. The tension emerges primarily in the seven uses of שׁוב where both Israel (30:1, 2, 8, 10) and Yahweh (30:3(2x), 8) are subjects of turning.[72] Israel turns, Yahweh turns to Israel and Yahweh turns Israel toward himself. It might be thought that the textual order and the כי-clauses suggest a cause-effect relationship between Israel's turning (vv. 1–2) and Yahweh's restoration (vv. 3–6). Yet, there are several reasons for our interpretation to maintain the overwhelming place of Yahweh's restoring initiative which gives way to Israel's obedient response and thereby retain Yahweh's sovereign discretion to give and withhold knowledge.

First, regardless of sequential order, it is necessary to affirm that Yahweh and Israel both turn. As regards the temporal כי-clauses in verses 1–2, it is more natural to the כי-construction to translate ושׁב in verse 3 with the apodeitic "then" than as a simple conjunctive "and".[73] In other words, these events are linked and Israel's turning to obedience is a required – though not necessarily causative – part of what it means for Israel to be restored. In fact, the whole framework in verses 1–10 clearly emphasises this aspect of mutual turning. Verses 8–10 reinforce the point that Yahweh's activity will and must be accompanied by turning (שׁוב) and obeying (שׁמע).[74] Israel is

---

[70] See McConville, *Deuteronomy*, 425.

[71] Mayes, *Deuteronomy*, 368 Miller, *Deuteronomy*, 208, 213; Brueggemann, *Deuteronomy*, 269. Cf. W. Brueggemann, "The Travail of Pardon: Reflections on *slh*", in B.A. Strawn/N.R. Bowen (ed.), *A God So Near* (Winona Lake, IN: Eisenbrauns, 2003) 283–97.

[72] On the centrality of שׁוב in this context, see Tigay, *Deuteronomy*, 283; Mayes, *Deuteronomy*, 368; McConville, *Deuteronomy*, 423; Miller, *Deuteronomy*, 212; Braulik, *Deuteronomium*, 219; G. Braulik, "Law as Gospel: Justification and Pardon According to the Deuteronomic Torah", *Interpretation* 38 (1984) 5–14, on p. 11;.

[73] Cf. Barker, "Israel", 183; Braulik, *Deuteronomium*, 219; McConville, *Deuteronomy*, 225; Waltke/O'Connor, *Hebrew Syntax*, 637.

[74] I agree with Thompson, *Deuteronomy*, 285 that, however urgent the *ordo salutis* is to a modern, confessional interpreter, we must consider the fact that the original setting did not necessarily focus on the chronological sequence as a means to derive causal implications. Cf. Merrill, *Deuteronomy*, 387.

again required to שׁוּב, שׁמע and שׁמר all the commandments given by Moses today (30:8–10). Brueggemann observes that throughout every division in this text, Israel is reminded of its need to "turn" and "obey" (vv. 1, 2, 8, 10).[75] Thus Israel's obligation to obey now and in the future is never lifted from the relationship, despite the divine declaration that Israel has and will again fail to keep faithfulness.

On the other hand, the textual ordering and content provide several ways to uphold the divine initiative in this relationship. The sequence of the narrative describes Israel's initial response in the cursed and dispersed places among the nations as sparked by the דברים which come upon Israel in exile (30:1); even before Yahweh's circumcision, his "words" (things) are an agent of renewal.[76] The "blessing and curse" in these "words" is a rejuvenating witness both to Yahweh's righteous judgment (the curses), and also to his רחם through which Israel can turn and Yahweh again שׂושׂ (delight) in blessing Israel as he did with "your fathers" (v. 9).[77] As covenant breakers, they will not have the right to שׁוּב, except that these דברים recall Yahweh's nature as one who restores unworthy apostates (cf. Exod 34:6). Israel's first turning is not out of nothing, but an effect of the דברים working this truth in their "hearts" (לבבך) to renew a right understanding of their predicament. This is the same prophetic purpose of the witness in Deuteronomy 32 (see below) wherein Israel's heart and mind are restored and awakened to truth as she responds by turning to Yahweh.

The heart of the passage (vv. 3–7) also exalts the priority of Yahweh's gracious restoration. These verses relate an exhaustive chain of divine restorative activity as Yahweh is made the subject of at least eight restorative verbs: שׁוּב (2x), קבץ (2x), רחם, לקח, יטב, בוא, רבה and מול. The last of these (מול, "circumcise") is used as an emphatic transformation of the command in 10:16 where Israel was initially required to "circumcise the foreskin of your heart". In that context (chapters 9–10) Israel's history testifies to her "stiff-necked" nature and an unwillingness to remain faithful. In this later and future context (30:6), Yahweh becomes the agent of renewing the hearts of a scattered nation. In other words, Yahweh's divine grace in circumcision encompasses Israel's own moral inabilities.[78]

Surely there is an inherent ambiguity to this mutual turning which must be sustained over against the tendency to find a NT Pauline reading doctrine of repentance here. The rhetorical ambiguity extends throughout Deuteronomy which revels in mystery, or as Olson says, is laden with "jux-

---

[75] *Deuteronomy*, 268.

[76] See Driver, *Deuteronomy*, 329.

[77] Exod 34:6–7 and Deut 28:63 present the dialectical relationship between Yahweh's just judgment and Yahweh's loving compassionate restoration with overturns the place of the guilty.

[78] Lemke, "Circumcision", 310, 315.

tapositions or paradoxes" of "*divine determination* and *human freedom*".[79] Specifically, Deuteronomy recalls both the need for Israel to circumcise (10:16) and Yahweh to circumcise (30:6); the obedience to things "*very difficult*" (29:22–28) and "*not difficult*" (30:11–14); Yahweh to circumcise and restore and Israel to "choose life" (30:6, 19); and things secret and things revealed (29:29).[80] The combination of these factors allows us to affirm the sense of Yahweh's all-compassing grace and yet an underlying tension grounded in Israel's call to obey in the light of past and future failure. The point is that even in the face of an "anti-Exodus" to a "new Egypt," Israel is never extracted from her place in a journey – and thus her participation – in Yahweh's gift of land and life.[81] The ambiguity and "secret things" in this extended context must, therefore be preserved, in order not to deprive Deuteronomy of its *present* hortatory/rhetorical force of demanding a choice.[82] As we will see now, the inattention to this hortatory objective can often distort the present concerns in 30:11–20 and the epistemological intentions of this text to make Yahweh present and known here and now.[83]

(2) Deuteronomy 30:11–14. Barker's extended study of Israel's faithless character represents some of the closest analysis of this difficult text. As far as possible, I will summarise his findings and indicate areas of disagreement which relate to Deuteronomy's epistemological impact for readers and hearers at Horeb, Moab and Canaan.

Verses 11–14 are typically regarded as a legal aside, apparently reverting to the present,[84] though Barker views it as a continuation of the future oriented prophecy in 30:1–11. I suggest that the rhetoric demands an understanding of circumcision that is present and continual and not merely eschatological. Diminishing the present setting only subverts Deuteronomy's emphatic intention to highlight the divine goodness of the torah over against the backdrop of Israel's moral/volitional impotence. The text is enclosed by two pairs of opposites:

30:11

כִּי הַמִּצְוָה הַזֹּאת אֲשֶׁר אָנֹכִי מְצַוְּךָ הַיּוֹם לֹא־נִפְלֵאת הִוא מִמְּךָ וְלֹא
רְחֹקָה הִוא׃

30:14

כִּי־קָרוֹב אֵלֶיךָ הַדָּבָר מְאֹד בְּפִיךָ וּבִלְבָבְךָ לַעֲשֹׂתוֹ׃ ס

[79] Olson, "Theology", 209.

[80] Ibid., 209. Cf. Braulik, "Law as Gospel", 12.

[81] Millar, "Place", 80.

[82] What McConville, *Deuteronomy*, 428 calls the "double function" of exhortation to present and future generations. The same choice in light of past failure is used in Psalm 78:5–8.

[83] Cf. Barker, "Israel". Barker does uphold the "ambiguity" in this text, but his reading is predominantly pessimistic, (pp. 241–43) – as it is in the books of the divided kingdom. However, in Deuteronomy, it is more ambiguous and even hopeful for the present generation.

[84] Craigie, *Deuteronomy*, 364; McConville, *Deuteronomy*, 429; and idem. *Grace*, 136–7. See below.

The focus of these pairs is to describe this מצוה and this דבר as something "not far" and "near" and something "not too difficult" that Israel "can do".[85] In what follows, it is necessary to consider carefully the integration of exegetical and theological factors which relate to the *doability* of the torah, the nearness or farness of the command, and the corresponding nature of "righteousness" in Deuteronomy.

(i) Doability and Difficulty. Verse 11 states that the commandment is לא־נפלאת, drawing on a word that is typically reserved for the mysterious or powerful acts of God.[86] In Deuteronomy, the root פלא has already been used to describe the powerful acts of Yahweh (28:59) and the judgment of cases "too difficult" for the Israelites that must be resolved by the Levitical Priests and judges (17:8–9). Though Barker does not follow the connection, it is not insignificant that priests as supervisors and handlers of the torah (17:18; 31:9, 24–25) should be able to judge righteously when cases are יפלא ממך (17:8). So it is certainly possible that the extended context, combined with the rarity of פלא, here elevates the *doability* of righteousness within this community as provided in the torah. The more prominent and central implication of the verse is its contrast to the "hidden things" in 29:29[28] wherein the מצוה (v. 11) or דבר (v. 14) represents the "revealed things" which are given "that you might do all the words of this law" (29:29) or "to do it" (30:14).[87] That is, in both passages this torah ("word") is something already given to Israel and already judged doable for past and present generations. This places the rhetorical concerns of the text in the present potential for torah-keeping in the land.

It is also necessary to resolve the "difficulty" in vv. 11–13 – from which this torah is free – and through which we gain a sharper perspective of the kind of problems Israel really faces. "Not too difficult" is often taken as ease of "understanding" the commandments.[88] Yet, we must remember Deuteronomy's counter-cultural interest to oppose ancient foreign law codes which proclaimed distant and inaccessible laws.[89] These laws, by contrast, are near and doable for Israel, which reflects the uniqueness of this God's presence. The references to "mouth" and "heart" (6:5–9) probably signal not the complexity of the law, but the essential intention for this law to encompass Israel's whole identity.[90] As such, Moses' present rhetorical assertion is that the law is "not [...] impossibly idealistic, impracticable, un-

85 Where מצוה signifies the whole Mosaic corpus in Deuteronomy Braulik, "Ausdrücke", 26–8.
86 Barker, "Israel", 227.
87 Sternberg, *Poetics*, 49.
88 Driver, *Deuteronomy*, 330; Thompson, *Deuteronomy*, 286; Merrill, *Deuteronomy*, 391; Keil/Delitzsch, "Pentateuch", 977.
89 Cairns, *Deuteronomy*, 265; Thompson, *Deuteronomy*, 286.
90 Driver, *Deuteronomy*, 331; Merrill, *Deuteronomy*, 391.

achievable".[91] The fault is not with the torah or its standards, but must lie within Israel's own nature. Yahweh and his torah are near, but Israel will not have them.

In the light of these present rhetorical interests, we can see how Barker's notion of doability impinges on his understanding of law-keeping and "righteousness". In the context of 30:15–20, Barker asserts that doing the torah is a matter of "trust", yet in verses 1–14, his interest in harmonising the text with Paul's eschatological conclusions in Romans 10 leads him to conceive of the righteousness of law-keeping as a matter of perfect compliance. This is because, contrary to the majority of interpreters, Barker's interests in NT theology compel him to limit the doability of the torah only to a future context of the circumcised heart by the Spirit of God.[92] This leads him to sense a dilemma between two views of doability:

> One view is that Israel's capacity to obey derives from its having received, learnt, and understood the torah which has been given to it. That is, the grounds are external to Israel, and involve both the easiness of the torah and its revelation The second view is that Israel's capacity to obey rests on a change of heart which enables obedience. In this case, the grounds are internal to Israel. Given our argument above that vv1–10 and vv11–14 are complementary, we argue for the latter of these two views.[93]

But this dilemma is foreign to Deuteronomy and misunderstands the rhetoric and theological nature of the torah for Israel. Deuteronomy's rhetoric portrays a power of these דברים and this תורה which actualise the realities of Yahweh's presence at Horeb.[94] They therefore appeal to Israel by the very fact that they can be on the heart (Deut 6:6; 11:18) as the principle agent of both Yahweh's presence and Yahweh's transformation. Receiving, learning and understanding the torah are not pitted against Deuteronomy's rhetoric of internal transformation, but are central to its aim; "in your mouth and in your heart" (v. 14) is the external torah made internal and transforming.[95]

There are further reasons to see this doability in a present context. Moses speaks to the present generation about the commandment given "today" (היום, v. 11) that is "not too difficult" (cf. 29:29). I agree with Barker, that the מול of the heart by Yahweh in 30:6 envisions a future and prophetic

---

91 Wright *Deuteronomy*, 290. He goes on to express this understanding in the mind of the psalmists who understood their righteousness in the law as "neither exaggerated nor exceptional. They arise from the natural assumption that ordinary people can indeed live in a way that is broadly pleasing to God and faithful to God's law, and that they can do so is a matter of joy and delight." Cf. also Brueggemann s "doable" *Deuteronomy*, 270 and Fretheim, "Law", 192 as opposed to von Rad's almost thoughtless "easy to obey", which does not tie the statement into the context *Deuteronomy*, 184.

92 "Israel", 229, 235. Cf also Braulik, "Law as Gospel", 14.. Note that Christians today admit to the same struggles with keeping the law.

93 "Israel", 222.

94 O'Donovan, *DN*, 151–53.

95 Braulik, *Deuteronomium*, 219; McConville, *Deuteronomy*, 429; Mayes, *Deuteronomy*, 370; Tigay, *Deuteronomy*, 286.

change of heart by which faithfulness to the torah will be kept; but we must be careful not to race past Moses' rhetoric to Pauline theology. What *does* Moses want to communicate to a generation who *is now* in a position of renewing grace to journey into the promised land? If the implicit value of this text is truly pessimistic,[96] as opposed to rhetorically pessimistic, then Moses' exhortations have little or no force.[97] But Deuteronomy 29–30 emphatically declares that Israel can keep this good torah today. Her failures, meanwhile, testify to her stiff-necked nature in Deuteronomy 1–30 (cf. Numbers) and her unwillingness to obey. The rhetoric of ability but unwillingness is meant to provoke Israel to obey and to turn to Yahweh in faith for help.

(ii) Nearness. This present doability also has a dimension of nearness (and "not far") in verses 11 and 14. Predictably for Barker, these are future oriented concepts which envision not divine incarnation but "rather" messianic death and resurrection symbolised by the eschatological circumcision of the heart in 30:6.[98] This offers a helpful corrective to readings which limit nearness only to divine incarnation. Yet I believe his future oriented reading leads him to overlook the obvious theophanic connections of the torah to Horeb, God's "glory" and to creation. The present hortatory force is empowered by the potential for present actualisation of the divine presence at Horeb[99] and this allows us to say, from a NT perspective, not "rather," but messianic transformation *and* eschatological incarnational nearness.[100]

(iii) Our understanding of nearness also goes back to what we have said about the "righteousness" of the torah when it is obeyed. For Barker, righteousness in Deuteronomy is "not an act but an attitude".[101] This is a false dilemma. There is a strong intertextual relationship between the "nearness" (קרב) of this דבר (v. 14) and the nearness of Yahweh (and righteousness of this law) when Israel obeys and keeps "all this torah" (4:5–8).[102] Indeed, the concept of "righteousness" (צדקה) is an emerging concept in the Pentateuch. Abraham is "counted" righteous for believing God's covenant promise in

---

96 "The exhortation does not presuppose Israel's ability." Barker, "Israel", 256.

97 Cf. to Joshua's speech where rhetorical pessimism (Josh 24:19) leads to a renewed response (v. 21).

98 Barker, "Israel", 231.

99 Cf. the exaltation of Sinai over Bashan as a symbol of presence in Psalm 68:7–18. See also A.A. Das, *Paul and the Jews* (Peabody, MA: Hendrickson, 2003), 80 for the connection between theophany, glory and redemption in Paul's theology of Messiah.

100 One wonders if an overemphasis on atonement theology has obscured the concerns with the larger theme of the restored created order R.F. Brown, "On the Necessary Imperfection of Creation: Iranaeus' *Adversus Haereses* IV, 38", *SJT* 28 (1975) 17–25. (25), has argued that "Pauline-Augustinian assumptions" have so elevated atonement and redemption theology that we have lost the re-creational role and function torah and the incarnate divine. Cf. also Rae, "Creation", 291.

101 Barker, "Israel", 94.

102 Cairns, *Deuteronomy*, 265; MacDonald, *Deuteronomy*, 79. 199; Millar, "Place", 182; Miller, *Deuteronomy*, 56, 215; Mayes, *Deuteronomy*, 370; Wright, *Deuteronomy*, 291.

Genesis 15:6. Yet Yahweh's statements to Abraham's visitors in Genesis 18 reaffirm Abraham's and Israel's means for blessing the nations by "doing *righteousness* and justice" (לעשׂת צדקה ומשׁפט, vv. 17–19). In other words, Abraham's mission in Genesis is to bring a trusting righteousness to the nations by keeping the *way* of Yahweh; it unites believing with obeying. As argued in chapter 3 above, obedience to the torah is a witness of Yahweh's nearness and the law's righteousness (צדק) (Deut 4:5–8).[103] Furthermore, Moses instructs parents to tell their children that careful obedience (שׁמר לעשׂות) will be "righteousness for us" (צדקה תהיה לנו, 6:25). The striking contrast when Israel is reminded that it is "not because of your righteousness" (לא בצדקתך) that Yahweh is giving the land (9:5–6) reminds Israel that they have never achieved the aims of the torah. But it does not in any way remove obedience from the concept righteousness. Like Genesis, Deuteronomy envisions law-keeping of this torah as righteousness which blesses and impresses the nations, yet sustains the necessity of faithful trust at the heart of righteousness itself.[104] Barker offers a Christian interpretation of Paul in Romans 3:21–30 and 10:5–8 where the righteousness of the law finds its *telos* in Christ. But that conclusion is not in Deuteronomy; instead we have a torah, as an agent of internalisation, with the power to reproduce both divine presence and obedient righteousness – an attitude distinguished by its acts. The torah psalms (Pss 1, 19, 50, 119) also refer to the law on the heart as an expression of righteousness that can come with faithfulness to torah.[105] The pessimism here is focused on Israel's prideful unwillingness to follow Yahweh in the past.[106] The imagery, then, has as much to do with humanity's refusal to imitate Yahweh in the garden as it does with a Messiah who will embody that imitation perfectly himself.

(3) 30:15–20. In the final section of this chapter, Moses makes a last appeal for Israel to choose the right path. The text combines the previous themes of faithfulness as trust and faithfulness as obedience from 30:1–14[107] where the liminal imagery provokes the need to choose between the path of "life", "good", and "blessing" or "death", "evil" and "curse" (vv. 15, 19). The good and righteous world of life in the land remains Deuteronomy's ideal picture of existence to which Israel is meant to aspire.

---

[103] Certainly, it is the statutes and ordinances which the nations proclaim as righteous (4:8), but the condition is that Israel has obeyed it in their sight (4:5).

[104] McConville, *Deuteronomy*, 116; Wright, *Deuteronomy*, 291.

[105] See Wright, *Deuteronomy*, 291.

[106] See A.A. Das, *Paul, the Law, and the Covenant* (Peabody, MA: Hendrickson, 2001), 94.

[107] On Israel's obligation to love (אהב, vv. 6, 16, 20) Barker says, Israel is "not so much deciding to do something as to receive something" (251–2), but he later confirms, "The priority lies with divine grace, though human responsibility is not lost" (256). Better to say that Israel is *receiving* the call and power to *perform* her created role.

The call to decision in 30:19 centres on the two worlds set before Israel where she is exhorted to "choose" (בחר)[108] life (cf. Josh 24:15). With this choice, "heaven and earth" are called as a "witness" against Israel. This recalls our original framework of Deuteronomy 29–32 and the three witnesses proscribed for Israel. A future covenant renewal in the land records the same principle when Joshua writes the previous events in the "book of the law" and sets up a stone to witness Israel's choice to obey (Josh 24:25–28). The ceremony in the book of Joshua draws out a panoramic view of torah, not just as law, but as the ongoing drama of Israel's covenant relationship with Yahweh which acts as a storied witness to future generations.

In Deuteronomy, the transformation of Moses' words to a torah-sepher establishes the second of three witnesses against Israel for her future disobedience (31:26) followed by the recalling of heaven and earth as an inclusio to the sermon (31:28). Chapter 30, therefore, serves as a rhetorical climax to the second witness (Moses' book) by opposing the doability and nearness of the torah (the means to actualise Israel's past realities) against Israel's own unfaithful inclination. This tension is sustained in Moses' song as the third and final witness which he is commanded to write in 31:21. As we will now see, this song reiterates the moral implications of Israel's failure to ground her knowledge in actualisation of the past.

3.1.2 The Song as a Witness to Morally Culpable Knowledge

According to Luyten, the song of Moses is "the most complex composition" of all the historical psalms in the OT.[109] Its form is an extended lawsuit (ריב), composed as a hymn of six to eight stanzas.[110] The hymn is also remarkably poetic, with 22 lines corresponding to the Hebrew alphabet.[111] The detail and imagery in these lines portray Moses at his very best – rhetorically and theologically. What is most significant for our purposes is that the song not only embraces the ריב structure, but much like the ancient treaty forms, Deuteronomy encompasses it with a vision of humanity recreated in cosmic vocation.[112] Making note of the witness theme, the hymn can be outlined as follows:

---

[108] It is significant that בחר is used 31 times in Deuteronomy, 29 of which Yahweh is the subject (cf. 23:17). Israel is now intended to choose Yahweh who has already chosen them (7:6). See Barker, "Israel", 238–9.

[109] J. Luyten, "Primeval and Eschatological Overtones in the Song of Moses (Dt 32:1–43)", in N. Lohfink (ed.), *Das Deuteronomium* (Leuven: Leuven University, 1985) 141–7, on p. 141.

[110] Cf. P.W. Skehan, "The Structure of the Song of Moses in Deuteronomy (32:1–43)", in Christensen (ed.), *Song* (1993) 156–68, on pp. 164–67; McConville, *Deuteronomy*, 451; Luyten, "Overtones", 341–44; Wright, *Deuteronomy*, 297–8.

[111] See Skehan, "Song", 167.

[112] McConville, *Deuteronomy*, 451. See also Luyten, "Overtones", 347 C.J.H. Wright, *Deuteronomy* (NIBC; Peabody, MA: Hendrickson, 1996), 297–8. But cf. G.E. Mendenhall, "Samuel's 'Broken *Rîb*: Deuteronomy 32", in Christensen (ed.), *Song* (1993) 169–80, on pp. 178–9 who labels the song a later "prophetic oracle" and neither a lawsuit or wisdom hymn.

32:1–3 Calling 'Heaven and Earth' as 'Witness' (עד) to Guilt
32:4–6 The Folly of Immoral Knowledge
32:7–14 Historical testimony
32:15–26 Indictment and Sentence
32:28–33 The Self-Deception of Immoral Knowledge
32:34–43 Vengeance and Divine Glory in the Primordial Design[113]

In going beyond the basic lawsuit format (32:1–26), Deuteronomy fashions its own version of Israel's history with Yahweh setting it within the larger scope of God's purposes in the created order. The poem's many wisdom themes are apparent both through the echoes of the creation myth and in God's condemnation of Israel's "foolishness" for failing to acknowledge their created purpose.

The song achieves its poetic and theological power primarily by appropriating mythical language and imagery from Genesis 1–11. Fisch's illuminating study analyses the extensive intertextual allusions and echoes between Deuteronomy 32 and Genesis 1–19 (creation, flood, dispersal of the nations, and Sodom and Gomorrah).[114] Thus Israel is indicted for following the path from creation (purpose and design) to faithlessness, dispersion and destruction: the path of death and curse (cf. Deut 30:15, 19).

The song begins by appealing to the "heavens" and the "earth" (Deut 32:1; Gen 1:1) as witnesses[115] to Yahweh's "teaching" which comes as rain and showers on the דשא and עשב (Deut 32:2; Gen 1:11–12).[116] Then the song calls Israel corrupt (שחת, 32:5), paralleling שחת as both "corruption" and "destruction" in the Flood narrative (Gen 6:11, 12, 13, 17; 9:11, 15). שחת is also used in the destruction of Sodom and Gomorrah (Gen 18:28, 31, 32) which is recalled in Deuteronomy 32:32. Sodom and Gomorrah also share the use of both אש (Deut 32:22; Gen 19:24) and the חפך of the people (Deut 32:20; Gen 19:21, 25, 29). Finally, the parallels extend to the drinking of "wine" יין in corruption (Gen 9:21, 24; 19:32–35; Deut 32:33) and the separation of the nations or peoples (Gen 10:5, 19; Deut 32:8).

The mythical language thus situates Israel's election and redemption within God's original cosmic designs for humanity. Like Adam and Eve, Israel was created קנה, made עשה, and established כון by God (32:6). Echoing Genesis 1:2, she was found in a chaos of a desert land and a "howling waste of wilderness" (32:10). She took path away from life in the garden to

---

113 There is little agreement on the structure. Craigie's divisions are possible but arbitrarily break up the flow of individual units *Deuteronomy*, 376–89. Cf. to Skehan's threefold division (1–14; 15–29; 30–43 "Song", 153–55.

114 In Fisch, *Poetry*, 55–79. See especially pp. 68–77. Sonnet, *Book*, 176. also uses Fisch to make these same connections.

115 Boston, "Influence", 198 notes that the heavens and earth are invoked eleven times in the OT – four times as witnesses – but only in Deut 32:1 to "hear".

116 These are the only occurrences of דשא in the Pentateuch and the only occasions where it is paired with עשב.

the path of death, dispersal and destruction.[117] Her failure to obey the torah thus amounts to dereliction of her created "vocation" in the world.[118] The condemning power in this passage comes from the way Israel is imagined like Adam and Eve, singled out to walk in fellowship with God (32:9). Israel's failure is thus the same as Adam and Eve's infidelity in the garden; it is not just a personal or even a national demise, but a refusal to carry out God's ultimate design for humanity (Gen 1:28–30).

3.1.3 Moral Wisdom in the Created Order

The wisdom-creation discourse sets Israel's future disobedience in the context of epistemological and moral guilt. This is evidenced most clearly in Deuteronomy 32:5–6 and 28–33 where we have strong images of Israel's response to her role within the the created order. Verses 5–6 correspond to similar language in Proverbs 8:22–31 where Yahweh created (קנה) wisdom. Yet here, the association is negative as the Israelites are "no longer sons" of the father who "created" (קנה) them. The indictment is framed in a combination of two sets of accusations. The first places the failure in moral categories where Israel's is "blemished" (מומם) and a "perverse and crooked generation" (דור עקש ופתלתל, v. 5). The second accusation interprets Israel's the moral failures in epistemological terms: "a people foolish and not wise" (עם נבל ולא חכם, v. 6).

This pairing of moral and epistemological categories is even more emphatic in a second passage which comes at the end of Yahweh's indictment and sentencing (vv. 7–26). Here Israel is shown to be like the "corrupt" (שׁחת) nations and the inhabitants of Sodom and Gomorrah who are reputed for their moral guilt. Yahweh's accusation in verses 28–29 again describes Israel in wisdom vocabulary:

כִּי־גוֹי אֹבַד עֵצוֹת הֵמָּה וְאֵין בָּהֶם תְּבוּנָה׃
לוּ חָכְמוּ יַשְׂכִּילוּ זֹאת יָבִינוּ לְאַחֲרִיתָם׃

They lack "counsel" (עצה) and "understanding" (תבונה); if they were "wise" (חכם) they would "perceive" (שׂכל) this and "understand" (בין) their end. There is no mistake that the wisdom tradition, which has the unique capacity to combine knowledge with obedience in the fear of Yahweh, has been appropriated here to articulate the nature of Israel's demise. This fact has attracted endless speculation about a wisdom redaction or a wisdom provenance to Deuteronomy.[119] We must not be distracted from the results of blending wisdom and covenant discourses in this way. Moral and epistemo-

---

[117] Fretheim thus rightly argues that Israel's law is not grounded in covenant or redemption but in the eternal designs of created order and created purpose "Law", 184–8. Cf. also Greidanus, "Dimension", 39–51.

[118] Fretheim, "Law", 184–5.

[119] Cf. Boston, "Influence"; Weinfeld, *D&DS*, 244–81; Brekelmans, "Influence"; Olson, "Theology", 7.

logical corruption are together grounded in the mythical ethos of created order.[120]

As such, these two passages allow us to tie Israel's behaviour directly to her worldview. By exchanging wisdom as virtuous knowledge and the right response to her created purpose, Israel has chosen the foolishness of prideful self-deception.[121] Her choice denies the realities of the created order and consequently rejects her ontological/cosmic role of being a blessing to the nations.

Israel's moral-cognitive failure allows us to expand upon what it means for the song and the book, as witnesses, to function within Israel's trans-generational community. There is certainly a tone of prophetic judgment in this song, but it must also be noted that it "ends with a good miracle",[122] or, in Fretheim's vocation-language it looks to the "openness of the future" to carry out God's work in the world.[123] The sentencing language of the song also performs a constituting function among the people of God as it restores wisdom's view of the created order and thereby preserves them in their place and purpose.[124] Miller says that, "It convicts as it instructs; it instructs as it convicts."[125] Fisch summarises song and witness this way:

> Nostalgia for the Golden Age is not what Moses means by "witness," but rather memory weighted with obligation. Nostalgia does not obligate; it fills the mind with a rosy image tinged with sadness. In that sadness we take a kind of consolation; we hide ourselves in "the soft vestments [...]". Memory is something else, not the ever-returning spring, coming to us again with the perennially blooming lilac, but a naked confrontation with a past that is terribly present in spite of the passage of years. We see the nakedness of Sodom and Gomorrah behind the bloom of Samaria' [...] ēdût [...] implies the recurrent awareness of a responsibility that comes from the individual's isolation from nature.[126]

So, while one can sense the pessimistic overtones at the end of Deuteronomy, that sense is simultaneously judgmental and restorative; "repetition" and not just "recollection".[127] Fisch says of Sodom,

> To remember that overthrow is to remember that it can be itself overthrown [...]. The desert is a place of burning but also of the burning bush [...]. To attend to such witnesses is to be denied the comforts of the pastoral, but there are compensations for

---

[120] Cf. Van Leeuwen, "Liminality", 121.

[121] Westphal, "Christian Philosophers", 217 says, "But everything we have learned from Marx and Freud (not to mention Augustine and Sartre) about self-deception suggests that we are most skillful at doing things without resolving to do them and thus without noticing that we are doing them precisely when we are doing something shameful". See also Wood, *Epistemology*, 61–6.

[122] Fisch, *Poetry*, 78.

[123] Fretheim, "Law", 188, 194.

[124] Kline, *Structure*, 92–3; Fisch, *Poetry*, 64; Cairns, *Deuteronomy*, 290–1.

[125] Miller, *Deuteronomy*, 225.

[126] *Poetry*, 58, 60.

[127] See above and Kirkegaard, *Fear/Repetition*, 131–2.

that as we wait, booted, our loins girded and staff in hand for the next unanticipated stage of the journey.[128]

Deuteronomy's rhetoric continually upholds the goodness of this torah in order that – over the course of the OT – a sharp contrast might be drawn between Israel's sin and the goodness of law.[129]

Returning to the epistemological implications of Israel's past and future rebellion, we find the torah and the song as witnesses – not just to guilt – but to need, grace and ongoing restoration through actualisation into Israel's created role. The pattern is a perpetual cycle. Israel's prideful self-deception is not a point in time, but the ever-present temptation to deny the rhythm of the seasons and the developmental niche designed for Israel to carry out her creative purposes. The "witness" of the song and of the torah bear judgment but also act as a self-reflective tradition in Israel's culture. Deuteronomy clearly informs Israel that she needs more than just a recollection of the past, but daily reflection on the finitude and fallenness of her nature. What she needs is a story that renews her encounter with Yahweh, gives her wisdom and thus restores her to her created purpose.

When we take the witnesses together, we can see that Deuteronomy 30:14 assures Israel not that she *cannot* obey but that she refuses to. The need for God's restoration of his chosen people is not unique to Moab but was evidenced repeatedly in Genesis (Gen 12:10–20; 16:1–6; 28:10–22; 32:9–21). Despite the universal intentions for Israel and humanity, Deuteronomy does not provide philosophical ideals, or a political constitution. Nor does it call for assent to complex theological truths. Instead it demands an attitude of dependence and humility which renews its faith through self-reflection, "turning" to God and obeying the torah. Deuteronomy is not an end in itself, but a major stage in an the OT narrative. In the end, the threat to Israel is not primarily that she will not keep the torah, but that she will refuse to acknowledge the torah-as-divine-presence as the internal heart-transforming agent by which Yahweh makes her stubbornness known to her and restores her freedom to flourish again in her vocation.[130] The witnesses are mirrors which reflect self-deception and the need to turn (30:1–2).

4. Deuteronomy and Beyond: A Book, A People and The Nations

Much like the frame-narrative structures in Job, Proverbs and Qohelet, the end of Deuteronomy solidifies the vision begun in its opening (chapters 1–3). Along the way the book has been drawing a distinction between what

---

[128] Fisch, *Poetry*, 79.

[129] On the necessity for upholding the progressive apprehension of Israel's failure in the OT, see Eichrodt, "Covenant", 317.

[130] Hahn, "Kinship", 98–9 states that the covenant at Moab, signified by the book of Deuteronomy, functions to renew and restore Israel after her failure at Beth Peor (Num 25; Deut 3:29; 4:3–4).

Israel has physically seen and heard and what she has spiritually understood. Anticipating future failures, Yahweh establishes three witnesses to testify to the present truths and knowledge which Israel will deny on her path to moral ruin. Chapters 31–34 leave a trail of concluding themes which strengthen the transition of the events at Moab into a future landscape where two paths offer the alternatives of seeing and seeing truly – of self-deception and faith. By focusing on the characters in these final scenes, we can make some concluding statements about the future which the Deuteronomic theology and rhetoric envision for Israel.

4.1 The Nations: גוים

One way to approach gentile nations in Deuteronomy is through the perspective of variously developing and maturing social and textual traditions.[131] Our concern focuses specifically on the of the narrative in the Pentateuch.[132] As we have seen, there are many factors internal to Deuteronomy which place it within the missional focus of Genesis (12:1–3; 18:18–19; 22:18). In chapter 2 above we demonstrated the international concerns of the knowledge of Yahweh in Exodus 1–15 where both Pharaoh and Egypt will "know" his identity. Deuteronomy reaffirms this universal mission of blessing to the nations which will be achieved in Israel's faithfulness to the torah (4:5–8). The glaring appearance of the חרם command in Deuteronomy 7 and 20 is better read as a rhetoric against evil than a nationalistic rationale for genocide. While it is careless not to reckon with the macabre reality of these laws, we must nevertheless appreciate the fuller social context in which they were given. The nine nations of "near" neighbours are to be eliminated (7:1–2, 24), but the nations surrounding Canaan can be spared if they make peace with Israel (20:10–11). These "far" nations intuitively have to represent the future audience of Israel's righteousness (4:5–8). The חרם command is therefore particularly focused and temporally constrained. Before and beyond this particular event, Deuteronomy stands in line with Israel's universal mission to carry the knowledge of Yahweh to the world. After all, Deuteronomy maintains a concern for the alien in the Sabbath law (5:12) and for all the poor in the land (cf. Deut 15:1–18), not just the Israelites.

Deuteronomy 32:43 is another passage with missiological significance. Unfortunately, the manuscript evidence yields three versions that differ with regard to the source and object of praise. The MT alone calls the גוים to praise Israel or to praise God with Israel whereas the LXX calls upon the

---

[131] Cf. C. Van Houten, *The Alien in Israelite Law* (JSOTSup 107; Sheffield: Sheffield Academic, 1991).
[132] Cf. Fretheim, "Law" and Wright, *Deuteronomy*, 8–17.

"heavens" (οὐρανοί) much like שמים in 4QDeut^{q}.[133] MacDonald's conclusion that the original is "unresolvable", seems quite reasonable.[134] Nevertheless, from what has been said so far, the reading of "nations" is also quite plausible. On contextual grounds, it is entirely possible that the gathering of the nations to praise Yahweh is in line with the cosmic restorative message of this song, especially in light of other OT passages which make the same claims (e.g. 1 Kings 8:41–3, 60; Ps 47:9; 67:1–7; Is 19:21–25).[135] Even if the text is amended along the lines of "heavens," it is significant that those things allotted to the nations for worship (4:19) should now be found praising Yahweh for his sovereignty over all peoples. Even the nations' "gods" praise Yahweh. Either way, the effect of the song only reinforces the cosmic, universal, and ontological aims for Israel – through the torah – in Yahweh's world.

4.2 Moses and his Successors

Just as Israel is the instrument of divine revelation to the nations, Moses has been the instrument of divine revelation to Israel. His death will create a void to be filled through the combination of a book, a song, a people, and Joshua, their leader. Torah, as argued thus far, represents the means to actualise the realities at Horeb and renew future generations. In these final chapters, Yahweh, the people and the torah are all joined in a narrative continuity which promises to sustain Israel in the future.[136]

We should, therefore, not lose sight of Moses' preeminence in the conclusion of the book. Contrary to Polzin who sees Moses' voice as undermined by the narrator,[137] there are several good reasons to see Moses as elevated by the anonymous voice in the frame.[138] For one, the narrator remains "offstage" and admires Moses, saying that "there has not since arisen in Israel a prophet like Moses" (34:10a). Second, the narrator retains Moses' unique access to Yahweh in meeting with him at Horeb (34:9) and seeing the "signs and wonders" in Egypt (34:10).[139] Third, the narrator makes a point of recording Moses' life of 120 years, which, with Genesis 6:3, draws together both the cursed state of post-garden life and the fullness

---

[133] Furthermore, MT has 4 lines while 4QDeut^{q} has 6 and LXX has 8. For a helpful comparison, see MacDonald, *Deuteronomy*, 92–4.

[134] Ibid., 94.

[135] For readings which develop "nations" as a part of the Pentateuchal vision, see McConville, *Deuteronomy*, 450; 459–60; Hahn, "Kinship", 115; Wright, *Deuteronomy*, 304–5 and J. Sailhamer, *The Pentateuch as Narrative: A Biblical-Theological Commentary* (Grand Rapids, MI: Zondervan, 1992), 475.

[136] Ricoeur, "Structure", 27 says, "Every tradition lives by grace of interpretation, and it is at this price that it continues, that is, remains living."

[137] *Moses and the Deuteronomist*, 34–72 (34).

[138] Whose anonymity itself is a sign of respect for Moses.

[139] Olson, *Deuteronomy*, 169; Cf. Sonnet, *Book*, 242; Coats, "Motifs", 185; Hahn, "Kinship", 99.

of life that Moses enjoyed before Yahweh. 120 is three full generations (Judg 3:11; 5:31) and the 3-fold repetition in 9–10, may also "be symbolic of his preeminence".[140] 120 is also more than Joseph's 110-year lifespan and 110 is the number of Egyptian wisdom ideal, which Moses also surpasses.[141] The resonances between Moses' final words and death with Jacob in Genesis 47–49 give him semi-patriarchal status as well.[142] Finally, Moses is a supreme prophet of Yahweh's words who has no equal (34:10–12; cf. 18:15).[143] This supremacy at the end of Deuteronomy reflects primarily upon the transition to Joshua but just as much upon Moses' torah which goes before Israel and upon which Joshua will depend.[144] Moses' authority and access to Yahweh are dispersed through the leadership and family to the entire community.

In the end, Deuteronomy ends with mixed signals. The high note of Moses at the fullness of life emphasises his unique legacy in the very words of Yahweh – written and spoken – that Israel might be able to retain the way to righteousness and divine presence trans-generationally. Likewise, his exaltation (31:2; 34:10–12) reflects the divine authority and transmission of Yahweh's voice in the torah. In the background, his unfaithfulness (32:51) and his mortality (34:5–6) remind Israel of their own unfaithfulness, judgment and need of restoration by the God of this torah.

5. Conclusion

In this chapter, I have argued that the tensions and ambiguities in Deuteronomy represent rhetorical and theological devices which engage readers and give them a sense of urgency. Most significantly, these final chapters *metamorphise* Moses' words from speech to writing, evidenced by the shift in the *Ausdrücke* from דברים to new terms. Chapters 27–31 contain a conspicuous surplus of references to ספר and כתב, where the eight references to ספר account for more than 90% of all uses in Deuteronomy and the twelve uses of כתב more than 50%. In this way, the narrative begins to move from speech to a book, from the fresh torah Moses receives from Yahweh to the

---

140 Cairns, *Deuteronomy*, 271. Cf. Braulik, *Deuteronomium*, 222; McConville, *Deuteronomy*, 477.

141 McConville, *Deuteronomy*, 438, 477; Braulik, *Deuteronomium*, 222.

142 Sonnet, *Book*, 202–9.

143 Driver, *Deuteronomy*, 424–5; Coats, "Motifs"; and Miller, "Moses", 248–50, who says, "By depicting Moses primarily as such a spokesman, the whole Book of Deuteronomy implicitly underscores the identification of prophecy with the communication of the divine word that is commanded. This is consistent with the Deuteronomic emphasis on the priority of the Word of God as the vehicle of divine presence and rule" (248).

144 S.D. McBride, "Polity", 69 calls the torah book a "surrogate for Moses himself." In this way, it connects to, and has the potential to renew the divine relationship (nearness) at Horeb. Cf. Miller, *Deuteronomy*, 56-57; Sonnet, *Book*, 40, 261; Hahn, "Kinship", 99–103.

future torah lived out in nameless generations of Israelites. The historical highlights of the past become liturgically renewed as Israel celebrates and obeys this torah in future generations. What has perhaps been most relevant for us is the way that Deuteronomy progressively imagines Yahweh, then Moses and the people speaking and writing the torah. The chain of imitation around the torah renew the יצר imitation in Genesis as the means to corporate knowledge.

The three witnesses in Deuteronomy 31–32 are also important signs which unite cosmic, epistemological and moral dimensions of the torah. On the one hand the witnesses judge Israel's failures in the past and the future. But the narrative of judgment is also rhetorical, providing the motivation for Israel to tell the story and renew her own identity. With the added tension of Moses' looming death, the torah-book becomes an increasingly necessary means to stay in touch with Israel's and humanity's ultimate purpose. Moses' song serves as one of these witnesses, but adds the unique quality of the wisdom tradition to the rest of the covenant and torah discourse so far. It reinforces the unity of knowledge, ethics and identity evidenced throughout Deuteronomy. But it also provides a helpful bridge to the material in the next two chapters.

CHAPTER SIX

Epistemology in Proverbs

1. Introduction

Here the two lines of our study converge; wisdom meets law. The relationship between the two is complex and has been heavily contested.[1] Even the fact that our study of wisdom begins with Proverbs is problematic, for many believe that the book defies a literary or holistic understanding.[2] In the first chapter, however, we critiqued such perspectives for their failure to give equal weight to the literary, ideological and aesthetic dimensions of the text. Whatever its internal contradictions, the book of Proverbs is an independent discourse, an aesthetic and theological collection which awaits commentary from the full "conflict of interpretations".[3] We have, therefore, chosen an inter-disciplinary hermeneutic for this study, for it provides a way for us to comment on the sophisticated blend of theology, rhetoric and aesthetics in the book.[4] As we shift to a study of epistemology in Proverbs, we will begin with a brief introduction to wisdom in the Old Testament, followed by a structural-theological analysis of Proverbs.

2. Wisdom

One of the goals of this study is to consider whether, and how, each particular use of חכם – and its roots – might be related to the larger theology of

---

1 Cf. J.L. Crenshaw, "Popular Questioning of the Justice of God in Ancient Israel", in idem; *Urgent Advice* (Macon, GA: Mercer, 1995) who describes a consistent "radical" and unpredictable character of God's acts in OT narrative, as seen in Genesis 18 (Abraham and Isaac; and Sodom and Gomorrah), Exodus 32 (Golden calf) and for David in Psalm 89 which contradict the tenets of traditional wisdom. Clements, *Changing World*, 34, 35, 47 sees wisdom as a reaction to the cultic world of torah. Cf. R.E. Murphy, "Assumptions and Problems in Old Testament Wisdom Research", *CBQ* 29 (1967) 407–18, on pp. 414–5.

2 W. McKane, *Proverbs: A New Approach* (OTL; SCM, 1970), 18, says Proverbs cannot "be accommodated within a single theological structure or unitary ethos" because of its tendency to conflicting perspectives (contradictions) on the same circumstances. B. Lang, *Wisdom and the Book of Proverbs* (New York: Pilgrim, 1986), 3, 15, sees a "random collection of didactic discourses" and denies that Proverbs is "a consciously constructed literary work".

3 Van Leeuwen, *Context and Meaning*, 15, says "Only upon the basis of a prior perception of unity of style, theme, language, usage of forms, and so on, is it possible for the critic to declare that a word, line or section is secondary or editorial. For without a clear notion of what *belongs* to a text one cannot judge what is foreign to it." Cf. pp. 30-32.

4 Long before Ricoeur and modern discourse theory, Archer Taylor's classic work *The Proverb* (1931) established the synthetic effects which proverbs take on when they are grouped in literary collections. On the book of Proverbs especially, cf. R. Alter, *The Art of Biblical Poetry* (U.S.A.: Basic Books, 1985), 163, 170–1.

the wisdom movement and genre as a whole. Words by their nature always express some specific and often nuanced meaning within a larger lexical range. Wisdom has the added complexity of being a major theological construct that develops throughout Israel's history. We must, therefore, explore the semantic range of חכם in the OT and then discuss why Proverbs has come to be viewed as the best representation of theological wisdom.

Even when the English "wise" and "wisdom" are being used as a translation for חָכְמָה (wisdom), חָכַם (become wise) and חָכָם (wise), there remains a cultural and semantic complexity in the Hebrew that does not correspond to modern English.[5] Owing to Greek influence, the English words refer primarily to intellectual categories. Fox thus defines wisdom as "the power of the human mind, both in its faculties and in the knowledge it can gain, hold and transmit. Wisdom both transcends the individual mind and resides within it".[6] But the חכם word group also expresses a comprehensive association of intellect, morality and skill.[7] More importantly, in most OT contexts, and for the wisdom material especially, wisdom, morality and skill are inseparably bound together.[8] Fox rightly identifies the "heart" as the seat of wisdom,[9] preserving the whole-person aspect of חכמה in the wisdom literature.[10] Wisdom can, therefore, equally apply to priests (Exod 28:3), craftsmen (Exod 31:6; 36:1-2), dream interpreters (Gen 41:29; Dan 2), traders (Ezek 28:4), and sagacity (2 Sam 13:3; Ezek 28:5).

The range in wisdom's semantic domain has led to a corresponding diversity within the history of interpretation. This is partly due to the fact that חכמה is difficult to define in a way that captures all of its OT uses.[11] Many scholars have thus pursued the historical and stylistic or semantic development of wisdom along the lines of historical-critical theories.[12] Fox's

---

5 M.V. Fox, "Wisdom in Qohelet", in L.G. Perdue/B.B. Scott/W.J. Wiseman (ed.), *In Search of Wisdom: Essays in Memory of John G. Gammie* (Louisville, KY: Westminster John Knox, 1993) 115–31, on pp. 115–6.

6 M.V. Fox, *Proverbs 1–9: A New Translation with Introduction and Commentary* (AB; New York: Doubleday, 2000), 3.

7 G.H. Wilson, "חכם", in W.A. VanGemeren (ed.), *NIDOTTE, 5 Vols. 2* (Grand Rapids/Carlisle, UK: Zondervan/Paternoster, 1997) 130–4.

8 Fox, "Wisdom in Qohelet", 116.

9 M.V. Fox, "Qohelet's Epistemology", *HUCA* 58/1 (1987) 137–55, on p. 143.

10 The heart (לב) designates more than the intellect in the wisdom literature, but includes the whole human orientation (Ps 111:10; Prov 4:23). See Bartholomew, *Reading*, 235 and E.S. Christianson, *A Time to Tell: Narrative Strategies in Ecclesiastes* (Sheffield: Sheffield Academic, 1998), 183–6.

11 J.A. Gladson, *Retributive Paradoxes in Proverbs 10–29* (Ann Arbor, MI: University Microfilms International, 1979), 62 suggests that "wisdom has an irreducible complexity about it".

12 R. Whybray, *The Intellectual Tradition in the Old Testament* (Berlin/New York: Walter de Gruyter, 1974), 3–4. There are many strengths in this work which can be put to use in a synchronic reading without unnecessarily assuming that wisdom must be grouped into old and late categories as does G.v. Rad, *Wisdom in Israel* (London: SCM, 1970), 11–2. Many of the sophisticated aspects of wisdom such as order and personification have been shown to be quite early, see K. Kitchen, *Ancient Orient and Old Testament* (Chicago: Inter-Varsity Press, 1966), 126. Wisdom was most likely applied contextually in the progression of Israel's history.

research on Qohelet develops the possibility of an author modifying the traditional sense of חכמה in order to organise experiences rationally.[13] Fontaine hypothesises that, because of the many possible linguistic and cultural origins of wisdom, several shades of meaning appear in the book of Proverbs alone.[14]

It is not our aim to resolve these problems, but rather to draw upon voices which have been muted in recent decades of research. Van Leeuwen's efforts to circumscribe the wisdom literature is perhaps the most fruitful way of moving us forward.[15] He suggests that wisdom has four "aspects, none of which may be lacking." Wisdom (1) "presupposes the fear of Yahweh/God", (2) "entails insight into and practice of generic patterns and norms for creation and creatures", (3) "entails knowledge of and appropriate action with reference to particular circumstances, institutions, persons and other creatures" and (4) "is traditional."[16]

3. Introducing Structure and Theology in Proverbs

Van Leeuwen's four aspects of wisdom are more easily identified in Proverbs than in the rest of the wisdom literature. Proverbs is, after all, a traditional didactic book, and most scholars recognize that the book aims to present wisdom in clear and persuasive way. The first nine chapters weave together cosmic images from Israel's mythical worldview[17] and parental (traditional), and liminal rhetoric from the parents instruction. Chapters 10–29 contain the bulk of the individual sayings whose role is to work out the

---

[13] M.V. Fox, *A Time to Tear Down and a Time to Build Up: A Rereading of Ecclesiastes* (Grand Rapids, MI/Cambridge: Eerdmans, 1999), 77 See next next chapter for a more extensive discussion of Qohelet's wisdom.

[14] C.R. Fontaine, "Wisdom in Proverbs", in L.G. Perdue/B.B. Scott/W.J. Wiseman (ed.), *In Search of Wisdom: Essays in Memory of John G. Gammie* (Louisville, KY: Westminster John Knox, 1993) 99–114, on p. 111.

[15] R.C. Van Leeuwen, "Wisdom Literature", in K.J. Vanhoozer/C.G. Bartholomew/Trier. Daniel/N. Wright (ed.), *Dictionary for Theological Interpretation of the Bible* (Grand Rapids, MI: Baker, 2005) 847–50.

[16] Ibid., 848–49.

[17] L.G. Perdue, "Wisdom in the Book of Job", in L.G. Perdue/B.B. Scott/W.J. Wiseman (ed.), *In Search of Wisdom: Essays in Memory of John G. Gammie* (Louisville, KY: Westminster John Knox, 1993) 73–98, on pp. 73–9; R. Scott, "The Study of the Wisdom Literature", *Interpretation* 24 (1970) 20–45, on p. 29; M.V. Fox, "The Innerstructure of Qohelet's Thought", in A.A. Schoors (ed.), *Qohelet in the Context of Wisdom* (Leuven, Belgium: Leuven University, 1998) 225–38, on p. 235, suggests "theoretical scaffolding", and Van Leeuwen a "map of reality" "Liminality and Worldview in Proverbs 1–9", *Semeia* 50 (1990) 111–44, on p. 111.

Clements' description of the wisdom worldview also connects wisdom with the ontology of creation, and therefore with all the nations of humanity; wisdom becomes universalised, *Changing World*, 20. Yet Clements fails to acknowledge the very explicit context of wisdom for Israel. By centring wisdom on the fear of יהוה, the God of creation, the writers of Proverbs contextualise wisdom within covenantal language. Torah is not explicitly abandoned.

wisdom worldview in the particularities of life. Chapters 30–31 close the book by again mixing cosmic themes with timely and local particularity.[18]

The common root for cosmic and practical forms of wisdom, as is typical in the ANE, is in the mythical worldview of creation and the created order.[19] On the one hand this worldview is grounded in a Yahwistic theology.[20] The ירא יהוה phrase occurs fourteen times in the book and has been carefully placed at key structural transitions to condition wisdom and guide it within theological boundaries (1:7, 29; 2:5; 8:13; 10:27; 14:27; 15:33; 19:23; 22:4; 31:30). Meanwhile, this phrase complements a theology of creation which runs throughout these chapters. The most direct statement in is Proverbs 3:18–20. Wisdom, as a cosmic feminine figure, promises to be a "tree of life" to those who "seize" her (3:18). Proverbs 3:19a then declares:

יְהוָה **בְּחָכְמָה יָסַר־אָרֶץ** כּוֹנֵן שָׁמַיִם בִּתְבוּנָה׃

The fact that wisdom is God's agent for creation (יצר) authenticates her ability to guide humanity into the whole moral-vocational realm of life in the world.[21] These two central tenets in Proverbs 1–9, the ירא יהוה phrase and its corresponding context of the created order, encourage readers to embrace Proverbs' worldview as a foundation for learning wisdom. O'Donovan says, "Wisdom, then, is not merely about creation order in the abstract. It is about the disclosure of creation order to the inquiring, believing and patient observer. It is about a painful process of making plain, which has, in its own terms, the character of a journey and a discovery."[22]

In summary, Proverbs 1–9 and 31 create an envelope for the book and situate the bulk of the individual proverbs within the cosmic, mythical worldview of created order. This symbolic, ideal wisdom is balanced by the

---

[18] Van Leeuwen, *Proverbs*, 24 is among others who see chapters 1–9 and 31 as an "interpretive frame".

[19] The relationship between wisdom and creation was first significantly developed by W. Zimmerli, "The Place and Limit of Wisdom in the Framework of Old Testament Theology", *SJT* 17 (1964) 146–58, and then more extensively by von Rad, *Wisdom*, 144–76. See also H. Schmid, "Creation, Righteousness, and Salvation", in B.W. Anderson (ed.), *Creation in the Old Testament* (Philadelphia/London: Fortress/SPCK, 1984 (Original in ZTK, 1973)) 102–17, on pp. 106–7; R.E. Murphy, *The Tree of Life: An Explanation of Biblical Wisdom Literature* (New York: Doubleday, 1990), 118–21.

[20] According to Van Leeuwen, *Proverbs*, 33, "With very few exceptions, Proverbs refers to God as [...] (Yahweh), the God who made covenant with Israel and lead the people through history [...]. The editors of Proverbs are very consistent in avoiding the suggestion that the God of the sages is any other than Israel's covenant God, Yahweh [...]. Perhaps the consistent use of 'Yahweh' was meant to forestall the idea that the God of Proverbs was not Israel's covenant God." The dating of the "Yahweh-Additions" as outlined by R. Whybray, *The Composition of the Book of Proverbs* (JSOTSup; Sheffield: JSOT, 1994), 61, 131, are discussed below.

[21] Van Leeuwen, "Liminality", 113 develops the idea of creation as the ground to a "Yahwistic worldview". Cf. Zimmerli, "Place and Limit", 151–3.

[22] O. O'Donovan, "Response to Craig Bartholomew", in C.G. Bartholomew, et al., *A Royal Priesthood?: The Use of the Bible Ethically and Politically* (Carlisle, UK/Grand Rapids, MI: Paternoster/Zondervan, 2002) 113–5, on p. 113.

more realistic material in chapters 10–29, where we encounter images of wisdom in the everyday world. The framing function of chapters 1–9 and 31, then, create the hermeneutic within which to wisdom interprets its way between experience and the created reality.[23] This allows the book to make an artistic portrayal of wisdom which grounds the moral order in the created order. Our aim now is to draw out the richness of this portrait.

4. Proverbs 1–9 and 31

Whybray suggests that wisdom developed throughout Israel's history such that autonomous human reason was gradually aligned with the gift of God's wisdom as expressed in Proverbs 1–9. This historical reading has since been questioned by literary readings which situate the chapters as a thematic introduction to the book.[24] It is increasingly acknowledged that the stylistic, thematic and linguistic features of the wise woman who fears Yahweh in Proverbs 31 form an obvious thematic inclusio for the extended proverb-poems and themes in chapters 1–9.[25] Even Whybray has since described these "affinities" as "unmistakable," creating a "framework" for the entire collection.[26] The effect, as argued here, is that the first nine chapters confront the reader or listener with a large scale divine map of reality, or worldview, which is grounded in the created order and communicated through a "coherence of metaphors".[27] The wise woman's behaviour in chapter 31 serves as an "embedded representation"[28] which exemplifies and summarises the hermeneutical process envisioned in chapters 1–30. That is, by interweaving several metaphors, chapters 1–9 lure the reader into a wisdom journey that encounters various circumstances before culminating in the ideal actualisation of wisdom of chapter 31.

The enticing capacity of the metaphors in Proverbs 1–9 are a central part of the proverbial worldview and essential to understanding its message. Perdue helpfully incorporates sociological tools to describe this performa-

---

[23] As O'Donovan, *Resurrection*, 87 argues, human knowledge of reality comes by "participation" in the created order and not by the "transcendence" of a disengaged knower.

[24] Whybray, *Intellectual Tradition*, 8. See also M.V. Fox, "Ideas of Wisdom in Proverbs 1–9", *JBL* 116 (1997) 613–33 and L.G. Perdue, *Proverbs* (Interpretation; Louisville, KY: John Knox, 2000), 62–3.

[25] See Wolters, *Valiant Woman*, 41 and Van Leeuwen, *Proverbs*, 263–4.

[26] *Composition of Proverbs*, 161, 159. See also his *The Book of Proverbs: A Survey of Modern Study* (Leiden: Brill, 1995), 110 where he shows that, although this parallel between 1–9 and 31 is increasingly accepted, there is no consensus on the meaning of the relationship. C.V. Camp, *Wisdom and the Feminine in the Book of Proverbs* (Sheffield: Almond, 1985), 186–208 calls 1–9 and 31 an "interpretive framework" to the book.

[27] Van Leeuwen, "Liminality", 111.

[28] Or, *duplication intérieure*; see Sonnet, *Book*, 79–80.

tive aspect in Proverbs as a "liminal" context where individuals and groups repeatedly encounter the two realms of "structure" and "anti-structure".[29]

The sociology of liminality creates an important bridge between ancient wisdom and law. In the case of wisdom, we can describe Proverbs 1–9 as a liminal beginning to a journey. Van Leeuwen thus appeals to liminality to link the array of metaphors (feminine, journey, and creational) with the structure and boundaries they represent on the wisdom journey.[30] Together these images represent a progression over and between the proper boundaries (ways, women, roads and houses) toward the way of life and not death, wisdom and not folly.[31] Epistemologically, we can appreciate how wisdom portrays knowing God, his world, and right and wrong as a function of participation in God's created order. To be wise is a matter of walking through life in the fear of Yahweh; it is to assume that he has a structure and order for the world that are necessary presuppositions to true understanding. In what follows, we analyse several passages in Proverbs 1–9 to demonstrate how their literary and theological design creates the liminal worldview we have just introduced.

4.1 ירא יהוה: Proverbs 1:1–7; 31:30

Proverbs welcomes its audience with an introductory prologue and purpose statement in 1:1–7.[32] The Solomonic figure and the father's voice in these verses serve to authenticate this book as traditional wisdom. The royal and paternal rhetoric in these voices also creates initial liminal tension that will continue through chapter 9. The address to the "son" (1:8, 2:1; 3:1; 4:1; 5:1; 6:20; etc.) is a typical image for the social setting of wisdom instruction, imagining an audience of more than just boys. Verses 4–5 indicate more broadly that the book is directed to both the "youth" (נער) and the "wise"

---

[29] L.G. Perdue, "Liminality as a Social Setting for Wisdom Instructions", *ZAW* 93 (1981) 114–26, on pp. 114–5 uses Victor Turner's social anthropology to analyse wisdom in its ancient social settings where limina are boundaries, limits or thresholds and "liminals" (individuals or groups) are challenged to move in and out of social levels (structure to anti-structure or structure to higher structure).

[30] On this two-fold imagery, see Van Leeuwen, "Liminality", 111–5. Cf. also Clements, *Changing World*, 25–7 who uses liminality to connect the proverbial characters to Israel's exilic and post-exilic setting and Brown, *Character in Crisis*, 152 who says, "Wisdom provides the inextricable link between family and community, no less youth and age."

[31] Cf. Perdue, *Proverbs*, 13.

[32] Most scholars agree that 1:1–7 consists of in an introductory prologue (vv. 1–6) and a declarative motto (v. 7) where verses 1–6 provide a uniquely "clear" statement of purpose. R.E. Murphy, *Proverbs* (WBC; Nashville, TN: Thomas Nelson, 1998), 5. See also Van Leeuwen, *Proverbs*, 33 who attributes the several key terms in this section to an effort to link Proverbs to Torah, Prophets and Psalms. On this intertextual function of Proverbs, see also Lang, *Wisdom*, 12 and D.J. Estes, *Hear, My Son: Teaching and Learning in Proverbs 1–9* (Cambridge/Grand Rapids, MI: Apollos/Eerdmans, 1997), 21.

(חכם)[33] – what Van Leeuwen delineates as the dual aims of "proleptic" and "parenetic" instruction.[34] The wise are instructed to increase in wisdom and the youth to learn to value and seek wisdom that can guide them as they move to a new level of maturity. All levels of readers, therefore, are invited to join the way of wisdom or suffer the consequences of the fool.

Thus enticed to embark on the wisdom journey (vv. 1–6) the audience encounters the most important clue to Proverbs' liminal structure in the "motto" of the proverbial collection:

Prov 1:7:

יִרְאַת יְהוָה רֵאשִׁית דָּעַת חָכְמָה וּמוּסָר אֱוִילִים בָּזוּ׃ פ

The phrase, ירא יהוה, stands out as an emphatic qualification for wisdom in all of Proverbs as is made clear by its literary and grammatical positioning in the prologue[35] and in its strategic repetition throughout the book (1:7,29; 2:5; 8:13; 10:27; 14:27; 15:33; 19:23; 22:4; 31:30).[36] This motto is typically considered a late addition to the book, yet the final collection very clearly intends to identify Yahweh as the one God wisdom and creation (cf. Sir 1:14).[37] And, even if we are able to identify an early wisdom phase, the "fear of Yahweh" phrase has been so carefully used throughout the composition (1:7; 9:10; 15:33; 16:6; 31:30) that diachronic readings quickly take us away from the literary and theological implications of the editing.[38] The combination of יהוה with the creation imagery in 3:19 and 8:22–31 parallels a similar tendency throughout the Pentateuch, Deuteronomistic history and the Writings to combine the divine epithets (Yahweh Elohim) and divine acts (creation and salvation) for theological reasons.[39] It is also common to overlook the fact that יהוה naturally evokes the underlying realities of Israel's national history as does the introduction by Israel's king

33 See Fox, *Proverbs 1–9*, 62–3 for the inclusion of the wise in the book's address. Perdue, *Proverbs*, 69f gives an extended explanation for these two different groups to whom the book is addressed. C.H. Toy, *Proverbs* (ICC; Edinburgh: T&T Clark, 1988), 7 unnecessarily regards this reference as a gloss out of context with the poem.

34 Van Leeuwen, "Liminality", 113–5.

35 Brown, *Character in Crisis*, 24 notes that this "all-embracing purpose statement" is made "particularly clear in the Hebrew, given the fact that each of the five bicola in vv. 2–5 is introduced with the preposition *l*ᵉ adjoined to the infinitive construct".

36 The phrase occurs fourteen times in Proverbs and directly qualifies wisdom at three structural transitions (1:7; 9:10; 15:33). Whybray, *Composition of Proverbs*, 29–33 rehearses the history of compositional possibilities for the phrase suspecting that it is a late addition that has grown out of progressive Yahwism.

37 Cf., however, Lang, *Wisdom*, 116–25.

38 Even though von Rad, *Wisdom*, 70 makes a strong distinction between old and new wisdom, he takes Yahweh to be applicable to both enterprises. And, although Whybray gives evidence of a pattern of "Yahweh Additions," he still concludes that "There is, however, no evidence of a systematic editing of the whole book for dogmatic or theological reasons" *Composition of Proverbs*, 31–3, 158.

39 See J. L'Hour, "Yahweh Elohim", *Revue Biblique* 81 (1974) 524–56 and Murphy, *Proverbs*, 255–58 who says, "While the notion is considered characteristic of 'later' wisdom (e.g. Prov 1–9), it is arbitrary to impose a limit since it appears also in ch. 10–29."

of wisdom, Solomon (Prov 1:1). Sirach and Baruch testify to the growing desire to accommodate creation and torah to wisdom (cf. Sir 16:29–17:12; 24:1–12, 23; Bar 3:9–14).[40] Wisdom is thus discovered in the Hebrew Bible as a part of the mythical-redemption narrative, not as a theoretical addition.[41] In the light of this extended OT and historical context, Murphy concludes: "There is no way of limiting 'fear of the Lord' to a given temporal pigeonhole."[42] The ירא יהוה phrase, by prefacing the book in this way, religiously and historically conditions the acquisition of wisdom throughout Proverbs.

The meaning of the phrase is central to the proverbial imagery, yet the range of possibilities must be addressed carefully. At the very least, "fear" must not be reduced to a single emotion, nor sentimentalized to remove all connotations of trembling.[43] Given the positioning and repetition of the phrase it is more appropriate to recognize "fear" as a theological keyword in Proverbs which links wisdom with a broader Yahwistic theology. Fear is used to communicate a range of meanings from "reverence",[44] love and obedience to "awe" and "dread."[45] The effect is to put the wisdom seeker in a reflexive position before God. We do not initiate wisdom, but acquire it in response to the creator God.

Wisdom's reflexive character is signified most strongly by the use of ראשית in the phrase. Fox divides the possible interpretations of ראשית into three senses: "(1) first in time; (2) principle, essence, chief part; or (3) the best part in quality and importance".[46] Fox and Van Leeuwen,[47] are right to emphasize the temporal sense both because the "fear of Yahweh" is not a part of wisdom but also because the repeated parallel in 9:10 replaces ראשית with תחלת, which much more clearly implies temporality. In phrasing the entry point to wisdom this way, the editors lead the reader to understand

---

[40] In fact, "the fear of the Lord" occurs more than fifty times in Sirach, leading A.A. Di Lella to identify the phrase as the heart of Ben Sira's wisdom, "The Meaning of Wisdom in Ben Sira", in L.G. Perdue/et al. (ed.), *In Search of Wisdom: Essays in Memory of John G. Gammie* (Louisville, KY: Westminster John Knox, 1993) 133–48.

[41] Crenshaw, "Concept", 205, too, places wisdom reflection in the obvious context of the national history of Israel. Cf. also J.J. Collins, "Proverbial Wisdom and the Yahwist Vision", *Semeia* 17 (1980) 1–17, on p. 12.

[42] Murphy, *Proverbs*, 256.

[43] See e.g. Perdue, *Proverbs*, 74.

[44] Or "religious piety", ibid., 76.

[45] Fox, *Proverbs 1–9*, 70 says, "There is, however, no indication that the concept has become so bland in Proverbs or that it has lost the connotation of real fear." He also develops the range of approaches that would be appropriate for each individual at each stage of life across the full spectrum of ethic, emotional and conscientious responses. Similarly, R. Whybray, *Wisdom in Proverbs: The Concept of Wisdom in Proverbs 1–9* (London: SCM Press LTD, 1965), 96 says, "The concept of 'fearing Yahweh' thus included every aspect of Israel's relationship to him: obedience, loyalty, worship, sacrifice and love." Toy, *Proverbs*, 10 prefers the more traditional fear as "dread" that giving full authority to the source of wisdom.

[46] Fox, *Proverbs 1–9*, 67.

[47] Toy takes it in the third sense while Murphy and Perdue opt for a combination of various senses.

wisdom as a journey with a "God-centred beginning";[48] it is the progressive life of the student through the liminal stages of maturation towards advanced stages of wisdom.[49] The reader stands on the threshold of a vital decision grounded in an encounter with this God and his history.[50]

The "fear of Yahweh" phrase rightly led von Rad to develop the many epistemological implications it has for wisdom. It mandates a religious way of entry for knowledge which stands in direct contrast to gnostic and Enlightenment dissolutions of the secular from the sacred,[51] faith from reason,[52] material from spiritual, or individual from community.[53] Von Rad explains that the responsive orientation of humanity to God

> contains in a nutshell the whole Israelite theory of knowledge [...]. [Israel] was, in all seriousness, of the opinion that effective knowledge about God is the only thing that puts man in a right relationship with the objects of his perception, that it enables him to ask questions more pertinently, to take stock of relationships more effectively and generally to have a better awareness of circumstances [...]. But we have already seen that Israel's understanding of truth was more comprehensive, that it included many more realities than that of modern man. We saw that for Israel there was only a single, unified world of experience in which the "real" phenomena in the foreground were more real than guilt or curse or divine blessing.[54]

So, knowledge from the mundane and concrete to the divine and abstract is correctly interpreted only in a subservient and religious approach to Yahweh.

We have also already made reference to the bridge created between the ontological foundation of wisdom in Yahweh's created order in chapters 1–9 and its living expression in the wise woman in Proverbs 31:10–31,[55] especially as it relates to the fear of Yahweh[56] and encloses the rest of the proverbial material in this uniquely religious frame. Wolters argues that the

---

48 Van Leeuwen, *Proverbs*, 34.

49 See M.V. Fox, "The Pedagogy of Proverbs 2", *JBL* 113/2 (1994) 233–43, on p. 238 who combines the fear of Yahweh with the advance to higher a social standing in wisdom.

50 O'Donovan, *Resurrection*, 157 distinguishes "moral" from "historical" authority whereby the latter onto logically captures ethics or wisdom within the progressive story and authoritative identity of the creating and redeeming God.

51 *Wisdom*, 67–8.

52 As described by R.E. Murphy, "Wisdom and Creation", *JBL* 104 (1985) 3–11, on p. 10.

53 Clements suggests that the religious aspect of Torah was necessary for a "true apprehension of wisdom", "Wisdom and Old Testament Theology", in John Day/R.P. Gordon/H.G.M. Williamson (ed.), *Wisdom in Ancient Israel* (Cambridge: Cambridge University Press, 1995) 269–86, on p. 284.

54 Rad, *Wisdom*, 67–8.

55 Wolters, *Valiant Woman*. Cf. also Camp, *Wisdom*, 188 who comments on the social value of feminine imagery: "It becomes hard to ignore the possibility that these texts were chosen to begin and end the book of Proverbs by virtue of that imagery. Far from being mere coincidence, this imagery should have crucial literary and theological claims to make with respect to the material it surrounds" (188).

56 Cf. Murphy, *Proverbs*, 258 who sees 31:30 as an "inclusion" with 1:8. Toy, *Proverbs*, 548f, however, thinks the mundane activities clash with the fear of Yahweh and instead adopts the LXX reading, "of intelligence".

form of the poem in Proverbs 31 is a heroic hymn resembling other Yahweh-hymns in the OT which celebrate the victorious acts of God. Yet here, the hero-God is replaced by a woman who embodies wisdom creating a polemical response to the surrounding abstract and rationalistic wisdom of Hellenistic thought: "The point of the song then becomes: not abstract theoretical wisdom rooted in impartial rationality is the praiseworthy ideal, but concrete practical wisdom rooted in the fear of the Lord."[57] The poem dismantles the secular/sacred distinction as the "mundane this-worldly activities" are combined with an "emphatically religious" fear of Yahweh.[58]

Based on the passages in Proverbs 1:7 and 31:10–31 (cf. 9:10), we conclude that wisdom and knowledge in Proverbs not only begin as a reflex to Yahweh's sovereign initiation – most especially in creation – but that this confidence in this knowledge comes by participation in the common life of the created order. Knowledge is, therefore, a matter of applying God's design for creation in every area of human existence – intellectual, religious, emotional, aesthetic and social.

4.2 Woman Wisdom, Creation and the Created Order

The theological and literary bridge between the woman in 31:10–31 and the prologue in 1–9 illumines the two sides of wisdom's liminal function in the book: wisdom in the daily life of the ideal woman and wisdom as a cosmic, expert witness in the order of creation.[59] These two images are a rhetorical means to communicate the urgency in getting wisdom. Speaking of Woman wisdom in Proverbs 8, Fox says, "Everything in the chapter serves the rhetorical goal of influencing the reader to desire wisdom. The reason the author declares that the earth's potentates avail themselves of wisdom is to make *you* want to bring this mighty and renowned resource into your own life."[60]

Van Leeuwen gives the most thorough account of these two feminine figures (cosmic and human), arguing that they create a "coherence of metaphors" which communicate a "map of reality" on two levels of human nature.[61] The first level is the "bi-polar human *eros* for the beauty of Wisdom, who prescribes life within limits, or for the seeming beauty of Folly,

---

57 *Valiant Woman*, 13. Wolters argues that the polemic against Hellenistic wisdom can be seen in the play between the participle צופיה (*sôp̄iyyāh*) in 31:27 and the Greek "*sophia*" (pp. 30–39).

58 Ibid., 15.

59 Camp, *Wisdom*, 74 aptly perceives the literary artistry in 1–9: "The word 'wisdom' and the implicit word 'woman,' then, interact in an extended metaphor throughout these poems, interpreting each other and producing new meaning in the process."

60 *Proverbs 1–9*, 293.

61 "Liminality", 111–6. I reverse the order of these levels from Van Leeuwen's material.

who offers bogus delights in defiance of created limits" (2:16–22; 5:7–9).[62] The second level is the "structure of boundaries or limits", corresponding to Woman Wisdom's role in creation. In order to appreciate the proverbial rhetoric involved, these two levels must be understood individually while keeping in mind their combined synthetic effects.[63]

4.2.1 Wisdom as Woman

In Proverbs *Eros* symbolises the intensive nature of decision-making along the liminal path of life. One needs a passion on par with the sexual libido to pursue wisdom for what she's worth. In the next section we will see that woman wisdom's relationship to creation – and created order – enables her to mediate this path through these boundaries towards the good life (3:19 and 8:22–31).[64] First we pause to reflect on how *eros* communicates liminal urgency. That is, wisdom as woman is able to appeal to the full range of human desire: she entices erotically (1–9); she appeals to the husband practically (31:10–12); she is admired by the children as the paragon of mothers (31:28–29); and is socially commended in community activities (31:10–31).[65] Her sexual essence not only suggests that (men) should love wisdom, but even more, that "Wisdom loves the wise".[66] Folly, too, is communicated with the same feminine eros (6:23–29; 7:1–27; Cf. Sir 9:1–9). The lure of wisdom and folly is an intense struggle for life.

There is of course some disagreement about the role of these feminine metaphors. Much of the debate surrounds the cosmological nature of wisdom relating to her origin, identity, and personification. As we will see below, Proverbs 3:19 portrays wisdom as God's tool in creation while in Proverbs 8:22–31 wisdom is created as an expert witness to the creation of

---

62 Van Leeuwen, "Liminality", 115. Cf. G.A. Yee, "'I Have Perfumed My Bed with Myrrh': The Foreign Woman ('Iššâ Zārâ) in Proverbs 1–9", *JSOT* 43 (1989) 53–68 who gives a full development of the the two women's speeches in chapters 1, 5, 7, 8 and 9 which form a chiastic "macrostructure" confronting the son in his decision to to choose between the paths of life and death. Like Van Leeuwen, she sees this macrostructure at the thematic centre of chapters 1–9. Cf. Perdue, *Proverbs*, 104 who takes woman wisdom as a rival for fertility goddesses in ANE religion.

63 Van Leeuwen concludes, "Thus recognition of cosmic structure or limits is inseparable from proper eros or direction. The images of Proverbs 1–9 thus create a symbolic world of good and evil where good means staying within prescribed religio-moral boundaries and evil means the trespassing of these limits [...]. Thus the roles of the actors in these chapters are wholly concerned with their eros for the opposed liminal images of roads, houses, and women" (116).

64 Cf. Fox, *Proverbs 1–9*, 293, 295 who says, on the delight wisdom takes in humanity (8:31), "The description of the reciprocal attraction between humanity and wisdom draws on language used in the description of the allures of the wife and the temptress [...]. Eros is the yearning for completion by filling a lack in oneself. In this sense, all statements of the reciprocal love between wisdom and mankind proclaim this 'intellectual eros'".

65 Camp, *Wisdom*, 79–123 develops the breadth of the imagery along the lines of "Wife and Mother", "Lover", "Harlot and Adulteress", and the "Wise Woman".

66 Fox, *Proverbs 1–9*, 295. On the erotic sexual rhetoric, see R.E. Murphy, "Wisdom and Eros in Proverbs 1–9", *CBQ* 50 (1988) 60–3.

the world. In both passages, she is clearly "personified" as a voice in the text who appeals to her audience to get wisdom. Attempts to identify her as a "person" or "revelation" or as Yahweh himself[67] are theologically loaded readings which often have serious disregard for the rhetorical and literary nature of these first nine chapters.[68] Instead, wisdom fits into the overall imagery in chapters 1–9 as a wooing woman *and* a mother figure familiar to the ancient world that first read about her. According to Camp:

> The Proverbs poems "introduce" the book not merely in some vague and general sense. Rather, by means of the device of personification, they do so with a very clear poetic purpose: the use of personification, insofar as it embodies the many in the one, asks the reader to seek the underlying unity of the multi-faceted expression of the proverb collection [...]. As a rhetorical device, personification thus has an effect that is similar to proverbial rhetoric, which also acts to integrate experience by imposing an order on the components of that experience.[69]

Camp's helpful correction pushes us forward from the obvious use of rhetoric in the personification to the more pertinent epistemological implications; how does personification relate not only to creation and the created order but more importantly to her ability to mediate knowledge of this order to humanity?

4.2.2 Wisdom as Expert Witness in Creation

The first intersection of feminine and creation imagery appears in God's appropriation of wisdom for his creative work (3:19–20). These verses conclude an appeal which begins in 3:13 aimed at persuading the one who gets wisdom of her pre-eminent value. The cosmological ending has climactic effects:

Prov 3:19–20

יְהוָה בְּחָכְמָה יָסַד־אָרֶץ כּוֹנֵן שָׁמַיִם בִּתְבוּנָה׃
בְּדַעְתּוֹ תְּהוֹמוֹת נִבְקָעוּ וּשְׁחָקִים יִרְעֲפוּ־טָל׃

Not insignificantly, these verses follow an identification of wisdom as the "tree of life" (v. 18) which resonates with the cosmic imagery of creation in

---

[67] Perdue and Lang both appeal tc ancient goddess imagery: Lang, in order to suspend wisdom as a created child who exists with the creator and above the creation, not the mediator of created order, Lang, *Wisdom*, 13–4, 65–6. Similarly, Murphy, "Creation", 9–11 identifies wisdom with "the Lord" or his revelation – not with the created order. Delitzsch calls her "the archetype of the world", the "mediatrix" who "mediated [...] God's word-creating work", *The Book of Proverbs* (Grand Rapids, MI: Eerdmans, 1983), 184, 94. On the debate regarding the personification or hypostasis of wisdom, see Camp, *Wisdom*, 23–68. For our purposes the distinctions are insignificant so long as wisdom is portrayed as a metaphor which both explains wisdom and lures the readers to acquire it.

[68] Cf. Van Leeuwen, *Proverbs*, 89.

[69] *Wisdom*, 215 Van Leeuwen, *Proverbs*, 96 says, "she exists both as a person who speaks and as cosmic reality".

Genesis 2.[70] Wisdom and creation are also related in Ps 104:5, 24; Jer 10:12; and Isaiah 40:12–17, yet none of these passages attempt to give an exhaustive account of the nature of wisdom's role.[71] The OT canon consistently betrays an underlying assumption about the relationship between wisdom and creation – one which I suggest is most clearly expressed in resonance between Proverbs 3 and 8. The cosmic praise of Yahweh's wisdom in Proverbs 3:19–20 is preceded by a praise of wisdom's value to humanity (vv. 13–18).[72] The emphasis is on a specific account of wisdom's role in the "heavens" (v. 19) and particularly on God's work to direct the "waters" (תהומות [...] ושחקים ירעפו־טל), apparently to nourish the earth.[73] Thus, God not only "established" creation by wisdom, but has done so in a way that brings life to the earth. Wisdom's expertise is augmented by the vitality she offers.

In other words, what we encounter in Proverbs 3 is a picture of wisdom in creation which accentuates the liminal imagery of ways, women and houses developing in the surrounding chapters. In this way, the narrative flow of Proverbs 1–9 gives way to increasing levels of poetic "intensification"[74] driven at the urgency of getting wisdom. Proverbs 8:22–31, therefore, sits in a position to add new exigency to this rhetorical development.

4.2.3 Proverbs 8:22–31

When the creation and feminine themes appear again in chapter 8, we find their relationship – and wisdom's epistemological role – significantly deepened. Here our main concern is with 8:22–31, the most intense section of an extended poem on the personification of wisdom (8:1–36). יהוה in verse 22 parallels יראת יהוה in verse 13 adding continuity to this poem and the introduction (cf. 1:7); but the theme in verses 22–26 concentrates specifically on wisdom's origins.[75] On the whole, Dell correctly recognises a general progression in this passage from the "cosmological God" to the "level of hu-

---

[70] The "tree of life" is only used elsewhere in Gen 2–3 and Revelation, with distant echoes in Ps 1 and Jer 17. Thus, not only is there a theological link between the Yahweh of wisdom and the God of creation, but more importantly wisdom is bound up in that interrelationship. Overlooking the strong cosmic mythology from Genesis, Fox, *Proverbs 1–9*, 158–9 says that she is only a "figure for vitality and healing". But, cf. Van Leeuwen, *Proverbs*, 53–4.

[71] Cf. Delitzsch, *Proverbs*, 95 who takes this passage as revealing both an attribute of Yahweh and as "characteristic of his actions". Fox *Proverbs 1–9*, 159, 161 appears divided in that he sees the wise action as God's "skill in craftsmanship" but attributes the purpose of the passage to wisdom and not to God. It is just as much about both, cf. A. Meinhold, "Gott und Mensch in Proverbien 3", *VT* 37 (1987) 468–77 and Van Leeuwen, *Proverbs*, 96 who demonstrates the "multireferential" role of wisdom gained in the larger canon as a whole.

[72] Van Leeuwen, *Proverbs*, 53–4; Meinhold, "Gott"; but cf. Fox, *Proverbs 1–9*, 161 who sees the passage relating only to wisdom and not to God.

[73] See Murphy, *Proverbs*, 22–3; Meinhold, "Gott", 470; Van Leeuwen, *Proverbs*, 53–4.

[74] See Alter, *Poetry*, 62–5 and 172.

[75] The speech ends with the new address in .v. 32, marked by ועתה.

manity" where the purpose of wisdom is "to teach and instruct humanity to find life".[76] Yet so much theological commentary falls short in its attempts to account for the specific relationships between wisdom, Yahweh and creation. As already argued regarding personification above, these concerns should fall under the rhetorical and liminal imagery that pervades chapters 1–9. Wisdom's reappearance with creation stands under the overall goal of these chapters to emphasise wisdom's (ontological) credentials.[77] Giving close attention to these credentials will enable us to make several conclusions about the purpose of this section (vv. 22–36) and its implications for knowledge in Proverbs 1–9.

The introductory stanza points to wisdom's origin, starting with verse 22:

יְהוָה קָנָנִי רֵאשִׁית דַּרְכּוֹ קֶדֶם מִפְעָלָיו מֵאָז׃

The use of the Hebrew root קנה evokes much disagreement, yet its function can be clarified by the surrounding context in chapter 8. As Fox observes, the predominant lexical association for קנה is clearly "to acquire" but also that the exact sense of the root – whether it be to create or to acquire – is "moot"[78] because the context clearly seeks to reveal wisdom's "origins".[79] Thus Fox's proposal that God acquired wisdom by creation appropriately combines the lexical, contextual and intertextual issues in this passage.[80] Rhetorically, the effect is to identify wisdom's place before and during Yahweh's creative activity thus securing her preeminence among all of God's created things and certifying the unique credentials of her teaching and instruction. She excels humanity in her witness to the "cosmic order" of all things.[81] She therefore bridges the ontological and the epistemological; her knowledge is knowledge of things as they are in reality.[82]

We see this more clearly in verses 27–29 where wisdom's credentials appear in a detailed comparison between the design of her teaching and the design of creation itself. The temporal and placial location of wisdom during creation allows her to see and report on the order established *there* and make it relevant *here and now*. Note the connection between 3:19, where God כון the heavens by wisdom (3:19), and the same כון of the heavens in

---

76 *Get Wisdom, Get Insight: An Introduction to Israel's Wisdom Literature* (Norwich, UK: Darton, Longman and Todd, 2000), 21 This is the opposite direction as the one in Prov 3:13–20, Meinhold, "Gott", 469.

77 Van Leeuwen, *Proverbs*, 92–3.

78 *Proverbs 1–9*, 179–80. Cf. also *BDB*, 888.

79 Fox, *Proverbs 1–9*, 279–80. Cf. Toy, *Proverbs*, 173; Murphy, *Proverbs*, 52 and Van Leeuwen, *Proverbs*, 92, 96.

80 Significantly, קנה is also used in this dual sense of acquiring at the origin in the creation references in Gen 4:1; 14:19, 22 and Deut 32:6. That Proverbs here is appealing to this polyvalent character of קנה in Pentateuchal contexts seems highly likely.

81 Van Leeuwen, *Proverbs*, 92.

82 See O'Donovan, *Resurrection*, 25–6, 190–1.

8:27a where she witnessed a circle drawn "on the face of the deep" (בחוקו,[83] v. 27b). The engraving imagery created by חק and הקק (vv. 27, 29) bridges the realities in the created order with the liminal and moral order: "to the seas God established a limit (חק) that they might not transgress his command, when he marked (בחוקו) the foundations of the earth" (v. 29). As such, the use of חק here indicates what Van Leeuwen calls the "boundaries within creation" or the "carved" worldview that frames human behaviour: "human boundaries have their warrant in divinely placed cosmic boundaries [...]."[84] The creation order in Proverbs 1–9 – into which God has placed the knowledge of reality – has a cosmic and mysterious nature which forbids immediate human access. Wisdom declares her unique access to the created design, but as she does so she reveals the strict conditions of her offer: one must approach in the fear of Yahweh. The pericope in chapter 8 thus connects the limits and order of God's creative acts with the expertise wisdom acquires in the realm of human affairs.

Because wisdom has the ability to mediate the "order" of reality to humanity, she is the key to the "bi-polar" experience of the human life, learning to align experience within the boundaries of creation. Love and joy adorn the path to wisdom: God "delights" in wisdom's activity (Prov 8:30),[85] she delights in the "generations of humanity" (v. 31). Wisdom's loving appeal to follow her in verses 1–21 are rejoined in verses 32–36 in order to sustain the overall liminal sense of "ways" and "boundaries" in Proverbs 1–9. Humans are bound to encounter a world of pluralities and wisdom assists us in uniting them into a navigable "pluriform" order.[86] Van Leeuwen's summary captures the basic point well: "Consequently, wisdom implies love within limits, freedom within form, and life within law."[87]

Yet the central section in verses 22–31 and the final chapter in Proverbs 1–9 help to remind the reader that wisdom is not an end in itself, but the means to relate to the creator and his cosmos. It is God's purpose in giving wisdom to communicate moral compliance with a certain cosmic design

[83] A Qal infinitive construct of חקק.

[84] Van Leeuwen, "Liminality", 117–9. Cf. also Delitzsch, *Proverbs*, 188 who regards חקק as an indication of the "graver's tools" that marked off the order of creation. His conclusion that wisdom herself "participated" in creation is an unnecessary extension of the imagery here. She is used by God (3:19) and watches (8:30f), but is not said to act. It is generally agreed that the thrust of vv. 27–29 is one of limits. See Fox, *Proverbs 1–9*, 284 who says "the essence of creation is separation and the marking of boundaries". Cf. also Perdue, *Proverbs*, 146–7.

[85] The translation of אמון is highly debated. Extensive treatments can be found in Fox, *Proverbs 1–9*, 285–9 and Van Leeuwen, *Proverbs*, 94f. Fox prefers to read it as an infinitive absolute "serving as an adverbial complement [...]": "I was growing up" because it requires no emendation to the Hebrew morphology. Van Leeuwen follows the Akkadian cognate *ummānu* to position wisdom "as the architect associate of Yahweh at the creation of the world". While most translations follow "child" or "craftsman" there does not seem to be enough evidence to be conclusive. What can be argued, following Fox, Murphy and Van Leeuwen is an emphasis on her position beside Yahweh and her activity as a delight to Yahweh.

[86] O'Donovan, *Resurrection*, 197.

[87] Van Leeuwen, *Proverbs*, 31.

through the intimacy of divine-human relationship.[88] The motto in Proverbs 9:10 resonates with 1:7 to frame the first nine chapters inside this common goal. The fear of Yahweh thus serves not only to condition the access to wisdom, but to signal the teleological goals of the divine human relationship in the created order – divine encounter. The feminine and liminal imagery along the way has served as a means to entice and guide readers into this relationship. With this sense of reality, the reading community is prepared to turn to a living interpretation and engagement of life – a hermeneutic of performance which is lived out in chapters 10–29.[89]

5. The "World as it Seems": Wisdom in Proverbs 10–29

In chapters 10–29 we find the main collection of proverbs. Generally speaking, individual proverbs are folk sayings with a tremendous range of social functions.[90] According to Van Leeuwen, proverbs are "*partial utterances*"[91] or, for Crenshaw, are like legal codes which are "suggestive, pointing the way without attempting to be exhaustive on any particular subject."[92] Alter says that Proverbs are syntactic parallel phrases which evoke a variety of responses upon repetition.[93] At the same time, proverbs can also be found in extended collections which, as Taylor says, should be seen as "literary monuments and not as mere assemblings of proverbial material."[94] It has been less common to grant this full context to the book of Proverbs, yet recent studies have begun to consider the individual proverbs in a *Sitz im Buch*[95] or *Sitz in der Literatur*[96] which serve as a frame for their referentiality and allow the limited extent of individual proverbs in 10–29 to represent a polyacoustic voice with a fuller meaning.

---

88 Cf. O'Donovan, *Resurrection*, 190.

89 O'Donovan, *Resurrection*, 190 states, "The moral agent approaches every new situation, then, equipped with the 'moral law' (which is how we shall refer to that wisdom which contains insight into the created order when it is formulated explicitly to direct decisions, i.e. deontically)."

90 A. Taylor, *The Proverb* (Cambridge, MA: Harvard University, 1931), 3 says defining a proverb "is too difficult to repay the undertaking; and should we fortunately combine in a single definition all the essential elements and give each the proper emphasis, we should not even then have a touchstone. An incommunicable quality tells us this sentence is proverbial and that one is not. Hence no definition will enable us to identify positively a sentence as proverbial [...]. Let us be content with recognising that a proverb is a saying current among the folk." Cf. similarly, R. Whybray, *Wealth and Poverty in the Book of Proverbs* (JSOTSup; Sheffield: JSOT, 1990), 73–4.

91 Van Leeuwen, "Wealth and Poverty", 29.

92 J.L. Crenshaw, *Education in Ancient Israel: Across the Deadening Silence* (London/New York: Doubleday, 1998), 230. See also, Murphy, *Tree*, 21 who says that proverbs are "open-ended" and "have several levels of meaning' where "hermeneutical possibilities emerge" in their hearing; Collins, "Proverbial Wisdom", 5–6 who recognises that proverbs are "paradigms" and not "natural laws".

93 *Poetry*.

94 Taylor, *The Proverb*, 174.

95 Van Leeuwen, *Context and Meaning*, 2.

96 Gladson, *Paradoxes*, 5.

Camp thus recognises the controlling nature of feminine imagery of the preceding chapters on the reading experience: "It becomes hard to ignore the possibility that these texts [Prov 1–9, 31] were chosen to begin and end the book of Proverbs by virtue of that imagery. Far from being mere coincidence, this imagery should have crucial literary and theological claims to make with respect to the material it surrounds."[97] Yet, as Van Leeuwen argues, this organising tendency is true not only for the feminine imagery, but also for the full feminine-creation-liminal nexus grounded in the various metaphors in Proverbs 1–9 (woman, ways, paths, death, life, etc). With creation as the root metaphor, these images give readers a "Yahwistic worldview" through which to interpret the individual sayings. This literary and theological approach to the proverbs suggests a new way to address the longstanding problems of retribution and theodicy in Proverbs through a more "aphoristic" or proverbial epistemology.

5.1 Retribution, Mystery and Crisis in Proverbs

We begin with a reconstruction of the common portrayal of Proverbs in the retribution and cause-effect nexuses.[98] The number and breadth of approaches to retribution, however, force us to group the major scholarly positions into three overarching views.

Crenshaw represents some of the stronger formulations of the problem. He believes that the evidence of social injustice historically becomes increasingly acute at the individual level causing the more community-driven appeals like torah and the prophets to appear anachronistic and overly simplistic. The national history surrounding the failures of David and the fall of Josiah led "late wisdom" to correct the incomplete accounting in early wisdom (Prov 10–29).[99] This acuteness corresponds to the development of Israel's theology from the earlier distant God, Elohim, to Yahweh, the personal "patron deity who had entered into an intimate relationship with the nation Israel".[100] The general response by the sages was to turn from theology to anthropodicy – a questioning not of God but of self where the

---

[97] *Wisdom*, 188. Cf. also Murphy, *Tree*, 137, who says, "This remarkable speech of Lady Wisdom seems to have a very deliberate purpose within the book; if Prov 1–9 is the "introduction" to the collections of individual sayings that follow, this powerful motivating figure sweeps all the practical wisdom of Israel into the orbit of her activity."

[98] Gladson, *Paradoxes*, 2–5 defines retribution as a relationship between "deed and expected consequence". Thus a "retributive paradox" is an "inconsistency or tension discernible in the deed-consequence formulation." With Gladson, I am arguing that Proverbs has been accused of a far more mathematical correlation than it actually embraces. Cf. Fox, *Proverbs 1–9*, 91–2.

[99] "Poverty and Punishment in the Book of Proverbs", in idem.; *Urgent Advice* (Atlanta: Macon, GA, 1995) 396–405, on p. 399 and Crenshaw, "Popular Questioning", 178–9.

[100] Crenshaw, "Concept", 196.

national creed changed from "Thus hath the Lord spoken" to the didactic form, "My son, listen to your father's advice".[101]

Crenshaw makes several methodological assumptions which are common in Proverbs' interpretation. First, he assumes that "creation faith" was not an early reality for Israel, but only a late response when the "crisis of meaning emerged".[102] But this assumption is challenged by scholars like Eichrodt who unites covenant with creation in Israel's historical response to theodicy.[103] This also comports with L'Hour's research cited above which illustrates the consistent use of Yahweh-Elohim and the creation-salvation theology throughout the torah, writings and prophets.[104] Crenshaw is not satisfied with this appeal to creation, calling it a "cop-out" when it is used in the divine speeches of Job 38–41.[105] This follows his own admitted preference to position anthropodicy or human understanding as the standard of epistemological justification for Job and his readers. Yet as we will see in Job and Qohelet, wisdom, grounded in the fear and trust of Yahweh (Prov 1:7; 3:5–7), opposes a certainty-driven rationalist need to satisfy the skeptic. Furthermore, Crenshaw seems unwilling to let a theology of creation transform Job's disposition from lament to praise.[106] But, as we noted in chapter 1, texts have the capacity (and purpose) to *influence* their interpretive audiences. Crenshaw wants to remain a "disengaged" exemption to this transforming potential of texts. Furthermore, the fact that Crenshaw attributes the problem to Proverbs almost always follows a divided reading of the book which separates chapters 10–29 from the frame and the sayings from their voice as a solitary collection.[107]

Eichrodt's theology represents a second view of retribution as it parallels several scholars who see a moderate response to retribution in Proverbs. While Eichrodt sees the father-son relationship of Jeremiah as a new level of intimacy that made the retribution problem more acute, he also affirms that wisdom's response to injustice is answered definitively in a renewed vision of the knowledge of God, of creation and of history.[108] A similar moderate approach to OT theology is applied to Proverbs, most extensively

---

[101] Crenshaw, "Popular Questioning".

[102] Ibid., 186.

[103] W. Eichrodt, "Faith in Providence and Theodicy in the Old Testament", in J.L. Crenshaw (ed.), *Theodicy in the Old Testament* (Philadelphia/London: Fortress/SPCK, 1983) 17–41, on p. 37 Cf. also Greidanus, "Dimension", 41–2; Niehaus, *Sinai*, 149.

[104] "Yahweh Elohim".

[105] Crenshaw, "Concept", 203–5.

[106] In the next chapter we cite Geller's observation that perspectives like Crenshaw's are a "failure to apprehend the ancient technique" of "arguments through juxtaposition rather than through logical exposition", "Where Wisdom", 102.

[107] Thus Crenshaw, "Poverty", 398 thinks it is astounding that Prov 1–9 make no mention of the poor. This is a common failure to miss literary effect of juxtaposing 1–9 and 10–29.

[108] Eichrodt, "Providence", 21, 37.

by Murphy and Whybray.[109] Murphy regards it as a "mistake" to deem the sages "simplistic" and "superficial" or to think that Proverbs is unaware of "life's inequalities"[110] upholding the sages' awareness of uncertainties and the "ambiguities in human affairs". However, he still holds some reservations and accuses Proverbs of accounting inadequately for the problem of the righteous suffering.[111] Whybray, too, allows the sages room; they give a "picture of society in which life is extremely precarious",[112] yet he does not work this out in a literary and theological reading of Proverbs.

An article by Collins marks a significant shift. While embracing the same limitations to OT wisdom as Murphy and Whybray, he pursues a more detailed description of the paradigmatic view of Proverbs which resists the common "dichotomy" between wisdom and biblical history.[113] Thus, like the OT prophets, he sees in Proverbs an internal "debunking tendency" against a false and overly dogmatic use of wisdom.[114] His approach begins a move away from atomistic readings of proverbs and the disconnected collections toward a more literary and synthetic view of the proverbial materials. Similarly, in his work on retributive paradoxes in Proverbs 10–29, Gladson suggests that sages of old *and* late wisdom[115] demonstrate an awareness of conflicts between retributive problems and the more dogmatic cause-effect scheme.[116] The sages' methods for dealing with a conflict between knowledge and experience are marked, not by direct theodicy, but by a more subtle juxtaposition of contrary truths which have a combined but inconclusive effect on the reader.[117] In effect, Gladson's methodology begins to do what is necessary for a sophisticated hermeneutical reading of Proverbs in that it appreciates the effect of the parts on the whole. Alter also alludes to this technique of juxtaposition as a common effort in OT narrative to portray artistically the "dialectical tensions" in the

---

[109] However, cf. also Dell, *Get Wisdom*, 19 who attributes an unavoidable 'tension" in Proverbs' approach to wisdom, and Perdue, *Proverbs*, 10–1 who recognises that retribution was not "mechanical" in the eyes of the sages.

[110] Murphy, *Proverbs*, 264f.

[111] Murphy, *Tree*, 11, 29.

[112] Whybray, *Wealth and Poverty*, 23–4, demonstrates the variety of voices that emerge in the individual proverbs thus making an assessment on the book's "position" on wealth and poverty or retribution inconclusive at best.

[113] Collins, "Proverbial Wisdom", 3, 10–2.

[114] Ibid., 1–17.

[115] Paradox is also evident in late wisdom, cf. Sir 5:1–5; 8:10–13; 13:17; 27:22–23; 28:17. See P.W. Skehan/A.A. De Lella, *The Wisdom of Ben Sira* (New York: Doubleday, 1987), 23.

[116] See, *Paradoxes*, 206 where he says, "The character of Proverbs renders unreliable any attempt to discriminate between diachronic and synchronic manifestations of these ambiguities. It is more likely that the wisdom tradition, particularly in its early stages, but continuous throughout its history, had deep inner tensions which were never fully resolved."

[117] Gladson, *Retributive Paradoxes*, 196, 288. Alter, *Poetry*, 164 calls these the "interesting" proverbs which stress "ambiguity" and a 'paradoxical image" upon the reader (p. 176).

reality of the created order.[118] Several passages in Proverbs 10–29 act in this fashion and indicate that a more comprehensive message emerges from the polyphony of voices, particularly when guided by the introductory material in chapters 1–9. The rest of this chapter will conduct a brief analysis of some of these passages.

5.2 Proverbs 26:1–12

The extended proverb-poem in 26:1–12 is not directly concerned with retribution theory but rather demonstrates the proverbial and aphoristic epistemology which is used to apply creational realities (Prov 1–9, 31) to particular and local circumstances. That is, we will find that the contradictory circumstances in this passage resonate with both the theology in chapters 1–9 and the more ambiguous material in Proverbs 25, thus creating for the reader a '"treatise" on "hermeneutics"'[119] – a poem on the interpretive necessity of wise living.

Structurally, verses 1–12 form a unit centred around the כסיל.[120] Van Leeuwen offers extensive evidence for the poetic and thematic unity of the poem highlighting their "intensive and cohesive force".[121] Because of this poem's unity, he understands the need to interpret the individual proverbs in vv 1–12 *about the fool* in light of the larger contextual aim: "contrary to most commentators [...] *it must be stressed that the poem concerns not just the* ksyl, *but the ksyl in his various relations*".[122] In other words, Proverbs 26:1–12 affirms that wisdom is not merely a matter of collecting facts but of learning to relate experience to declared realities.

Looking closely at the poem, the proverbial rhetorical in verse 1 introduces the hermeneutical nature of the poem in verses 1–12. Instead of a

---

118 In *The Art of Biblical Narrative* (New York: Basic Books, 1981) Alter describes "parallel dialectical tensions" between "divine plan" and "disorderly character" (promise failed and fulfilled) where human nature, as imagined in the Bible "is a function of its being conceived as caught in the powerful interplay of this double dialectic between design and disorder, providence and freedom. The various biblical narratives in fact may be usually seen as forming a spectrum between the opposing extremes of disorder and design" (33). Here we see a "bundle of paradoxes, encompassing the zenith and the nadir of the created world" requiring "special cunning attentiveness in literary representation" (147). On poetry see ibid., *Poetry*, 177–9.

119 Van Leeuwen, *Context and Meaning*, 99.

120 For unity in vv. 1–12, see Murphy, *Proverbs*, 198; Perdue, *Proverbs*, 225; Toy, *Proverbs*, 471–4; and less decisively Delitzsch, *Proverbs*, 173.

121 *Context and Meaning*, 95–9, (his emphasis). Besides the use of כסיל- which is only absent from verse v.2 – he gives evidence for unity based upon key sounds (following the consonants in כסיל), words, and key phrases. He says, "The most dramatic phrase repetition (with some variations of the verb) appears in the contradictory Admonitions in vv 4a, 5a: *'l t'n/'nh ksyl k'wltw.*" He concludes that "the repetitions in 26:1–12 fit their context and must be granted their intensive and cohesive force" (96).

122 Ibid., 90. Cf. Murphy, *Proverbs*, 198–9 who follows Van Leeuwen at almost every point in his interpretation. He adds parenthetically that the "dichotomy" between the wise and the fool is "too neat" and "part of an educational ploy" (198). I can only assume that he is referring to Van Leeuwen's interest in getting beyond the fool to the hermeneutical ambitions of the poem.

verb or traditional Hebrew sentence structure, this verse offers four nouns in two sets of leading comparisons: "Like snow in summer or rain in harvest" (כשלג בקיץ וכמטר בקציר :). This leaves the reader inquisitively poised for the concluding statement which comes with climactic force: כן לא־נאוה לכסיל כבוד ("so not fitting for a fool is honour"). "Snow in summer" and "rain in harvest" in verse 1a thus leave us pondering the improprieties, even before coming to the semantic parallel in 1b: לא נאוה. This confirms the negative calculations developed in the readers' imagination. The comparisons in verses 2–3 reinforce the original point, which is to illustrate circumstances which do not "fit" (נאוה).[123] At the turn of the Enlightenment, Francis Bacon reflected his sense of two ways of knowing: the aphorisms of the ancients and the methods of the enlightenment: "Aphorisms, representing a knowledge broken, do invite men to inquire further; whereas Methods, carrying the show of a total, do secure men, as if they were at farthest."[124]

Verses 4–5 stand out as a small summary of the poem; each saying provides a pair of oppositions which outline negative images of the fool in various circumstances. In this extended context, this otherwise troublesome verse-pair can be reappraised on the basis of thematic interrelations, especially as the verses correspond to v. 12.[125]

Prov 26:4–5

אַל־תַּעַן כְּסִיל כְּאִוַּלְתּוֹ פֶּן־תִּשְׁוֶה־לּוֹ גַם־אָתָּה׃
עֲנֵה כְסִיל כְּאִוַּלְתּוֹ פֶּן־יִהְיֶה **חָכָם בְּעֵינָיו**׃

Prov 26:12

רָאִיתָ אִישׁ **חָכָם בְּעֵינָיו** תִּקְוָה לִכְסִיל מִמֶּנּוּ׃

The point of the parallel verses (4–5) is that one must walk delicately in answering a fool in order to avoid a tragic role reversal. The oppositional scenario depicted here resists absolute or dogmatic characterisations of proverbs – or a deed-consequence schema – but it also reinforces the open-ended character to the search for wisdom.[126] Van Leeuwen and Murphy recognise that this juxtaposition, especially given the unity of the poem, resonates with verses 1 and 12. The thematic introduction of נאוה ("fittingness,")[127] in verse 1 starts the imaginative process and verse 12 rejoins and explains the poem as marked by the repetition of חכם בעיניו from verse 5. The one wise in his own eyes is the object of avoidance in verse 5 and the paradoxical result of the wise becoming introspective or individualistic in

[123] Verse 2 is the only verse lacking the Hebrew כסיל, yet its attention to "fittingness" gives it a place in the context.

[124] F. Bacon, *Advancement of Learning*, 2.6–7.

[125] A point accepted by both Murphy and Van Leeuwen, but otherwise ignored by most commentators.

[126] Murphy, *Proverbs*, 203 says that there is an "ambiguity [...] that should probably be left open" (199) and that the purpose of the verses, in conjunction with v. 12 are part of an aim to "educate readers to the ambiguities of life".

[127] BDB has "comely" or "seemly". The two other uses in Proverbs (17:7; 19:10) carry the same idea.

their pursuit of wisdom in verse 12. Both are examples of the "fittingness" which wisdom provides. Van Leeuwen's interpretation of the passage draws the various interrelationships in the context together:

> "Not fitting" is that which upsets the order of nature and society [...]. *N'wh* is not the order of creation (including society) itself. Rather *n'wh* seems to designate states of affairs which are in harmony with the creational standards which hold for them [...] thus while what is *n'wh* always befits the order which holds for it, this order itself is no simple thing. It needs to be discerned by the wise [...]. This concern is essentially a hermeneutical one. Wisdom, to a very large extent, is a matter of interpreting people, events, situations, actions in relation to norms for existence [...]. Thus Prov 26:4–5 takes the problem of fittingness (vv 1–3), which the wise man is ordinarily expected to master, and formulates it in a contradictory way which exposes the limits of wisdom. Anyone who thinks he has an infallible answer to the dilemma is himself "wise in his own eyes."[128]

The combined effect of this poem, in its thematic and theological opposition between the wise and the fool, resonates outwardly with the parallels in 3:5–7. The one "wise in his own eyes" (3:7a) is the opposite of one who "fears Yahweh" (3:7b, cf. 1:7) and the one who trusts in Yahweh (3:5a) is opposed to one who trusts in his *own* understanding (3:7b).[129] Following a sequential-literary reading, the Yahwistic worldview mapped out in Proverbs 1–9 now finds realistic application in the mystery and ambiguity of life. To navigate this mystery, the wise start in wonder – with a fear of Yahweh that encounters him in their interpretation of the world. They, in turn, live with a balance between individuality and "otherness" which makes all knowledge hermeneutical.[130]

Murphy follows Van Leeuwen's interpretation closely, yet he makes the strange conclusion that, apart from 26:1–12, "Nowhere else is the 'danger' of wisdom explored."[131] I have already made reference to the more than 100 incidences of paradox which Gladson identifies in Proverbs 10–29 in order to correct the scholarly trend which attributes a "crystal cage" optimism to Proverbs. In a lengthy section devoted to proverbial contexts of "Divine Inscrutability" Gladson reinforces the limits of human wisdom in Proverbs (16:1–9, 25; 20:9, 24; 21:2 and 25:2)[132] which confirm the inherent "danger" in wisdom. These less frequent passages are, nevertheless,

---

128 *Context and Meaning*, 99–101. Cf., however, Murphy's rejection of "order" in the nature of the wisdom search, *Proverbs*, 266.

129 Murphy and Van Leeuwen both make this connection to 3:5–7.

130 Van Leeuwen, *Context and Meaning*, 105 says, "As the viewer looks at the other, the other is himself engaged in a fatal act of self-perception [...]. It is finally the failure of self-knowledge that defines the fool. Because such a person does not know himself, he is prone to seeking *kbwd* which is beyond his limits."

131 *Proverbs*, 201. He seems unable to sustain this claim, for in a later context he associates 26:1–12 with the same anti-individualistic warnings on wisdom found in 3:5–7; 28:25–27 (203).

132 Gladson, *Paradoxes*, 220–37.

what Alter called "interesting"[133] proverbs for the way they arrest the reader just when he or she has become lulled into complacency by the predictability of several proverbs in a row. When placed together, one can see how these passages achieve the same (though weaker) effect of contradictory juxtaposition we will encounter in Job and Qohelet.

"A gracious woman obtains honor, and violent men[134] obtain riches" (11:16)
"The fallow ground of the poor yields much fruit, but it is swept away through injustice" (13:23)
"The wicked take a bribe in secret (bosom), to pervert the ways of justice" (17:23)
"Who can say 'my heart is clean, I am pure from my sin?'" (20:9)
"Every way of man is upright in his own eyes, but Yahweh weighs hearts" (21:2)

Proverbs 16:1–9 is another lengthy poem which, although not as strong as 26:4–5, also confirms the ambiguities of human "ways" and "planning" which are, in the end, held under God's control. In doing so, human freedom and the uncertainties of the lived life are preserved without defaulting to the precision of retributive absolutism.[135] These passages interrupt the otherwise predictable flow in Proverbs 10–29, reminding readers that wisdom embraces the bi-polarity of experience in the midst of ambiguity. Bacon's reasons for retaining aphoristic thinking in spite of the popularity in Enlightenment methodology, are a fitting summary of Proverbs 10–29:

[…] yet I have avoided so to do, because this delivering of knowledge in distinct and disjointed aphorisms doth leave the wit of man more free to turn and toss, and to make use of that which is so delivered to more several purposes and applications. For we see all the ancient wisdom and science was wont to be delivered in that form; as may be seen by the parables of Solomon, and by the aphorisms of Hippocrates […].[136]

5.3 Proverbs 30

Finally, Agur's speech in Proverbs 30 is one of many more passages in the collection which evidence something of a "debunking tendency"[137] against "crystal cage" optimism and dogmatic uses of wisdom. The extended poem bridges the collection of sayings and admonitions (10–29) with the decisive and concluding frame elements in 31:10–31. There is no consensus as to where this poem ends and consequently, "its very meaning and purpose have received radically contrary interpretations".[138]

---

133 *Poetry*, 164.
134 Cf. to Murphy, *Proverbs*, 79 who takes עריצים as "strong men".
135 Cf. Gladson, *Paradoxes*, 229–31; Murphy, *Proverbs*, 118–9; Toy, *Proverbs*, 319 and Van Leeuwen, *Proverbs*, 157–8.
136 F. Bacon, *Preface to Maxims of the Law* (.
137 Collins, "Proverbial Wisdom", 1, 13.
138 Van Leeuwen, *Proverbs*, 250. Interpretations include skepticism, agnosticism, atheism, and humble resolve (cf. Job 42:1–7). Van Leeuwen takes this last option. The further difficulty is not just the radical con-

Taking Agur as an outright skeptic undercuts the Yahwistic theology and liminal imagery that pervades the rest of the book. It is not difficult to discern the connections between Agur and the contradictory juxtapositions in previous chapters. Despite his reservations about wisdom, Agur (vv. 1–33) maintains a religious approach to life. He recommends humility (vv. 1–4; 11–14; 32–33), wonder (vv. 18–31), and reverence for Yahweh and his word (vv. 5–6, 9). At the very least, these words reinforce the "dangerous" nature of wisdom and that Yahweh must be approached in fear and humility. O'Donovan, commenting here on the connection between Proverbs 8:15 and 30:24–28, recognises Agur's contribution to a theological use of wisdom:

Wonder and incomprehension are not the first aspect of Wisdom that is usually spoken of; yet they are, it seems to me, fundamental to the wisdom project [...]. There is a paradigm in nature, too, for the spontaneous sociality of creatures, an ability to organise and fend for themselves without the pretentiousness of rule: and set beside such models, are we not invited to think that the strutting cock and the king striding before his people have a touch of the ridiculous about them? In the lizard who creeps into kings' palaces we have an ironic metaphor for the role of wisdom itself, unpretentious but infinitely versatile. The reptilian wise man who finds his way across the trackless rock will insinuate himself into the pretentiousness of power and make it possible to do something to the point. "By *me* kings reign". Standing by the king's right hand is the advisor, the one who knows the world outside the palace, the link between the king and the cosmos.[139]

Reading Proverbs 10–30 alongside chapters 1–9 and 31 as we have done here invites correction to the more popular generalisations about the contradictions in the book.[140] At the most basic level, von Rad seems justified in saying that the wise "place their pupils within the sphere of influence of varied and partly contradictory experiences of life", such that Job and Ecclesiastes are not a "whole phase of wisdom".[141] Yet, at the same time, what we find in Proverbs is not just the dialectic of dogmatism and mystery, or dissent within warring traditions, but an artistic portrayal of wisdom through the unity of its polyphonic voices. These many voices express the

tent but, according to Murphy, *Proverbs*, 227, there is no way to decide where Agur's speech actually stops or if it does, before v. 33. Gladson, *Paradoxes* interprets the chapter this way: "Thus Agur illustrates what happens when the divine mysterium, generally viewed positively in Prov 10–29, gets turned around and effectually paralyses the wisdom enterprise. At the very limit of human knowledge, where answers are so desperately craved, ultimate questions remain suspended in a dark and painful silence" (302). Agur embodies skepticism in "seed form" (297). R. Gordis, *The Book of Job* (New York: Jewish Theological Seminary of America, 1978), 539 comments: "Both Koheleth and Agur ben Yakeh (Pr. 30:1ff.), are unable to make peace with the impassable limits placed upon man's understanding of the universe and they constantly lament man's ignorance". 539

[139] O'Donovan, "Response to Craig Bartholomew", 113, 115.

[140] Murphy, *Proverbs*, 262 says that "If one considers that very many of these sayings were handed down by oral tradition, no true context is possible [...] proverbs can be at war with each other."

[141] *Wisdom*, 106, 110.

full range of bi-polar experiences in an attempt to resolve daily perceptions in the light of God's declared reality. This polyphonic character of wisdom can be found both *within Proverbs* and *within the cohesive wisdom genre of the OT.*[142] While Gladson's work on Proverbs helpfully illustrates the intentional juxtaposition of differing views of reality, he does not tie these voices into the literary and theological whole.[143] Van Leeuwen, however, says: "In my judgment, the contradictions in question are not ultimately evidence for contrary social groups or worldviews. Rather, whatever their historical origin, within Proverbs they have come to express *one* broad worldview which acknowledges the conflict of dogma and experience, yet maintains both."[144] When Proverbs is allowed to maintain the polyphonic expression of order, liminality, mystery and the fear of Yahweh, it presents a complementary but incomplete voice in the wisdom literature which grounds the more severe struggles in Job and Qohelet.[145]

6. Conclusion

Murphy rightly warns "What a mistake it is to deem the sages simplistic!"[146] Our interdisciplinary hermeneutic has helped us not to underread the book of Proverbs. We have argued most importantly that Proverbs 1–9 and 31 create a frame to the book and serve as a key to interpretation of what lies within the sayings and admonitions in 10–29. This frame provides a worldview grounded in a theology of creation which intentionally combines the salvation history (Yahweh) with the theology of Elohim's created world-order. The frame also makes an enticing and often erotic appeal to listeners to embark on the journey to wisdom while, at the same time, establishing the theological limits and boundaries of knowledge. The "fear of Yahweh" is, therefore, more than just conditioning knowledge; it qualifies wisdom as a reflexive response of humanity before the wise, creator God. In this way, the proverbial epistemology is like Torah in the way it is

142 Or what Crenshaw, *Education (1998)*, 221–7 (221) calls a "literary canon". While his concept is more social than literary, he nevertheless entertains the idea that these books represented a literary curriculum for ancient Israel. The same idea can be found in Whybray's "common tradition" and "distinct intellectual strand in Israel's life". Whybray, *Intellectual Tradition*, 54, 70. See also Rad, *Wisdom*, 70.

143 See *Paradoxes*, 265 where he says, "Because the anomalies were part and parcel of the unfolding of life, they stand unsystematically sprinkled throughout Prov 10–29 largely without the benefit of special structural or linguistic markers".

144 Van Leeuwen, "Wealth and Poverty", 26.

145 Note our account of the juxtaposition of Gen 1 with Gen 2–3 and chapter 2, see Alter, *Narrative*, 141–3, S. Niditch, *Oral World and Written Word* (Louisville, KY: Westminster John Knox, 1996), 25–38 and N. Stahl, *Law and Liminality in the Bible* (JSOTSup; Sheffield: JSOT, 1995), 27–36. Stahl's larger project develops the "multiplicity," "polyphonics" and "ambivalence" created by this narrative technique.

146 Murphy, *Proverbs*, 264.

grounded in ontology and engaged in a relationship with the creator and his creation.

With the frame around chapters 10–29, the sayings and admonitions represent an application of the worldview in chapters 1–9 to the experiences of life. The flow mimics the bi-polar experience of wisdom in life. The message in Proverbs 26:1–12 about "fittingness" exemplifies the lost epistemology of aphoristic or hermeneutical thinking. Knowledge is not merely the product of methods and universal systems, but is grounded in the local and particular as well.

The proverbs thus deny the certainty and dogmatism sought by skeptics. In their variety, they represent the range of voices that constitute the multivalency of the wisdom literature. With the creation order setting the boundaries and limits of human morality and knowledge, the knower is to recognize the ambiguity and mystery that are inherent in human life. Still, Proverbs' voice is traditional and foundational and therefore limited in its aim. As such, we can see how significant a literary and theological reading can be not only for the wisdom literature, but for a canonical reading of the OT. Like Psalm 73, the wisdom literature allows for a journey into the mysterious (Job) and enigmatic (Qohelet), but it never forgets the foundations of wisdom that give unity to human knowledge in the creator's world.

CHAPTER SEVEN

Epistemology in Ecclesiastes and Job

1. Introduction

In the Old Testament, Ecclesiastes has been the crown prince of epistemological studies.[1] The contradictions, radical conclusions and passionate desire for knowledge not only make it an appropriate candidate for such study, but also put its message in sharp contrast with the rest of the OT and especially Proverbs. Job too exemplifies a problem, if not a crisis, with the confident form of wisdom in Proverbs. This chapter rehearses the epistemological study of Ecclesiastes and Job, seeking to clarify its relationship to the ways of knowing we have encountered so far.

2. Epistemology in the Wisdom Literature

2.1 Wisdom and the Wisdom Literature

We begin by setting Job and Ecclesiastes[2] in their context as wisdom literature. By general consensus, the book of Proverbs is "traditional" OT wisdom. As we discussed in the last chapter, Proverbs has a strong sense of optimism, order and divine sovereignty. "Wisdom" is a way of knowing God's order for the world and knowing how to live ethically and fittingly within that order – to discern the human task in the world.

It is, therefore, logical to identify Proverbs' use of חכמה as the central and traditional understanding of wisdom.[3] This is crucial to the study that follows, for we will find that Job and Ecclesiastes have a tendency to press Proverbs' optimism and to extend the semantic range of wisdom.[4] For example, Fox suggest that Qohelet modifies the traditional sense of חכמה in

---

[1] I. Nordheimer (1838) appears to be the first to address Qohelet's philosophy and epistemology, though he is largely left alone in this interest until the late twentieth century. See C. Ginsberg, *The Song of Songs and Coheleth* (New York: KTAV, 1970) for the history of interpretation in Ecclesiastes.

[2] Hereafter "Qohelet," following the title in the Hebrew canon. Some authors refer to the book as Qohelet(h) while others only use Qohelet(h) when talking about the speeches in the middle of the book (1:2 or 1:12–12:8). I will use Qohelet and Ecclesiastes interchangeably, only differentiating the Qohelet character from the frame-narrator when the argument requires it.

[3] M.V. Fox, *Proverbs 1–9: A New Translation with Introduction and Commentary* (AB; New York: Doubleday, 2000), 29–30.

[4] Note our caution in the last chapter about the common tendency to overemphasise the mainline position of Proverbs, thus portraying Job and Ecclesiastes as reactions to the failures of traditional wisdom.

order to organise experiences rationally.[5] Christianson confirms not only a variety among OT uses of חכמה, but also that it is especially evident in Qohelet's application of the term.[6] The meaning of wisdom, and its relationship to Proverbs (traditional wisdom), propels us forward with questions about epistemology in Ecclesiastes and Job.

3. Epistemology in Qohelet

Because of Qohelet's unusual style and contradictory content, there is no consensus on the book's literary structure. At the least, Ecclesiastes introduces the wisdom sayings of an Israelite king seeking wisdom (Eccl 1–2). The next ten chapters conduct a sequence of observations, laments and wisdom instructions, followed by a more reserved conclusion that "the end of the matter" is to "fear God and keep his commandments" (12:13). Our interest in epistemology here seeks to read Ecclesiastes keeping the following four threads intact in the overall message: epistemology, rhetoric, structure and the use of *a priori* wisdom concepts.

We pause briefly to orient these threads to the structure of Ecclesiastes in which their operate. There are four basic approaches to outlining Ecclesiastes. The most extreme view denies any structure in Qohelet and prefers to see a collection of sources, interpolations and annotations.[7] A more moderate group of scholars sees an edited central body with one or more obviously appended epilogues. Crenshaw, for example, describes Ecclesiastes as a less unified combination of Qohelet's central message – an author portraying a persona from a distance – and two disassociated epilogists in the frame (1:1–2a; 7:27 and 12:8–14).[8] Third, it is increasingly common to interpret Ecclesiastes through the structure of a frame-narrative. Fox, Longman, Christianson and Bartholomew are among many who adopt this structure, though with different interpretations of the epistemology and theology in the book.[9]

---

5 M.V. Fox, *A Time to Tear Down and a Time to Build Up: A Rereading of Ecclesiastes* (Grand Rapids, MI/Cambridge: Eerdmans, 1999), 77.

6 E.S. Christianson, *A Time to Tell: Narrative Strategies in Ecclesiastes* (Sheffield: Sheffield Academic, 1998), 100f.

7 See Seow, *Ecclesiastes*, 39–40 for a summary of the various approaches.

8 *Education in Ancient Israel: Across the Deadening Silence* (London/New York: Doubleday, 1998), 225–6. R. Gordis, *Koheleth – The Man and His World* (London: Jason Aronson, 1995) and G. Ogden, *Qoheleth* (Readings – A New Biblical Commentary; Sheffield, England: Sheffield Academic, 1987) have similar approaches to the structure.

9 M.V. Fox, "Frame-Narrative and Composition in the Book of Qohelet", *HUCA* 48 (1977) 83–106., sees the frame (1:1; 7:27; 12:8–14) integrated with Qohelet's speeches in way that allows the reader to evaluate the book through the narrator's eyes. A reader can agree with the book but disagree with Qohelet (103–4). Christianson, *Time*, 73–125 applies a full frame-narrative reading with the added complexity of a

Not only is Fox largely responsible for popularising frame-narrative readings, he has also been the most prolific contributor to studies on Qohelet's epistemology, and a strong advocate for the role of Qohelet's rhetoric in the book. He chooses to describe Qohelet's epistemological process as thoroughly experiential and empirical.[10] For him, Qohelet is a sage emerging from the teachings of the wisdom tradition who becomes perplexed by the problem, and particularly the obscurity, of meaning.[11] His (Fox's) attention to the rhetorical cues allows him to see Qohelet's empiricism as strategic, operating through a modified use of חכמה, to expose and redefine meaning – what Fox calls tearing down and building up.[12]

Fox locates Qohelet's epistemological and rhetorical method in a struggle to find meaning – a struggle which grows out of the idealism of his inherited wisdom tradition: absolute retribution and a predictable and repeatable means for attaining wisdom and righteousness.[13] The clash of the traditional foundations in his "inherited world construction" with his own experiences of reality subject him to an existential crisis.[14] The result is an autobiographical and poetic narrative[15] which waivers between advice to enjoy the good (2:24; 3:12 ,22; 5:17[18]; 8:15; 9:7–9) and mysterious or despairing conclusions in the recurrent הבל passages.

Qohelet's salient rhetorical flare is marked by his 38 uses of הבל – over half of all the OT uses – and this repetition is a key to Qohelet's epistemology. Fox takes הבל to mean "absurd"[16] which signals a strong departure from Qohelet's intervening positive judgments. Unlike Crenshaw,[17] however, Fox takes the intervening rhetoric *not* as a contradictory antithesis with traditional wisdom, but as an attempt to augment his tradition with the

---

Solomonic guise (p. 128–165). This contributes significantly to the reading experience forcing the reader to consider issues of authority and national history in the evaluation of Qohelet's epistemology. Furthermore, like Deuteronomy and Job, Qohelet's frame-narrative pattern tells a story in a way that the (loose outlines of) plot control the reading.

10 See especially "Qohelet's Epistemology", *HUCA* 58/1 (1987) 137–55; "Wisdom in Qohelet", in L.G. Perdue/B.B. Scott/W.J. Wiseman (ed.), *In Search of Wisdom: Essays in Memory of John G. Gammie* (Louisville, KY: Westminster John Knox, 1993) 115–31; "The Innerstructure of Qohelet's Thought", in A.A. Schoors (ed.), *Qohelet in the Context of Wisdom* (Leuven, Belgium: Leuven University, 1998) 225–38; *Time*, 70–1; and *Qohelet and His Contradictions* (JSOTSup 71; Sheffield: Almond, 1989), 79–120.

11 Fox, *Time*, 133–4.

12 Ibid., 3, 77, 133–4; "Innerstructure", 225.

13 Cf. chapter 3 below and M.V. Fox, "The Pedagogy of Proverbs 2", *JBL* 113/2 (1994) 233–43; Fox, "Innerstructure", 235.

14 Fox, "Innerstructure", 234.

15 I use the term "narrative" loosely here; though the story lacks a traditional plot it still has a central message, a central character and continuity of rhetorical method. Cf. Christianson, *Time*.

16 *Time*, 35. The meaning of הבל is highly disputed, despite common translations of "vain" and "vanity." Ogden argues for "enigmatic" and "mysterious," *Qoheleth*, 17–22. Longman prefers "meaningless," *The Book of Ecclesiastes* (NICOT; Grand Rapids, MI: Eerdmans, 1998), 32. Bartholomew senses a "paradoxical," "enigmatic," and "metaphorical" sense, *Reading*, 267, 166.

17 For Crenshaw the contradictions signify Qohelet's rejection of traditional wisdom.

admission that, in the human view of reality, things *appear* contradictory.[18] The problem is not with traditional wisdom but with "what happens *to* wisdom" in the finite world of human reality:[19] "Qohelet is not complaining that things are not enduring or valuable or worthy or useful enough but is rather lamenting the refractory, paradoxical, cussed quality of reality."[20] Thus Qohelet "is introducing a radical innovation into the notion of wisdom: [...] that one may use his independent intellect to discover new knowledge and interpret the data of individual experience."[21] For Fox, Qohelet's struggle can be summarised as a yearning to explore and understand epistemology[22] – to uncover the preconditions of knowledge[23] and meaning which he finds lacking in traditional wisdom.

Crenshaw has interacted extensively with Fox's attempt to understand Qohelet's epistemology, though his approach is far less systematic. He confirms Qohelet's use of empirical judgments, but describes the structure, epistemology and nature of traditional epistemology differently. Against Fox's frame-narrative reading, he proposes a group of editors who try to relocate Qohelet's works within traditional views of wisdom and torah.[24] This maintains the distance of a third-person story hidden behind a character in the narrative to complicate Qohelet's epistemology and accentuate the personal crisis with traditional views.[25] Crenshaw thus agrees with Fox about the highly individual and personal nature of Qohelet's crisis, but rejects the consistency Fox finds between the body, the frame and the book. At times he seems to reject Fox's more optimistic attempt to relate Qohelet to the wisdom tradition.[26]

Crenshaw's work, however, is significant for the attention it gives to Qohelet's *a priori* knowledge: "The simple truth is that Qoheleth accepted an astonishing variety of transmitted teachings without submitting them to the test of experience [...]. In light of overwhelming evidence of *a priori* knowledge in Qoheleth's teaching, it may be necessary to qualify the claim that a new era of empirical knowledge dawned when he appeared on the scene."[27] In other words, Crenshaw's allusions to traditional wisdom revisit our interest in worldview and ideology as pre-conditioning factors in one's epistemology.

---

[18] Fox, "Innerstructure", 226.
[19] Ibid., 229.
[20] Ibid., 227.
[21] Fox, *Time*, 76.
[22] Ibid., 71f.
[23] Fox, "Innerstructure", 229.
[24] Crenshaw, *Education (1998)*, 225–7.
[25] J.L. Crenshaw, "Qoheleth's Understanding of Intellectual Inquiry", in A. Schoors (ed.), *Qohelet in the Context of Wisdom* (Leuven, Belgium: Leuven University, 1998) 205–24, on p. 211.
[26] See the ambiguities in Crenshaw's position below.
[27] Crenshaw, "Understanding", 212ff (213).

In this light it is interesting how Crenshaw's (and Fox's) view of this *a priori* knowledge lead to inconsistent attempts to relate Qohelet to the more "conventional" wisdom tradition. At times Crenshaw wants to say that Qohelet "denies the very premises on which wisdom ordinarily took its stand", that the epilogists portray the Qoheleth as a "radical teacher" with a "profound skepticism",[28] and that he discerns "no moral order at all".[29] At other points he says that Qohelet's epistemology differs only "in degrees" from Proverbs; that he "resists a particular kind of wisdom" but does not "[oppose] wisdom as such";[30] and that Job and Qohelet share a "common understanding" with other wisdom books.[31] It is more than likely that Qohelet's wisdom, like Job, undermines several common assumptions which developed in the wisdom tradition, but it does not undermine wisdom itself or commend a new (radical) movement altogether.[32] In the end, Crenshaw seems to want to emphasise that, somehow, Qohelet leaves many of the traditional tenets of wisdom untested in order to build upon them with his own investigation of knowledge (like Fox) while at the same time rejecting the conventional program for wisdom.

So although Fox and Crenshaw claim to differ on the degree to which Qohelet seeks to depart from or amend the wisdom tradition, the actual disagreement is sometimes negligible. Nevertheless, their attention to Qohelet's rhetoric relates to the very important relationship between epistemology and ontology and the degree to which traditional wisdom accords with reality. They both characterise Qohelet as a "realist" who wants to express the way things *look* in contrast to what Proverbs say they *are*.[33] Significantly, they see Qohelet caught in a balance between what has been declared and what he sees, unable to reconcile the two.[34] What is most striking (more for Crenshaw than Fox), in this light, is the inadequate attempt to account comprehensively for the structural, rhetorical, theological and epistemological aspects of the book especially as they resonate and echo with Proverbs and with their larger OT context. OT epistemology, as I have argued throughout this study, is embedded in a particular epic-narrative plot and worldview which guides and determines the reception of the individual books; epistemological studies in Ecclesiastes research have largely neglected this fact.

---

28 Crenshaw, *Education (1998)*, 162, 227, 242.

29 *Ecclesiastes* (OTL; London: SCM, 1988), 29.

30 Crenshaw, "Understanding", 206 (224), 212.

31 Crenshaw, *Education (1998)*, 162f.

32 Ibid., 162.

33 Crenshaw, *Ecclesiastes*, 29 says, "To be sure, he sets the private interpretations of reality over against conventional wisdom." Cf. Fox, *Contradictions*, 32, 93, 117.

34 Ogden, *Qoheleth*, 14. also describes Qohelet as a "realist" who calls subsequent generations to ponder life's mysteries while still holding firmly to optimistic aspects of the wisdom tradition.

Nevertheless, by giving attention to frame-narrative structure and the relationship between rhetoric, epistemology and ontology, Fox has initiated the move towards more holistic readings. This has paved the way for other scholars to make formative contributions. Christianson, Bartholomew, Longman and, in some ways, Lohfink all adopt the frame-narrative as key to understanding Qohelet's meaning.[35] Their approach to the frame, however, has been taken in three directions: reinforcing the ironic undercurrents of Qohelet's dialogue (Bartholomew); polemicising the epistemologies of Qohelet and the frame narrator (Longman);[36] and antithetically advancing or nuancing Qohelet's message (Christianson).

Bartholomew argues that the narrator exposes Qohelet's egocentric and ironic use of חכמה in contrast to its familiar use in the wisdom tradition.[37] Qohelet's search for certainty (1:13; 3:11) underlies the ironic failings of his חכמה and allows the frame narrator to reinforce the limits of pure empirical reasoning and the futility of individual autonomy.[38] Like Crenshaw, Bartholomew is particularly interested in the positive *and* negative judgments made by Qohelet, yet he argues for a more careful reading of the *a priori* material which signifies, at least at one level, clear unity between Qohelet and the more traditional narrator. He also interprets הבל as a metaphor (translating it as "enigma"), replacing the strong sense of pessimism with a more ambiguous reading. This allows him to close the distance between Qohelet and the frame.[39] Bartholomew is certainly right to call for a careful reading of the rhetoric, structure and (traditional) *a priori* assumptions when attempting to describe Qohelet's epistemology. And while Crenshaw only argues for one epistemology in the book, his disregard for the relationship between Qohelet and the frame leaves too many questions unanswered. The analysis which follows assumes the frame-narrative structure and thereby attempt to resolve some of the differences perceived in Qohelet's rhetorical and theological strategy.[40]

---

35 Christianson, *Time*, 123–5. Conservative scholars have followed the majority of those in history by seeking two voices rather than a frame. See M.A. Eaton, *Ecclesiastes* (Downers Grove, IL/Leicester, England: InterVarsity, 1983), 36–40. Cf. however, Longman, *Ecclesiastes* and Bartholomew, *Reading*.

36 Longman, *Ecclesiastes*, 38–9, 85 puts Qohelet against the wisdom tradition and the frame narrator in a position to correct him with orthodoxy.

37 Bartholomew, *Reading*, 229–37.

38 Ibid., 262f.

39 Ibid., 139–71.

40 On rhetoric and structure, see R. Whybray, *Ecclesiastes* (NCBC; Grand Rapids, MI: Eerdmans, 1989), 19–20 and Fox, "Unsought Discoveries: Qoheleth 7:23–8:1a", *Hebrew Studies* 19 (1978) 26–38, on p. 26, who says, "A combination of exegesis and rhetorical analysis is thus most likely to lead to an optimal understanding of a literary text." In this light, Bartholomew opposes the historical-critical emphases in interpretation that neglect the literary artistry in the book: "recognition of the literary craftedness of Ecclesiastes is crucial for its interpretation". *Reading*, 228. In other words, "unity", rather than "simplicity," focuses us on poetics and rhetoric.

3.1 A New Proposal for Qohelet's Epistemology

Among many candidates, I have chosen to analyse two passages in which Qohelet's rhetoric is accentuated by the message in the frame. Epistemological studies tend to be unclear about these relationships and thus fail to account adequately for the intra-textual dynamics in Qohelet and the related intertextual relationships between the wisdom books. By clarifying these relationships, Qoheleth's epistemology can be better understood, and its relationship with the other wisdom books can be advanced in the direction of a "polyphonic" reading[41] where multiple voices contribute to the sound of OT wisdom.

Apart from the presence of a frame, the structure in Qohelet is inherently difficult to describe. Ogden says, "The conclusion that Qoheleth is a unitary work does not necessarily imply that it has a definable structure [...]" and, on the other hand, "We shall discover that there are in the individual pericopes, structural features which suggest that the book is not devoid of structure, however difficult precise description of that structure may prove to be".[42] Bartholomew, nevertheless keeps us focused on the book's artistry and "literary craftedness."[43] Reading Ecclesiastes for poetics and artistic points us toward the important use of rhetoric, attitudes, gaps, tones and parallels that give clues to the overall meaning.[44] Above all, we will show that this passage sets the tone for the book in the way that it employs an ironic or sarcastic rhetoric and the guise of a "divided self" in support of a undervalued theme in traditional wisdom (12:13–14).

3.1.1 Ecclesiastes 1:12–2:26

While some prefer to divide 1:12–2:26 into smaller pericopes,[45] and others treat the text as a whole,[46] I take it as a single pericope consisting of three sub-units (1:12–18; 2:1–11; and 2:12–26) united by an over-arching theme:

---

[41] See A.C. Thiselton, "Communicative Action and Promise in Hermeneutics" in R. Lundin/C. Walhout/A. Thiselton (ed.), *The Promise of Hermeneutics* (Grand Rapids, MI: Eerdmans, 1999) 133–239, on pp. 172–82. Cf. G.E. Schnittjer, "The Narrative Multiverse Within the Universe of the Bible: The Question of 'Borderlines' and 'Intertextuality'", *WTJ* 64 (2002) 231–52, on p. 251, who says: "Thus rightful 'surplus of meaning' is not different meanings – polyphonic – but extensions of the meaning – polyacoustic – through innerbiblical intertextuality". Schnittjer argues that Polyacoustic readings come from a single authority, whereas the presence of multiple authorities or reading communities represents polyphonics. As with its use in musical theory, my use of "polyphonic" does not imply dissonance. Cf. liminality and polyphony in N. Stahl, *Law and Liminality in the Bible* (JSOTSup; Sheffield: JSOT, 1995).

[42] Ogden, *Qoheleth*, 11–2.

[43] Bartholomew, *Reading*, 228.

[44] Lohfink *Qoheleth* (Minneapolis, MN: Fortress, 2003), 7–9, acknowledges the frame, yet offers suggestions for structuring the book either logically or chiastically. While insightful, these seem forced and fail to account for the more artistic and rhetorical character of the book.

[45] Bartholomew, Delitzsch, Fox, Longman, Ogden and Provan.

[46] Christianson, Crenshaw, Gordis, Lohfink (1:12–3:15), Seow and Whybray. While Lohfink may find a continuity in the theme of anthropology that takes him past 2:26 in the unit, 3:1 introduces a major shift from the 1st-person rhetorical search that pervades chapter 2 especially. See my analysis on individuality below.

Qohelet's desire to search (דרשׁ) and explore (תוּר) *all things* by wisdom (בחכמה, 1:13).[47] On the surface, Qohelet's initial tone and language align him with traditional wisdom, to בקשׁ and קנה wisdom (Prov 2:2–4; 4:7). Yet his search is slightly more desperate and than and extreme than what we hear in Proverbs. For one, Qohelet claims to be wiser than all before him in Jerusalem (1:16; 2:9). Second, it is not wisdom that Qohelet wants (cf. Prov 4:7) so much as את־כל־המעשׂם (1:13) *by* wisdom.[48] Also, the extraordinary boast of a wise man, where humility would be more natural (Prov 26:12), combined with the enigmatic beginning to the book (1:2–11) are signals to that Qohelet's posture may not comport well with traditional wisdom.[49] A hint of irony even starts to emerge as Qohelet's דרשׁ and חכמה seem to undermine the wisdom in Proverbs.

This ironic tone is, in fact, the key to Qohelet's method. Irony "is saying one thing and meaning the opposite"; it is a "criticism which perceives an incongruity in things as they are [...]".[50] Qohelet creates irony by juxtaposing his *a priori* worldview alongside his experiential knowledge without offering an explanation. Which does he mean? The question hangs over the text as the monologue progresses. Each juxtaposition intensifies the rhetoric with irony and the need for resolution.[51]

Significantly, 1:13–2:26 is preceded by the frame-narrator's introduction in 1:1–11 where the reader is lead to wonder at the meaning of the endless cycles of toiling, generations, sun, wind, streams, speaking and remembering that yield nothing new.[52] This introduction, too, is a piece of subtle irony in that it *concludes* that there is nothing new at the *beginning* of the book. Qohelet's personal introduction to his search is marked by two more peculiar techniques which provide additional clues that his use of חכמה is not what it seems to be, but rather is ironically disengaged and self-destructive.

---

[47] With few exceptions, most take the phrase בחכמה adverbially: "by wisdom," "through wisdom," "wisely" (Longman), "with the help of knowledge" (Lohfink), making the object of the search על כל־אשר נעשׂה תחת השׁמים. Seow, *Ecclesiastes*, 120 points out that in the other uses of בחכמה in Ecclesiastes (2:3; 7:23; 9:15) the ב "always indicates agent or instrument [...] and not the object of any verb." The same is true for other occurrences of the phrase throughout the OT. Cf. Longman, *Ecclesiastes*, 77, 79–80 and the circumstantial uses of ב in Waltke/O'Connor, *Hebrew Syntax*, 196–7.

[48] Cf. כל־אשר נעשׂה (v. 13).

[49] Longman, *Ecclesiastes*, 79–80 says that Qohelet's appraisal of the search as "evil" shows a "radical discontinuity" with the wisdom tradition of Proverbs.

[50] Bartholomew, *Reading*, 230. I.J. Spangenberg, "Irony in the Book of Qohelet", *JSOT* 72 (1996) 57–69, on p. 60 however, argues that the irony arises from Qohelet's "skeptical stance" towards the "*claims and hopes of the original wisdom teachers*".

[51] H. Fisch, *Poetry With a Purpose: Biblical Poetics and Interpretation* (Bloomington, IN: Indiana University, 1988), 173–4 regards these breaks in the irony as a central part of his strategy to undermine his divided subjectivity.

[52] I follow Fisch's interpretation that these cycles indicate the inescapable and "trapped" or "enclosed" thinking that leads to הבל, *Poetry*, 167. Cf. also Seow, *Ecclesiastes*, 113–17 who notices the alternating pattern of: human activity – nature – human activity, which leads the reader through all the cycles in creation in order to make a conclusion about the limits of human knowledge.

(1) First, 1:13–2:16 reveals Qohelet's conspicuous hyper-subjectivity. The combination of first-person verbs and pronouns are unparalleled in the OT and the rest of Ecclesiastes. Christianson notes that the emphases are both in the grammar and the "narrative posture".[53] He concludes that over 80% of the verses in chapter 2 have first-person word forms – by far the highest in the OT (chapter 8 has the second highest frequency at 40%).[54]

Scholars are increasingly noting the statistic, but few work it out interpretively. Crenshaw mentions the "selfishness" in the text without further comment.[55] Fox, Seow and Longman attribute the first-person occurrences to the genre of ancient royal autobiography, though Longman's interpretation favours the royal parallel over against the "emphatic" subjectivity.[56] He is so focused on the historical parallels behind the text that he misses the obvious clues to the ironic rhetoric within it. Furthermore, Longman is among others who believe the presence of (Solomonic) kingship disappears after chapter 3,[57] underreading the poetic unity in the text and leading to two obvious problems. First, he fails to account for Solomon's union with the first-person emphasis. The first-person emphasis remains strong throughout (cf. chapter 8). Second, if Solomon's character disappears, is Qohelet still an autobiography? And if so, in what shape does the subjective voice proceed?

Fox and Seow[58] avoid these autobiographical dilemmas by focusing as much on the royal fiction as on the linguistic anomalies in Qohelet's rhetorical context. They recognise that while the ancient, royal genre leads one to anticipate an account of great success, Qohelet's search reveals the failure (or enigmatic character) of his wisdom. This, as Seow says, is ironically "contrary to the purpose of royal propaganda".[59] We are left with a paradoxical use of royal autobiography. Christianson draws out the epistemological implications of Qohelet's royal autobiography and subjectivity, saying:

> What is most important about the first-person narrative stance [..] is that it remains formally unchanged and unbroken from 1.12 to the frame narrator's appearance at 12.8. That stance, which makes Ecclesiastes unique in the biblical canon, contributes to the observational quality of Qohelet's narration and provides the anchor of his experience. Consequently it is likewise the anchor of his proleptic question and the

---

[53] Christianson, *Time*, 34.

[54] Ibid., 41. There are two weakness in this analysis: that it relies on English chapter divisions and that it looks at verses rather than words or pericopes. He thus over-represents the first person voice in the first pericope and underplays the transition at 1:12. Statistically, the text from 1:12–2:26 still has almost 80% of its words in first-person voice, with only the poetry in verses 15 and 18 lacking any such forms.

[55] Crenshaw, *Ecclesiastes*, 25.

[56] Longman, *Ecclesiastes*, 83.

[57] Cf. ibid., 5.

[58] Cf. also Bartholomew and Christianson.

[59] *Ecclesiastes*, 144. Fox, too, recognises the ironic character of Qohelet's autobiography and suggests it underlies the entirety of Qohelet's speeches, *Time*, 154–5.

sense of mystery that it helps to create. The narratorial voice is integral, therefore, to the functionality of events and, as we have seen, to the coherence of the narrative as a whole.[60]

From Christianson's point of view, the first-person voice unites the narrative and engages the reader in Qohelet's self-reflective exercise.[61] In expressing his thoughts this way, "Qoheleth transcends himself"[62] and his divided-self operates in a hyper-subjective mode of reasoning which opens our eyes to the "formation of the self".[63] Here we encounter a rare anticipation of the Cartesian, egocentric knower who raises his reason above his "self" to find certainty. He wants to think about himself *and* the "other" within himself and connect it to "other's" through his book.[64] Fox, too, says of this unique empiricism, "He is not only exploring, but also observing himself explore."[65]

Much like Christianson, Brown suggests that Qohelet's self-consciousness is meant to encourage progress in our intellectual and moral character. But he gets there by a caricature of traditional wisdom in Proverbs as an archaic and simplistic deed-consequence schema in need of challenge and advancement.[66] As such, Qohelet's intellectual discovery apparently escapes the naivete of the past and instead "places a high value on the role of the individual and personal intellect to make moral coherence of one's life and world".[67] It is true that the subjective tone engages the reader, but Brown misreads the rhetoric and irony and thus makes Qohelet a celebrity for charting a new path. Qohelet does occasionally *appear* to abandon tradition and history in his individualistic pursuit of knowledge, but his reasons for doing so require a better account of his method.

In sum, the interpreters so far variously and sometimes awkwardly try to address the problems of subjectivity, irony, rhetoric and structure. Fisch provides a fresh way forward. Recognising Qohelet's explicit division of his self in an effort to understand reality and meaning, he articulates the kind of irony that results:

---

[60] Christianson, *Time*, 42 Cf. W.P. Brown, *Character in Crisis: A Fresh Approach to the Wisdom Literature of the Old Testament* (Grand Rapids, MI/Cambridge: Eerdmans, 1996), 148.

[61] Christianson also demonstrates a shift from first-person to second person emphases that starts after chapter 2 and is complete by chapters 11 and 12, *Time*, 243–45. However, the larger question I aim to answer is: 'what is being done to Qohelet's persona in the first two chapters with the emphatic use of these ironic and subjective signs?

[62] Ibid., 211.

[63] E.S. Christianson, "Qohelet and The/His Self Among the Deconstructed", in A.A. Schoors (ed.), *Qohelet in the Context of Wisdom* (Leuven, Belgium: Leuven University, 1998) 425–33, on p. 428.

[64] Christianson, ibid., 428–30 shows how the writing and reading process transcends the postmodern deconstructive process of self reflection. Instead Qohelet shows our own self formation through our vision of his self. On the role of the "other" in aesthetics, see G. Steiner, *Real Presences* (Chicago: University of Chicago, 1989), 200–32.

[65] Fox, *Time*, 78.

[66] *Character in Crisis*, 134. This perspective on Proverbs is critiqued in Chapter 6 above.

[67] Ibid., 148.

We may say that here we have fundamental irony or aporia: even as the philosopher contemplates himself as the passive *object* of a universal *process*, his active contemplation of this process in the language of philosophy detaches him from the process, affirms his freedom and independence as a *subject*. We are in fact somewhere near the very ground and origin of all irony.[68]

Fisch thus brings Qohelet's strategy closely in line with his semantic tools demonstrating that the first-person language nuances his search and his wisdom inside a mood of wavering irony which deconstructs his hyper-subjectivity in the process.

(2) The divided self and the ironic tone are also evident through Qohelet's use of his לב to get wisdom. לב is used 12 times in 1:12–2:26, a frequency 13.8 times greater than the rest of the book.[69] Several concomitant rhetorical devices thus converge in this section, yet the effect is rarely noted.[70] Qohelet's heart is used from a distant, "divided" position in order to apply it to a host of actions and circumstances: he spoke (דבר) to (with) his heart (1:16; 2:15 [2x]), gave (applied, נתן) his heart (1:13, 17; 8:9, 16; 9:1), explored (תור) (2:3), tested it with pleasure (שׂמחה) (2:1), did not withhold it from pleasure (שׂמחה) (2:10), and turned (סבב) it to despair (יאשׁ) (2:20). Fox summarises: "His heart, for its part, "sees" wisdom (1:16), conducts itself in wisdom (2:3), and receives pleasure."[71] The heart becomes the lone instrument of an unbounded epistemological search for meaning and pleasure. Yet as Christianson points out, לב first appears in Qohelet's introduction (1:13)[72] along with the first use of חכמה and the beginning of the first-person emphasis. In this way, the text seems carefully crafted to combine the observational, even empirical, individual and exhaustive character of Qohelet's searching heart and his disengaged wisdom.

Paralleling Fisch's observation that this process presents a unique and ironic use of חכמה,[73] Bartholomew offers another account for the rhetorical and semantic factors at play. לב has been taken up by a wise man in the exhaustive pursuit of all things; he wants certainty. Drawing out the irony, Bartholomew asks, "is this energy directed towards 'guarding his heart'?" (Prov 4:23), or trusting in Yahweh (Prov 3:5–7)?[74] Bartholomew concludes

---

68 Fisch, *Poetry*, 169.

69 Fox, *Time*, 78.

70 Crenshaw, *Ecclesiastes*, 72 merely notes the intellectual character of the term, similar to Longman, *Ecclesiastes*, 78. Ogden at least remarks that the use is peculiar to Qohelet, *Qoheleth*, 36. By translating לב as "mind" and חכמה as "understanding," Lohfink shows his recognition of the unique uses in Qohelet, yet the translation (into German or English) consequently deprives them of their semantic play and ironic force in the Hebrew, *Qoheleth*, 19. Commenting on 1 Sam 1, Sternberg says, "Much of the beauty of the irony in this chapter lies in its covertness [...]. With the irony overarticulated, this passage falls between translation and interpretation." *Poetics*, 195, 525.

71 Fox, *Contradictions*, 87.

72 Christianson, *Time*, 195.

73 Fisch, *Poetry*, 159.

74 Bartholomew, *Reading*, 236.

that he does neither, but is rather intentionally identifying his rationalist לב with the conceited fool (cf. Prov 28:26).[75] Conventional wisdom (i.e. Proverbs) for Bartholomew has a "bi-polarity" by which the individual balances experience against the *a priori* traditional worldview. Qohelet lacks this bi-polarity, having the attitude "anything less than certainty is ignorance".[76] The lack of bi-polarity accentuates the ironic clues in the text.

Returning briefly to analysis in the last chapter, we can flesh out several ways that Proverbs provides a contrast for Qohelet's use of לב and חכמה:

Prov 3:5–7

בְּטַח אֶל־יְהוָה **בְּכָל־לִבֶּךָ** וְאֶל־בִּינָתְךָ אַל־תִּשָּׁעֵן׃
בְּכָל־דְּרָכֶיךָ דָעֵהוּ וְהוּא יְיַשֵּׁר אֹרְחֹתֶיךָ׃
אַל־תְּהִי חָכָם בְּעֵינֶיךָ יְרָא אֶת־יְהוָה וְסוּר מֵרָע׃

Prov 4:23

מִכָּל־מִשְׁמָר נְצֹר לִבֶּךָ כִּי־מִמֶּנּוּ תּוֹצְאוֹת חַיִּים׃

Eccl 1:13

וְנָתַתִּי אֶת־לִבִּי לִדְרוֹשׁ וְלָתוּר בַּחָכְמָה עַל **כָּל־אֲשֶׁר נַעֲשָׂה** תַּחַת הַשָּׁמָיִם הוּא | עִנְיַן רָע נָתַן אֱלֹהִים לִבְנֵי הָאָדָם לַעֲנוֹת בּוֹ׃

In these and other passages of Proverbs, the heart is guarded in service to Yahweh, whereas Qohelet's unbounded heart searches desperately (assigning such a task to the human vocation). He seeks to explore and set his heart to understanding, but Proverbs warns against the fool expressing his own לב (18:2) or trusting in his own לב (28:26; cf. 28:11). Furthermore, Qohelet not only thinks he is wise,[77] but the wisest of all (Eccles1:6; cf. 2:9). Proverbs warns that there is more hope for a fool than the man who is wise in his own eyes (Prov 26:12).[78] The sets of passages above are also contrasted by their use of the inclusive construct ־כל: all your heart, all your ways, all diligence, all things done under the sun.[79] Against the emphatic warnings created by the constructs in the proverbs, the construct phrases in Ecclesiastes communicate the exhaustive nature of Qohelet's search (1:12–14, 16; 2:9–11). It is not necessary to think that Qohelet has these direct parallels in mind as he writes (though it is possible).[80] Ecclesiastes has been very carefully written and it is more than reasonable to conclude that Qohelet works out of a "corporate memory" of torah and traditional wisdom. His

---

75 See R.C. Van Leeuwen, "Wealth and Poverty: System and Contradiction in Proverbs", *Hebrew Studies* 33 (1992) 25–36, on p. 34.

76 Bartholomew, *Reading*, 234.

77 Or, "*took* himself," depending on how Qohelet is relating his method.

78 R.C. Van Leeuwen, *Context and Meaning in Proverbs 25–27* (SBL.DS; Atlanta, GA: Scholars Press, 1988), 103 says that "wise in his own eyes" (26:12) is the "tacit converse" of "The Fear of the Lord" in Prov 3:5–7.

79 See this observation in D. Winston, "Hellenistic Jewish Philosophy", in D.H. Frank/O. Leaman (ed.), *History of Jewish Philosophy* (London: Routledge, 2003) 38–61, on p. 39.

80 Lohfink describes the "textual affiliation" and "public" character of writings that allows underlying principles in texts to be engaged without direct linguistic parallels. See "Was There a Deuteronomistic Movement"? 39–40.

speech in 1:12–2:26 reveals an intentional and subtle set of intertextual plays and echoes which set out a depiction of the heart, of Yahweh and of wisdom that align in ironic opposition to Proverbs. He is overdoing his private subjective search in every way and the effect compromises his own conclusions.[81]

3.1.2 Ecclesiastes 5:1–7 [4:17–5:6]

So far I have demonstrated the inconsistent or broken irony in Qohelet's speeches that indirectly affirms the order and foundations of traditional wisdom. While this irony represents Qohelet's divided-self, it is also a genuine expression of his experiential journey. The speech in 1:12–2:26 shows Qohelet at the peak of his irony as he voices his experience of the "refractory, paradoxical, cussed quality of reality".[82] But Qohelet does not regard the experience anti-realistically,[83] as continually reaffirmed by the breaks in his rhetoric which reveal an underlying, *a priori* view of reality behind his thoughts. In light of such a passage in Ecclesiastes 3:16–17, Fisch says, "In such verses we reach the limits of irony as the mind vibrates to a different need and a different purpose. For a moment the ego-centered direction is abandoned and another takes its place – a disinterested indignation at the world's wrongs, a quite nonphilosophical passion for judgment and righteousness."[84]

We must, then, ask why Qohelet occasionally breaks his enigmatic moods with these turns to fixed realities. Speaking to these occasions, Fox argues that Qohelet never invokes the sages' conclusions, but only quotes them in support of his own conclusions.[85] Contrary to Fisch, he does not really see Qohelet breaking stride with his radical empiricism. Yet this misses the obvious turn from empirical (observational) statements to the faith based declarations of what Qohelet assumes to be true. It is these unexpected turns from empirical to rational/traditional judgments which force readers to question Qohelet's epistemological foundations and his relation to his tradition.

In Ecclesiastes 5:1–7[4:17–5:6], Qohelet quotes and interacts with traditional material in a way that allows us to comment on his view of tradi-

---

[81] Winston, "Philosophy", 40, says, Qohelet's "demand for rationality constitutes the heart of the mainstream tradition in Greek philosophy. For a philosopher like Nietzsche, 'the fanaticism with which all Greek reflection throws itself upon rationality betrays a desperate situation,' and is 'pathologically conditioned.' In any case, it is this fundamental drive for rationality that prevents Qohelet from ignoring the ineluctable absurdity that characterizes the human enterprise as a whole and thus sharply distinguishes his approach from that of the Jewish wisdom tradition," citing Nietzsche, *The Twilight of the Idols*, 10:478 in W. Kaufman, *The Portable Nietzsche* (New York, Viking: 1954).

[82] Fox, "Innerstructure", 227.

[83] Cf. Fox, *Contradictions*, 90–5 and Bartholomew, *Reading*, 234.

[84] Fisch, *Poetry*, 173.

[85] Fox, *Time*, 76.

tional wisdom.[86] There is almost universal agreement on the beginning and end of this pericope.[87] It begins a change of tone from reflection to ethics[88] – from observation to affirmation. The pericope is enclosed by two imperatives, שׁמר (4:17[5:1]) and ירא (5:6[7]) as well as being marked by intertextual affirmations of conventional wisdom and torah. Thematically, the passage is also enclosed by two sentences which express Qohelet's overall purpose in this passage. 4:17a[5:1a] acts as an introduction to the pericope: שׁמר רגליך כאשׁר תלך אל־בית האלהים,[89] summarizing the attitude that is required for those who seek to do religious or cultic service,[90] and 5:6[7] closes the admonitions with a similar summary statement: כי את־אלהים ירא.[91] Both phrases are closely affiliated with the central admonitions and metaphors of traditional wisdom instruction, especially רגל and ירא.[92]

Added to that, the specific admonitions,[93] while modifying the language of the source texts, appropriate warnings and ideas from both torah and wisdom sayings to caution the attitude and "words" of those who approach God (Num 15:3; Deut 23:22–24; 24:4; Prov 1:15; 20:25).[94] The overall

---

86 R.E. Clements, "Wisdom and Old Testament Theology", in John Day/R.P. Gordon/H.G.M. Williamson (ed.), *Wisdom in Ancient Israel* (Cambridge: Cambridge University Press, 1995) 269–86, on p. 280 says in relation to 5:6[7] in the wisdom corpus that "cultic language concerning holiness appears only in a very restrained manner, although the cult is taken unquestioningly to be a proper part of he order of life".

87 Crenshaw, *Ecclesiastes*, 114 places vv 7–8 into this pericope. Cf. R. Whybray, *Ecclesiastes* (NCBC; Grand Rapids, MI: Eerdmans, 1989), 91 who stops at v. 6 he acknowledges a continuity in form from 4:17 to 5:8, but opts to stay with thematic indicators to close the pericope.

88 See Seow, *Ecclesiastes*, 197. The shift is also evident in the larger structure from 1:2–4:16 and 4:17 to 6:9.

89 Whybray, *Ecclesiastes*, 91 takes it as four "related" admonitions, but Seow seems closer to the overall sense grouping the various admonitions under two warnings to watch your steps and fear God in 4:17 and 5:6, *Ecclesiastes*, 197.

90 I do not think it matters whether בית האלהים in 4:17 refers to the temple or the synagogue. Lohfink, *Qoheleth*, 74–5 makes the more contextual observation that the admonitions are dealing with religious activity in general, not just sacrifice or formal worship, especially as reinforced by the transcendent nature of God as "wholly other" in v. 5.1. Cf. Seow, *Ecclesiastes*, 197.

91 cf. Fox, *Time*, 233.

92 Van Leeuwen, "Liminality" describes a worldview in Proverbs comprised of two paths, two ways, and two women which are to be navigated with the fear of Yahweh. On the imagery of רגלים see also Seow, *Ecclesiastes*, 197–8. It is also significant that this presents a parallel between the speech-admonitions in Proverbs and Qohelet's enigmatic attitude towards דברים.

93 There are several minor textual difficulties and some corresponding challenges in translation. Scholars are not agreed about what יודעים לעשׂות רע implies about fools doing evil: whether they do not know *how* or do not know *that* they are doing it, etc (4:17). Furthermore, the meaning of ענין in 5:2 is contested as are the meanings and forms of המלאך and האלהים. While clarifications at each of these points may illumine the passage, one cannot be decisive on most points, and none of the various options detracts from the major thematic flow of this text, Cf. Fox, *Time*, 230–1 and Seow, *Ecclesiastes*, 193–7.

94 Crenshaw, *Ecclesiastes*, 116 however, says that the "advice" in 4:17, "neither recommends nor discounts traditional piety [...]" but goes on to conclude about v. 6 that "Fear of God results in few words, faithfulness in paying vows if one ever resorts to them, and generally to conduct that does not invite punishment" (118). Following the observations made especially by Bartholomew but also Lohfink and Longman, it is better to see these traditional sayings in conjunction with the overall theme of the book as taken up in my position below.

"attitude" or "fear"[95] in these admonitions is reinforced by the visual picture of distance between God in heaven and humans in the earth below (5:2[1]). Some take this picture as an emphasis on divine otherness[96] and Gordis oddly regards it as typical of "unbelief";[97] yet the more reasonable explanation assigns two levels to Qohelet's rhetorical strategy as he affirms both the transcendent nature of the divine *and* the felt-distance in his own experience. This two-fold response can also be observed in Qohelet's ironic allusion to Yahweh's presence through his absence in אלהים.[98]

The breaks in Qohelet's experiential process and individual authority emerge throughout his speeches (cf. 2:24; 3:12–13; 5:18–20; 8:12–13; 9:7–10; 11:1–12:8). While the uncertainty in his tone[99] signals the experiential outcome of his search for certainty it also functions as a rhetorical device to keep his audience in suspense. Against the backdrop of his tone, however, the reader is struck by Qohelet's positive conclusions in matters of the cult, wisdom and the fear of God.[100] These conclusions are not empirical *observations*, but statements of what he *knows to be true* and ultimate – the fear of God. But how does he know these things? And if his method is skeptical, radical or purely empirical, what does he gain by confirming the supposed target of his struggle?

The patterns of irony and repetition in these speeches prevent us from dismissing the traditional affirmations as many are prone to do. It makes more sense to take references like את אלהים ירא as a subversive way to

---

[95] Fox, *Time*, 229–30 makes note of all of the major indicators of "trepidation" in 4:17; 5:2 and 5:6 but he still regards the overall theme as vows while sacrifices and speech are secondary themes. Longman, *Ecclesiastes*, 148 sees the text as admonitions of the cult addressing sacrifices, prayers and vows. While giving close attention to the detail in these warnings, Seow, *Ecclesiastes*, 197 helpfully sustains the overall theme of "attitude" before God. These settings provide a platform for Qohelet to make his larger point about the divine human relationship. Cf. also Lohfink, *Qoheleth*, 75 who senses Qohelet's larger motives.

[96] Cf. Seow, *Ecclesiastes*, 198 and Lohfink, *Qoheleth*, 75. The idea here is that the torah promises both the transcendence and immanence of Yahweh (Deut 4:7, 36 etc.) and that by emphasizing only distance and transcendence, Qohelet seek a reform of religion. Even if this is true, it is complicated by the fact that Qohelet wants both to affirm and caution the legitimate approach (קרב) of the worshiper (4:17). The meaning of the Hebrew קרב is occasionally contested or nuanced, but Fox, *Time*, 230, shows how the root clearly resonates with contexts of intimacy between God (Ps 34:19; 85:10; 119:151) and the worshiper (Num 16:10; Ps 148:14; Ezek 43:19; Lev 10:3). Furthermore, Fox confirms that Qohelet's attention to distance is to maintain "God's heavenly vantage point" as necessary for those who bring vows (231).

[97] Gordis, *Koheleth*, 238.

[98] By using אלהים throughout the book (37 times) Qohelet ironically alludes to the "absence" of Yahweh in his experience (cf. Esther). Fisch, *Poetry*, 162, sees this frequent use of אלהים not only as the absence of Yahweh, but further as the absence of covenant: "That bond of relation which gives meaning to a world, purpose to human life, and shape to history, is implied by a kind of pointed silence, by an absence that seems to cry out and draw attention to itself. It denies itself, paradoxically, through the bleakness and emptiness of an existence in which it is never affirmed."

[99] Cf. Longman, *Ecclesiastes*, 148–9.

[100] Because Fox says that, "Qohelet never abandons moral and religious principles or repudiates the principle of divine justice", his distinction between "quoting" and "invoking" the sages' advice amounts to an unnecessary qualification. *Time*, 229.

deconstruct the fruitless, disengaged rhetoric which dominates the speech in 1:12–2:26. The ultimate function of these subversive phrases is finally confirmed in the conclusion (12:13–14). Like the present passage (5:1–7[4:17–5:6]), these phrases also mark the "shared view of reality" between wisdom and law and expose the moments in Qohelet's thought which are obscured by his empirical, hyper-subjective epistemology.[101] Behind his irony and the הבל judgments lie principles of divine created order which re-centre Qohelet's thought and permits his more sober conclusions. Right and wrong, good and bad, etc. are not arbitrary categories for Qohelet, but principles grounded in the reality of God's created order which allow these desperate but rational comparisons to be made.

In summary, the analysis here shows that the structural-frame, *a priori* material and irony create a self-destructive rhetoric which give way to the fear of God conclusions. These conclusions are only a subversive voice until they are strongly proclaimed as the ultimate lesson of wisdom in Ecclesiastes 12:13–14. Fisch helpfully explains:

> the idea that would assign these closing verses of Ecclesiastes [12:13f] to another editor or author should be resisted. The skeptical rejection of skepticism is the final twist of Qohelet's super-irony. It gives us an ego that has ironized itself away and has abdicated the self-sufficient thinking of the ḥākām [...]. The proper study of mankind is man, Qohelet seems to say. But ironically, this penultimate verse of the book explodes such a humanistic pretension. To fear God and keep his commandments becomes "the whole of Man" or, we may say, what is left of man when his ego has been ironized away.[102]

When the egocentric guise is "exploded," so also is the autonomous, rational, "disengaged" search for certainty that seeks to transcend tradition, history, community and the fear of Yahweh. Qohelet's experience is real, but his wavering rhetoric in the end serves to expose temptations to elevate wisdom above God and his created order. Ecclesiastes, then, need not be taken as a rejection of wisdom but just as well serves as one of several "polyacoustic voices" in OT wisdom which express wisdom in a harmony of many perspectives. As we turn to the epistemological analysis of Job's rhetoric below, we will find this polyacoustic nature of wisdom expanded in another.

---

[101] Bartholomew, *Reading*, 259, says, "Order and and instruction/torah go hand-in-hand, and obedience requires both a good creation and instruction. The point is that wisdom literature assumes certain ethical principles which are not just read off creation but are often very similar to the principles found in Law [...] wisdom and law share and underlying and often tacit presupposition of a 'carved' creation order. This is their shared reality." 260

[102] Fisch, *Poetry*, 175. Cf. Bartholomew, *Reading*, 260 for a similar conclusion.

4. Epistemology in Job

Like Ecclesiastes, Job provides a test of wisdom in the throes of life and, in its own way, serves to affirm the reliability of the created order. As a whole Job is a lengthy and complex narrative about the problems of justice, righteousness, suffering and evil.[103] At present, there are no focused studies on the epistemology of Job. Still the story stimulates endless scholarly discussion on the theory and limits of wisdom and knowledge. Our concern here is not to fill this void, but rather to draw upon aspects of Job that contribute to our study of Hebraic epistemology, notably those elements which demonstrate an engagement with traditional wisdom and knowledge in God's created order.

The poetic discourse (Job 3–42:6) is set within a conspicuous prose frame (chapters 1:1–2:12 and 42:10–17).[104] Within the frame, Job is depicted as a righteous man (1:1, 8–9; 2:3; 42:7–8) who becomes the pawn in a divine confrontation with the Satan. The bulk of the poetry (ch. 1–25) reports three cycles of speeches between Job and his friends Eliphaz, Bildad and Zophar whose speeches defend rigid views of divine retribution. Chapter 28 stands out both for its appeal to wisdom in creation and for its shift in form and tone that can be seen in Job's pleading.[105] In chapters 32–37 Elihu rebukes Job for justifying himself against God and the three friends for their failures to answer Job correctly. This "deliberate anticlimax" increases anticipation and heightens God's climactic response to Job's request for a mediator (38–41).[106] God's response takes place in two speeches which parallel his two appearances in the courts (chapters 1–2), and Job's double restoration (42:7–17). In this way the speeches bring the narrative to a true climax with an extended rhetorical justification of his wisdom, order and transcendent knowledge. Significantly, the hidden divine courts in chapters 1–2, where God agrees to test Job's allegiance, provides both suspense and the key to interpreting the intervening 38 chapters. The frame-narrator gives the audience several epistemological points of view which he withholds from the main characters. They lack our perspective to resolve their debate. The end result is a "multiplicity" and "diver-

---

[103] Job's genre is debated, but the book maintains substantial thematic parallels with other wisdom texts: vocabulary, creation and order of the cosmos, divine knowledge, human knowledge and the doctrines of divine reward/retribution.

[104] N.C. Habel, *The Book of Job* (OTL; London: SCM, 1985), 25–7. Some assign Job's speech in chapters 25–31 to the frame, especially because of the frame narrator's voice in 25:1; 26:1 and 27:1. On Chapter 28 and the frame, cf. Gordis, *Job*, 298.

[105] Many see chapter 28 as a late addition, cf. Habel, *Job*, 392 and J.E. Hartley, *The Book of Job* (NICOT; Grand Rapids, MI: Eerdmans, 1988), 26f. É. Dhorme, *A Commentary on the Book of Job* (Nashville, TN: Thomas Nelson, 1984 (original 1926)), li. Cf. however, R.S. Fyall, *Now My Eyes Have Seen You: Images of Creation and Evil in the Book of Job* (Leicester/Downers Grove: InterVarsity, 2002) who shows how chapter 28 resonates with the plot and surrounding narrative (65–70; 90–1).

[106] Habel, *Job*, 33.

gence" of perspectives which give the plot its persuasive force and "motivate the progress of the tale."[107]

Three of these sections stand out as shifts in the epistemological flow of the narrative and will be examined briefly here: the friends' speeches, Job's wisdom poem in chapter 28 and the divine speeches of chapters 38–41.

4.1 Job's Comforters

The three friends are most easily characterised by their opposition to Job's self-justification, owing to their "crystal-cage" view of justice and retribution.[108] The debate is sparked by Job's first poetic lament in chapter 3 where he curses "light" and "day" (the day of his birth) as subtle critique of God's creation.[109] Not only are most of the six days of Genesis 1 evident in Job's speech, but his lament is also laden with imagery of death: the womb, grave, shadows and darkness. Brown illumines the significance of the anti-creation pattern:

> By calling for a reversal of creation, Job curses not only a particular day on the calendar, his birthday, but the extension of all creation itself, signified by light, the first act of creation (Gen 1:3) [...]. Moreover, the reference to the seven days during which Job's friends dare not speak is a counterecho to the Priestly Creation account, in which all creation is brought about and structured by the divine speech (Gen 1:1–2:4a).[110]

Creation order, therefore, sets the tone for the ensuing narrative. Eliphaz, for example, immediately defends retribution theology (4:7–9,17). So do Bildad (8:3–7, 13, 20) and, even more emphatically, Zophar (11:4–6, 13–20).[111] All of these figures represent a rigid view of traditional wisdom (8:8–12; 15:9–10; 17–19) which holds an almost mathematical view of divine retribution and deed-consequence outcomes.[112] As the plot builds, the

---

[107] Sternberg, *Poetics*, 172.

[108] Cf. also Polzin, "Framework", 184–5; A. Lo, *Job 28 as Rhetoric* (VTSup 98; Leiden/Boston: Brill, 2003), 63–5.

[109] The antithetical parallels to Gen 1 and 3 are unmistakable, such that Job's view of his plight is contrary to the very order and fabric of the created order. See M. Fishbane, "Jeremiah 4:23–26 and Job 3:3–13: A Recovered Use of the Creation Pattern", *VT* 21 (1971) 151–67, on p. 153 and Fyall, *Eyes*, 102–05.

[110] Brown, *Character in Crisis*, 61.

[111] The friends come to offer consolation and are ironically pushed into their defense of divine retribution. Job comes only with lament and is pushed into the desire for a legal hearing in the presence of God. These oppositions are central to the narrative plot, see Habel, *Job*, 30–1.

[112] Dhorme, *Job*, cxxxiv–cxxxv; Hartley, *Job*, 38, 44; and Habel, *Job*, 61f Compare L.G. Perdue, "Wisdom in the Book of Job", in L.G. Perdue/B.B. Scott/W.J. Wiseman [ed.], *In Search of Wisdom: Essays in Memory of John G. Gammie* [Louisville, KY: Westminster John Knox, 1993] 73–98, on p. 88 believes that the friends have a "darker" view than just retribution. Zophar's view of depravity in chapter 11 is morose indeed. Cf. however, E.A. Phillips, "Speaking Truthfully: Job's Friends and Job", Unpublished paper Presented at The Evangelical Theological Society; 2004) who sees the friends' arguments simultaneously upholding a true side to covenant fidelity in the created order, yet spoken in the wrong "*context*" (5).

tension becomes unavoidable: popular ("traditional") views of God and justice do not match the human experience of reality. Dhorme suggests that this was inevitable:

> [the stories of Israel's history] form the basis of the speeches of Job's friends [...] the really typical feature of this book is precisely that it passes through the crucible of a critical and penetrating mind orthodox, accepted ideas. Job will firmly deny the truth of all short-sighted explanations. His friends seek to apply normal solutions to the exceptional case. We are at a stage of development when thinkers have subjected to the verification of experience a religious philosophy which is far too *a priori*. The debate between Job and his friends represents the clash between observations based on daily experience and a tradition satisfied with outmoded aphorisms.[113]

Perdue also portrays Job in an experiential test of traditional wisdom that results in an "intellectual crisis of faith".[114] This common tendency to attribute this conflict to the inadequacies of "traditional wisdom," however, cannot be easily sustained under the close scrutiny of Job's rhetoric and plot.[115] As Phillips perceptively notes, even Zophar's first speech introduces a self-deflating irony: after arguing for the *inscrutable* ways of God's wisdom (11:7–12), he then proceeds to abuse Job for not acknowledging the *clear* conclusions in divine wisdom (11:13–20).[116] In this way, the narrative progressively displays the friends' perspective of a popular and overly simplistic application of traditional wisdom to the complex and varied circumstances of life. Job's desire to resolve the ambiguities in his circumstances turns to his own "wisdom" through an extended series of apologies, prayers, complaints and reflections in chapters 26–31.[117]

4.2 Chapter 28: The Heart of Job's Last Speech

At the centre of Job's last reply, chapter 28 captures a turn from apologetic to a reflection on wisdom, accentuating the book's richness in "discrepancy and juxtaposition".[118] The chapter differs from the surrounding context in its tone,[119] content and form,[120] particularly as Job moves from lament and

---

113 Dhorme, *Job*, cxxxv.

114 "Wisdom in the Book of Job", 88f. Habel calls it a 'conflict between belief and experience'. *Job*, 62.

115 In his study on Prov 10–29 Gladson, *Paradoxes*, 3 says, "What these sheer numbers indicate is a more serious pluralism in early wisdom than previously recognized, that the crisis in retribution in wisdom smoldered long before Job and Qoheleth, and that the locus of dissent was internal rather than external."

116 Phillips, "Speaking", 4.

117 Polzin, "Framework", 183. Or what was described above as a bi-polarity in Proverbs and Qohelet which balances experience against the tenets of wisdom.

118 Ibid., 182.

119 Habel, *Job*, 392 describes the tone as more "measured, lyrical and controlled" than the surrounding speeches and Hartley, *Job*, 373 suggests that the "abstract, reflective tone" is so different from the friends that it must be Job's voice.

120 Many scholars regard chapter 28 as a foreign or late addition to the original narrative. For a review of these theories, see Lo, *Job 28*, 2–21. Cf. also E.M. Good, *In Turns of Tempest: A Reading of Job* (Stanford,

self-justification to, what Habel calls, "a self-contained and measured reflection on access to wisdom".[121] The chapter also parallels the divine speeches in 38–41 and has affinities with chapter 1 making it both a bridge between the first and second halves of the book and a thematic marker which anticipates the conclusion.[122] Interpreters, however, have typically struggled with several aspects of this poem, most of which extend beyond the scope of this study.[123] We are particularly concerned with two of these problems and how they can be resolved in the light of the rhetoric in the book: the nature of the contradictory juxtapositions in the context of Job 22–31 and the problem of 28:28.

(1) Contradictory juxtaposition: In the first section (vv. 1–11), Job begins with ancient mining terminology, cataloging the successful attempts by human craft to discover the precious, hidden treasures of earth. His search parodies the friends' simplistic and scientific approach to theology, but it also sets an antithetical standard against which wisdom will be contrasted.[124] Habel says that for each of the sought treasures in this section, there is a "place," a "way or means of access" and "process of discovery".[125] The parody of the friends is brought to light as the mysterious "place" (מקום) of wisdom is contrasted to the success of craft (28:12):

[126]וְהַחָכְמָה מֵאַיִן תִּמָּצֵא וְאֵי זֶה מְקוֹם בִּינָה׃

This question, repeated again in verse 20,[127] is the "nucleus" of the chapter.[128] Thus, enclosed by the repeated question the second major section emphasizes the inaccessibility of wisdom by common means. It cannot be found by exploration (vv. 13–14) or purchased with earthly wealth (vv. 15–19).[129]

CA: Stanford University, 1990), 290. Fyall, *Eyes* and Habel, *Job*, 38–9, argues for its structural continuity with the surrounding chapters.

[121] Habel, *Job*, 392.

[122] Habel, ibid., 393 shows how סור רע in 28:28b forms an inclusio with 1:1. Gordis, *Job*, 298 notes the many parallels with the God-speeches, though he thinks the hymn is out of place, prematurely introducing the conclusion. Cf. also Hartley, *Job*, 373 who calls it a "bridge" text.

[123] According to Lo, *Job 28*, 5 there are four problems: (1) authorial style, (2) "Job's mouth" (voice), (3) pre-mature climax, and (4) the problem of 28:28.

[124] Good, *Tempest*, 290–1 sees four parts of a spiral that go from technological knowledge to ignorance. By the end of the chapter the "scientific" and "technological" approaches in this section are shown to be antithetical to the religious and moral form of true wisdom (292).

[125] See Habel, *Job*, 393–6, who argues that the three motifs which apply to human craft do not apply to human wisdom. Only God knows the place, access and process to getting wisdom directly.

[126] "*But* where shall she be found and where is the *place* of understanding". The introductory *waw* is adversative, see Hartley, *Job*, 378 and Gordis, *Job*, 308. Also חכמה is emphatic here, following Habel's translation. *Job*, 388.

[127] The change from תמצא to תבוא marks a shift from human searching (1–11) to the divine origin (vv 21–27).

[128] Hartley, *Job*, 379. L.G. Perdue, *Wisdom in Revolt: Metaphorical Theology in the Book of Job* (Sheffield: JSOT, 1991), 242 also recognises the questions as the "theme" of the chapter.

[129] The imagery is Hartley's, *Job*, 380. The antithesis between human craft and wisdom is strengthened here by the fact that neither the methods of human craft, nor the great treasures themselves can get wisdom.

When the question is repeated in verse 20, it transitions the chapter to the third section (vv. 20–27) which declares God's unique access to wisdom. When read in light of Proverbs 3:19 and 8:22–31, this section affirms the corresponding centrality and mystery of wisdom in creation, with an added caveat.[130] While traditional wisdom is grounded in a theology of creation, Job 28 warns that wisdom is not therefore acquired like the material elements in creation. Wisdom belongs to God and is given by him. It is God alone who knows the מקום, and the way to it (דרכה v. 23).[131] The passage parodies the friends' tendency to rely too readily on empirical and rational conclusion and brings the dialogues to a climax. The resulting tension between voices, as with Qohelet, is best understood in the light of the book's overall rhetorical savvy. As Lo points out, "Contradictory juxtapositions within the context of Job 28 (ch. 22–31) are part of the rhetorical strategy to expose the friends' inadequate perspective by highlighting the contradictions between traditional theology and actual experience."[132] That is, rhetorical analysis reveals Job in traditional wisdom's bi-polar process of encountering experiences in the light of declared realities.[133] In sum, the juxtapositional tone does not detract from the book but rather constitutes its very essence. True wisdom is committed to the struggles in the experienced life and is not satisfied with simplistic answers.

(2) Second, we are concerned with the problems of Job 28:28. According to Lo, these are: (1) the introduction to ויאמר לאדם, (2) the use of אדני rather than יהוה and (3) the dissonance between 1–27 and v. 28.[134] The first two problems have little impact on our epistemological investigation and have been answered well by Lo and others.[135] Our primary concern is with the rhetorical dissonance between 1–27 and 28 and consequently between Job 28 and Job 22–31. Rather than seeing this dissonance as a fault or problem with the plot, a rhetorical sensitivity to contradictory juxtaposition allows us to see this verse as creating the conflict in the plot which begs for eventual resolution.

That is, according to Job 28, the particular uniqueness of wisdom – and climactic conclusion to this chapter – is the conditional means for accessing it. Job says in verse 28: "Behold, the fear of Adonai, this is wisdom and turning aside from evil is understanding." Humans are given wisdom on the

---

130 Cf. von Rad, *Wisdom*, 148.

131 Habel, *Job*, 394–5 and Hartley, *Job*, 382 note the significance of these nouns in light of human craft in vv. 1–11.

132 *Job 28*, 20–1.

133 Lo cites Sternberg's plot analysis to augment her reading. Commenting on the multiple perspectives, Sternberg helpfully states, "No ignorance, no conflict; and no conflict, no plot". *Poetics*, 173.

134 Lo, *Job 28*, 11.

135 See Gordis, *Job*, 538; Habel, *Job*, 400–1 and Lo, *Job 28*, 11–4. Many manuscripts have יהוה and some have יהוה אדני. The unusual phrase could be intended to draw a distinction for the friends, a mark of the book's foreign setting, or a copyists emendation.

basis of "fear" and turning from evil. Significantly, it is Job's mouth which confesses this doctrine; Job has been willing to submit to a wisdom without answers – a lesson which his friends have denied. Furthermore, in the surrounding narrative, this distinction between Job and his friends is dramatically reinforced by the very fact that he prays to God in the midst of his plight (6:8–9; 19:7; 30:20; 31:35; 40:3–5; 42:1–6).[136] That is, although Job's tone alternates through contradictory perspectives, he is distinguished by his commitment to accept mystery, to struggle with his God and to appear in the divine courts.

Clearly Job and his friends part ways in their approach to wisdom and it is common to see this as pointing to two kinds of wisdom – either the wisdom of Proverbs against the wisdom of Job or God's wisdom against humanity's wisdom.[137] This needs to be phrased carefully. An opposition between Job and Proverbs must not arise from a simplistic reading of Proverbs, as we argued in the last chapter. Habel is on better ground when he suggests the that passage emphasises two "ways" or "modes" to wisdom, rather than two kinds of wisdom.[138] It is God who sets wisdom in creation and requires divine worship as a prerequisite for learning it. Humanity does not have unconditional access to wisdom, but must go to God in ירא and סור מרע in order to get it. Job's own conclusion in 28:28 resonates with his character in 1:1 as one who ירא אלהים and סור מרע, and who prays to God in crisis, in contrast to his friends' whose haste to answer eclipses their fear and leads to the misinterpretation of Job's situation, as made clear in chapter 42.[139] Before we draw conclusions, however, we need to consider Job's argument in chapters 22–27 and his demand for a legal hearing in chapters 29–31. Job 28 and 28:28 are an ambiguous pause that invites resolution.

4.3 The Divine Speeches

Like Job 28, the four chapters of the divine speeches in 38–41 evoke a contrast between divine wisdom and the limits of human knowledge in a way

[136] Phillips, "Speaking", 9–11. On this basis, Phillips suggests translating אלי נכונה in 42:7 and 8 as "unto me" rather than "about me" or "concerning me".

[137] Some believe that the pessimistic character in vv. 13–19 opposes the optimism in Prov 2:1–7. On this basis, the wisdom in Job is an advance of traditional wisdom, see Habel, *Job*, 389. Others see two kinds of wisdom in this chapter, appealing to the absence of the definite article in v. 28 as opposed to vv. 12 and 20 and/or the difference between what God can know and what humanity can know. See Good, *Tempest*, 282; Gordis, *Job*, 539 and Hartley, *Job*, 383–4.

[138] Habel, *Job*, 401. The misunderstanding is partly due to the identification of the object of the four verbs in v. 27 as wisdom rather than creation. Yet, in the rest of the OT, the four verbs in v. 27 are only used of creative acts and never of wisdom. See S.L. Harris, "Wisdom or Creation? A New Interpretation of Job 28:27", *VT* 33 (1983) 419–27, who argues that there is no evidence for two kinds of wisdom in Scripture. There is one wisdom set in creation by the creator (Prov 3:19–20), p. 424. Thus God controls the access to wisdom (Job 28:24–27), and his creatures must come submissively and obediently to him to get wisdom and understanding (426).

[139] Habel, *Job*, 64.

that reinforces the beauty and danger manifest both in creation and in human wisdom. The more than 80 rhetorical questions are designed not to rebuke Job so much as to invite him, and the audience, to reflect on Job's experience through a corrected view of wisdom.[140]

The questions also initiate the transition to the closing frame and bring the narrative to a close.[141] Fox discerns three types of rhetorical questions in these addresses.[142] First, there are questions of the "who" type that obviously point back to God as the source of the universe. Second, there are "what" questions ("Does the rain have a father?" 38:28) probing the limits of Job's certainty and all revealing that Job does not have an answer.[143] The third set of questions ("Have you ever [...]?") require a humble response to things Job cannot do or has not seen. Similar to what was accomplished in Qohelet, the general consensus among scholars is that these chapters continue what Job began in chapter 28 – reinforcing the limits of human wisdom.[144] God's response to Job's plea for a legal hearing turns him back to contemplate the implications of creation, and thereby recontextualises the foundations employed by Job to bring his case forward.[145]

This theological turn to creation and the limits of wisdom allows the questions to drive home a fundamental wisdom lesson. Fox thus thinks that the rhetorical questions and the limits of human knowledge are a means for the narrator to draw attention to the depth and transcendence of divine wisdom.[146] Habel, too, concludes that the narrative portrays God's primordial wisdom as created by God to be a companion governing the order of the cosmos. Although "primordial wisdom" is not accessible to humanity its existence is made known by the rules it has placed in the cosmos.[147] These rules are not the mechanical rules complacently embraced by the "wisdom"

---

[140] Fox contrasts the effects of an indicative approach with the rhetorical method and the benefits of the latter in the narrator's purpose, "Job 38 and God's Rhetoric", *Semeia* 19 (1981) 53–61, on p. 58.

[141] See Dhorme, *Job*, xxxi–xxxii and Habel, *Job*, 26. In an interesting survey of tragedy, Fisch, *Poetry*, 41–2 categorizes Job as a creation story paralleling Genesis 1–3 with a typical Hebraic ending: the tragic hero is fully restored.

[142] Fox, "Job 38", 58–9. This is in addition to a few direct questions that have the same effect.

[143] G. Vall, "From Whose Womb Did the Ice Come Forth?: Procreation Images in Job 38:28–29", *CBQ* 57 (1995) 504–13, argues that the most logical answers to the connected set of four questions in Job 38:28–29 insinuate mystery not divinity. That is, in answer to the first question, God is the founder of the waters, but the remaining questions are not answered by an appeal to God as the source, but that human language and metaphors cannot describe the reality of what God does and knows (513).

[144] Besides, Fox and Vall, see Crenshaw, *Education (1998)*, 215–6, Habel, *Job*, 535–7, and Gordis, *Job*, 298.

[145] For this reason, I believe conclusions like those of Hartley (487–489) and G.W. Parsons, "The Structure and Purpose of Job", *BSac* 138 (1981) 139–57, which describe the aim of the book as reinforcing relationship, submission and sovereignty fail to account for the larger framework in which these themes are communicated – divine wisdom.

[146] Fox, "Job 38", 60. Cf. also S.A. Geller, "Where is Wisdom?" in Idem.; *Sacred Enigmas* (London: Routledge, 1996) 87–107, on p. 102 who sees the argument as one made by "juxtaposition" rather than by "logical exposition".

[147] Habel, *Job*, 68–9.

of Job's friends, but are divinely ordained and beyond human control. Epistemologically, Habel sees humanity in a state of mystery, unable to perceive the fullness of primordial wisdom, yet beckoned to enter into a relationship with Yahweh that includes the possession of human wisdom and the knowledge of the true and free nature of this wisdom over against mechanical blind submission to rules. In a slightly different way, Hartley concludes that the revelation of divine wisdom exposes the friends' "erroneous" conclusions and false use of wisdom that was based upon a simplistic view of divine retribution.[148]

In the end, Good is right to see the story of Job as an "open text" that stimulates more questions and ideas than it answers.[149] The fact that the narrator tells such a lengthy story reinforces the point that in order for wisdom to guide the way through pain and mystery it must be in a bi-polar effort to balance experience with traditional wisdom tenets. Wisdom and knowledge in Job are a matter of participation in the created order with spiritual/religious devotion to the creator. Gordis, who regards chapter 28 as part of the conclusion with the divine speeches, explains that "(t)his existential experience of the pattern of the natural order serves as the basis of his faith in the rationality and meaning of the moral order. This implication, derived by analogy, is not an exercise in logic; it is the unanswerable result of a deep emotional experience".[150] Bartholomew puts it this way:

> The resolution of Job's enigmatic suffering comes through personal encounter with God himself, and particularly with God as transcendent creator. Indeed, in 38–41 the doctrine of creation functions as the key to theodicy. Somehow, this personal encounter resolves at an existential level Job's desperate struggle with the radical exceptions to the act-consequence structure that he has experienced, and he finds his relationship with God immeasurably deepened and his prosperity restored.[151]

In sum, the epistemology in Job, like Qohelet, aims to oppose false ways of knowing. Human knowledge is not found in the simple, rationalist, certainty-driven model of Job's friends; it is a dynamic part living with a worldview that balances experience with reality. The oppositional juxtaposition of perspectives confirms both the existence of a divine reality (and wisdom), but also the inability for humanity to see that reality as God sees it (Job 28). The doctrine of creation is a steady reminder of the bi-polar nature of life which leads the knower into a humble encounter with the creator in the fear of God.[152]

---

[148] Hartley, *Job*, 544–5.

[149] Good, *Tempest*, 179.

[150] Gordis, *Job*, 539.

[151] C.G. Bartholomew, "A God for Life, and Not Just for Christmas!" in P. Helm/C. Trueman (ed.), *The Trustworthiness of God: Perspectives on the Nature of Scripture* (Leicester: Apollos, 2002) 39–57, on p. 51.

[152] Cf. the "theodicy of soulmaking" and "phenomenology" at the heart of this book, Carmy/Schatz, "Bible", 23–5.

5. Conclusion

The modern tendency to set Proverbs against Ecclesiastes and Job has, in many ways, resulted from an inattention to the storied worldview of the ancient world. Our epistemological study has sought to refresh the contours of that worldview and hear these books in a new way. This chapter examined the important relationships between Ecclesiastes frame-narrative structure, irony and *a priori* material in order to explain the epistemology at work in the book. While it is possible to see Qohelet at odds with the tradition, there is also good reason to expect a more complicated message – one which carefully pits הבל statements against carpe diem sayings in order to draw an audience into an unresolved bi-polar experience. Qohelet's הבל expressions, instead of opposing his search for wisdom, are an ironic way of exposing the failures of an ambitious epistemology in order to reinforce the need for a bi-polar vision that resolves the gap between experience and received theology. The answer to the ambiguities in the world is not perfect or better knowledge, but "to fear God and keep his commandments" (12:13; cf. 2:24; 4:17–5:12, etc.) in the search for wisdom.

Job, too, presents a test of traditional wisdom against the perceptions of the lived life. The fact that Proverbs' optimism is already nuanced in a way that debunks mathematical approaches to retribution and reality, sets the friends up as too ambitious in their readiness to equate "the world as it seems" with the doctrines of "the world the way it really is." The friends simply fail to embrace the limits of human understanding and they drive Job to seek an answer from the divine courts. God's answer to Job undercuts the human proclivity to certainty and scientific rationalism, representing human knowledge in the context of encountering God their creator through their life in the world.

Clearly, wisdom and knowledge are front and centre in the wisdom books, while they are implicit in the narratives of the torah. Yet both traditions reinforce the mythical worldview of God and his creation, presence and wisdom as the context for human knowing. Our final chapter will provide a new perspective on the relationship between this traditions and their reception in the modern world.

CHAPTER EIGHT

Conclusion
Wisdom and Torah in Historical Perspective

1. Introduction

We began this study by setting Hebrew torah and wisdom in the context of the history of epistemological and phenomenological thought, and then we proceeded to examine these two traditions largely independently. This concluding chapter aims to summarise the study thus far and draw conclusions along several lines. We are initially interested in re-thinking the historical, cultural and religious relationship between wisdom and torah in the light our epistemological study. Second, we will briefly consider how epistemological reflection on the Deuterocanonical texts and the New Testament inform our study before finally integrating our conclusions with the historical development of epistemology outlined in the first chapter. We begin with a summary of the journey thus far.

2. Summary: The Epistemology of Wisdom and Torah

There is an unusual complexity in asking epistemological questions of ancient, pre-theoretical texts. We therefore chose a method which embraces the "conflict of interpretations" as it makes us maximally aware of the range of disciplines which inform our study. I also concluded that it was necessary to focus our method on Israel's mythical and symbolic approach to narrative, wisdom and law. We thus set the Israelite torah within the mythical framework of the creation of the world, the fall of humanity and the choice of Abraham's family to carry out God's teleological purposes. Torah for Israel, therefore, embodies the ethical demands of the garden to live between the antithesis of "good" and "evil." At stake is the ethical embodiment of the human *yeṣer*, that is, the human responsibility to submit to Yahweh as co-creators.

Wisdom literature also grounds knowledge in the mythical view of creation and Yahweh's primordial designs for the world. But instead of the national and covenantal particularity which we find in the torah, wisdom portrays knowledge with a universal relation to the created order. Still this universal perspective is not alternative option to torah; rather, the wisdom tradition grounds its whole enterprise on the "fear of Yahweh." Wisdom and knowledge cannot acquired apart from the religious faith and world-view in which torah is also rooted. How exactly, then, do these traditions differ? We seek to answer this question under five headings: ontology, ideology, liminality, hermeneutics and ethics.

2.1 Ontology and the Created Order in Wisdom and Torah

We have observed throughout this study that the epistemologies exhibited in Deuteronomy and the wisdom literature are alike engaged in the ontological realities of the created order. To be epistemologically engaged in ontology is to say that knowledge is acquired and justified on the basis of a preconceived understanding of reality (its origin, purpose, structure, etc.), and not with a move to "disengaged" objectivity. At the same time, these two traditions relate to their common ontology in different ways, and we are now in a position to present a brief comparison between wisdom and torah they situate knowledge in the *a priori* worldview of a Yahwistic faith.

Deuteronomy represents the realities of creation order in terms of the covenantal and patriarchal intentions for Israel amidst the nations.[1] This aspect of Israel's divinely-created vocation is most poignant in Moses's song (Deut 32) which portrays Israel's covenant infidelity as a violation of Yahweh's larger created purposes. So, while creation order provides the backdrop for the song, the national and storied side of Deuteronomy's ontology is obviously focused on Israel's particular role in a way that we do not find in the wisdom literature. Furthermore, Israel's knowledge of Yahweh and his will are rooted in the demand to actualise ancient relationships and traditional notions of reality, signified most prominently by the theophany at Horeb (cf. Deut 5:22–28).[2] Moses' words and torah are also Yahweh's words and torah and together these represent the means for Israel to renew Moses' theophanic realities at Horeb throughout all future generations.

The natural or creational foundation for the law is well attested, and James Barr attempts to use this fact along with evidence in laws in other ancient cultures to ground law in nature.[3] But in doing so, Barr is not careful in the way he relates the theological and juridical decrees in the torah to Israel's understanding of the created order. Barr's position forbids us from resolving contradictory approaches to law and nature in the ancient world.

---

1 The vision in Gen 12:1–3 and 18:17–19 is echoed not only in the classic text in Deut 4:5–8 but also in almost 50 references to the patriarchs in Deuteronomy.

2 As argued in chapters 2–5 above.

3 Barr, "Law", 9–13. What O'Donovan calls a confusion of epistemology and ontology, *Resurrection*, 19–20.

Is the source of different laws to be attributed to the cultures within nature? or to nature itself? Apart from the created order, how does one draw the line between culture and nature? Moreover, how would Barr attempt to handle the cross-cultural judgments imagined in the universal claims in Israel's torah? In other words, while the universal ontology of Yahweh's created order can account for the particular and temporary חרם-laws in Deuteronomy 7 and 20, pure natural law is unable to legislate such particularity and conditionality at the temporal level; natural law has no means to single out one nation or culture for ontological or teleological purposes. O'Donovan and Van Leeuwen avoid problems like Barr's by recognising that Yahweh – as the sole transcendent being – must be the one to reveal such universal and particular laws to humanity.[4] Israel's torah, then, is not a natural law nor is it merely a cultic-legal recitation; it claims to be a transcendent, divinely revealed "*comprehensive* moral viewpoint" that Yahweh gives to his subjects *within* creation.[5] Law comes not from within, but from without, and orders the particulars in nature from above.

Understood in this way, torah gives form to the diversity of the created order, founding the divine-human relationship upon the principles which unify the creation. The Greeks also sought principles which united their ontology – for Plato, the Ideas were organised around justice and Aristotle more loosely identified the concept of *eudemonia* as the centre of human meaning. In the torah, love stands at the head of the unifying principles for creation.[6] Yahweh's redemption of Israel – and therefore of the creation (Gen 12:1–3) – is motivated by his loving nature and loving activity (Exod 34:6–7; Deut 7:6–8, 10:15, 32:9–43). And as a response to Yahweh's actions, he obliges them with a corresponding command to love him (Deut 6:4–9; 10:15–20), a command which stands symbolically over the whole torah (cf. Matt 22:34–40; John 3:16). Torah grounds knowledge not primarily in the logical or juridical spheres, but in the relational and religious.

Creation order also provides an ontological foundation for knowledge in the wisdom literature. In chapters 6 and 7, we noted the strength of this foundation in passages like Job 28; 38–42 and Proverbs 1–9; 26. Not only does woman wisdom have her place before creation (Prov 8:22–26) – mak-

---

4 For O'Donovan, *Resurrection*, 34–5, something "teleological" is needed to rise above the "generic" relationships between the created beings. Cf. Van Leeuwen, "Liminality", 132 and the similar observation by Fox, *Contradictions*, 97 that the wisdom literature in this case sees law grounded in created order (about which Barr is correct) but that humanity is not epistemologically equipped to go directly to creation to extract wisdom and a natural law.

5 O'Donovan, *Resurrection*, 200. Cf. Van Leeuwen, "Liminality", 120; von Rad, *Wisdom*, 166.

6 O'Donovan, *Resurrection*, 222–24. See also Millar, "Place", 56 and Geller, "Wisdom", 32. Cf. the history of post-Kantian philosophy and its search to find unifying principle behind Kant's dualisms: language in Hamann, representation in Reinhold, the will in Fichte, being in Heidegger, the indifference point (force of life) in Schelling, religion in Schleiermacher, the spirit in Hegel, power in Nietzsche, praxis for Marx, the unconscious for Freud and play in Derrida. See Beiser, *Fate*, 43 and Critchley, *Continental Philosophy*, 31.

ing her an expert of the order formed there – but she also testifies to the wisdom embedded in creation (3:19–20). Wisdom's expert testimony is made on the basis of the "carved" (חק) sphere she saw designed for the seas (8:27–29), and this corresponds to her ability to reveal humanity's created vocation to pursue life and favour from Yahweh (8:32–36).[7] Unlike torah, wisdom is not depicted in the political or national goals of Israel's covenant, but as an address to the family and society in general to interpret and respond to their carved place in the world order. Wisdom, therefore, mediates the design within God's covenant with creation to humanity in order to facilitate the ongoing process of perception and response to things as they really are.[8]

In summary, because wisdom and torah are both grounded in the created order, they operate on the basis of a shared worldview[9] or a shared "map of reality".[10] This does not reduce torah to wisdom as perhaps happened in post-exilic Judaism. Schäfer, for example, rightly observes that wisdom and torah guide humanity to live in "harmony" with the created order;[11] yet to equate wisdom and torah on this basis[12] is to misrepresent their fundamental distinctions as they emerge in the narrative contours of the OT. With its cosmic origins wisdom supersedes torah and mediates the social "perception that every novelty, in its own way, manifests the permanence and stability of the created order, so that, however astonishing and undreamt of it may be, it is not utterly incommensurable with what has gone on before".[13] Torah, on the other hand, provides the same stability through covenant actualisation where Israel's unique relationship with Yahweh at Horeb is renewed in each generation. In torah, Israel alone is given the command to enact capital justice on Yahweh's behalf (Deut 7; 20). Torah goes *through Israel* to the world while wisdom precedes Israel and embraces the covenant with humanity *in creation*.

Thus, while wisdom and torah are distinguished between universal and national contexts, they are both grounded in the human boundaries and limits of the created order,[14] which involves the ultimate vision of humanity to be restored in Yahweh's order and Yahweh's land (Gen 11:8; Deut 32:8; Job 28; Prov 8:22–29; Ps 74:17; Jer 31:35–36; cf. Acts 17:24–6).

---

7 Van Leeuwen, "Liminality", 123.

8 Ibid., 116.

9 Bartholomew, *Reading*, 259.

10 Van Leeuwen, "Liminality", 111. Cf. also von Rad, *Wisdom*, 148–59.

11 P. Schäfer, "Wisdom Finds a Home: Torah as Wisdom", in J.H. Charlesworth/M.A. Daise (ed.), *Light in a Spotless Mirror* (Harrisburg, PA: Trinity Press International, 2003) 26–44, on p. 38. See also Van Leeuwen, *Context and Meaning*, 99ff; Fretheim, "Law", 190.

12 Schäfer, "Wisdom", 42.

13 O'Donovan, *Resurrection*, 189.

14 Van Leeuwen, "Liminality", 120.

2.2 Ideology, Worldview and Certainty in Wisdom and Torah

If ontology is a view of reality, or "the world as it really is," then epistemology describes the human means and limitations to access the knowledge in this reality. In both wisdom and torah, we have found the human ability to see "the world as it really is" inhibited by the ambiguities of life and distorted by the ideologies of idolatry and evil. Autonomous and scientific approaches to knowledge typically seek to get beyond all ambiguity and distortion to satisfy the skeptical demand for certainty – in effect to be disengaged. As such, critical wisdom like Job and Ecclesiastes is often conceived as a response to the ambiguity (retributive paradoxes) for which early wisdom and torah could not provide an account.

However, in chapter 6 above, I suggested that a careful study of Proverbs does not allow the book to be reduced to naive or simplistic views of causality and retribution. Van Leeuwen's work, for example, organises proverbial sayings into "quadrants" which express multiple contradictory perspectives on retribution and causality[15] and exemplify a complex worldview through polyphonic voices. He concludes, "In my judgment, the contradictions in question are not ultimately evidence for contrary social groups or worldviews. Rather, whatever their historical origin, within Proverbs they have come to express *one* broad worldview which acknowledges the conflict of dogma and experience, yet maintains both."[16]

In the same way, Deuteronomy has often been aligned with Proverbs for its apparent simplicity or inadequate attention to reality in its retributive theology.[17] However, Olson and McConville are among others who have disputed such overly simplistic interpretations of retribution in the Deuteronomic theology, especially as the book presents the tension between unconditional promise and the conditional demand to obey and prosper.[18] While neither Deuteronomy nor Proverbs are simplistic, we can say that, in contrast to the prophets, Qohelet and Job, these books are constrained to address general admonitions for the conduct of the good life. Deuteronomy, in the Pentateuchal tradition and political and covenantal context, is concerned with *corporate* and *historical* behaviour on the social and international scale, whereas Proverbs' rooting in the familial/social sphere of the created order deliberates the *individual* response to experience at the human level.[19]

So, despite a general optimism, both books portray paradoxes between justice and injustice, promise and obligation, and certainty and mystery;

---

15 Cf. also Gladson, *Paradoxes*.

16 "Wealth and Poverty", 26, and Van Leeuwen, *Context and Meaning*, 47. Cf. Wright, *Ethics*, 346.

17 See Murphy, *Tree*, 29 and Gammie, "Retribution", 11–2. Cf. McConville, *Deuteronomy*, 43–4.

18 McConville, *Deuteronomy*, 43; Olson, *Deuteronomy*, 175–6; Olson, "Theology", 213. Cf. Gammie's argument that Deuteronomy cannot be reduced to such simplicity, "Retribution", 12.

19 See J.A. Baker, "Deuteronomy and World Problems", *JSOT* 29 (1984) 3–17, on p. 10.

both books depict the unavoidable problems of knowing amidst human diversity and moral fissures of human life. Social and historical theories aimed at minimising these paradoxes, reducing them to random textual development, or assigning them to historical ideologies, simply fail to acknowledge the self-involving theological-rhetoric of these books. Gaps, contradiction, repetition and paradox are not – or in any case, not only – to be taken as evidence for social evolution through conflict, but more importantly as literary and rhetorical social-pragmatic functions which entice the reader to join Israel's covenant story in faith, or to embark on the wisdom journey in the fear of Yahweh. They encompass author and reader in a relationship which fosters contemplation and response. Our hermeneutical approach highlighted the rhetorical power of these books and their theological aims to engage readers in unique ways.

If one surrenders the inclination to oppose these traditions and instead enters into a relationship that listens to them in the social context of OT story and OT theology, the problems with retribution, ambiguity, ideology and certainty can be seen to be a part of Israel's effort to tell a coherent national story. Initially, torah provided the way for Israel to actualise the identity and vocation established for her at Horeb. As Israel breaks her covenants with Yahweh, she loses her corporate identity and this gives way to the isolation of the individual and the contemplation of evil. The emerging dominance of the individual in Job, Qohelet and the prophets laments the loss of corporate and covenant "memory" and longs for a return to corporate identity.[20] However, neither tradition functions alone, nor does one provide a univocal perspective on reality. Instead the wisdom books work in harmony to depict the bi-polar experience between the "real" (Prov 1–9) and the problems of perception amidst ambiguity (Prov 10–29), tragedy (Job) and the loss of meaning (Qohelet). Certainty lies not in Qohelet or Deuteronomy or Proverbs, but in a concert of voices which capture the full range of experiences and perspectives on justice, suffering, promise and

[20] O'Donovan, *DN*, 80, says, "It is important to understand the emergence of the individual in Israel historically, but equally important not to succumb, as we have said, to "Whig history supposing that the trend from community to individual could simply be extrapolated to authorise any kind of radical individualism as its final term. For what Israel affords is a strong concept of the individual on a quite different basis from the individualism of the West. The community is the aboriginal fact from beginning to end, shaping the conscience of each of its members to greater or lesser effect. But when the mediating institutions of government collapse, then the memory and hope which single members faithfully conserve provide a span of continuity which can reach out towards the prospect of restructuring. The fractured community which fashioned the individual's conscience is sustained within it and renewed out of it [...]. *To generalise, as we have done before, we must say that the conscience of the individual members of a community is a repository of the moral understanding which shaped it, and may serve to perpetuate it in a crisis of collapsing morale or institution* [...]. The conscientious individual speaks with society's own forgotten voice." Cf. also H. Fisch, "Qohelet: A Hebrew Ironist" in Idem, *Poetry*.

hope.[21] In both torah and wisdom, then, knowledge acquisition is constituted in a particular relationship between the knowledge and history of a community and the individual's status within that community.

2.3 The Liminal Rhetoric in Wisdom and Torah

I have also made several references to the liminal aspects of wisdom and torah. Liminality captures the sociological boundaries, transitions and "rights of passage" faced by communities and individuals who are engaged in their respective worlds.[22] In effect, liminality is some of the strongest evidence that these traditions view knowledge through a similar, modest epistemology. That is, Deuteronomy and the wisdom literature, perhaps more than most OT books, embody this transitional aspect of humanity to the effect that it weaves the epistemological experience of reading and hearing into the ontological realities of the story behind these texts.

Deuteronomy itself has several layers of liminal imagery and we find that their combined effect accentuates the need for actualisation. We have already identified the overall metaphor of journey – prominent mostly in chapters 1–3,[23] which embodies the decisions and activity in a faithful life before Yahweh.[24] In addition to the historical boundaries (Horeb to Moab) and geographical boundaries (Horeb, Moab, Shechem and the future "place" of chapter 12), Israel is commissioned to actualise the realities at Horeb primarily through the writing imagery (Deut 6:4–9; 11:18–29; 17:18; 27:3; 31:9, 24).[25] Just as Yahweh writes at Horeb to separate Israel as a holy people (5:22), Moses and Israel write to renew and secure the Horeb relationship for each generation, thereby creating a "transcendent community"[26] of Yahweh's people through liminal rights of passage.

Some of the strongest liminal rhetoric comes in Moses' song (Deut 32). As Israel is charged to cross geographical and historical thresholds, she is simultaneously forbidden from crossing boundaries of holiness. In her past and future disobedience, Israel crosses these forbidden limits, shatters the historical progress established in the patriarchs (32:7, 17), and maligns the

---

[21] D. Willard, "Hermeneutical Occasionalism", in R. Lundin (ed.), *Disciplining Hermeneutics* (Leicester: Apollos, 1997) 167–72, on pp. 171–2 suggests that the history of interpreting communities give way not to propositional certainty, but to interpretive confidence based upon an active (obedient) spiritual community which brings multiple perspectives together.

[22] Cf. van Gennep, *Rites*, 3.

[23] These chapters depict the future boundary "crossing" through עבר – a root used more in in these three chapters than anywhere else in Deuteronomy. The second highest use is in chapter 27 which depicts the liminal writing ceremony at Shechem – see below.

[24] Millar, "Place", 31–2. See also Miller, *Deuteronomy*, 9–11, 19–21 and Brueggemann, *Deuteronomy*, 22–5. On the nature of the 'way' in Deuteronomy and wisdom, see Lindars, "Torah", 129–30.

[25] Sonnet, *Book*, 222–3.

[26] McBride, "Yoke", 291.

order set for the nations in creation (32:8, 18). Yahweh's character, on the other hand, is depicted through a series of boundary-crossing metaphors: rock, eagle, father, mother, spouse, divine warrior.[27] Olson concludes: "It is a tapestry that weaves new patterns out of old cloth, a new covenant out of old forms".[28] Deuteronomy gives Israel a national tradition which encounters reality through distinctively liturgical patterns. Dangerous boundaries are crossed by seeking God's design for rhythm and harmony in the created order.

We also studied the liminal character of the Proverbial rhetoric as communicated through what Van Leeuwen dubbed a "two-fold metaphoric system" of ways, houses and women.[29] Liminality in Proverbs portrays the bipolar nature of the wisdom search. Wisdom is embedded in the creation order and given by God to mediate the worldview needed for the journey toward the right end (5:4, 11; 14:12; 16:25) or to the path of "life" (2:8–9, 20; 3:23; 4:11, 18, etc.), thus avoiding the way of folly and "death" (1:15, 16, 19; 2:19; 4:19). Further, Proverbs 8:22–29 envisions the "carved" placed of human existence amidst the divinely created boundaries; and Proverbs 26:1–12 ushers humanity into the process of sensing and responding to life's situational boundaries through the "fittingness" (נאוה) of humble wisdom.[30]

Torah and wisdom, therefore, are alike for the enticing and seducing rhetoric they create through their liminal themes and metaphors.[31] As argued above, however, this does not equate the two traditions.[32] In the process of actualisation, torah communicates its boundaries in terms of holiness, journey, geography, and the international relationships which offer both the opportunity for blessing and the temptation to idolatry. Proverbs, however, uses its liminal metaphoric imagery to reinforce the boundaries encountered at the family and social level. As seen with Solomon's reign in 1 Kings 1–11, these functions of wisdom and torah are theologically and narratively interdependent. Torah on Israel's hearts enables them to exercise wisdom to achieve social justice and order.[33]

---

[27] Olson, *Deuteronomy*, 143 who also observes that Yahweh takes up the form of the unclean "eagle" (נשר, Deut 14:12) and the agent of conquering judgment (28:49) to become a clean animal of strong protection (32:11).

[28] Ibid., 143.

[29] "Liminality", 114–6.

[30] Van Leeuwen, *Context and Meaning*, 99–106. See "Hermeneutics" below.

[31] Cf. J. Malfroy, "Sagesse et Loi dans le Deutéronome", *VT* 15 (1965) 49–65, on p. 52; McConville, *Deuteronomy*, 42 and Barker, "Israel", 240 who recognises "choice" at the centre of the intersection between these two genres.

[32] Cf. Clements, "Wisdom and OT", 283 and *People*, 21–5, 89–105 who offers a creative suggestion that torah changed into wisdom to account for the secular surroundings of Jewish diaspora. When national identity is lost, morality is guided by wisdom. Much of this is true except that it blurs the institutional boundaries between wisdom and torah where Israel in the dispersion is still a people in the cursed and waiting people of torah's eschatological hope. Torah and wisdom both still have their place in exile and dispersion.

[33] O'Donovan, *DN*, 112–3.

2.4 The Hermeneutics of Epistemology

The liminal imagery common to wisdom and torah evokes the open world of choices which face individuals and communities. The construct of choices in their diverse and changing worlds give these two traditions hermeneutical contexts which provide another means to compare them. In the first chapter, we saw that the "ambitious" and rationalist spirit of the Enlightenment seeks knowledge "disengaged" from history, tradition and community in order to achieve epistemological certainty. On the other hand, the continental and romantic philosophies of the Enlightenment emphasise knowledge as "engaged" in the ontological aspects of history, community and tradition. Hermeneutics, therefore, is concerned with the operations of understanding as humans go about the knowing and interpreting process. While the OT does very little to abstract and address these issues theoretically, I have argued in the last six chapters that it has nevertheless presented its way to knowledge and its verification of knowledge in a hermeneutical way. In both wisdom and torah, we have identified material which allows us to describe the kind of interpretive activity they endorse and the way in which they describe the structure of human understanding. It is the particular hermeneutical character of wisdom which torah appropriates to guide and preserve Israel's knowledge.

In chapters 6 and 7 above I argued that the individual "crisis-genre" of Job and Qohelet and the liminal metaphorical imagery in Proverbs act to entice readers into a performative hermeneutic. Thus, rather than gaining wisdom and knowledge primarily through a systematic method, the wisdom literature communicates knowledge to the reader who journeys with Job, Qohelet and the wise sons and daughters addressed in Proverbs. Reason is not excluded, but it is set within a larger interdisciplinary matrix, focused on right relationship to God and his creation.

Our study of Proverbs considered the explicit hermeneutical intentions of Proverbs 26:1–12 – what Van Leeuwen calls a "'treatise' on the 'hermeneutics' of wisdom".[34] In this extended proverb-poem the "fittingness" of things in nature (26:1–3) sets a platform for the fitting answer of a fool (26:4–5) and for the identifying a fool based on the fool's self-appraisal (26:11–12). The apparently contradictory requirements of verses 4–5 (answering a fool according to his folly) are in fact an application of verses 1–3 where "wisdom is [...] a matter of interpreting people, events, situations, actions in relation to norms for existence".[35] Thus the wisdom in Proverbs 26:1–12 speaks to both the interpretive side of hermeneutics and to the ethical and conditional nature of understanding in changing contexts in the social sphere of human life.

---

[34] Van Leeuwen, *Context and Meaning*, 99.

[35] Ibid., 100.

Together the wisdom books speak within Israel's structures as a collection of *polyphonic voices*.[36] Proverbs 1–9 communicates the foundational sayings and admonitions as guides for life. Proverbs 10–29, Job and Qohelet portray the bi-polar nature of hermeneutics amidst suffering (Job) and in the search for meaning (Qohelet). As such, the wisdom literature is a group of "productive" texts[37] whose meaning is found not in an accumulation of truths and facts, but in the bi-polar relationship humans live before God and his world.

That Deuteronomy relies on this same bi-polar, experiential aspect of human life in the world in its presentation of torah, can be observed along several lines. Most significantly, torah's connection to transcendent, ontological realities allows it to interpret the world for Israel. Torah thus acts as a hermeneutic, but at is does so, it provides Israel with the means to perform ethically before the nations, resulting in their ascribing "wisdom" and "understanding" to Israel and "righteousness" to the torah (Deut 4:6–8). In other words, torah lived out in Israel's local and national context appears to the nations as a witness to a *common* sense of world order. McConville helpfully notes that צדיק in the mouths of the nations (4:8) envisions "God's right ordering of all things (see 6:25). The Decalogue, therefore, is a summary transformation of God's creative ordering of the world into commands for living for the people he has redeemed from slavery in Egypt."[38] In this way, torah communicates ontological realities in a missional way. As torah provides the means for Israel to interpret God and the world, her obedience to its demands speak universally to the nations about Yahweh's divine order (wisdom).

Moreover, in chapter 4 above I demonstrated the hermeneutical and ideological character of prophetic interpretation in Deuteronomy 13:15 and 18:15–20. The assurance that Israel will encounter both true and false prophets requires her to live in constant interpretation. The truthfulness of the prophet is decided on a two-fold test of the prophet's message and the outcome of any predicted signs. The process envisioned is not a simple one. It requires Israel to use Moses' torah as the means to validate or refute prophetic messages on the basis of historical criteria recorded by Moses at Moab, thus hermeneutically preserving Israel's identity (at Horeb) against the distortions of ideology, evil and idolatry.

Furthermore, the relationship between the Decalogue in Deuteronomy 5 and the statutes and ordinances in Deuteronomy 12–26 also exhibit an hermeneutical understanding of the application of torah. For one, it is obvious that Yahweh's ten words are ready for expansion to the specifics and parti-

[36] See Thiselton, "Communicative Action", 172–82 and Stahl, *Law*, 12.
[37] Thiselton, "Communicative Action", 171.
[38] *Deuteronomy*, 121.

cularities of Israel's life in the land as Yahweh gives Moses the laws for the future.[39] McConville aptly notes that the transition from the Decalogue to statutes and ordinances "inaugurates a hermeneutical process, according to which provisions may be adapted to new situations".[40] Second and related to this, the Mosaic laws in Deuteronomy already implement as many as 22 changes from Exodus and Leviticus.[41] As observed in chapter six above, the canonising aspect of Deuteronomy's torah is conditioned by the changing needs and contexts of Israel's liminal journey.[42] Israel lives in a tension between the certainty of the canon and the newness and contingency of the journey. We cited Ricoeur earlier for his observation that "Every tradition lives by grace of interpretation, and it is at this price that it continues, that is, remains living."[43] The tension that results from new social and moral dilemmas compels Israel to pursue a hermeneutical response to past horizons; she must use wisdom to renew the realities of the past and thereby understand the present.

Hermeneutics thus gives us another means to sustain the parallels and distinctions in wisdom and torah. In Barr's conception of natural theology, he distinguishes torah from wisdom on the basis of revelation and non-revelation.[44] In reality however, wisdom begins with the fear of Yahweh and is given by God himself (Prov 2:5–6). Wisdom is thus a revelation to individuals and groups which is able to guide the proper obedience of torah[45] and that which describes the righteous and orderly outcome of events which torah has been kept (Deut 4:8).

Schäfer sees the constantly changing contexts of life as the environment where torah – in interpretation and application – becomes the "embodiment of wisdom"; wisdom is the "Oral Torah" which completes the "Written Torah".[46] In this way of stating it, wisdom and torah retain an epistemological interdependence. Torah envisions and creates space for a hermeneutical application fulfilled by wisdom's interpretive expertise – to face newness with consistency.[47]

---

39 One should note the connection between Deut 5:33 where Moses received further commands from Yahweh and Deut 11:32–12:1 where Moses delivers those commands to Israel.

40 McConville, *Deuteronomy*, 217.

41 Fretheim, "Law", 199 cites Dale Patrick, *Old Testament Law*, Atlanta: JKP (1985) for this figure.

42 Cf. however, Levinson, *Deuteronomy*, 15, 151–57, who describes the Deuteronomic interest to "transform", "replace" and "subvert" the cultic book of the covenant for its own political interests. Yet he fails to recognise the explicit hermeneutical conventions endorsed by Deuteronomy itself. Levinson's desire to see "charlatans [...] under the table" is an unnecessary and overly suspicious reading. Cf. Fretheim, "Law", 198–9 for a similar critique.

43 "Structure", 27.

44 "Law", 14–6.

45 Braulik, "Wisdom", 9; Miller, *Deuteronomy*, 56–7.

46 "Wisdom", 31, 34.

47 Cf. O'Donovan, *Resurrection*, 189.

2.5 The Ethics of Understanding

We can finally comment on the similar way these two traditions unite epistemology with ethics and the moral nature of human understanding. I have already introduced Westphal's suggestion that sin was an "epistemological category".[48] That Israel's cosmic, mythical worldview was grounded in the good and evil use of the human *yeṣer* demonstrates that ethics and knowing were always inseparable for Israel. Here we make some brief comparisons between ethics in wisdom and torah.

Turning again to the oft-cited passage in Deuteronomy 4:5–8, we find knowledge and ethics together in the promise that Israel's obedience to the torah (vv. 5, 8) will be interpreted as "wisdom and understanding" in the eyes of the nations (vv. 6–8). Braulik sees this passage "reinterpreting" the original legal righteousness into a "*religious and ethical attitude*".[49] This reading, however, is dominated by historical critical concerns that stop short of working out the textual implications within an ancient, mytho-poetic and theological worldview. Deuteronomy's rhetoric works holistically to set torah-keeping in the context of creation order and God's mission to all creation – the nations included. The rhetoric in fact works out of a theological foundation seen throughout the Pentateuch, most notably where the righteous behaviour of Abraham's will be a source of blessing to the nations (Gen 18:17–19). In the full context of the Pentateuch, the torah has not been abandoned or reinterpreted by wisdom, but appropriated through creative rhetoric which unites religion, ethics, morality and theology in the "formation and maintenance of a communal infrastructure".[50] Israel's appreciation for the cosmic power of the torah motivates her obedience and characterises her history as an ethical call to fulfill God's designs for creation.[51]

Like Deuteronomy 4:5–8, the Shema (6:4–5) threads Israel's relationship with God into a historical and ethical fabric. Israel's self-understanding is rooted in a story about Yahweh, a story which transcends the stories and gods of the nations.[52] To love Yahweh, then, is a call to ethical monotheism[53] and, in an eschatological sense, to missional monotheism.

The closing frame in Deuteronomy 30–32 returns to the historical and ethical texture of Israel's national story. The rhetoric in chapter 30 emphasises the *goodness* and doability of the torah in order to expose Israel's own pride and folly for refusing to keep it. Deuteronomy 32 captures that refusal

---

48 Westphal, "Sin". See also Das, *Paul, Law*, 258ff and Schnabel, *Law and Wisdom*, 231–344.

49 Braulik, "Wisdom", 12.

50 Brueggemann, *Deuteronomy*, 22. Cf. also, Crüsemann, *Torah*, 10; McConville, "Place", 108; Millar, "Place", 55–6; Wright, *Deuteronomy*, 5.

51 Wright, *Deuteronomy*, 12; Crüsemann, *Torah*, 367.

52 See Kearney, *Wake of Imagination*, 395.

53 See Ricoeur, *Symbolism of Evil*, 120.

in a dramatic display of wisdom vocabulary which resonates with Proverbs 8:22–31. Israel's folly (lack of wisdom) and sinfulness are interpreted as a breach of the created order (32:5–6, 28–29).[54] Here Deuteronomy's juridical and political tradition uses wisdom to reveal the disparity between Israel's ethical vision and the moral design of Yahweh's created order. The decision to disobey the torah is a moral determination to reject the cosmic boundaries set for humanity.

The practical guidance in Proverbs, especially by way of the instruction in chapters 1–9 and 26, is also conditioned by an ethical context.[55] Like Deuteronomy 32, Proverbs 1–9 identifies the decision to choose wisdom or folly as a matter of sin or obedience and life or death (1:7, 10, 16, etc.). Furthermore, woman wisdom's ability to guide humanity in righteousness (8:32–36) is based upon her observation of wisdom in the created order (3:19–20, 8:22–31). Proverbs thus clearly places its sense of moral order within the larger structure of the created order. The "treatise" on hermeneutics in Proverbs 26, then, is best interpreted within the theology creation in Proverbs 1–9. Wisdom is a matter of *fittingness*, the right time and the right place, while folly is a rejection of harmony and order. The fool who glorifies himself and is wise in his own eyes (26:12) is evidence of a love of disorder and a lack of fit. Wisdom thus connects individual and social morality to the ontology of the created order.

Wisdom and torah, then, share the same cosmic worldview which sets individual folly and pride alongside national pride and covenant infidelity as matters of distorting the moral structures of the created order. Folly in these two books is a state of pride-induced blindness which leads to sin, death and curse. Only torah explicitly articulates the narrative framework of Yahweh's future discipline and restoration; torah is the means through which Yahweh renews Israel's wisdom and respect for her role in God's cosmic plans to bless the nations (Deut 30:15; 32:47; Prov 2:19, 4:23).

2.6 Post-Exilic Epistemology

In order to give close readings to the texts in question, this study has focused on the epistemology in the Hebrew Bible. While it lays a foundation for studies in Second Temple, New Testament and later Christian and Rabbinical writings, each of these areas merits extensive study on its own. We can, nevertheless, venture tentatively into a few of these texts in an effort to demonstrate how the findings here could be carried forward.

---

[54] See Fisch, *Poetry*, 78; Fretheim, "Law", 183–200.

[55] Gladson, *Paradoxes*, 60. Cf. Brown, *Character in Crisis*, 8.

Sirach, Baruch and The Wisdom of Solomon provide some of the most exciting material to continue a phenomenological study because of the way they draw upon the well established traditions in wisdom and torah in order to communicate their message. It is, in fact, well recognized that wisdom becomes the predominate framework within which torah and Israel's history are re-interpreted.

In our study of Deuteronomy I suggested that the ontological realities of God's presence (theophany) formed the symbolic centre of Israel's torah. The torah not only guided Israel into *knowing* how to walk within the creation, but it served ultimately to renew Israel's relationship with a God who comes near. So too in the Deuterocanonical books, presence remains a core feature of Israel's belief. Wisdom's search for a "resting place" and an "inheritance" (Sir 24:7–8, NRSV) echoes the search by Noah's dove (Gen 8:8–9);[56] and in turn Israel's and Yahweh's own longing for a place to dwell (Deut 3:18–20, 12:1–11; 25:19).[57] The theme of presence appears in Baruch 3:37 and in a lengthy narrative in the Wisdom of Solomon, especially in 11:2–19:22 where wisdom performs a midrashic interpretation of the exodus from Egypt and desert wanderings.[58] The book ends with the hope that harmony will come in a new creation (19:18–21) and then a summary praise that wisdom has been with Israel in all "at all times and in all places" (v. 22, NRSV). While there is a great diversity in these books, we can see that the land and creation remain formative elements in Israel's self-identity. Wisdom provides the hermeneutic for Israel to interpret her changing world, a hermeneutic which embraces the holistic bond between knowledge, place and divine presence.

The late wisdom books show an acute awareness of the ambiguities of life amidst the loss of king, land and national identity. Yet, their means for coping with dispersion and exile reinforce the narrative (mythic) inclinations which we have observed throughout this study, most especially in Deuteronomy and Proverbs. In Sirach 16 and 17, Ben Sira recounts much from Genesis 1–3 related to human origins in creation. The passage in 17:1–14 echoes the many themes we identified under the heading of imitation and divine knowledge. For example, with explicit awareness of Genesis 1:26–30, Sirach 17:1–4 rehearses God's work to create humanity and assign them their role in the cosmos as co-creators:

The Lord created human beings out of the earth
and makes them return to it again

---

56 Cf. P.W. Skehan/A.A. De Lella, *The Wisdom of Ben Sira* (New York: Doubleday, 1987), 333.

57 Sheppard, *Wisdom*, 39–45.

58 M. Kolarcik, S.J., *New Interpreters Bible V: Wisdom of Solomon* (Nashville, TN: Abingdon, 1997), 441.

He gave them a fixed number of days,
but granted them authority over everything on the earth
He endowed them with strength like his own
and made them in his own image
He put the fear of them in all living beings,
and gave them dominion over beasts and birds (NRSV)

Once again echoing Genesis 2:17 and 3:1–14, Sirach 17:7 states that God "filled them with "knowledge and understanding, and showed them good and evil". The human *yeṣer*, as we have said throughout, is the moral and epistemological role that God has assigned to humanity as stewards of the creation. Ben Sira's shift to the torah in verses 10–14 depends upon this sense of the *yeṣer*, thus identifying the covenant and the torah as God-given measures for Israel – as humanity's representative – to choose the "law of life" (v. 10) and avoid "all evil" (v. 14),[59] motivated, no less, by God's majestic theophany on the mountain (v. 13). We will return to the idea of wisdom's presence on the throne in the heavens (Sir 24:4) in our reflections on NT literature below.

Finally, we make note of the explicit design in these late wisdom books to interpret or perhaps reinterpret torah through a hermeneutic of wisdom. Sirach 17:10–14 is one clear example of this tendency, but here we should also give our attention to Baruch 3:9–4:4 and Sirach 24 as further evidence that a theological wisdom-hermeneutic was at work Second Temple period.

While the author of Baruch is known for his immense literary references to the Hebrew Bible, this passage (3:9–4:4) makes explicit use of the language in Proverbs 8, Job 28 and Deuteronomy 30. Sheppard helpfully observes that Baruch's intention is to apply the wisdom themes of "searching" and "finding" to the context the torah in Deuteronomy 30.[60] As we noted extensively in chapters 2–5 above, the torah in Deuteronomy is to be "heard," "written," "observed," "remembered," and "kept" – one is never said to "find" the torah.[61] Meanwhile some of the strongest imagery in the wisdom books is the search: finding (מצא) or not finding wisdom (Prov 2:4–5; 3:13; 8:12, 35; Job 28:12–13). Baruch exchanges the *nearness* of the torah (Deut 30:14) for the availability of wisdom as the result of God's provision (Bar 3:36). And what is this wisdom for Israel? "She is the book of the commandments of God, the law that endures forever" (4:1). This text clearly invites extended analysis, but we can at least agree with Sheppard that "One part of the literature offers a theological vitality to clarify another."[62]

---

59 See Sheppard, *Wisdom*, 82–3 who connects these themes, noting that Ben Sira uses God's eternal wisdom to identify torah as God's teaching after Eden to guide humanity to life; torah, unlike wisdom, is not eternal.

60 Ibid., 84–99.

61 Ibid., 92–93.

62 Ibid., 99.

A major part of this theological vitality is that torah and wisdom share a common belief in that God's revelation is deeply rooted in cosmic (creational) realities. That is, according to these books, we know God as he has revealed himself in creation, in history and in his covenants and commands.

Sirach 24 is the most familiar place where wisdom and torah are identified. The first 22 verses parallel the long hymn in Proverbs 8 as well as Proverbs 1:20–33; Job 28 and Wisdom 6–10. The dominant metaphor for wisdom here is that of a prolific tree which the "Creator" planted in Israel (24:8-12), "grew tall," "gave forth perfume," and produced "abundant fruit" (vv. 13–17). I do not think that philological arguments are necessary to see the "tree of life" resonant among these images of creation, fruit and life. In the mythical framework of the ancient Near Eastern mind, the continuity between Eden's trees and this tree of wisdom (cf. Prov 3:18) goes without saying.[63] Wisdom promises all that God had originally intended for humanity.

The second major section (verses 23–29), identifies wisdom with "the book of the covenant of the Most High God, the law that Moses commanded us as an inheritance for the congregations of Jacob" (24:23). The connection between wisdom and torah is strengthened by the repetition of the "Most High" in verses 2, 3 and 23 which are all likely drawing upon Deuteronomy 33:4 "Moses commanded to us a torah, as a possession for the assembly of Jacob." As we have emphasised throughout this study, in Deuteronomy Yahweh is transcendent but comes near in his torah, and Ben Sira seems to be very clear in presenting wisdom in this same Deuteronomic rhetoric; she is on a throne in the heavens (Sir 24:3–4), but has come near at Yahweh's bidding (Sir 24:8–12, 51:26). As we saw above, Baruch 3:9–4:4 provides additional evidence that wisdom and torah come together in this way. Wisdom, though, is not just near abstractly, but is God's cosmic revelation of his original intentions for humanity, namely to walk with them in harmony (Gen 3:8). The unique naming of the Pishon, Tigris, Gihon and Euphrates in Sir 24:25–26 recalls not just the particularity of Genesis 2, but the emplacement of humanity in a paradise uniquely designed for them. Schnabel suggests that the identification of wisdom and torah in this context communicate their "double character: both realms have a cosmological and salvation-historical aspect."[64] The literature clearly

---

[63] While J.L. Crenshaw, *New Interpreter's Bible V: The Book of Sirach* (Nashville, TN: Abingdon, 1997), 759 immediately notes the mythical (narrative) hermeneutic at work here, and even Eden with its four rivers, he opposes this new legal revelation to the creation theology of Job, Proverbs and Ecclesiastes. I cannot see how such a corrective move would make sense for Ben Sira, since creation imagery is some of Ben Sira's most reliable evidence for the goodness of wisdom. Crenshaw fails to appreciate that for Sirach, wisdom and torah are inter-interpretative within the context of the created order. See Sheppard, *Wisdom*, 60, who finds cultic practice and wisdom in harmony in Sirach 24.

[64] *Law and Wisdom*, 90.

assumes a unity between creation and covenant, albeit, a reinterpretation of the covenant and Israel's future does take place.

Ricoeur helpfully proposes a framework for the development from Torah to Oral Torah in the dominant tradition of Pharisaism. He suggests that the torah was "revelation" to Israel – an "instruction" which manifests God to Israel in an ethical bond.[65] Yet in a desire to move beyond "law" to torah as instruction for life in every circumstance, the Pharisean sages divinised casuistry and thus "placed too high a value on a precise type of judgment, discernment [...]".[66] The imaginative pole of the *haggadah* (*yeṣer hatob*) in which the sages contemplated instruction theologically, was eventually sidelined by a fear of the *yeṣer hara* and a corresponding zealous construction of practical ethics. In turn, Pharisaism gradually became a system for ethics and less a wisdom tradition which contemplated the mythical foundations of the created order.

This explains a lot about much of the Mishnaic and early Christian theological writings. Yet despite Pharisaism's dominance, the creative wisdom tradition sustained its presence in throughout the second temple period and beyond. We have seen this in Sirach, Wisdom and Baruch, but it is made especially clear in the New Testament writings which followed. The influence of the Deuterocanonical wisdom books on the New Testament literature has not gone unnoticed. It is particularly strong in the Pauline[67] and Johannine literature as well as in Hebrews. We will briefly review some of the wisdom and torah motifs in Paul, marking significant evidence of a Hebraic ontological and ethical foundation for knowledge which we have been working with so far.

A brief look at the macro-structure of Romans is most enlightening. While 1 Corinthians and Colossians are easily identified for their wisdom motifs, Paul's concern in Romans is with the gospel and the law. Interestingly, however, Paul states that his mission (which is outlined at length in the first chapter), is to the "wise and the foolish" (1:14). This word pair could refer to a number of things; Fitzmyer connects it with the whole range of humanity.[68] But Paul could have just stayed with "Greeks and Barbarians" or added another merism. More likely, the choice of vocabulary follows the typical Pauline tendency speaking within a theology of creation. The theme of creation order, in fact, dominates the condemnation for sin in 1:18–30 where we also find another allusion to this word pairing: "professing to be wise, they became fools." Cranfield follows Calvin's reading that Greek philosophy is not in view here, but more likely the human tendency

---

[65] *Symbolism of Evil*, 127.

[66] Ibid., 133.

[67] By "Pauline," I do not mean that the books all belong to Paul's hand. I am merely following the traditional way of naming the 13 epistles.

[68] J.A. Fitzmyer, *Romans* (Anchor Bible; New York: Doubleday, 1993), 251.

to wisdom and folly recorded in Genesis 3:6 and 11:4.[69] Paul is setting up a cosmic theology within which he deals with the gospel, sin, election and righteousness.

Wisdom themes also dominate Romans 9–11. Paul's wisdom, in fact, allows him to reinterpret the torah in light of the Christ in 10:4–7, where allusions to Proverbs 30, Baruch and Sirach are all very likely.[70] Schnabel says of 10:6–7: "The parallel with Bar 3,29–30 is striking where Deut 30:12–13 is interpreted in terms of wisdom and has therefore often been used as substantiation of the assumption that Paul implies here the identification of Christ with divine wisdom: Paul has replaced wisdom with Christ as the object or person searched for."[71] The climactic hymn in 11:33–36 renews this cosmic framework once more, giving glory to the "wisdom and knowledge of God", before Paul closes the book with two probable wisdom references in 16:19 and 25–27. In verse 19 Paul exhorts the church at Rome to be "wise in what is good and innocent in what is evil." The pairing of good and evil could obviously free from theological connotations, but that these are Paul's final words, and that he has articulate such a strong creation theology in Romans 1 and through the Pauline corpus is certainly suggestive. The book ends with a blessing and a doxology (vv. 25–27). The blessing is by the God of "my gospel" which is a part of the "revelation of the mystery" about the Gentiles and the doxology is to the "only wise God" – all phrases which echo 11:33. It might be argued that these themes are weaker than in other Pauline letters, but it is nevertheless significant that they show up as they do in Paul's longest theological treatise on salvation.

When we come to Colossians and 1 Corinthians, it is much clearer that wisdom has become a hermeneutic for Paul to understand Christ's work in creation and in history. The antithesis between wisdom and folly in Corinthians is known to be a rhetorical critique of Greek, intellectual wisdom. But we will direct our focus here briefly to Colossians 1:15–20 where creation theology and epistemological orientation are more prevalent:

> He is the image of the invisible God, the firstborn of all creation; for in him all things in heaven and on earth were created, things visible and invisible, whether thrones or dominions or rulers or powers – all things have been created through him an for him. He himself is before all things, and in him all things hold together. He is the head of the body, the church; he is the beginning, the firstborn from the dead, so that he might come to have first place in everything. For in him all the fullness of God was

---

[69] *Romans* (ICB; Edinburgh: T&T Clark, 1975), 119.

[70] See B.I. Witherington, *Jesus the Sage: The Pilgrimage of Wisdom* (Minneapolis, MN: Fortress, 2000), 320–30 for a thorough summary of Paul's use of Wisdom, Sirach and Baruch in Romans 1–2 and 9–11. One major point which bears upon our concerns is that Romans envisions the Christ as the "end of the law" (Rom 10:4) insofar as it points to Christ as God's wisdom and righteousness.

[71] *Law and Wisdom*, 248.

pleased to dwell, and through him God was pleased to reconcile to himself all things, whether on earth or in heaven, by making peace through the blood of his cross. (NRSV)

Significantly, this passage follows Paul's prayer for "wisdom" and "knowledge" in verses 9–14, setting his message within an Hebraic epistemology. That is, Proverbs suggests that the wise need wisdom (1:5–6) and that "the beginning of wisdom is get wisdom" (Prov 4:6–7), but also that God is the source of wisdom (2:6–7). Faithful to the proverbial worldview, Paul seeks wisdom from God through prayer and humility; this knowledge is acquired spiritually. The content of Paul's wisdom message is focused on Christ as wisdom – that is as key to the origin, meaning and order of the created world. Paul calls Christ the "beginning" (ἀρχή) (1:18; Prov 8:22) who is "before all things" (Colossians 1:17; Prov 8:23) in order to interpret him through the image of the personified figure of wisdom in Proverbs. Furthermore, Christ as the "image of God" (v. 15) and as God made to "dwell" with humanity (1:19), not only recall the creation of humanity in Genesis 1:26–27,[72] but also the theme of divine presence which we have identified as foundational to the creation myth and divine narrative. In this way, Christ is the new bridge between God and humanity, the new wisdom through whom humanity may know God and his plan for the world.[73]

This run through Second Temple and New Testament literature, while brief, has nevertheless demonstrated the continuing power of the cosmic myth of creation to provide the framework for Israel to interpret the changing world around her and renew a sense of national identity. In contrast to epistemology in modern interpretation, Israel's aim was not driven by systematic reason or scientific analysis of history. Though they were cognizant of history, and logical in their mindset, their way of knowing began by orienting the community to a common story of the totality of things. This certainly gets more complicated in subsequent centuries where Greek philosophy diversifies wisdom and epistemology greatly. We thus stop here and turn to a concluding section in which we will draw upon the epistemological distinctives which we have identified in Hebraic thought and relate them to the history of ideas outlined in the first chapter.

3. The Hebraic Epistemology[74] Today

As we end this study we are in a position to relate our conclusions about the Hebraic phenomenology to the way our modern culture goes about know-

---

72 See F. Bruce, *Colossians, Philemon and Ephesians* (Grand Rapids, MI: Eerdmans, 1984), 58.

73 On this "sapiential" reading, see also Schnabel, *Law and Wisdom*, 258.

74 By "Hebraic" I intend to denote the broad religious and cultural worldview, spanning countless centuries, which is rooted in the texts of the Hebrew Bible.

ing things. Most of these conclusions are intended to be suggestive, providing space for more detailed research on these important issues.

Overall it is fair to say that the mythical and cosmic structures of Israel's worldview allow wisdom and torah to work within one holistic view of God and history. As we have already stated, these traditions have different roles within Israel's culture. Nevertheless, their common sense of holisms is also uniquely comprehensive in its origin. Israel's knowledge is "of the whole"[75] as it uses creation and creation order to understand the relationships between things and the structure within which they meet. Things coinhere in the Hebraic mind, and a mythic narrative about the world is the means for this to happen.

The dualisms in Platonic thought resist this kind of inherent unity and thus allow knowledge to be thought of apart from issues of ethics, relationships and history. The Enlightenment and movements of Modernity too reduced knowing to sensory and intellectual aspects without a consistent means even to relate these features of human identity. Post-Enlightenment epistemology is also uniquely individualistic and autonomous; each person is freely empowered to create the structures for thought. Here community, relationship, and tradition all lose their place in the knowing process. Does the Hebraic worldview have something productive for us today? If so, how would it speak into our world?

I think it begins with an affirmation of the mythical/storied framework for knowing that has been underemphasized today.[76] Not only does *narrative* provide a unique (and memorable) way to organise our logic (reason), but it also embraces the role of *aesthetics*, *emotions*, *history* and *faith* in the knowing process. The power of poetry as a form of theology, philosophy and therapy has been lost in many ways today, but the history of literature tells us something about the dynamic way aesthetics and poetics shape a culture's way of knowing and believing.[77] These Hebraic notions were at the heart of Hamann and Herder's response to Immanuel Kant in the Eighteenth century. Knowledge, they claimed, was more human, or *creaturely* than Kant's transcendental rationalism allowed. It has organic dimensions that cannot be reduced to logic, categories and systems alone.

The Hebraic mind also proposes a different way to encounter our histories. While facts, dates and movements are all important, there seems to be a lost sense of joy in embracing the mysterious chains of ideas and traditions that have been provided to us through our families and cultures. This

[75] R.P. O'Dowd, "A Chord of Three Strands: Epistemology in Job, Proverbs and Ecclesiastes", in M. Healy/R. Parry (ed.), *The Bible and Epistemology* (Carlisle, UK: Paternoster, 2007) 65–87, on pp. 70–3.

[76] See R. Kearney, *On Stories* (London: Routledge, 2002).

[77] See Sidney, J. A. Van Dorsten (ed.), *A Defence of Poetry* (Oxford: Oxford University Press, 1991 (1966)) and Umberto Eco's chapter "The Poetics and Us" in *On Literature* (Orlando: Harcourt, 2002), 236–54.

recognition is central to understanding modern Islam, the struggles in Eastern European and African nations and the ongoing effort to resolve religious and geographical contests with Native American and First Nations cultures in North America. Different faiths orient these cultures to unique worldviews and frameworks within which knowledge is gained and believed. Engaging at this historical faith level is essential today.[78]

Wisdom and torah also share the common motto of the "fear of the Lord". This seemingly heavy, outdated phrase is apt to be overlooked in phenomenology today. But if we could refresh it, it would remind us of the place of wonder and of the "other" in our journey to knowing. The Enlightenment emphasis on the individual too easily feeds attitudes of autonomy, academic narcissism and political divisiveness. Wonder situates *us* before *others* and, for those religiously optimistic, before the Other.

The storied and communal grounds for knowing in Hebraic thought thus highlight the *ethical* and *relational* aspects of knowing. Might there be overlooked benefits for the individual in seeking knowledge in the midst of community? The relational question also prompts individuals to reflect on ways that our knowing – and the rhetoric we use to express it – has communal effects which are often ethical in nature. Knowing is a responsibility as much as it is a process.

With major environmental and energy-related crises burdening generations of the twenty-first century, the Hebraic mind offers us a way to relate our *land* and *place* to the way we know things. Certainly epistemology and national resources are both important today, but how often are they brought into a common conversation? Does it matter for the way we know whether we live surrounded by nature and silence or by asphalt, metal and industrial noise? And, are there larger national, cultural and ethical structures which can help us to move forward on such issues? The central concern for the "place" where Israel will live and worship in Deuteronomy suggests that food, culture, community and knowing were all intertwined. The Passover celebration certainly possesses some rich connections to our cultural, national and historical identity. When people live in famine or on a fast-food diet, apart from feasts in the community and family, it affects the way they reason and the way they hope. One searches in vain to find discussions about the centrality of the meal and the table to a community's tradition-forming process within Enlightenment philosophy. When the meal, food, community and place are thus marginalised in favor of intellectual processes, something about the human way of knowing is drastically misrepresented.

---

[78] As is argued by Richard Kearney in *Strangers, Gods and Monsters: Interpreting Otherness* (London: Routledge, 2003), a book which tackles some of the major crises in modern culture in search of paths to peace.

In sum, almost all of these issues which were a part of Israel's epistemology are alive and well today: ecology, aesthetics, ethics, faith, reason, story, community, and politics. What has been lacking, perhaps, is a creative effort to explore their interrelationships. The Hebraic cosmology gave the world an origin and a purpose within which to relate these aspects of life. And, in doing so, it provided the nation with a trajectory, a form of hope and a respect for the dignity of humanity in the world. The complexities which face present and future generations, I would argue, have much to learn from the ancient Hebrew writings.

4. Conclusion

The compass of this investigation has been immense indeed. But, as I hope is evident by now, such interdisciplinary study proves to be extremely fruitful and should become more of the norm in biblical and religious studies today. Our primary aim here has been to explore the epistemology within Israel's ancient traditions of wisdom and torah. No doubt there were many literary and religious movements in Israel, not least *within* these two traditions themselves. But I have argued that the ideological and theological evolution within and between these traditions has, in most cases, been greatly overplayed. The broad perspective employed here has allowed us to see that we have a range of aesthetic, historical and religious documents that work within a shared worldview – a worldview of creation and creation order. Wisdom and torah serve as revelation about the divine, about the structures in creation and about the ethical behaviour appropriate to living before this God and in this world.

From my perspective, the most fecund outcome of this study is the way that the Hebraic epistemology fosters a healthy exercise of meta-critique; it leads us to question the critique itself, asking questions about the faith, ethics, religion, history and worldview that shape our lives and our work in academe. We are likely aware now, more than any time in recent history, that academic work is inseparable from the political, social and cultural issues we face in the world today. A more robust view of epistemology positions us as individual knowers humbly within our global community with a respect for the plurality of factors that influence the way we act, think and believe.

Bibliography

Alston, W.P., "On Knowing That We Know: The Application to Religious Knowledge", in C.S. Evans/M. Westphal (ed.), *Christian Perspectives on Religious Knowledge* (Grand Rapids, MI: Eerdmans, 1993) 15–39.

———, *Perceiving God: The Epistemology of Religious Experience* (Ithaca, NY/ London: Cornell University, 1991).

Alter, R., *The Art of Biblical Narrative* (New York: Basic Books, 1981).

———, *The Art of Biblical Poetry* (New York: Basic Books, 1985).

Aristotle, *The Nicomachean Ethics* (New York: Penguin Books, 2004).

Bacon, F., *Advancement of Learning*, http://etext.library.adelaide.edu.au/b/bacon/ francis/b12a/.

———, *Preface to Maxims of the Law*, http://books.google.com/books?vid= OCLC 06792219&id=HU_mpfEWO_IC&pg=PA3&lpg=PA3&dq=Bacon+Maxims&as_brr =1&ie=ISO–8859–1#PPA7,M1

Baker, D.W., "Scribes as Transmitters of Tradition", in A.R. Millard/J.K. Hoffmeier/D.B. Baker (ed.), *Faith, Tradition, and History* (Winona Lake, IN: Eisenbrauns, 1994) 65–77.

Baker, J.A., "Deuteronomy and World Problems", *JSOT* 29 (1984) 3–17.

Barker, P., "Faithless Israel, Faithful Yahweh in Deuteronomy", PhD Dissertation Bristol University, 1995.

Barr, J., "Biblical Law and the Question of Natural Theology", in T. Veijola (ed.), *The Law in the Bible and in Its Environment* (Helsinki: Finnish Exegetical Society, 1990) 1–22.

———, *Holy Scripture: Canon, Authority, Criticism* (Philadelphia, PA: Westminster, 1983).

———, *The Semantics of Biblical Language* (Oxford: Oxford University, 1961).

Bartholomew, C.G., "Before Babel and After Pentecost: Language, Literature and Biblical Interpretation", in C.G. Bartholomew/C. Greene/K. Möller (ed.), *After Pentecost: Language and Biblical Interpretation* (Grand Rapids, MI: Zondervan, 2001) 131–70.

———, "A Christian World-View and the Futures of Evangelicalism", in C.G. Bartholomew (ed.), *The Futures of Evangelicalism* (Leicester, UK: InterVarsity, 2003) 194–220.

———, "A God for Life, and Not Just for Christmas!" in P. Helm/C. Trueman (ed.), *The Trustworthiness of God: Perspectives on the Nature of Scripture* (Leicester: Apollos, 2002) 39–57.

———, *Reading Ecclesiastes: Old Testament Exegesis and Hermeneutical Theory* (AnBib; Rome, Italy: Pontifical Biblical Institute, 1998).

———, "Three Horizons: Hermeneutics from the Other End – An Evaluation of Anthony Thiselton's Hermeneutic Proposal", *EJT* 5 (1996) 121–35.

Barton, S.C., "New Testament Interpretation as Performance", *SJT* 52 (1999) 179–208.

Bauckham, R., *Bible and Mission: Christian Witness in a Postmodern World* (Carlisle, UK: Paternoster, 2003).

Beckwith, F.J., "Limited Omniscience and the Test for a Prophet: A Brief Philosophical Analysis", *JETS* 36 (1993) 357–62.

Beiser, F.C., *The Fate of Reason: German Philosophy from Kant to Fichte* (Cambridge, MA/London: Harvard University, 1987).

Bennett, H.V., *Injustice Made Legal: Deuteronomic Law and the Plight of Widows, Strangers, and Orphans in Ancient Israel* (Grand Rapids, MI: Eerdmans, 2002).

Blenkinsopp, J., *Wisdom and Law in the Old Testament* (Oxford: Oxford University, 1983).

Block, D.I., "How Many is God? An Investigation Into the Meaning of Deuteronomy 6:4–5", *JETS* 47 (2004) 193–212.

Bockmuehl, M., "Reason, Wisdom and the Implied Disciple of Scripture", in D.F. Ford/G. Stanton (ed.), *Reading Texts, Seeking Wisdom* (London: SCM Press, 2003) 53–68.

———, *Seeing the Word: Refocusing New Testament Study* (Grand Rapids, MI: Baker Academic, 2006).

Booth, W.C., *The Rhetoric of Fiction* (Chicago: University of Chicago, 1983 [1961]).

Borgen, P., "The Gospel of John and Philo of Alexandria", in J.H. Charlesworth/ M.A. Daise (ed.), *Light in a Spotless Mirror* (Harrisburg, PA: Trinity International, 2003) 45–76.

Boston, J.R., "The Wisdom Influence Upon the Song of Moses", *JBL* 87 (1968) 198–202.

Bowker, J.W., "Religions as Systems", in *Believing in the Church: Essays by Members of the Church of England* (London: SPCK, 1983) 159–89.

Braulik, G., "Die Ausdrücke für 'Gesetz' im Buch Deuteronomium", in idem.; *Studien Zur Theologie Des Deuteronomiums* (Stuttgart: Katholisches Bibelwerk, 1988) 11–38.

———, *Deuteronomium* (NEB; 2 vols.; Würzburg: Echter Verlag, 1986–1992).

———, "Deuteronomy and Human Rights", in idem.; *The Theology of Deuteronomy* (N. Richland Hills, TX: BIBAL, 1994) 131–50.

———, "Deuteronomy and the Birth of Monotheism", in idem.; *Theology* (1994) 99–130, 237–47.

———, "Law as Gospel: Justification and Pardon According to the Deuteronomic Torah", *Interpretation* 38 (1984) 5–14.

———, "The Sequence of the Laws in Deuteronomy", in D. Christensen (ed.), *A Song of Power and the Power of Song* (Winona Lake: IN: Eisenbrauns, 1993).

———, *The Theology of Deuteronomy: Collected Essays of Georg Braulik* (BIBAL Collected Essays; N. Richland Hills: BIBAL, 1994).

———, "Weisheit, Gottesnähe und Gesetz", in *Studien zur Theologie des Deuteronomiums* (Stuttgart: Katholisches Bibelwerk, 1988) 53–93.

———, "Wisdom, Divine Presence and Law: Reflections on the Kerygma of Deut 4:5–8 (1977)", in idem.; *Theology* (1–25, 199–214, 1994).

Braybrooke, D., "Ideology", in P. Edwards (ed.), *The Encyclopedia of Philosophy 4* (London/New York: Collier Macmillan, 1972) 124–7.

Brekelmans, C., "Deuteronomy 5: Its Place and Function", in N. Lohfink (ed.), *Das Deuteronomium* (Leuven: Leuven University, 1985) 164–73.

———, "Wisdom Influence in Deuteronomy", in D.L. Christensen (ed.), *Song of Power* (Winona Lake: Eisenbrauns, 1993) 123–34.

Brenner, A., "Job the Pious? The Characterization of Job in the Narrative Framework of the Book", *JSOT* 43 (1989) 37–52.

Brown, P./Levinson, S.C., *Politeness: Some Universals in Language Usage* (Cambridge: Cambridge University, 1987).

Brown, R.F., "On the Necessary Imperfection of Creation: Iranaeus' *Adversus Haereses* IV, 38", *SJT* 28 (1975) 17–25.

Brown, W.P., *Character in Crisis: A Fresh Approach to the Wisdom Literature of the Old Testament* (Grand Rapids, MI/Cambridge: Eerdmans, 1996).

———, "*Creatio Corporis* and the Rhetoric of Defense in Job 10 and Psalm 139", in W.P. Brown/S.D. McBride (ed.), *God Who Creates* (Grand Rapids, MI: Eerdmans, 2000) 107–24.

———, *Ecclesiastes* (Interpretation; Louisville, KY: John Knox Press, 2000).

Bruce, F., *Colossians, Philemon and Ephesians* (Grand Rapids, MI: Eerdmans, 1984).

Brueggemann, W., *Deuteronomy* (AOTC; Nashville: Abingdon, 2001).

———, *Theology of the Old Testament: Testimony, Dispute, Advocacy* (Minneapolis, MN: Fortress, 1997).

———, "The Travail of Pardon: Reflections on *slh*", in B.A. Strawn/N.R. Bowen (ed.), *A God So Near* (Winona Lake, IN: Eisenbrauns, 2003) 283–97.

Buber, M., *Good and Evil* (New York: Scribner, 1952).

———, "People Today and the Jewish Bible: From a Lecture Series", in M. Buber/F. Rosenzweig (ed.), *Scripture and Translation* (Bloomington, IN: Indiana University, 1994) 4–21.

Cairns, I., *Deuteronomy: Word and Presence* (ITC; Grand Rapids, MI: Eerdmans, 1992).

Callaway, P.R., "Deut 21:18–21: Proverbial Wisdom and Law", *JBL* 103/3 (1984) 341–52.

Camp, C.V., *Wisdom and the Feminine in the Book of Proverbs* (Sheffield: Almond, 1985).

Carmichael, C.M., "Deuteronomic Laws, Wisdom, and Historical Traditions", *JSS* 12 (1967) 198–206.

———, *The Laws of Deuteronomy* (Ithaca, NY/London: Cornell University, 1974).

———, *The Origins of Biblical Law: The Decalogues and the Book of the Covenant* (Ithaca, NY/London: Cornell University, 1992).

Carmy, S./D.Schatz, "The Bible as a Source of Philosophical Reflection", in D.H. Frank/O. Leaman (ed.), *History of Jewish Philosophy* (London: Routledge, 2003) 13–37.

Caws, M.A., *Reading Frames in Modern Fiction* (Princeton, NJ: Princeton University, 1985).

Chaplin, J., "Prospects for an 'Evangelical Political Philosophy'", *ERT* 24.4 (2000) 354–73.

Charlesworth, J.H., "Lady Wisdom and Johannine Christology", in J.H. Charlesworth/M.A. Daise (ed.), *Light in a Spotless Mirror* (Harrisburg, PA: Trinity Press International, 2003) 92–133.

Childs, B.S., *The Book of Exodus* (Louisville, KY: Westminster, 1974).

———, *Introduction to the Old Testament as Scripture* (Philadelphia: Fortress, 1979).

———, *Memory and Tradition in Israel* (London: SCM, 1962).

Christensen, D.L., *Deuteronomy 1:1–21:9* (WBC; Dallas, TX: Thomas Nelson, 2001).

———, “Form and Structure in Deuteronomy 1–11”, in Norbert Lohfink (ed.), *Das Deuteronomium* (Leuven: Leuven University, 1985) 135–44.

Christensen, D.L.(., *A Song of Power and the Power of Song: Essays on the Book of Deuteronomy* (Winona Lake, IN: Eisenbrauns, 1993).

Christianson, E.S., “Qohelet and The/His Self Among the Deconstructed”, in A.A. Schoors (ed.), *Qohelet in the Context of Wisdom* (Leuven, Belgium: Leuven University, 1998) 425–33.

———, *A Time to Tell: Narrative Strategies in Ecclesiastes* (Sheffield: Sheffield Academic, 1998).

Clements, R.E., *God's Chosen People: A Theological Interpretation of the Book of Deuteronomy* (London: SCM, 1968).

———, “Wisdom and Old Testament Theology”, in John Day/R.P. Gordon/H.G.M. Williamson (ed.), *Wisdom in Ancient Israel* (Cambridge: Cambridge University, 1995) 269–86.

———, *Wisdom for a Changing World: Wisdom in Old Testament Theology* (Berkeley, CA: Bibal, 1990).

Clifford, R.J., “The Hebrew Scriptures and the Theology of Creation”, *Theological Studies* 46 (1985) 507–23.

Clines, D.J., *The Theme of the Pentateuch* (JSOTSup 10; Sheffield: Sheffield Academic, 1978).

Clouser, R.A., *The Myth of Religious Neutrality: An Essay on the Hidden Role of Religious Belief in Theories* (Notre Dame, IN/London: University of Notre Dame, 1991).

Coats, G.W., “Legendary Motifs in the Moses Death Reports”, in Christensen (ed.), *Song* (1993) 181–91.

Collins, J.J., “Proverbial Wisdom and the Yahwist Vision”, *Semeia* 17 (1980) 1–17.

Craigie, P.C., The Book of Deuteronomy (NICOT; Grand Rapids, MI: Eerdmans, 1976).

Cranfield, C., *Romans* (ICB; Edinburgh: T&T Clark, 1975).

Crenshaw, J.L., “The Acquisition of Knowledge in Israelite Wisdom Literature”, *Word and World* 7/3 (1987) 245–52.

———, *New Interpreter's Bible V: The Book of Sirach* (Nashville, TN: Abingdon, 1997).

———, “The Concept of God in Old Testament Wisdom”, in idem.; *Urgent Advice* (Macon, GA: Mercer, 1995) 191–205.

———, “The Deuteronomist and the Writings”, in L.S. Schearing/S.L. McKenzie; *Those Elusive Deuteronomists: The Phenomenon of Pan-Deuteronomism* (JSOTSup 268; Sheffield: Sheffield Academic, 1999) 145–58.

———, *Ecclesiastes* (OTL; London: SCM, 1988).

———, “Education in Ancient Israel”, *JBL* 104 (1985) 601–15.

———, *Education in Ancient Israel: Across the Deadening Silence* (London/New York: Doubleday, 1998).

———, “Method in Determining Wisdom Influence Upon ‘Historical’ Literature”, *JBL* 88 (1969) 129–42.

———, *Old Testament Wisdom: An Introduction* (Louisville, KY: Westminster John Knox, 1981).

———, “Popular Questioning of the Justice of God in Ancient Israel”, in idem.; *Urgent Advice* (Macon, GA: Mercer, 1995).

———, "Poverty and Punishment in the Book of Proverbs", in idem.; *Urgent Advice* (Macon, GA: Mercer, 1995) 396–405.

———, "Qoheleth's Understanding of Intellectual Inquiry", in A. Schoors (ed.), *Qohelet in the Context of Wisdom* (Leuven, Belgium: Leuven University, 1998) 205–24.

———, *Urgent Advice and Probing Questions: Collected Writings on Old Testament Wisdom* (Macon, GA: Mercer, 1995).

———, "Wisdom and Authority: Sapiential Rhetoric and Its Warrants", in idem.; *Urgent Advice* (Macon, GA: Mercer, 1995) 326–43.

Critchley, S., *Continental Philosophy: A Very Short Introduction* (Oxford: Oxford University, 2001).

Crüsemann, F., *The Torah: Theology and Social History of Old Testament Law* (Edinburgh: T&T Clark, 1996).

Currid, J.D., *Ancient Egypt and the Old Testament* (Grand Rapids, MI: Baker, 1997).

Das, A.A., *Paul and the Jews* (Peabody, MA: Hendrickson, 2003).

———, *Paul, the Law, and the Covenant* (Peabody, MA: Hendrickson, 2001).

Delitzsch, F., *The Book of Proverbs* (Grand Rapids, MI: Eerdmans, 1983).

Dell, K., *Get Wisdom, Get Insight: An Introduction to Israel's Wisdom Literature* (Norwich, UK: Darton, Longman and Todd, 2000).

Derrida, J., "Force of Law: 'The Mystical Foundation of Authority'", in D. Cornell/M. Rosenfeld/D.G. Carlson (ed.), *Deconstruction and the Possibility of Justice* (New York: Routledge, 1992) 3–67.

Descartes, R., *Discourse on Method and Related Writings* (London/New York: Penguin Books, 2003).

DeVries, S.J., *Yesterday, Today and Tomorrow: Time and History in the Old Testament* (London: SPCK, 1975).

Dhorme, É., *A Commentary on the Book of Job* (Nashville, TN: Thomas Nelson, 1984 [original 1926]).

Di Lella, A.A., "The Meaning of Wisdom in Ben Sira", in L.G. Perdue (ed.), *In Search of Wisdom: Essays in Memory of John G. Gammie* (Louisville, KY: Westminster John Knox, 1993) 133–48.

Dillard, R., "Review: Moshe Weinfeld: Deuteronomy and the Deuteronomic School", *WTJ* 36 (1974) 263–9.

Dittmar, L., "Fashioning and Re-Fashioning: Framing Narratives in the Novel and Film", *Mosaic* 16.1–2 (1983) 189–203.

Driver, S.R., *A Critical and Exegetical Commentary on Deuteronomy* (ICC; Edinburgh: T&T Clark, 1902).

———, *An Introduction to the Literature of the Old Testament* (Gloucester, MA: Peter Smith, 1972).

Dubin, L.C., "The Social and Cultural Context: Eighteenth-Century Enlightenment", in D.H. Frank/L. Leaman (ed.), *History of Jewish Philosophy* (London: Routledge, 2003) 636–59.

Dumbrell, W.J., *Covenant and Creation: A Theology of Old Testament Covenants* (Carlisle, UK: Paternoster, 1984).

Eaton, M.A., *Ecclesiastes* (Downers Grove, IL/Leicester, UK: InterVarsity, 1983).

Eco, U., *On Literature* (Orlando: Harcourt, 2002).

Eco, U./Rorty, R./Culler, J./Brooke-Rose, C./Collini, S. (ed.), *Interpretation and Overinterpretation* (Cambridge: Cambridge University Press, 1992).

Eichrodt, W., "Covenant and Law: Thoughts on Recent Discussion", *Interpretation* (1966) 302–21.

———, "Faith in Providence and Theodicy in the Old Testament", in J.L. Crenshaw (ed.), *Theodicy in the Old Testament* (Philadelphia/London: Fortress/ SPCK, 1983) 17–41.

Enns, P., *Exodus* (NIVAC; Grand Rapids, MI: Zondervan, 2000).

———, "Law of God", in W.A. Van Gemeren (ed.), *NIDOTTE, 5 Vols. 4* (Grand Rapids, MI: Zondervan, 1997) 893–900.

Eslinger, L., "Exod 6:3 in the Context of Genesis 1–Exodus 15", in L. Regt/J. de Waard/J.P. Fokkelman (ed.), *Literary Structure and Rhetorical Strategies in the Hebrew Bible* (Assen: Van Gorcum, 1996) 188–98.

———, "Freedom or Knowledge? Perspective and Purpose in the Exodus Narrative (Exodus 1–15)", *JSOT* 52 (1991) 43–60.

Estes, D.J., *Hear, My Son: Teaching and Learning in Proverbs 1–9* (Cambridge/ Grand Rapids, MI: Apollos/Eerdmans, 1997).

Evans, C.S., *The Historical Christ and the Jesus of Faith* (Oxford: Clarendon, 1996).

Evans, C.S./Westphal, M., "Introduction", in Idem. (ed.), *Christian Perspectives on Religious Knowledge* (Grand Rapids, MI: Eerdmans, 1993) 1–14.

Feldman, S., "Spinoza", in D.H. Frank/O. Leaman (ed.), *History of Jewish Philosophy* (London: Routledge, 2003) 612–35.

Fisch, H., *Poetry With a Purpose: Biblical Poetics and Interpretation* (Bloomington, IN: Indiana University, 1988).

Fischer, G./Lohfink, N., "Diese Worte sollst du summen: Dtn 6,7 Wedibbartā Bām – ein verlorener Schlüssel zur Meditativen Kultur in Israel", in N. Lohfink (ed.), *Studien zum Deuteronomium und zur deuteronomistischen Literatur 3* (Stuttgart: Katholisches Bibelwerk, 1995) 181–203.

Fischer, G., "Exodus 1–15 – Eine Erzählung", in M. Vervenne (ed.), *Studies in the Book of Exodus* (Leuven: Leuven University, 1996) 149–78.

Fish, S., *Is There a Text in This Class? The Authority of Interpretive Communities* (Cambridge, MA: Harvard University, 1980).

Fishbane, M., "Jeremiah 4:23–26 and Job 3:3–13: A Recovered Use of the Creation Pattern", *VT* 21 (1971) 151–67.

———, *Text and Texture: Close Readings of Selected Biblical Texts* (New York: Schocken, 1979).

Fitzmyer, J.A., *Romans* (Anchor Bible; New York: Doubleday, 1993).

Fontaine, C.R., "Wisdom in Proverbs", in L.G. Perdue/B.B. Scott/W.J. Wiseman (ed.), *In Search of Wisdom: Essays in Memory of John G. Gammie* (Louisville, KY: Westminster John Knox, 1993) 99–114.

Ford, D.F., "Jesus Christ, the Wisdom of God (I)", in D.F. Ford/G. Stanton (ed.), *Reading Texts, Seeking Wisdom* (London: SCM, 2003) 4–21.

Foucault, M., *The Order of Things* (New York: Vintage Books, 1994).

Fox, E., *The Five Books of Moses: Genesis, Exodus, Leviticus, Numbers, and Deuteronomy* (The Schocken Bible vol. 1; New York: Schocken Books, 1997).

Fox, M.V., "Bible Scholarship and Faith-Based Study: My View", *SBL Forum* (2006).

———, *Ecclesiastes* (JPS; Philadelphia: Jewish Publication Society, 2004).

———, "Frame-Narrative and Composition in the Book of Qohelet", *HUCA* 48 (1977) 83–106.

———, "Ideas of Wisdom in Proverbs 1–9", *JBL* 116 (1997) 613–33.
———, "The Innerstructure of Qohelet's Thought", in A.A. Schoors (ed.), *Qohelet in the Context of Wisdom* (Leuven, Belgium: Leuven University, 1998) 225–38.
———, "Job 38 and God's Rhetoric", *Semeia* 19 (1981) 53–61.
———, "Job the Pious", *ZAW* 117 (2005) 351–66.
———, "The Pedagogy of Proverbs 2", *JBL* 113/2 (1994) 233–43.
———, *Proverbs 1–9: A New Translation with Introduction and Commentary* (AB; New York: Doubleday, 2000).
———, *Qohelet and His Contradictions* (JSOTSup 71; Sheffield: Almond, 1989).
———, "Qohelet's Epistemology", *HUCA* 58/1 (1987) 137–55.
———, "Review of C. Bartholomew, Reading Ecclesiastes: Old Testament Exegesis and Hermeneutical Theory", *Interpretation* 54 (2000) 195–6.
———, *A Time to Tear Down and a Time to Build Up: A Rereading of Ecclesiastes* (Grand Rapids, MI/Cambridge: Eerdmans, 1999).
———, "Unsought Discoveries: Qoheleth 7:23–8:1a", *Hebrew Studies* 19 (1978) 26–38.
———, "Wisdom in Qohelet", in L.G. Perdue/B.B. Scott/W.J. Wiseman (ed.), *In Search of Wisdom: Essays in Memory of John G. Gammie* (Louisville, KY: Westminster John Knox, 1993) 115–31.
Fretheim, T.E., *Exodus* (Interpretation; Louisville, KY: John Knox, 1991).
———, *God and World in the Old Testament: A Relational Theology of Creation* (Nashville: Abingdon, 2005).
———, "Law in the Service of Life: A Dynamic Understanding of Law in Deuteronomy", in B.A. Strawn/N.R. Bowen (ed.), *A God So Near* (Winona Lake, IN: Eisenbrauns, 2003) 183–200.
———, "The Reclamation of Creation: Redemption and Law in Exodus", *Interpretation* 45 (1991) 354–65.
Fromm, E., *You Shall be as Gods: A Radical Reinterpretation of the Old Testament in Its Tradition* (Chicago/New York: Holt, Rinehart and Winston, 1966).
Fyall, R.S., *Now My Eyes Have Seen You: Images of Creation and Evil in the Book of Job* (Leicester/Downers Grove: InterVarsity, 2002).
Gadamer, H.G., *Truth and Method* (2nd ed.; New York: Crossroad (Sheed and Ward), 1985 (1975 English Translation; 1960 German)).
Gammie, J.G., "The Theology of Retribution in the Book of Deuteronomy", *CBQ* 32 (1970) 1–12.
Ganssle, G.E., "Introduction: Thinking About God and Time", in idem. (ed.), *God and Time: Four Views* (Carlisle, UK: Paternoster, 2001) 9–27.
Ganssle, G.E., *God and Time: Four Views* (Carlisle, UK: Paternoster, 2001).
Geller, S.A., "Fiery Wisdom: The Deuteronomic Tradition", in idem.; *Sacred Enigmas* (London: Routledge, 1996) 30–61.
———, "Literature, History and Religion", in idem.; *Sacred Enigmas* (London: Routledge, 1996) 168–94.
———, "Where is Wisdom?" in idem.; *Sacred Enigmas* (London: Routledge, 1996) 87–107.
Gennep, A.v., *The Rites of Passage* (London/Henley: Routledge and Kegan Paul, 1977).
Ginsberg, C., *The Song of Songs and Coheleth* (New York: KTAV, 1970).
Gladson, J.A., *Retributive Paradoxes in Proverbs 10–29* (Ann Arbor, MI: University Microfilms International, 1979).

Good, E.M., *In Turns of Tempest: A Reading of Job* (Stanford, CA: Stanford University, 1990).

Gordis, R., *The Book of Job* (New York: Jewish Theological Seminary of America, 1978).

———, *Koheleth – The Man and His World* (London: Jason Aronson, 1995).

———, "The Social Background of Wisdom Literature", *HUCA* 18 (1944) 77–118.

Gottwald, N.K., *The Hebrew Bible – A Socio-Literary Introduction* (Philadelphia: Fortress, 1985).

Goudoever, J.v., "The Liturgical Significance of the Date in Dt 1,3", in N. Lohfink (ed.), *Das Deuteronomium* (Leuven: Leuven University, 1985) 145–8.

Grant, J.A., *The King Exemplar: The Function of Deuteronomy's Kingship Law in the Shaping of the Book of Psalms* (Atlanta: Society of Biblical Literature, 2004).

Greidanus, S., "The Universal Dimension of Law in the Hebrew Scriptures", *Sciences Religieuses* 14 (1985) 39–51.

Grenz, S.J., *A Primer on Postmodernism* (Grand Rapids, MI/Cambridge: Eerdmans, 1996).

Grondin, J., *Introduction to Philosophical Hermeneutics* (New Haven, CT/London: Yale University, 1994).

Haack, S., "'The Ethics of Belief' Reconsidered", in M. Steup (ed.), *Knowledge, Truth, and Duty* (Oxford: Oxford University Press, 2001) 21–33.

Habel, N.C., *The Book of Job* (OTL; London: SCM, 1985).

———, "He Who Stretches Out the Heavens", *CBQ* 34 (1972) 417–30.

Habermas, J., *Knowledge and Human Interests* (Boston: Beacon, 1971).

Hahn, S.W., "Kinship by Covenant: A Biblical Theological Study of Covenant Types and Texts in the Old and New Testaments", PhD dissertation Marquette University, 1995).

Hamilton, J.M., *Social Justice and Deuteronomy: The Case of Deuteronomy 15* (SBLDS; Atlanta, GA: Scholars, 1992).

Hamilton, V.P., *Genesis 1–17* (NICOT; Grand Rapids, MI: Eerdmans, 1990).

Hamlyn, D., "History of Epistemology", in Paul Edwards (ed.), *Encyclopedia of Philosophy 3* (8 Volumes; New York/London: Macmillan, 1967) 8–38.

Hardy, D.W., "Reason, Wisdom and the Interpretation of Scripture", in D.F. Ford/G. Stanton (ed.), *Reading Texts, Seeking Wisdom* (London: SCM Press, 2003) 69–88.

Harris, S.L., "Wisdom or Creation? A New Interpretation of Job 28:27", *VT* 33 (1983) 419–27.

Hartley, J.E., *The Book of Job* (NICOT; Grand Rapids, MI: Eerdmans, 1988).

Hasker, W., "Proper Function, Reliabilism, and Religious Knowledge: A Critique of Plantinga's Epistemology", in C. Evans/M. Westphal (ed.), *Christian Perspectives on Religious Knowledge* (Grand Rapids, MI: Eerdmans, 1993) 66–86.

Hauerwas, S., *The Peaceable Kingdom* (Notre Dame, IN: University of Notre Dame, 1983).

Hawkes, T., *Structuralism and Semiotics* (London: Methuen, 1977).

Hays, R.B., *The Conversion of the Imagination* (Grand Rapids, MI: Eerdmans, 2004).

Healy, M., "What the Heart of Man Has Not Conceived", PhD Dissertation Rome: Gregorian University, 2000).

Heidegger, M., John Macquarrie and Edward Robinson (tran.); *Being and Time* (New York: Harper and Row, 1962).

Helm, P., "Divine Timeless Eternity", in G. Ganssle (ed.), *God and Time* (Carlisle, UK: Paternoster, 2001) 28–60.

Holladay, W.L., *Jeremiah 1: Jeremiah 1–25* (Philadelphia: Fortress, 1986).

Holmes, S.R., *Listening to the Past: The Place of Tradition in Theology* (Carlisle, UK/Grand Rapids, MI: Paternoster/Baker, 2002).

Jeffrey, D.L., "(Pre) Figuration: Masterplot and Meaning in Biblical History", in C.G. Bartholomew/et al. (ed.), *Behind the Text* (Leicester, UK: Paternoster, 2003) 363–93.

Joyce, P., "Proverbs 8 in Interpretation (I): Historical Criticism and Beyond", in D.F. Ford/G. Stanton (ed.), *Reading Texts, Seeking Wisdom* (London: SCM, 2003) 89–101.

Kant, I., *The Critique of Pure Reason* (New York: Macmillan, 1965).

———, "What is Enlightenment", in *The Philosophy of Kant* (New York: The Modern Library, 1949) 132–9.

Kass, L., *The Beginning of Wisdom* (Chicago: University of Chicago, 2003).

Kearney, R., *Dialogues with Contemporary Continental Thinkers: Paul Ricoeur, Emmanuel Levinas, Herbert Marcuse, Stanislas Breton, Jacques Derrida* (Manchester: Manchester University, 1984).

———, *The God Who May Be* (Bloomington, IN: Indiana University, 2001).

———, *On Stories* (London: Routledge, 2002).

———, *Strangers, Gods and Monsters: Interpreting Otherness* (London: Routledge, 2003).

———, *The Wake of Imagination* (New York: Routledge, 1988).

Keel, O., *The Symbolism of the Biblical World: Ancient Near Eastern Iconography and The Book of Psalms* (New York: Seabury, 1978).

Keil, C./Delitzsch, F., "Pentateuch", *Biblical Commentary on the Old Testament: The Pentateuch (1866)* (Vol 1; Nashville: Hendrickson, 2001).

Kirk, J.A./et al., "Epistemological Trends in the West", in A.J. Kirk/K.J. Vanhoozer (ed.), *To Stake a Claim* (New York: Orbis Books, 1999) 3–17.

———, "The State of Claims to Rationality", in A.J. Kirk/K.J. Vanhoozer (ed.), *To Stake a Claim* (New York: Orbis Books, 1999) 35–52.

———, "The State of Claims to Truth", in A.J. Kirk/K.J. Vanhoozer (ed.), *To Stake a Claim* (New York: Orbis Books, 1999) 18–34.

Kirkegaard, S., *Fear and Trembling/Repetition* (Princeton, NJ: Princeton University, 1983 [1843]).

Kitchen, K., *Ancient Orient and Old Testament* (Chicago: InterVarsity Press, 1966).

Kline, M.G., *The Structure of Biblical Authority* (Grand Rapids, MI: Eerdmans, 1972).

Koch, K., "Is There a Doctrine of Retribution in the Old Testament", in J.L. Crenshaw (ed.), *Theodicy in the Old Testament* (Philadelphia/London: Fortress/SPCK, 1983) 57–87.

Kolarcik, M., S.J., *New Interpreters Bible V: Wisdom of Solomon* (Nashville, TN: Abingdon, 1997).

Koyzis, D.T., *Political Visions and Illusions: A Survey and Christian Critique of Contemporary Ideologies* (Downers Grove, IL: InterVarsity, 2003).

Kreisel, H., "Moses Maimonides", in D.H. Frank/O. Leaman (ed.), *History of Jewish Philosophy* (London: Routledge, 2003) 245–80.

Kuhn, T.S., *The Structure of Scientific Revolutions* (Chicago/London: University of Chicago, 1996 (1962)).

L'Hour, J., "Yahweh Elohim", *Revue Biblique* 81 (1974) 524–56.

Labuschagne, C.J., "Divine Speech in Deuteronomy", in Christensen (ed.), *Song* (1993) 375–93.

Lang, B., *Wisdom and the Book of Proverbs* (New York: Pilgrim, 1986).

Lash, N., *Theology on the Way to Emmaus* (London: SCM, 1986).

Lemke, W.E., "Circumcision of the Heart: The Journey of a Biblical Metaphor", in B.A. Strawn/N.R. Bowen (ed.), *A God So Near* (Winona Lake, IN: Eisenbrauns, 2003) 299–319.

Lestition, S., "Kant and the End of the Enlightenment in Prussia", *The Journal of Modern History* 65 (1993) 57–112.

Levinson, B.M., *Deuteronomy and the Hermeneutics of Legal Innovation* (Oxford: Oxford University, 1998).

Levinson, S.C., *Pragmatics* (Cambridge: Cambridge University, 1983).

Lindars, B., "Torah in Deuteronomy", in P.R. Ackroyd/B. Lindars (ed.), *Words and Meanings: Essays Presented to Winton Thomas* (Cambridge: Cambridge University, 1968) 117–36.

Lo, A., *Job 28 as Rhetoric* (VTSup 98; Leiden/Boston: Brill, 2003).

Lohfink, N., "Bund als Vertrag im Deuteronomium", *ZAW* 107 (1995) 215–39.

———, "Der Bundesschluss im Land Moab: Redaktionsgeschichtliches zu Dt 28:69–32:47", *BZ* 6 (1962) 32–56.

———, *Das Deuteronomium: Enstehung, Gestalt und Botschaft* (BETL; Leuven: Leuven University, 1985).

———, "Das Deuteronomium: Jahwegesetz oder Mosegesetz?" in idem.; *Studien zum Deuteronomium und zur deuteronomistischen Literatur 3* (SBAB 20; Stuttgart: Katholisches Bibelwerk, 1995) 157–65.

———, "Distribution of the Functions of Power: The Laws Concerning Public Offices in Deuteronomy 16:18–18:22", in D. Christensen (ed.), *Song of Power* (Winona Lake, IN: Eisenbrauns, 1993).

———, "Dtn 12,1 und Gen 15,18: Das dem Samen Abrahams Geschenkte Land Als der Geltungsbereich der Deuteronomischen Gesetze", in idem.; *Studien zum Deuteronomium und zur deuteronomistischen Literatur 2* (Stuttgart: Katholisches Bibelwerk, 1991) 257–85.

———, "Die *Huqqîm Ûmišpātîm* im Buch Deuteronomium und ihre Neubegrenzung Durch Dtn 12,1", in idem.; *Studien zum Deuteronomium und zur deuteronomistischen Literatur 2* (Stuttgart: Katholisches Bibelwerk, 1991) 229–56.

———, "Moab oder Sichem – wo wurde Dtn 28 nach der Fabel des Deuteronomiums proklamiert?" in idem.; *Studien zum Deuteronomium und zur deuteronomistischen Literatur 4* (Stuttgart: Katholisches Bibelwerk, 2000) 205–18.

———, *Qoheleth* (Minneapolis, MN: Fortress, 2003).

———, *Theology of the Pentateuch: Themes of the Priestly Narrative and Deuteronomy* (Edinburgh: T&T Clark, 1994).

———, "Verküngkigung des Hauptgebots in der jüngsten Schicht des Deuteronomiums (Dt 4, 1–40)", in idem.; *Studien zum Deuteronomium und zur deuteronomistischen Literatur 1* (Stuttgart: Katholisches Bibelwerk, 1990) 167–91.

———, "Was There a Deuteronomistic Movement?" in Linda S. Schearing and Steven L. McKenzie (ed.), *Those Elusive Deuteronomists: The Phenomenon of Pan-Deuteronomism* (JSOTSup 268; Sheffield: Sheffield Academic, 1999) 36–66.

Lonergan, B.J., *Method in Theology* (London: Darton, Longman & Todd, 1972).
Longman, T.III., *The Book of Ecclesiastes* (NICOT; Grand Rapids, MI: Eerdmans, 1998).
Lubac, H.D., *Medieval Exegesis* (Grand Rapids, MI: Eerdmans, 1998).
Luyten, J., "Primeval and Eschatological Overtones in the Song of Moses (Dt 32:1–43)", in N. Lohfink (ed.), *Das Deuteronomium* (Leuven: Leuven University, 1985) 141–7.
MacDonald, N., *Deuteronomy and the Meaning of 'Monotheism'* (Tübingen: Mohr Siebeck, 2003).
MacIntyre, A., *Whose Justice? Which Rationality?* (Notre Dame, IN: University of Notre Dame, 1988).
———, *After Virtue* (Notre Dame, IN: University of Notre Dame, 1984).
Malfroy, J., "Sagesse et Loi dans le Deutéronome", *VT* 15 (1965) 49–65.
Marcus, J., "Mark 4:10–12 and Marcan Epistemology", *JBL* 103 (1984) 557–74.
Mayes, A., "Deuteronomistic Ideology and the Theology of the Old Testament", *JSOT* 82 (1999) 57–82.
———, *Deuteronomy, NBC* (Grand Rapids, MI/London: Eerdmans/Marshall, Morgan & Scott, 1979).
———, *The Old Testament in Sociological Perspective* (London, UK: Marshall Pickering, 1989).
———, "On Describing the Purpose of Deuteronomy", *JSOT* 58 (1993) 13–33.
Mays, J.L., "'Maker of Heaven and Earth': Creation in the Psalms', in W.P. Brown/S.D. McBride (ed.), *God Who Creates* (Grand Rapids, MI: Eerdmans, 2000) 75–86.
Mays, J.L., "Justice: Perspectives from the Prophetic Tradition", *Interpretation* 37 (1983) 5–17.
McBride, S.D., "Polity of the Covenant People; The Book of Deuteronomy", in D. Christensen (ed.), *Song of Power* (Winona Lake: Eisenbrauns, 1993) 62–77.
McBride, S.D.J., "The Yoke of the Kingdom: An Exposition of Deuteronomy 6:4–5", *Interpretation* 27 (1973) 273–306.
McConville, J.G., "1 Kings Viii 46–53 and the Deuteronomic Hope", *VT* 42 (1992) 67–79.
———, *Deuteronomy* (AOTC; Leicester/Downer's Grove, IL: InterVarsity, 2002).
———, "Deuteronomy: Torah for the Church of Christ", *EJT* 9 (2000) 33–47.
———, *Grace in the End: A Study in Deuteronomic Theology* (Grand Rapids, MI: Zondervan, 1993).
———, *Law and Theology in Deuteronomy* (JSOTSup 33; Sheffield: JSOT, 1984).
———, "Metaphor, Symbol and the Interpretation of Deuteronomy", in C.G. Bartholomew/et al. (ed.), *After Pentecost* (Carlisle, UK/Grand Rapids, MI: Paternoster/Zondervan, 2001) 329–51.
———, "Time and Place and the Deuteronomic Altar-Law", in J.G. McConville/ J.G. Millar; *Time and Place* (Sheffield: Sheffield Academic, 1994) 89–139.
McConville, J.G./Millar, J.G., *Time and Place in Deuteronomy* (JSOTSup; Sheffield: Sheffield Academic, 1994).
McKane, W., *Proverbs: A New Approach* (OTL; SCM, 1970).
McKay, J., "Man's Love For God in Deuteronomy and the Father/Teaching – Son/Pupil Relationship", *VT* 22 (1972) 426–35.
McLuhan, M., *The Classical Trivium* (Corte Madera, CA: Gingko, 2006).
Meinhold, A., "Gott und Mensch in Proverbien 3", *VT* 37 (1987) 468–77.

Mendenhall, G.E., "Samuel's 'Broken *Rîb*': Deuteronomy 32", in Christensen (ed.), *Song* (1993) 169–80.

Merrill, E.H., *Deuteronomy* (NAC; Nashville, TN: Broadman & Holman, 1994).

Middleton, J.R., *The Liberating Image: The Imago Dei in Genesis 1* (Grand Rapids, MI: Brazos, 2005).

Milbank, J., "Knowledge: The Theological Critique of Philosophy in Hamann and Jacobi", in J. Milbank/C. Pickstock/G. Ward (ed.), *Radical Orthodoxy: A New Theology* (London/New York: Routledge, 1999) 21–37.

Milbank, J./et al., *Radical Orthodoxy: A New Theology* (London/New York: Routledge, 1999).

Milgrom, J., *Leviticus 23–37* (New York: Doubleday, 2000).

Millar, J.G., "'A Faithful God Who Does No Wrong: History, Theology, and Reliability in Deuteronomy", in P. Helm/C. Trueman (ed.), *The Trustworthiness of God* (Leicester, UK: Apollos, 2002).

———, "Living at the Place of Decision: Time and Place in the Framework of Deuteronomy", in J.G. McConville/J.G. Millar; *Time and Place* (Sheffield: Sheffield Academic, 1994) 15–88.

Millard, A., "Story, History, and Theology", in A.R. Millard/J.K. Hoffmeier/D.B. Baker (ed.), *Faith, Tradition, and History* (Winona Lake, IN: Eisenbrauns, 1994) 37–64.

Miller, D.B., "Qohelet's Symbolic Use of הבל", *JBL* 117 (1998) 437–54.

Miller, P.D., *Deuteronomy* (Interpretation; Louisville, KY: John Knox, 1990).

———, "Deuteronomy and Psalms: Evoking a Biblical Conversation", *JBL* 118/1 (1999) 3–18.

———, "Faith and Ideology in the Old Testament", in F. Cross/W.E. Lemke/P.D. Miller (ed.), *Magnalia Dei: The Mighty Acts of God* (New York: Doubleday, 1976) 464–79.

———, "'Moses My Servant' The Deuteronomic Portrait of Moses", *Interpretation* 41 (1987) 245–55.

———, "The Poetry of Creation: Psalm 104", in W.P. Brown/S.D. McBride (ed.), *God Who Creates* (Grand Rapids, MI: Eerdmans, 2000) 87–103.

———, "The Poetry of Creation: Psalm 104", in W.P. Brown/S.D. McBride (ed.), *God Who Creates* (Grand Rapids, MI: Eerdmans, 2000) 87–103.

Moore, B., *The Scribal Contribution to Dt., 4, 1–40* (Michigan: University Microfilms International Research, 1976).

Morgan, M.L., "Mendelssohn", in D.H. Frank/O. Leaman (ed.), *History of Jewish Philosophy* (London: Routledge, 2003) 660–81.

Morris, W. (ed.), *The American Heritage Dictionary of the English Language* (Boston: Houghton Mifflin, 1979).

Murphy, R., "Israel's Wisdom: Dialogue Between the Sages", in J.H. Charlesworth/M.A. Daise (ed.), *Light in a Spotless Mirror* (Harrisburg, PA: Trinity Press International, 2003) 7–25.

Murphy, R./Huwiler, E., *Proverbs, Ecclesiastes, Song of Songs* (NIBC; Peabody, MA: Hendrickson/Paternoster, 1999).

Murphy, R.E., "Assumptions and Problems in Old Testament Wisdom Research", *CBQ* 29 (1967) 407–18.

———, "The Personification of Wisdom", in J. Day/R.P. Gordon/H.G.M. Williamson (ed.), *Wisdom in Ancient Israel* (Cambridge: Cambridge University Press, 1995) 222–33.

———, *Proverbs* (WBC; Nashville: Thomas Nelson, 1998).

———, *The Tree of Life: An Explanation of Biblical Wisdom Literature* (New York: Doubleday, 1990).

———, “Wisdom and Creation”, *JBL* 104 (1985) 3–11.

———, “Wisdom and Eros in Proverbs 1–9”, *CBQ* 50 (1988) 60–3.

Nardoni, E., *Rise Up O Judge: A Study of Justice in the Biblical World* (Peabody, MA: Hendrickson, 2004).

Nash, R.H., *Social Justice and the Christian Church* (Milford, MI: Mott Media, 1983).

Naugle, D.K., *Worldview: The History of a Concept* (Grand Rapids, MI/Cambridge: Eerdmans, 2002).

Neusner, J., *A Theological Commentary to the Midrash: Sifré to Numbers and Sifré to Deuteronomy* (Studies in Ancient Judaism; Lanham, NY/Oxford: University Press of America, 2001).

Nicholson, E.W., *Deuteronomy and Tradition* (Oxford: Basil Blackwell, 1967).

Niditch, S., *Oral World and Written Word* (Louisville, KY: Westminster John Knox, 1996).

Niehaus, J.J., *God at Sinai: Covenant and Theophany in the Bible and Ancient Near East* (Grand Rapids, MI: Zondervan, 1995).

O’Donovan, O., *The Desire of the Nations: Rediscovering the Roots of Political Theology* (Cambridge: Cambridge University Press, 1996).

———, “Response to Craig Bartholomew”, in C.G. Bartholomew/et al. (ed.), *A Royal Priesthood?: The Use of the Bible Ethically and Politically* (Carlisle, UK/Grand Rapids, MI: Paternoster/Zondervan, 2002) 113–5.

———, *Resurrection and Moral Order: An Outline for Evangelical Ethics* (Leicester, England: InterVarsity, 1986).

———, *The Ways of Judgment* (Grand Rapids, MI: Eerdmans, 2005).

O’Dowd, R.P., “Frame Narrative”, in D. Reid/T. Longman/P. Enns (ed.), *Dictionary of Old Testament Wisdom, Poetry and Writings* (Downers Grove: InterVarsity, Forthcoming).

———, “Memory on the Boundary: Epistemology in Deuteronomy”, in M. Healy/R. Parry (ed.), *The Bible and Epistemology* (Carlisle, UK: Paternoster, 2007) 3–22.

———, “Nathan MacDonald: Deuteronomy and the Meaning of ‘Monotheism’”, *EJT* 13 (2004) 66–7.

———, “A Chord of Three Strands: Epistemology in Job, Proverbs and Ecclesiastes”, in M. Healy/R. Parry (ed.), *The Bible and Epistemology* (Carlisle, UK: Paternoster, 2007) 65–87.

Ogden, G., *Qoheleth* ((Readings – A New Biblical Commentary); Sheffield: Sheffield Academic, 1987).

Olson, D.T., *Deuteronomy and the Death of Moses: A Theological Reading* (Minneapolis, MN: Fortress, 1994).

———, “How Does Deuteronomy Do Theology? Literary Juxtaposition and Paradox in the New Moab Covenant in Deuteronomy 29–32”, in B.A. Strawn/N.R. Bowen (ed.), *A God So Near* (Winona Lake, IN: Eisenbrauns, 2003) 201–13.

Palmer, R.E., *Hermeneutics:* (Evanston, IL: Northwestern University Press, 1969).

Parker, K., “Solomon as Philosopher King? The Nexus of Law and Wisdom in 1 Kings 1–11”, *JSOT* 53 (1992) 75–91.

Parsons, G.W., "The Structure and Purpose of Job", *BSac* 138 (1981) 139–57.
Patrick, D., "Is the Truth of the First Commandment Known by Reason?" *CBQ* 56 (1994) 423–41.
Perdue, L.G., "Liminality as a Social Setting for Wisdom Instructions", *ZAW* 93 (1981) 114–26.
———, *Proverbs* (Interpretation; Louisville, KY: John Knox, 2000).
———, *Wisdom in Revolt: Metaphorical Theology in the Book of Job* (Sheffield: JSOT, 1991).
———, "Wisdom in the Book of Job", in L.G. Perdue/B.B. Scott/W.J. Wiseman (ed.), *In Search of Wisdom: Essays in Memory of John G. Gammie* (Louisville, KY: Westminster John Knox, 1993) 73–98.
———, *Wisdom Literature: A Theological History* (Louisville, KY: Westminster John Knox, 2007).
Perry, M., "Literary Dynamics: How the Order of a Text Creates Its Meanings", *Poetics Today* 1 (1979) 35–64.
Phillips, E.A., "Speaking Truthfully: Job's Friends and Job", Unpublished paper presented at The Evangelical Theological Society: 2004).
Placher, W.C., *Unapologetic Theology: A Christian Voice in a Pluralistic Conversation* (Louisville, Kentucky: Westminster John Knox, 1989).
Plantinga, A., "Divine Knowledge", in C.S. Evans/M. Westphal (ed.), *Christian Perspectives on Religious Knowledge* (Grand Rapids, MI: Eerdmans, 1993) 40–65.
———, *Warranted Christian Belief* (New York/Oxford: Oxford University Press, 2000).
Plato, *The Republic* (New York/London: Penguin Books, 2003).
Polak, F., "Theophany and Mediator: The Unfolding of a Theme in the Book of Exodus", in M. Vervenne (ed.), *Studies in the Book of Moses* (Leuven: Leuven University, 1996) 113–47.
Polanyi, M., *Personal Knowledge: Towards a Post-Critical Philosophy* (New York: Harper and Row, 1964 (1958)).
Polzin, R., "The Framework of the Book of Job", *Interpretation* 28 (1974) 182–200.
———, *Moses and the Deuteronomist: A Literary Study of the Deuteronomic History* (Bloomington, IN: Indiana University, 1980).
Popkin, R.H., "Michel Eyquen de Montaigne", in P. Edwards (ed.), *Encyclopedia of Philosophy 5* (New York: Collier-Macmillan, 1972) 366–68.
Pressler, C., "Certainty, Ambiguity, and Trust: Knowledge of God in Psalm 139", in B.A. Strawn/N.R. Bowen (ed.), *A God So Near* (Winona Lake, IN: Eisenbrauns, 2003) 91–9.
Provan, I.W., *Ecclesiastes, Song of Songs* (NIVAC; Grand Rapids, MI: Zondervan, 2001).
———, "Ideologies, Literary and Critical", *JBL* 114 (1995) 585–606.
Quine, W., "Epistemology Naturalized", in H. Kornblith (ed.), *Naturalizing Epistemology* (Cambridge, MA: MIT, 1994) 15–31.
Rad, G.v., *Deuteronomy* (OTL; Philadelphia: Westminster, 1966).
———, *Genesis* (Philadelphia, PA: Westminster, 1961).
———, "The Joseph Narrative and Ancient Wisdom", in idem.; *Problem* (1953) 292–300.
———, *Old Testament Theology OT Theology* (New York/London: Harper and Row, 1962).

———, *The Problem of the Hexateuch and Other Essays* (London: SCM, 1966).

———, "The Promised Land and Yahweh's Land in the Hexateuch", in idem., *Problem* (London: SCM, 1943) 79–93.

———, "Some Aspects of the Old Testament World-View", in idem.; *Problem* (London: SCM, 1964) 144–65.

———, "There Remains Still a Rest for the People of God: An Investigation of a Biblical Conception", in idem.; *Problem* (London: SCM, 1933) 94–102.

———, *Wisdom in Israel* (London: SCM, 1970).

Rae, M.A., "Creation and Promise: Towards a Theology of History", in C.G. Bartholomew/et al. (ed.), *Behind the Text* (Leicester, UK: Paternoster, 2003) 267–99.

Ricoeur, P., "Existence and Hermeneutics", in *The Conflict of Interpretation* (Evanston, IL: Northwestern University, 1974) 3–24.

———, *Hermeneutics and the Human Sciences* (Cambridge: Cambridge University, 1981).

———, *Husserl: An Analysis of His Phenomenology* (Evanston, IL: Northwestern University, 1967).

———, *Interpretation Theory: Discourse and the Surplus of Meaning* (Fort Worth, TX: Texas Christian University, 1976).

———, "The Problem of Double Meaning", in *The Conflict of Traditions* (Evanston, IL: Northwestern University, 1974) 62–78.

———, "Structure and Hermeneutics", in *The Conflict of Interpretations* (Evanston, IL: Northwestern University, 1974) 27–61.

———, *The Symbolism of Evil* (Boston: Beacon, 1967).

Robinson, J.M., "Hermeneutic Since Barth", in J.M. Robinson/J.B. Cobb Jr. (ed.), *The New Hermeneutic* (New York: Harper and Row, 1964) 1–77.

Rogerson, J.W., "Discourse Ethics and Biblical Ethics", in *The Bible in Ethics: The Second Sheffield Colloquium* (Sheffield, England: Sheffield Academic Press, 1995) 17–26.

———, *Old Testament Criticism in the Nineteenth Century: England and Germany* (London: Fortress, 1984).

Rorty, R., *Contingency, Irony, and Solidarity* (Cambridge: Cambridge University Press, 1989).

Rosenzweig, F., "The Secret of Biblical Narrative Form", in M. Buber/F. Rosenzweig (ed.), *Scripture and Translation* (Bloomington/Indianapolis: Indiana University, 1994) 129–42.

Russell, B., "Epistemic and Moral Duty", in M. Steup (ed.), *Knowledge, Truth, and Duty* (Oxford: Oxford University Press, 2001) 34–48.

Sailhamer, J., *The Pentateuch as Narrative: A Biblical-Theological Commentary* (Grand Rapids, MI: Zondervan, 1992).

Schäfer, P., "Wisdom Finds a Home: Torah as Wisdom", in J.H. Charlesworth/ M.A. Daise (ed.), *Light in a Spotless Mirror* (Harrisburg, PA: Trinity Press International, 2003) 26–44.

Schmid, H., "Creation, Righteousness, and Salvation", in B.W. Anderson (ed.), *Creation in the Old Testament* (Philadelphia/London: Fortress/SPCK, 1984 (Original in ZTK, 1973)) 102–17.

Schnabel, E.J., *Law and Wisdom from Ben Sira to Paul: A Tradition Historical Inquiry Into the Relation of Law, Wisdom, and Ethics* (Tübingen: Mohr Siebeck, 1985).

———, "Law and Wisdom: In the Mishnaic System", *BTB* 17 (1987) 104–11.

Schnittjer, G.E., "The Narrative Multiverse Within the Universe of the Bible: The Question of 'Borderlines' and 'Intertextuality'", *WTJ* 64 (2002) 231–52.

Schultz, C., "The Cohesive Issue of Mišpāt in Job", in J.E. Coleson/V.H. Matthews (ed.), *Go to the Land I Will Show You: Studies in Honor of Dwight. D. Young* (Winona Lake: Eisenbrauns, 1996) 159–75.

Scott, R., "The Study of the Wisdom Literature", *Interpretation* 24 (1970) 20–45.

Seitz, C.R., "The Call of Moses and the 'Revelation' of the Divine Name", in idem.; *Word Without End* (Grand Rapids, MI: Eerdmans, 1998) 229–47.

Seow, C.-L., *Ecclesiastes* (AB; New York: Doubleday, 1997).

Sheppard, G.T., *Wisdom as a Hermeneutical Construct: A Study in the Sapientializing of the Old Testament* (Berlin/New York: BZAW de Gruyter, 1980).

Skehan, P.W., "The Structure of the Song of Moses in Deuteronomy (32:1–43)", in Christensen (ed.), *Song* (1993) 156–68.

Skehan, P.W./De Lella, A.A., *The Wisdom of Ben Sira* (New York: Doubleday, 1987).

Sonnet, J.-P., *The Book Within the Book: Writing in Deuteronomy* (Leiden/New York: Brill, 1997).

Sosa, E., "Reflective Knowledge in the Best Circles", in M. Steup (ed.), *Knowledge, Truth and Duty* (Oxford/New York: Oxford University, 2001) 187–203.

Spangenberg, I.J., "Irony in the Book of Qohelet", *JSOT* 72 (1996) 57–69.

Sperber, D./Wilson, D., *Relevance: Communication and Cognition* (Second ed.; Oxford: Blackwell, 1995).

Stahl, N., *Law and Liminality in the Bible* (JSOTSup; Sheffield: JSOT, 1995).

Steiner, G., *Real Presences* (Chicago: University of Chicago, 1989).

Sternberg, M., "Biblical Poetics and Sexual Politics: From Reading to Counterreading", *JBL* 111 (1992) 463–88.

———, *The Poetics of Biblical Narrative* (Bloomington, IN: Indiana University, 1987).

———, "Time and Space in Biblical (Hi)Story Telling: The Grand Chronology", in R. Schwartz (ed.), *The Book and the Text: The Bible and Literary Theory* (Oxford: Blackwell, 1990) 81–145.

Strawn, B.A., "Keep/Observe/Do – Carefully – Today! The Rhetoric of Repetition in Deuteronomy", in B.A. Strawn/N.R. Bowen (ed.), *A God So Near* (Winona Lake, IN: Eisenbrauns, 2003) 215–40.

Talmon, S., "'Wisdom' in the Book of Esther", in Literary Studies; *Literary Studies in the Hebrew Bible* (Jerusalem/Leiden: The Hebrew University, 1993) 419-455.

Tarnas, R., *The Passion of the Western Mind: Understanding the Ideas That Have Shaped Our World View* (New York: Ballantine Books, 1991).

Taylor, A., *The Proverb* (Cambridge, MA: Harvard University, 1931).

Taylor, C., "Aristotle's Epistemology", in S. Everson (ed.), *Epistemology* (Cambridge: Cambridge University, 1990) 116–44.

Taylor, C., "Language and Human Nature", in *Human Agency and Language: Philosophical Papers 1* (Cambridge: Cambridge University, 1985) 215–47.

———, *The Malaise of Modernity* (Toronto: Anansi, 1991).

Thiselton, A.C., "'Behind' and 'In Front Of' the Text: Language, Reference and Indeterminacy", in C.G. Bartholomew/et al. (ed.), *After Pentecost: Language and Biblical Interpretation* (Carlisle, UK/Grand Rapids, MI: Paternoster/ Zondervan, 2001) 97–120.

———, "Communicative Action and Promise in Hermeneutics", in R. Lundin/C. Walhout/A. Thiselton (ed.), *The Promise of Hermeneutics* (Grand Rapids, MI: Eerdmans, 1999) 133–239.

———, *A Concise Encyclopedia of the Philosophy of Religion* (Oxford: Oneworld, 2002).

———, "Knowledge, Myth and Corporate Memory", in *Believing in the Church: Essays by Members of the Church of England Doctrine Commission* (London: SPCK, 1983) 45–78.

———, *New Horizons in Hermeneutics: The Theory and Practice of Transforming Biblical Reading* (Grand Rapids, MI: Zondervan, 1992).

———, *The Two Horizons: New Testament Hermeneutics and Philosophical Description* (Grand Rapids, MI/Carlisle, UK: Eerdmans/Paternoster, 1983 [1980]).

Thompson, J.A., *Deuteronomy* (TOTC; Leicester, UK: InterVarsity 1974).

Thompson, J.B., "Editor's Introduction", in idem. (ed.), *Hermeneutics and the Human Sciences* (Cambridge: Cambridge University, 1981) 1–26.

Tigay, J.H., *Deuteronomy, Debarim* (JPSTC; Philadelphia: Jewish Publication Society, 1996).

Torrance, T.F., *Reality and Evangelical Theology: The Realism of Christian Revelation* (Downers Grove, Illinois: InterVarsity Press, 1982).

Toulmin, S., *Cosmopolis: The Hidden Agenda of Modernity* (Chicago: University of Chicago, 1990).

Toy, C.H., *Proverbs* (ICC; Edinburgh: T&T Clark, 1988).

Traber, C., "In Perfect Harmony? Escaping the Frame in the Early Twentieth Century", in E. Mendgen/et al. (ed.), *In Perfect Harmony: Picture and Frame, 1850–1920* (Amsterdam: Van Gogh Museum, 1995) 221–47.

Tucker, G.M., "Deuteronomy 18:15–22", *Interpretation* 41 (1987) 292–7.

Vall, G., "From Whose Womb Did the Ice Come Forth?: Procreation Images in Job 38:28–29", *CBQ* 57 (1995) 504–13.

Van Leeuwen, R.C., "Building God's House: An Exploration in Wisdom", in J. Packer/S.K. Soderlund (ed.), *The Way of Wisdom: Essays in Honor of Bruce K. Waltke* (Grand Rapids, MI: Zondervan, 2000) 204–11.

———, *Context and Meaning in Proverbs 25–27* (SBL.DS; Atlanta, GA: Scholars Press, 1988).

———, "Liminality and Worldview in Proverbs 1–9", *Semeia* 50 (1990) 111–44.

———, *New Interpreters Bible V: Proverbs* (Nashville: Abingdon, 1997).

———, "Proverbs 30:21–23 and the Biblical World Upside Down", *JBL* 105 (1986) 599–610.

———, "Scribal Wisdom and Theodicy in the Book of the Twelve", in L.G. Perdue/B.B. Scott/W.J. Wiseman (ed.), *In Search of Wisdom: Essays in Memory of John G. Gammie* (Louisville, KY: Westminster John Knox, 1993) 31–49.

———, "Wealth and Poverty: System and Contradiction in Proverbs", *Hebrew Studies* 33 (1992) 25–36.

———, "What Comes Out of God's Mouth: Theological Wordplay in Deuteronomy 8", *CBQ* 47 (1985) 55–7.

———, "Wisdom Literature", in K.J. Vanhoozer/C.G. Bartholomew/Trier. Daniel/N.T. Wright (ed.), *Dictionary for Theological Interpretation of the Bible* (Grand Rapids, MI: Baker, 2005) 847–50.

———, "Wisdom Literature", in K.V. Vanhoozer/C.G. Bartholomew/D.J. Treier/ N.T. Wright (ed.), *Dictionary for Theological Interpretation of the Bible* (Grand Rapids, MI: Baker, 2005) 847–50.

Van Pelt, M.V./Kaiser, W.C., "הגה", in W. VanGemeren (ed.), *NIDOTTE 1* (Grand Rapids, MI: Zondervan, 1997) 1006–8.

VanGemeren, W.A., (ed.), *New International Dictionary of Old Testament Theology and Exegesis 5 vols.* (Grand Rapids, MI: Zondervan, 1996).

Vanhoozer, K.J., *Is There a Meaning in This Text?: The Bible, The Reader, and the Morality of Literary Knowledge* (Grand Rapids, MI: Zondervan, 1998).

———, "Lost in Interpretation? Truth, Scripture, and Hermeneutics", in A. Köstenberger (ed.), *Whatever Happened to Truth* (Wheaton, IL: Crossway, 2005) 93–136.

———, "The Trials of Truth: Mission, Martyrdom, and the Epistemology of the Cross", in A.J. Kirk/K.J. Vanhoozer (ed.), *To Stake a Claim* (New York: Orbis Books, 1999) 120–56.

Vanier, J., *Becoming Human* (New York: Paulist, 1998).

Verheij, A., "Paradise Retried: On Qohelet 2:4–6", *JSOT* 50 (1991) 113–5.

Wallace, D.F., "Tense Present: Democracy, English, and the Wars Over Usage", *Harpers* (April 2001) 39–58.

Waltke, B., *Proverbs 1–15* (NICOT; Grand Rapids, MI: Eerdmans, 2004).

Waltke, B./O'Connor, M., *An Introduction to Biblical Hebrew Syntax* (Winona Lake, IN: Eisenbrauns, 1990).

Warner, S., "An Epistemology of 'Participating Consciousness': Overcoming the Epistemological Rupture of Self and World", *Religious Education* 93 (1998) 189–205.

Watson, F., *Paul and the Hermeneutics of Faith* (London: T&T Clark, 2004).

———, *Text, Church and World: Biblical Interpretation in Theological Perspective* (Grand Rapids, MI: Eerdmans, 1994).

Weinfeld, M., *Deuteronomy 1–11* (AB; New York: Doubleday, 1991).

———, *Deuteronomy and the Deuteronomic School* (Winona Lake, IN: Eisenbrauns, 1992 (Oxford: Clarendon, 1972)).

———, "Judge and Officer in Ancient Israel and in the Ancient Near East", *IOS* (1977).

———, *Social Justice in Ancient Israel and in the Ancient Near East* (Jerusalem: Magnes, 1995).

Welch, A.C., *The Code of Deuteronomy: A New Theory of Its Origin* (London: James Clark & Co., 1924).

Wellhausen, J., *Prolegomena to the History of Ancient Israel* (Gloucester, MA: Peter Smith, 1973 (1885)).

Wenham, G., "The Date of Deuteronomy: Linch Pin of Old Testament Criticism, Part 2", *Themelios* 11 (September 1985) 15–8.

———, "The Date of Deuteronomy: Linch-Pin of Old Testament Criticism", *Themelios* 10 (April 1985) 15–20.

Wenham, G.J., "Deuteronomy and the Central Sanctuary", in Christensen (ed.), *Song* (1993) 94–108.

———, *Genesis 1–15* (Word Biblical Commentary; Waco, TX: Word, 1987).

———, *Story as Torah: Reading the Old Testament Ethically* (Edinburgh: T&T Clark, 2000).

Westphal, M., "Christian Philosophers and the Copernican Revolution", in C. Evans/M. Westphal (ed.), *Christian Perspectives on Religious Knowledge* (Grand Rapids, MI: Eerdmans, 1993) 161–79.

———, "Taking St. Paul Seriously: Sin as an Epistemological Category", in T.P. Flint (ed.), *Christian Philosophy* (Notre Dame, IN: University of Notre Dame, 1990) 200–26.

Whybray, R., *The Book of Proverbs: A Survey of Modern Study* (Leiden: Brill, 1995).

———, *The Composition of the Book of Proverbs* (JSOTSup; Sheffield: JSOT, 1994).

———, *Ecclesiastes* (NCBC; Grand Rapids, MI: Eerdmans, 1989).

———, *The Intellectual Tradition in the Old Testament* (Berlin/New York: Walter de Gruyter, 1974).

———, *Wealth and Poverty in the Book of Proverbs* (JSOTSup; Sheffield: JSOT, 1990).

———, *Wisdom in Proverbs: The Concept of Wisdom in Proverbs 1–9* (London: SCM Press LTD, 1965).

———, "The Wisdom Psalms", in John Day/R.P. Gordon/H.G.M. Williamson (ed.), *Wisdom in Ancient Israel* (Cambridge: Cambridge University Press, 1995) 152–60.

Willard, D., "Hermeneutical Occasionalism", in R. Lundin (ed.), *Disciplining Hermeneutics* (Leicester, UK: Apollos, 1997) 167–72.

Wilson, G.H., "Preknowledge, Anticipation, and the Poetics of Job", *JSOT* 30 (2005) 243–56.

———, "חכם", in W.A. VanGemeren (ed.), *NIDOTTE, 5 Vols. 2* (Grand Rapids, MI/Carlisle, UK: Zondervan/Paternoster, 1997) 130–4.

Wilson, I., *Out of the Midst of the Fire: Divine Presence in Deuteronomy* (SBL.DS; Atlanta, GA: Scholars, 1995).

Winston, D., "Hellenistic Jewish Philosophy", in D.H. Frank/O. Leaman (ed.), *History of Jewish Philosophy* (London: Routledge, 2003) 38–61.

Witherington, B.I., *Jesus the Sage: The Pilgrimage of Wisdom* (Minneapolis, MN: Fortress, 2000).

Wittgenstein, L., *Philosophical Investigations* (2nd ed.; Oxford: Blackwell, 2001 (1958)).

Wolf, H., "הגה", in R.L. Harris/G.L. Archer/B.K. Waltke (ed.), *Theological Wordbook of the Old Testament 1* (Chicago: Moody Press, 1980) 205.

Wolters, A., *Creation Regained: Biblical Basics for a Reformational Worldview* (Grand Rapids, MI: Eerdmans, 1985, 2005).

———, *The Song of the Valiant Woman: Studies in the Interpretation of Proverbs 31:10–31* (Carlisle, UK: Paternoster, 2001).

Wolterstorff, N., "Can Belief in God be Rational", in A. Plantinga/N. Wolterstorff (ed.), *Faith and Rationality: Reason and Belief in God* (Notre Dame, IN/ London: University of Notre Dame, 1983) 135–86.

———, *Divine Discourse: Philosophical Reflections on the Claim That God Speaks* (Cambridge: Cambridge University Press, 1995).

———, *Reason Within the Bounds of Religion* (Grand Rapids, MI: Eerdmans, 1984).

———, "The Remembrance of Things (Not) Past: Philosophical Reflections on Christian Liturgy", in T.P. Flint (ed.), *Christian Philosophy* (Notre Dame, IN: University of Notre Dame, 1990) 118–61.

Wood, W.J., *Epistemology: Becoming Intellectually Virtuous* (Leicester, England: Apollos, 1998).

Wright, C.J.H., *Deuteronomy* (NIBC; Peabody, MA: Hendrickson, 1996).
———, *God's People in God's Land: Family, Land, and Property in the Old Testament* (Exeter/Grand Rapids, MI: Paternoster/Eerdmans, 1990).
———, *Knowing Jesus Through the Old Testament* (Downers Grove, IL: InterVarsity, 1992).
———, "Mission as Matrix for Hermeneutics and Biblical Theology", in C.G. Bartholomew/et al. (ed.), *Out of Egypt* (Grand Rapids, MI: Zondervan, 2004) 102–43.
———, *Old Testament Ethics for the People of God* (Leicester, UK: InterVarsity, 2004).
Wright, N.T., *Jesus and the Victory of God* (Minneapolis, MN: Fortress, 1996).
———, *The New Testament and the People of God* (Minneapolis, MN: Fortress, 1992).
Yamauchi, E., "The Current State of Old Testament Historiography", in A.R. Millard J.K. Hoffmeier/D.B. Baker (ed.), *Faith, Tradition, and History* (Winona Lake, IN: Eisenbrauns, 1994) 1–36.
Yee, G.A., "'I Have Perfumed My Bed with Myrrh': The Foreign Woman ('Iššâ Zārâ) in Proverbs 1–9", *JSOT* 43 (1989) 53–68.
Yerushalmi, Y.H., *Zakhor: Jewish History and Jewish Memory* (Seattle/London: University of Washington, 1996).
Young, F., "Proverbs 8 in Interpretation (2): Wisdom Personified", in D.F. Ford/ G. Stanton (ed.), *Reading Texts, Seeking Wisdom* (London: SCM, 2003) 102–15.
———, "Proverbs 8 in Interpretation (2): Wisdom Personified, Fourth-Century Christian Readings: Assumptions and Debates", in D.F. Ford/G. Stanton (ed.), *Reading Texts, Seeking Wisdom* (London: SCM, 2003) 102–15.
Zagzebski, L., "Recovering Understanding", in M. Steup (ed.), *Knowledge, Truth, and Duty: Essays on Epistemic Justification, Responsibility, and Virtue* (Oxford: Oxford University Press, 2001) 235–51.
Zimmerli, W., "I Am Yahweh", in W. Brueggemann (ed.), *Yahweh* (Atlanta: John Knox, 1953) 1–28.
———, "Knowledge of God According to the Book of Ezekiel", in W. Brueggemann (ed.), *I Am Yahweh* (Atlanta: John Knox, 1954) 29–98.
———, "The Place and Limit of Wisdom in the Framework of Old Testament Theology", *SJT* 17 (1964) 146–58.

Index